Communication in China

STATE AND SOCIETY IN EAST ASIA
Series Editor: Elizabeth J. Perry

Communication in China

Political Economy, Power, and Conflict

Yuezhi Zhao

ROWMAN & LITTLEFIELD PUBLISHERS, INC.
Lanham • Boulder • New York • Toronto • Plymouth, UK

ROWMAN & LITTLEFIELD PUBLISHERS, INC.

Published in the United States of America
by Rowman & Littlefield Publishers, Inc.
A wholly owned subsidary of The Rowman & Littlefield Publishing Group, Inc.
4501 Forbes Boulevard, Suite 200, Lanham, Maryland 20706
www.rowmanlittlefield.com

Estover Road, Plymouth PL6 7PY, United Kingdom

British Library Cataloguing in Publication Information Available

Library of Congress Cataloging-in-Publication Data

Zhao, Yuezhi, 1965–
  Communication in China : political economy, power, and conflict / Yuezhi
Zhao.
      p. cm. — (State and society in East Asia)
  Includes bibliographical references and index.
  ISBN-13: 978-0-7425-1965-7 (cloth : alk. paper)
  ISBN-10: 0-7425-1965-1 (cloth : alk. paper)
  ISBN-13: 978-0-7425-1966-4 (pbk. : alk. paper)
  ISBN-10: 0-7425-1966-X (pbk. : alk. paper)
  1. Communication policy—China. 2. Mass media policy—China. 3.
Communication—China. 4. Mass media—China. I. Title.
  P95.82.C6Z43 2008
  302.23′0951—dc22

                                                                    2007037635

Printed in the United States of America

♾️™ The paper used in this publication meets the minimum requirements of
American National Standard for Information Sciences—Permanence of Paper
for Printed Library Materials, ANSI/NISO Z39.48-1992.

For Jianxing, Linda, my mother Qin Yujiao,
and in memory of my grandfather Qin Chaoxin,
a famine victim in 1961

Contents

Acknowledgments

Two individuals, Dan Schiller and Elizabeth Perry, played instrumental roles in the making of this book. Dan Schiller helped me out of the agony over working on my "old" research focus on the Chinese media and "new" research focus on Chinese telecommunications by suggesting that I write a "quick and small" book on the Chinese media as a follow-up to my 1998 book, *Media, Market, and Democracy in China,* when I found myself remaining preoccupied with developments in this area. I not only owe the idea of this book to Dan, but also have benefited enormously from him for many of the ideas in it. Dan read and commented on an earlier draft of this manuscript and helped me to develop and clarify my thinking on the issues I have been grappling with throughout the years. I cannot thank him enough for his generous support and sustained intellectual engagement. All remaining problems and potential inconsistencies, of course, are mine.

When the originally envisioned "quick and small" book went out of control and became a 10-chapter monster after my many years of shooting a moving target, Elizabeth Perry not only advised me to cut it down to the current 6-chapter structure, but also intervened at a crucial moment of the publication process for it to be published at its current length. Liz invited me to publish this book in her State and Society in East Asia series with Rowman & Littlefield when I first mentioned the idea of this book to her in 2000. I am very grateful for her encouragement, patience, and incisive editorial stewardship throughout this book's protracted process of transformation. I am extremely fortunate to have the opportunity to work with her.

I would like to thank Susan McEachern, the book's acquisition editor at Rowman & Littlefield, for her patience, flexibility, and care for this project, and Jehanne Schweitzer, the book's production editor, for her efficiency, professionalism, and willingness to accommodate my busy traveling schedule in the last stages of the book's production. I also acknowledge the contribution of an anonymous reviewer whose extensive comments and criticisms challenged me to revisit a number of my arguments. Although I have ended up reinforcing my analysis, critical comments from somebody who works from a different theoretical framework are at times very helpful.

Numerous other individuals outside and inside China formed an enlightening and supportive intellectual community for me to pursue the ideas in this book. Outside China, I benefit from scholarly exchanges with Ruoyun Bai, Paula Chakravartty, Joseph Chan, Timothy Cheek, Yik-chan Chin, John Downing, Chien-san Feng, Eric Florence, Anthony Fung, Yu Huang, Chin-Chuan Lee, Bingchun Meng, Zaharom Nain, Zhongdang Pan, Manjunath Pendakur, Jack Linchuan Qiu, Richard Levy, Jing Wang, Xin Xin, Gehao Zhang, and Jonathan Zhu, among others.

I am extremely fortunate to have many friends and acquaintances inside China's communication industries and academy. Their generosity in sharing their insights and in helping me with my research was indispensable. Several of them even took the trouble to send books and other useful research material to me in Canada. Although I am unable to name them all here, I wish to acknowledge the following individuals: Bu Wei, Chen Lidan, Chen Weixing, Guo Zhenzhi, Hu Zhengrong, Huang Dan, Li Bin, Lu Xinyu, Lu Ye, Shan Bo, Shao Peiren, Song Jianxin, Sun Wusan, Wang Yihong, Wang Yunpeng, Wu Fei, Xia Qianfang, Xu Jilin, Yan Bofei, Yang Xiaoyan, and Zhan Jiang. I would like to make a special tribute to Shen Li, who enlightened me with her insights and whose premature death in 2006 saddened me deeply. I learned a great deal from the wide-ranging discussions I had with a number of my university classmates—many of whom are media executives and practicing journalists—during my various gatherings with them, including our 20-year class reunion gathering at Hainan Island in 2004. In particular, I thank Chen Jianqi, Dong Rui, Gong Aiqiang, Huang Xuxiao, Li Miao, Li Xuming, Liu Qingdong, Peng Lai, Tian Linzhu, Wang Fei, Wang Xiaoying, Zhang Tianjian, and Zhao Liping.

I am indebted to the intellectual nourishment I received from teaching at the University of California, San Diego, between 1997 and 2000, where the Department of Communication and China Studies Program combined to provide me with the most inspiring and enriching academic environment. I not only initiated this book project in San Diego, but also acquired some of its intellectual foundations there. I also benefited greatly from the

School of Communication at Simon Fraser University for the position of Canada Research Chair in the Political Economy of Global Communication. This position provided me with much-needed research time and the necessary financial resources to complete this book. In particular, I thank Martin Laba for his generosity and Catherine Murray for her spirited collegial support. I am grateful to Zoë Druick, Kirsten McAllister, and Fiona Jefferies, who invited me to present my work at their public lecture series, allowing me to test my ideas in front of a "home audience." I should also thank Dal Yong Jin, who read the entire manuscript and suggested places to cut, when I was trying very hard to shorten the manuscript. Lucie Menkveld and Monique Cloutier provided efficient and friendly support in administrative tasks relating to the book's research and publication. I thank them both.

Generous invitations by China scholars and communication scholars for article contributions and scholarly research presentations provided invaluable opportunities for me to expand my empirical foci and develop the analysis in this book over the years. Although the fast-moving nature of the subject matter and the different contexts eventually made it impossible for me to publish these articles in a book form, this book draws on a number of these articles and I am very grateful to the following individuals for the opportunities to write these articles and make research presentations on the book's themes: Ann Anagnost, Shan Bo, Andrew Calabrese, Nick Couldry, James Curran, Michael Curtin, Jan Ekecrantz, Richard Ericson, Merle Goldman, Larry Gross, Lindhoff Håkan, Chin-Chuan Lee, Colin Leys, Perry Link, Richard Madsen, Catherine McKercher, Vincent Mosco, Graham Murdock, Zaharom Nain, Leo Panitch, Elizabeth Perry, Paul Pickowicz, Lena Rydholm, Dan Schiller, Hemant Shah, Colin Sparks, Slavko Splichal, Pradip Thomas, Daya Thussu, Janet Wasko, Gu Xin, and Dingxin Zhao. Sadly, Jan Ekerantz, who hosted my visit to Stockholm University in December 2004 and published a fascinating article on the Chinese media's coverage of the World Economic Forum and the World Social Forum in early 2007, passed away in summer 2007.

Three student assistants, Andy Hu, Yan Liang, and Rob Prey, provided excellent research and editorial assistance at various stages of the book project. Other graduate students and visiting scholars, including Arthur Aginam, Abu Jafar Bhuiyan, Mark Cote, Greig de Peuter, Rob Duffy, Wei Gao, Dong Han, Ying-fen Huang, Li Na, Xinren Li, Guoxin Xing, and Yin Liangen, have been generous in sharing their ideas and relevant information. Kathi Cross, Arthur Aginam, and Rob Duffy were brilliant when I asked them to serve as my "focus group" in the final attempt to come up with a meaningful title for the book.

As always, I am deeply indebted to personal friends and family members. Daniel Say and Jim Uhl sent me steady flows of news updates about developments in China. DeeDee Halleck, a friend and a former colleague, also frequently sent me useful news updates on China's Internet throughout the years. Huang Weiping and Chen Qunhua provided me with accommodations and offered warm friendship when I was writing parts of the manuscript in Hangzhou in the summer of 2005. My sister Weichun helped me with newspaper archival research at the Zhejiang Library, and I could not have completed this work without the unconditional love and support of my husband, Jianxing, my daughter, Linda, and my mother, Qin Yujiao.

Introduction

Feng Xiujü, 64 years old, handicapped and recently widowed, with a laid-off son and a daughter-in-law who lacks an urban household registration and dares not have a child, is no doubt a most peripheral member of Chinese society. Yet, Feng also represents a constituent element of the Chinese communication system. When I took the book's cover photo on July 1, 2007, Feng, the woman on the right bottom corner, had operated this makeshift newsstand on a street corner in the Chaowai Neighborhood of Beijing's Chaoyang District for 19 years. Nothing seems to be more mundane than this Beijing street scene. And yet, nothing is more symbolic of the central themes of this book.

Next to her makeshift newsstand and partially visible in the photo is a super-modern newspaper and periodical booth, attended by a young woman and carrying the corporate logo of China Post, the state newspaper distributor and retailer. Rather than being hired by China Post, however, this young woman was hired by the family of Zhang Laikuan, who works in the Chaowai Neighborhood Office of the Chaoyang District and had obtained the operating license for this booth through official connections. By hiring somebody else to attend the booth, the Zhang family makes a profit.

If things had gone in Feng's favor in the Chinese Communist Party's project of building and developing "socialism with Chinese characteristics"—a slogan invoked by general party secretary Hu Jintao 52 times in his report to the party's 17th national congress on October 15, 2007[1]—she should be the one inside the fancy booth, while her makeshift newsstand

1

should have vanished many years ago from this busy street corner in Beijing's posh business and diplomatic district. As I wrote in my 1998 book, *Media, Market, and Democracy in China: Between the Party Line and the Bottom Line*, the return of private newspaper vendors in urban China in the late 1970s symbolized the arrival of a media market and the end of China Post's monopoly in newspaper distribution and retailing.

By 2000, two major structural and historical forces had gathered into a storm behind the backs of Feng and her family, who have depended on the newsstand to sustain their livelihoods since the late 1980s. First, the Chinese media industry had started a recentralization drive and China Post had strived to reclaim the state's share in the newspaper distributing and retailing markets. Second, as Beijing geared up for the 2008 Olympics, makeshift newsstands such as Feng's were seen as incompatible with its image as a world-class city. The result was that uniformly manufactured newspaper booths, as seen in the photo, were rented out by the state to individual street vendors. Under official policy, existing newsstand operators such as Feng and laid-off workers were to be given priority in the allocation of these booths. In reality, however, those with power seized the opportunity to grab the operating licenses of these booths, re-renting them for profit-making purposes, driving poor and powerless existing operators such as Feng out of business, or to less desirable locations.

Feng had lost an opportunity to move into a booth earlier when she was told that she needed to come up with a one-time deposit of 10,000 yuan, an astronomical figure for her, and a monthly rental fee of 800 yuan, an extremely high figure in relation to the potential revenue of the operation (she later found out that the actual monthly rental fee was 300 yuan, and she insisted that officials lied to her so that she would voluntarily opt out). In November 2000, in the final drive to "beautify" Beijing for the Olympic bid, Feng was told by the newspaper retailing company to submit a drawing of her street corner and was promised a new booth in the same location. However, this never happened. The booth went to the well-connected Zhang family; Zhang's wife had already operated a lucrative lottery ticket booth near the district government office.

Since then, Feng has sustained a protracted struggle to continue her makeshift newsstand operation on that very street corner. She occupied the new booth for eight days and nights in freezing Beijing winter weather when it was first put up. When her cart was once again turned upside down by a member of the Zhang family, she mustered all her energy to smash a brick into the Zhang family booth behind her, breaking a glass window. She appealed to the Beijing municipal and Chaoyang District handicapped people's associations. She went to the Chaoyang District municipal office, kneeling in front of officials for a resolution of the conflict. Chaoyang municipal officials predictably sent her case back to the Chaowai Neighborhood Office, the very jurisdiction in which the

Zhang family has its power base, or in the words of Feng, "back to Zhang Laikuan's household." She also sought justice through the local media. The power of the Zhang family and their ability to retain the state-owned booth in the face of Feng's repeated appeals is obvious. However, Feng's ability to sustain her resistance and to continue to operate her makeshift newsstand in apparent violation of local administrative orders is also remarkable. Driving Feng's determined resistance is her normative expectations about what a socialist system should be and her outrage at the injustice of the current system. As she stated in an appeal letter addressed to "concerned responsible persons":

> Zhang Laikuan abused the power of his office. He colluded with the newspaper retailing company and the district government offices and bullied ordinary folks like us. Where is justice? A socialist country of ours should not tolerate this kind of rotten officials. . . . I demand that justice be returned to a handicapped person, so that my family can continue to survive.[2]

Apart from her inner sense of economic and social justice, Feng has also drawn her strength from the solidarity of ordinary people on the street. In her letter, she described how, when her newsstand was turned upside down and newspapers scattered all over, people on the streets helped to collect the papers. In fact, I first met Feng in the summer of 2001 when I bought a newspaper from her and saw a tearful Feng being comforted by two customers after her newsstand operating license, which had been taken away by officials for an "annual check," was not returned to her on time, making her worried that it might be revoked forever. Since then, I would visit her every time I went to Beijing. During a 2002 trip, a middle-aged woman recounted how she had supported Feng by boycotting the Zhang family booth. In June 2004, I witnessed a middle-aged, male, laid-off worker helping Feng to sell newspapers. When I returned in January 2005, an old lady had come to lend a hand to Feng because the laid-off worker had become sick and could no longer come. The old lady said that she lived in the neighborhood as a well-off retiree, and she found her companionship to Feng meaningful. When I visited again on July 1, 2007, two retired women, as well as the male laid-off worker I had encountered before, came to lend a hand at different times. Meanwhile, McDonald's, which has an outlet just a few steps away from Feng's newsstand, had mounted its bright protective umbrellas for her. If McDonald's has turned Feng's newsstand into a space for advertisement and the promotion of transnational corporate benevolence, to the local community in this highly mobile and seemingly impersonal street corner, Feng and her newsstand have become of a symbol of defiance and a site of local solidarity.

This street scene signifies a whole range of broad issues. It is about the mutual constitution between a particular configuration of state and market power and the Chinese citizenry in the era of globalization. It is about new developments in China's three decades of market reforms and the displacement of owner-operators such as Feng in the ongoing world historical processes of capitalist "accumulation by dispossession."[3] It is about contradictions between the promises of "socialism with Chinese characteristics" and the actual practices of political economic power in the system. It is also about resistance and social contestation. The nature of domination and resistance at the present, however, is more multifaceted than that of the 1989 era, which was symbolized by the famous man-versus-tank Beijing street scene.[4] In place of the anonymous young and educated urban male—the perfect signifier of a political and civil subject in the liberal democratic discourse—we have Feng, a poor and handicapped old woman from the ranks of China's subaltern classes. In the place of the tank, an unambiguous symbol of the repressive and singular force of the Chinese state, we have the modern newspaper booth and the localized web of political and economic power relations it carries, as well as Feng's multifaceted relationship with the state, manifested in her normative expectations from and legitimate claims over the state, and her relationships with local state offices and agents. It is about the social dimensions and the human faces of the grand narratives of Chinese modernization, "China's rising," China's democratization, and China's global reintegration. More specifically, it is about the necessity and importance of reinserting a social analysis in grasping China's spectacular emergence as a global economic power, because the story about contemporary China is also the story of the reconstitution of class relations in China, and as Dutton has put it, it is the story of "not just the new mercantile class that has grown rich with reform, but also of the subaltern classes that have not"[5] and, I should add, those in between or who considered themselves to be in between. Finally, it is about the dynamics of Chinese society, the resilience of subalterns like Feng in China's relentless march toward modernization and global reintegration. It is about her relationships with her customers, ordinary pedestrians, her supporters, and their search for meaning and community. This is a relationship of solidarity, and yet it is also one of ambivalence, tension, and even division, as manifested in Feng's uneasy encounter with the hired attendee inside the Zhang family's booth, a rural migrant whose precarious presence in the urban space is predicated upon Feng's potential displacement in that very space.

THE BOOK'S TOPIC AND CONTEXT

This book, a sequel to my 1998 book, can be seen as an extended version of the above story: about the mutual constitution between the communication system, the party-state, and Chinese society in the context of accelerated market reforms and global reintegration, marked, among other milestones, by China's accession to the World Trade Organization (WTO) in 2001 and Beijing's successful bid to stage the 2008 Olympics. In my 1998 book, I analyzed how the struggle for the democratization of the Chinese media system in the initial reform era culminated in 1989 and how the violent repression that year was followed by a process of rapid commercialization after Deng called for accelerated market reforms in 1992, resulting in a fusion of political control and the market imperative in the media. In this book, I situate the Chinese communication system in the evolving state-society nexus in post-1989 China and analyze the dynamics of communication, the formation of class and other forms of power relations, and social contestation during a period of deepening market reforms.

The broad context for this analysis is "the neoliberal revolution" and the forging of the "market state"[6] in the global political economy since the late 1970s and the Chinese state's attempt, as a result, to construct a "socialism market economy"—although David Harvey, emphasizing how reform-era Chinese political economy "increasingly incorporates neoliberal elements interdigitated with authoritarian centralized control," has called it "neoliberalism with Chinese characteristics."[7] Within this context, neoliberalism is not "just a reincarnation of laissez-fair sentiment or a simple neo-classical attachment to the idea of the inherent efficiency of markets."[8] Nor is it merely the economic policies of market liberalization, deregulation, privatization, and fiscal austerity associated with the "Washington Consensus" and the "shock therapy" and "structural adjustment programs" applied to Russia and other transitional economies, to which China is seen as an exception.[9] Rather, neoliberalism has been understood in contemporary social theory as a governmentality that "relies on market knowledge and calculations for a politics of subjection and subject-making"[10] and "a concept of a larger social and political agenda for revolutionary change" that "aimed at nothing less than extending the values and relations of markets into a model for the broader organization of politics and society."[11] As a response to the crisis of accumulation in Western capitalism in the 1970s and a potential antidote to threats to the capitalist social order posed by the "embedded liberalism" of the post–World World II period and the radical social movements of the late 1960s and early 1970s, neoliberalism is "nothing less than a defining movement of our age"[12] and "a *political* project to re-establish the conditions for capital accumulation" and restoring capitalist class power.[13] Moreover, as analysts such as Harvey and Robison agree, there are inconsistencies and tensions between neoliberalism as a political economic theory and the actual practices of neoliberalization in various countries. Consequently, the theoretical utopianism of the neoliberal argument has worked primarily either as "a system of justification and legitimation for whatever needed to be done"[14] to restore or newly create the power of an economic elite or as a means for the more general "instrumental harnessing of the market state to serve various institutional or private interests."[15]

To be sure, China is not an openly committed neoliberal capitalist social formation. Nor did the post-Mao leadership launch the economic reforms with an ideological commitment to neoliberalism.[16] The socialist legacies and promises of the Chinese state must be taken seriously, and it would be a mistake to simply equate the Chinese state with neoliberal market authoritarian states elsewhere in the world.[17] Nevertheless, neoliberal ideas have been influential in China as the post-Mao leadership addressed the specific crises of state socialism and searched for new ways to develop the country while ensuring its own grip on power.[18] In particular, the defining characteristics of neoliberal governmentality, that is, the infiltration of market-driven truths and calculations into the domain of politics, have in many ways characterized China's post-1989 accelerated transition from a planned economy to a market economy. Specifically, the Chinese state has been pragmatically deploying what Aihwa Ong has identified as the twin modalities of the neoliberal governmentality—"neoliberalism as exception" and "exceptions to neoliberalism"—in its attempt to build a "socialist market economy."[19] While "neoliberalism as exception" is deployed to subject certain populations, places, and socioeconomic domains to neoliberal calculations to maximize entrepreneurial dynamism and facilitate interactions with global markets, "exceptions to neoliberalism" are invoked in political decisions to "exclude populations and places from neoliberal calculations and choices" to either protect social safety nets or to strip away all forms of political protection.[20] To apply Ong's concepts to the Chinese media system, the establishment of a market-oriented urban subsidiary newspaper by a party organ can be seen as the application of "neoliberalism as exception." On the other hand, the ban on the establishment of a newspaper as an independent market entity can be seen as an "exception to neoliberalism."

This book not only offers an analysis of both the institutional and discursive dimensions of the Chinese communication system under the influence of neoliberalism beginning in the early 1990s under the Jiang Zemin leadership, but also provides a portrayal of the broader Chinese political economy and the changing dynamics of Chinese society through the prism of communication. In particular, I foreground the fact that the Chinese party-state has not only embraced the market rationality and committed to the unleashing of individual entrepreneurial freedoms and other new sources of private power and interests, but also set in motion— either directly sanctioned or indirectly failed to constrain—a whole range of neoliberal and predatory practices involving "accumulation by dispossession," from the privatization of state-owned enterprises to the seizure of farmlands, and from the commodification of a wide range of cultural forms to the destruction of the environmental commons. The resultant "new society,"[21] one of the most inequitable in the world (ranked 90th of 131 countries by the United Nations in a 2005 report),[22] has been characterized by a fractured structure, acute divisions along class, rural/urban, ethnic, and regional cleavages, and heightened conflicts. The Hu Jintao leadership, recognizing that social instability had reached the "red line" after it came to power in late 2002 and assumed full control of the Chinese state in late 2004 (when Hu assumed control of the Chinese military), has intensified its attempts to stabilize such a fluid, and indeed potentially explosive, social field for more sustainable development of the Chinese political economy. This is the terrain and context that the rapidly transforming Chinese communication system helps to shape and in which this system is embedded.

THE BOOK'S FRAMEWORK AND SCOPE

"Today the sweep and import of communication have become virtually uncontained. To study communication," as Dan Schiller put it, "is to make arguments about the forms and determinants of sociocultural development as such."[23] Rather than study Chinese communication institutions and processes in isolation and in a framework that focuses on political control alone, this book draws upon the tradition of critical communication scholarship, which aims to develop an integrative framework that is capable of "relating the various levels of the mass communication processes, both to each other and to the central dimensions of social structure and social processes."[24] As British media scholars Peter Golding and Graham Murdock noted, such an approach entails three key concerns.

First, this approach entails a focus on the relations between the unequal distribution of control over systems of communications and wider patterns of inequality in the distribution of wealth and power, particularly "between the mass media and the central axis of stratification—the class structure."[25] This point is particularly relevant to contemporary China, where accelerated market reforms have not only accentuated preexisting political, economic, and social inequalities, but have also created new forms of social inclusion and exclusion, engendering rapid processes of social stratification and class polarization.

Second, such an approach addresses the processes of legitimation, through which the prevailing structures of advantage and inequality are presented as natural and inevitable. Again, this concern is paramount in studying contemporary Chinese communication. How has the party-state managed to avoid a near-death experience and sustain its rule since 1989? How does the party address the question of legitimacy? How are capitalistic social relations installed, understood, legitimated, or not legitimated in a socioeconomic system that not only resulted from a communist revolution and experienced its radical aftermath, the Cultural Revolution, but also continues to call itself "socialist"? What is the role of communication, culture, and ideology in this process?

Third, this approach foregrounds social conflicts. As Golding and Murdoch went on to say,

> These processes of incorporation and legitimation do not work in an entirely smooth and uninterrupted manner, however. On the contrary, gaps and contradictions are constantly appearing between what is supposed to be happening and what is actually taking place, between what has been promised and what has been delivered. Into these cracks and fissures flow currents of criticism and movements of contestation. Our third and final starting point, then, is with the sources of social dissent and political struggle, and with the dialectical relations between challenge and incorporation.[26]

In the case of China, to say that the process is not "entirely smooth and uninterrupted" is certainly an understatement. Rather, China's social transformation is boiling with—even constituted by—political economic contradictions, social conflicts, and ideological and cultural tensions. On the one hand, the reform era has witnessed the progressive expansion of market relations and the pragmatic implementation of neoliberalism as a "technology of governing" whereby "governing activities are recast as non-political and nonideological problems that need technical solutions."[27] On the other hand, oppositions against neoliberal developments continue to surface at every turn of the reform process in politics and ideology. Most notably, intensive ideological and policy struggles within the elite resulted in the "first debate on reform" between 1982 and 1984, which legitimated a "planned commodity economy," the "second debate on reform" between 1989 and 1992, which ended with Deng's imposition of the no-debate curse—that is, there should be no debate about whether reform policies are capitalist or socialist—and accelerated market-oriented reforms under the banner of constructing a "socialist market economy."[28] Within Chinese society, as Elizabeth Perry and Mark Selden have observed, the reform process has engendered multifaceted conflicts and myriad arenas of resistance at every stage, from tax riots, labor strikes, and interethnic clashes to environmental, anticorruption, and gender protests, legal challenges, pro-democracy demonstrations, local electoral disputes, religious rebellions, and even mass suicides. Moreover, "the emerging patterns of conflict and resistance" have "stimulated and shaped significant dimensions of the reform programme itself."[29]

As the processes of social stratification, class polarization, and cultural displacement accelerate in a rapidly globalizing context since the signing of China's WTO accession agreement with the United States in 1999, the frequency and velocity, as well as the breadth and scope, of these "hydra-headed" conflicts and resistance have also intensified at both elite and popular levels. Outside China and from the underground, the Falun Gong movement, which exposes the profound cultural contradictions of the Chinese reform process, has been a permanent thorn in the side of the Chinese party-state since its massive 1999 sit-in outside the Zhongnanhai party headquarters.[30] The movement escalated its struggles in the early 2000s by hacking into Chinese communication systems and publishing its infamous "Nine Commentaries" in 2004, a polemical critique of the Chinese Communist Party from a Cold War–inspired, ultra-right political perspective. The "obtrusive" figure of the Falun Gong reporter/protester Wang Wenyi interrupting Chinese president Hu Jintao's address at his official reception hosted by U.S. president George Bush on the White House's southern lawn on April 20, 2006, was the latest high-profile episode of this sustained conflict. Inside China, as elite and popular debates about the future direction of the reform process intensified since 2004, the number of officially recorded "mass incidents"—a euphemism for riots and uprisings by a wide range of disenfranchised and dispossessed social groups—reached 74,000 during 2004 and 87,000 in 2005, up from 58,000 in 2003 and 10,000 in 1994,[31] including the widely known Dongzhou village case in Guangdong, in which the police shot at least three villagers to death.[32]

The extraordinary situation in China is that a state that was forged in a communist revolution and still claims to build socialism has been pursuing, in the words of Arif Dirlik, "a paradigm of development that was the product of capitalism," thus turning socialism into "a cover for policies of development inspired by capitalism."[33] Such a unique historical condition has meant that the objective processes of neoliberal "accumulation by dispossession" and the consequences of rapid class polarization and cultural dislocation have been subjectively experienced by a population that has been educated in the socialist ideology of equality, social justice, and the rightness, if not the liberal legal right, of rebellion. Despite official blackouts of news on "mass events" and the media's relentless promotion of economic prosperity and cultural festivity, China's different social classes experience and feel an acute sense of class conflicts. As an unusually candid survey conducted by the Chinese Academy of Social Sciences revealed, China's urban population expressed a strong sense of social conflict along major political economic cleavages. The survey revealed that 79.1 percent feel various degrees of conflicts between capital and labor, 78.1 percent feel conflicts between officials and the ordinary people, and

75.8 percent feel conflicts between the rich and the poor.[34] Moreover, the population groups that identify themselves as either at the top or at the bottom of the class structure tend to perceive stronger social conflicts along these dimensions.[35] Not only does there exist "apparent mutual hostility between the rich and the poor," but "a significant proportion of those who self-identify as being at the top of the social structure are unwilling to shoulder the responsibility of helping the poor."[36] In fact, nearly 50 percent of those polled opposed increasing taxation to alleviate poverty.[37] Considering the urban bias of the survey, which was conducted in the metropolitan centers and provincial capitals, the actual sense of class division is probably much sharper. This heightened level of sensitivity toward social division and injustice on the part of the lower classes, as well as the arrogance of the rich and the powerful, is precisely what explains why a traffic incident involving a BMW driver and a peasant in Harbin turned into the explosive "BMW incident" in the Chinese media and cyberspace in 2003. The same reasons also explain why an ostensibly "purely pedestrian" encounter between a self-proclaimed ranking government official and a lowly porter in Sichuan Province turned into the October 18, 2004, "Wanzhou uprising" in which tens of thousands of ordinary people stormed the city square and set fire to the city hall.[38] As I will show in this book, by this time a broader ideological and policy debate about the future of China's reform, the "third debate on reform," was already under way in the Chinese media and ideological field.

The party-state's relentless efforts at control and the members of Chinese society's persistent challenges against such control in the realm of communication are two sides of the same conflicted historical process, which unfolds through both state and society. In this book, I not only describe the making of authoritarian formations in the Chinese communication system and the role of communication in the constitution of "China's new order,"[39] but also analyze the unfolding dynamics of communication politics and the uneven terrains over which various social forces struggle for their respective stakes during China's epochal transformation. In doing so, this book continues and extends the themes in my previous book in a number of ways.

First, while China's communication system is my focal point, I situate it within the wider field of Chinese social relations, particularly the political, economic, and social struggles of China's elite and popular social forces and their discourses, consciousnesses, and lived experiences.

Second, the materiality and economic dimension of communication, symbolized by Feng's dependence on selling newspapers to sustain her livelihood, assumes critical importance. I treat communication not only as a key dimension of Chinese politics, but also as an increasingly important sector of the Chinese economy, a site of capital accumulation, as well as a crucial means of social organization and class and identity formation in the current era of "informationalized capitalism."[40] My analysis encompasses not only the news media, but also China's rapidly expanding and converging telecommunication, information, and entertainment industries. The Internet, which has emerged as the system's most dynamic part since the late 1990s, also figures significantly.

Third, I locate the evolving dynamics of power and contestation inside and around the Chinese communication system within the broader global political economy and the ongoing currents of global capital and cultural flows. From the Chinese state's release of a jailed journalist in response to international pressures to the entry of foreign media capital and the pivotal role of Lang Xianping, a transnationally located scholar, in stirring up a media and Internet debate on the direction of state enterprise reform and triggering the much broader "third debate on reform" between 2004 and 2006, the interaction between Chinese and global forces constitutes a key dimension of this study.

Finally, I historicize developments in the Chinese communication, state, and society nexus since the 1990s and analyze how the institutional and ideological legacies of Chinese socialism continue to cast a long shadow over them.

In all these ways, I aim to examine the institutions, processes, and contents of contemporary Chinese communication across and beyond the binary conceptual grids of state and market, global and local, structure and agency, elite and popular, left and right, and class and nation, as well as liberal-pluralist-inspired questions about whether the state is powerful and autonomous and whether the media serve state power.[41] In particular, I engage issues regarding the nature of the Chinese state and analyze it in relation to its historical legacy and its constitution as *both* a political singularity ruled by the Communist Party as a socially penetrating organization with "a massive power base across social cleavages"[42] *and* a multifaceted and "ever shifting assemblage of planning, operations, and tactics increasingly informed by neoliberal reason to combat neoliberal forces in the world at large."[43] In other words, I foreground a concept of the Chinese state as a contradictory entity and as a site of struggle between competing bureaucratic interests, divergent social forces, and different visions of Chinese modernity.[44] As it sustains and is sustained by both its revolutionary legacy and the imperative of bureaucratic self-preservation, it is also simultaneously transforming and being transformed by internal and external social forces.

THE BOOK'S ORGANIZATION AND OBJECTIVES

The book is based on research conducted both inside and outside China between 1998 and early 2007, including documentary research, media content analysis, more than half a dozen field trips, and nearly 200 formal and informal interviews with journalists, policy makers, private media operators, and academics.[45]

Chapters 1 through 4 foreground the political economic and ideological transformations in the Chinese communication system and the complicated ways in which these have been shaped by the broader Chinese political economy and ongoing social struggles, on the one hand, and have contributed to the reconstitution of new Chinese social relations and social consciousnesses, on the other. Chapters 5 and 6 examine the structure and the substance of the highly fluid and rapidly transforming Chinese "public sphere" in the form of case studies.

Specifically, chapter 1 analyzes the reconfiguration of the party-state's regime of political, bureaucratic, regulatory, ideological, and normative power in the Chinese communication system in response to accelerated commodification, intensified ideological and social struggles, and rapid technological developments. Chapter 2 describes the economic transformation of state media and cultural institutions and processes of state capital formation and class formation within and through the media and cultural fields. Together, these two chapters delineate the political economic and ideological makeup of the Chinese communication system: while the party-state has reacted to challenges from below by persistently reinventing and tightening up control of the system, it has also strategically and irreversibly transformed it into a pivotal site of market-oriented development. In turn, this creates the conditions and sets the limits for the involvement of transnational and domestic private capital in this system, further transforming Chinese social relations and reconfiguring the ideological and cultural fields.

Consequently, chapter 3 examines the global reintegration of the Chinese communication system and the political economic and sociocultural implications of this integration, with a focus on communication and transnational class formation, on the one hand, and the articulation and containment of various nationalistic discourses, on the other. Chapter 4 historicizes and analyzes the formation of domestic private media capital and its implications.

To deepen the analysis in the first four chapters, chapter 5 focuses on media and Internet mobilization around civil rights and legal justice and the question of rural and urban social division through two case studies. The first case revolves around Sun Zhigang, a young graphic designer who was beaten to death in a police detention center for rural migrants in

Guangzhou in 2003. The second case concerns the politicization of the criminal case of Wang Binyu, a rural migrant worker who was executed by the state for killing four people after failing to get his unpaid salary. Chapter 6 examines the political, economic, and ideological structuring of China's media and Internet discourses over the issues concerning property rights reform and the ownership of the means of production in the "Lang Xianping Storm" in late 2004, which triggered the "third debate on reform" regarding the fundamental directions of China's social transformation in the subsequent two years. The conclusion revisits many of the main themes in the book's six main chapters while updating developments in Chinese communication politics from late 2006 to the Chinese Communist Party's 17th national congress in October 2007.

Although I invoke the Habermasian concept of the "public sphere" in this context, these case studies are not designed to measure the Chinese "public sphere" against some dehistoricized and idealized notion in which unequal power relations are bracketed and "all members of polity" have ownership, while the role of the state is presumably limited to one of keeping such a public sphere "functioning and fair."[46] Following scholars such as Nancy Fraser, who has critiqued Jürgen Habermas's original formulation, I take for granted observations about the exclusionary nature of the "bourgeois public sphere" as it emerged historically in the Western European context.[47] I also accept the crucial point that "the emergence of a bourgeois public was never defined solely by the struggle against absolutism and traditional authority, but . . . addressed the problem of popular containment as well. The public sphere was always constituted by conflict."[48] That is, the "bourgeois public sphere" is the institutional vehicle for a major historical transformation in the nature of political domination from one based primarily on acquiescence to superior force to one based on consent supplemented with some measure of repression. This recognition of the exclusionary and class-dominated nature of the actually existing "bourgeois public sphere" and its antagonistic relationship with subaltern publics is not meant to dismiss its historical achievements, nor to reject its democratic promises and widespread appeals across a wide range of social classes, let alone to belittle both the courage and sincerity of its proponents. Rather, such a recognition is necessary because it historicizes the "public sphere" and provides the necessary vantage point from which to particularize and denaturalize any universalistic claims of an emerging Chinese bourgeoisie aiming to replace the party to establish hegemonic rule over Chinese society in the current historical conjuncture.

Once again, the peculiar situation in China is that a party-state, which at its founding claimed to represent the national bourgeoisie but comprised primarily a variety of counter-bourgeois publics—peasants, workers, women, ethnic groups, nationalists, as well as socialists and communists—is simultaneously re-engendering a bourgeoisie. Moreover, this process took off in the aftermath of the disastrous experiment with the radical leftist politics of "proletariat power" aimed to eliminate any bourgeois elements during the Cultural Revolution.[49] The contradictory nature of China's party-state formation, its tumultuous and complicated historical legacies, and the balance of power in contemporary Chinese society mean that popular containment, as much as struggle against an authoritarian state, may have become the political priority of the newly re-engendered Chinese bourgeoisie, which has not only yet to cut its umbilical cord with the party to become a "class for itself," but also has been officially incorporated into the party through the so-called three represents (*sange daibiao*) doctrine. This doctrine, first articulated in 2000 and codified into the party's Constitution in 2002, repositions the party from a supposedly working-class vanguard to a party of "the Chinese people and the Chinese nation," including China's rising capitalist, technocratic, managerial, and professional strata.[50] As I will demonstrate in chapters 5 and 6, profound antagonisms among different social classes, the party's legitimation imperative, and the political economy of China's media and Internet systems, together with the Chinese bourgeoisie's dual imperative of class containment and opposition against authoritarian state power, intersect in complicated ways to shape the terms and dynamics of media and Internet discourses on civil rights, economic and social rights, legal justice, and property rights—key issues in the contestation over China's future.

The book aims to accomplish a twofold objective: to foreground the central role of communication in the processes of China's social transformation and to shed light onto these processes through the prism of communication. I hope to provide not only a portrayal of the Chinese communication system beyond Western news headlines about the jailing of another Internet activist or the gold rush dreams of yet another global media mogul, but also a snapshot of Chinese state-society relations at a moment of great dynamism and uncertainty. In particular, I hope to describe a state of unsettled elite division and fortifying intra-elite complicity, heightening social conflict and popular contestation and, above all, intricate complexity.

As the following pages will show, this is a China in which the party-state acts as well as reacts. This is a China in which class relations and class conflicts redefine social dynamics apart from and under the control of the party-state. This is a China in which uneven development and rural impoverishment, alongside corruption, privatization of social assets, and dismantling of an already inadequate and unevenly distributed system of social security in crucial domains such as education, medical care, pensions, and housing have become major sites of political contestation. This is a China in which authoritarian and even neofascistic tendencies visibly continue, along with democratic and socialist projects, not only under the auspices of the party-state, but sometimes despite it. Above all, this is a China in which the stakes in controlling and accessing the means of social communication have never been so high and "the power to discourse" (*huayu quan*) has never been so central to the unfolding process of social struggle.

NOTES

1. The 17th Party Congress update: Top Buzzwords and the Science of Claps, shanghaiist.com/2007/10/18/17th_party_cong.php (accessed 20 Oct. 2007).

2. Handwritten letter obtained from Feng Xiuju, 8 Jan. 2005, Beijing.

3. As David Harvey argues, this concept foregrounds "the continuous role and persistence of the predatory practices of 'primitive' or 'original' accumulation within the long historical geography of capital accumulation." See David Harvey, *The New Imperialism* (Oxford: Oxford University Press, 2003), 144. These practices range from the commodification of land and the forceful expulsion of peasant populations to the conversion of common, collective, and state forms of property rights into exclusive private property rights to the commodification of cultural forms, histories, intellectual creativity, and the depletion, and even wholesale commodification, of nature. Harvey, *The New Imperialism*, 145.

4. Michael Dutton, *Streetlife China* (Cambridge: Cambridge University Press, 1998), 17.

5. Dutton, *Streetlife*, 3.

6. Richard Robison, ed., *The Neo-Liberal Revolution: Forging the Market State* (New York: Palgrave Macmillan, 2006).

7. David Harvey, *A Brief History of Neoliberalism* (New York: Oxford University Press, 2005), 120.

8. Richard Robison, "Neo-Liberalism and the Market State: What Is the Ideal Shell?" in Robison, ed., *The Neo-Liberal Revolution*, 4.

9. Joseph Stiglitz, *Globalization and Its Discontents* (New York: Norton, 2002); for relevant discussion, see Huang Ping and Cui Ziyuan, *Zhongguo yu quanqiuhua: Huashengtun gongshi huanshi Beijing gongshi* (China and Globalization: The Washington Consensus or the Beijing Consensus) (Beijing: Shehuikexue wenxian chubanshe, 2005).

10. Aihwa Ong, *Neoliberalism as Exception: Mutations in Citizenship and Sovereignty* (Durham, N.C.: Duke University Press, 2006), 13.

11. Richard Robison, "Preface," in Robison, ed., *The Neo-Liberal Revolution*, vii; Robison, "Neo-Liberalism and the Market State," 4.

12. Robison, "Preface," vii.

13. Harvey, *A Brief History*, 19, emphasis in the original.

14. Harvey, *A Brief History*, 19.

15. Robison, "Introduction," in Robison, ed., *The Neo-liberal Revolution*, xiii.

16. As Harvey commented, whether China's transition to a market economy and its historically contingent articulation with the neoliberal turn in the advanced capitalist world "was all a matter of conscious though adaptive planning ('groping the stones while crossing the river' as Deng called it) or the working out, behind the backs of the party politicians, of an inexorable logic deriving from the initial premises of Deng's market reforms, will doubtless long be debated." *A Brief History*, 122.

17. For further elaboration, see Yuezhi Zhao, "Neoliberal Strategies, Socialist Legacies: Communication and State Transformation in China," in *Global Communication: Toward a Transcultural Political Economy*, ed. Paula Chakravartty and Yuezhi Zhao (Lanham, Md.: Rowman & Littlefield, 2007); see also Elizabeth J. Perry, "Studying Chinese Politics: Farewell to Revolution?" *China Journal* 57 (Jan. 2007): 1–22, for a discussion of the limits of comparing China's "revolutionary authoritarianism" with other forms of authoritarianism.

18. For analyses of the influence of neoliberal ideas in Chinese intellectual discourses and policies, see Wang Hui, *China's New Order*, ed. Theodore Hunters (Cambridge, Mass.: Harvard University Press, 2003); Harvey, *A Brief History*; Ong, *Neoliberalism as Exception*; Shaun Breslin, "Serving the Market or Serving the Party: Neo-liberalism in China," in Robison, ed., *The Neo-Liberal Revolution*, 114–134; Huang Ping, Yao Yang, and Han Yuhai, *Women de shidai* (Our Times) (Beijing: Central Compilation & Translation Press, 2006). For analyses of the influence of neoliberalism in Chinese media, see Yuezhi Zhao, "'Enter the World': Neo-Liberalism, the Dream for a Strong Nation, and Chinese Press Discourse on the WTO," in *Chinese Media, Global Contexts*, ed. Chin-chuan Lee, 32–56 (London: RoutledgeCurzon, 2003); Yuezhi Zhao, "The Rich, the Laid-off, and the Criminals in Tabloid Tales: Read All about It!" in *Popular China: Unofficial Culture in a Globalizing Society*, ed. Perry Link, Richard P. Madsen, and Paul G. Pickowicz, 111–135 (Lanham, Md.: Rowman & Littlefield, 2002).

19. Ong, *Neoliberalism as Exception*.

20. Ong, *Neoliberalism as Exception*, 4.

21. Sun Liping, *Duanlie: Ershishiji jiushi niandai yilai de Zhongguo shehui* (Fractured: Chinese Society since the 1990s) (Beijing: Shehui kexue wenxian chubanshe, 2003); Sun Liping, *Shiheng: Duanlieshehui de yunzuo luoji* (Imbalance: The Logic of a Fractured Society) (Beijing: Shehui kexue wenxian chubanshe, 2004).

22. Jonathan Manthorpe, "Communist Party Divided on Dealing with Dissidents," *Vancouver Sun*, 30 Jan. 2006, E3.

23. Dan Schiller, *Theorizing Communication: A History* (New York: Oxford University Press, 1996), vii.

24. Peter Golding and Graham Murdoch, "Theories of Communication and Theories of Society," *Communication Research* 5, no. 3 (July 1978): 353.

25. Golding and Murdoch, "Theories," 353.

26. Golding and Murdoch, "Theories," 353.

27. Ong, *Neoliberalism as Exception*, 3.

28. For accounts of these debates, see Joseph Fewsmith, *China since Tiananmen: The Politics of Transition* (Cambridge: Cambridge University Press, 2001) and Ma Licheng and Ling Zhijun, *Jiaofeng: Dangdai Zhongguo sanci sixiang jiefang shilu*

(Cross-Sword: A Record on the Three Movements of Thought Liberation in Contemporary China) (Beijing: Jinri Zhongguo chubanshe, 1998). Note the shift in ideological frame in characterizing and defining the "three debates" from that of Ma and Ling, two market liberals who chronicled China's reform-era ideological struggles in terms of three consecutive "thought liberation" movements from the socialist ideology and characterized the Jiang Zemin leadership's embrace of privatization in the "private versus public" debate of 1997 as the third "thought liberation" (after the "truth debate" in 1978 and the "socialist versus capitalist" debate in 1992).

29. Elizabeth J. Perry and Mark Selden, "Introduction: Reform and Resistance in Contemporary China," in *Chinese Society: Change, Conflict and Resistance*, 2nd ed., ed. Elizabeth J. Perry and Mark Selden, 1–22 (London: RoutledgeCurzon, 2003).

30. Yuezhi Zhao, "Falun Gong, Identity, and the Struggle for Meaning Inside and Outside China," in *Contesting Media Power: Alternative Media in a Networked World*, ed. Nick Couldry and James Curran, 209–224 (Lanham, Md.: Rowman & Littlefield, 2003).

31. Geoff Dyer, "Shanghai Property Boom Brings Eviction Protests," *Financial Times*, 13 Aug. 2005, news.ft.com/cms/s/d344a728-0b86-11da-9939-00000e2511c8 .html (accessed 20 Aug. 2005).

32. Mark Magnier, "Farmers Stand Tall against China's Land Grab," *Vancouver Sun*, 20 Apr. 2006, A13.

33. Arif Dirlik, *Marxism in the Chinese Revolution* (Lanham, Md.: Rowman & Littlefield, 2005), 157, 9.

34. Li Peilin, Zhang Yi, Zhao Yandong, and Liang Dong, *Shehui chongtu yu jieji yishi* (Social Conflicts and Class Consciousnesses) (Beijing: Shehui kexue wenxian chubanshe, 2005), 136–138.

35. Li et al., *Shehui chongtu*, 138–142.

36. Li et al., *Shehui chongtu*, 171, 174–175.

37. Li et al., *Shehui chongtu*, 179.

38. Joseph Kahn, "China's 'Haves' Stir the 'Have Nots' to Violence," *New York Times*, 31 Dec. 2004, www.nytimes.com/2004/12/31/international/asia/31china .html?ex=1105499763&ei=1&en=c02ce9731dcd462b (accessed 31 Dec. 2004).

39. Wang Hui, *China's New Order*.

40. Dan Schiller, *How to Think about Information* (Urbana: University of Illinois Press, 2007).

41. As Jing Wang has argued, the crucial question is not whether the state is powerful or not, but what is the intention and purpose of state power. See Jing Wang, "The State Question in Chinese Popular Cultural Studies" *Inter-Asia Cultural Studies* 2, no. 1 (2001): 35–52.

42. Lin Chun, *The Transformation of Chinese Socialism* (Durham, N.C.: Duke University Press, 2006), 220.

43. Ong, *Neoliberalism as Exception*, 99.

44. Zhao, "Neoliberal Strategies, Socialist Legacies."

45. While I have provided the names and dates of some interviews, confidentiality requires me to leave out the specific names of interviewees and, in some cases, exact dates and locations of interviews.

46. Daniel C. Lynch, *After the Propaganda State: Media, Politics, and "Thought Work" in Reformed China* (Stanford, Calif.: Stanford University Press, 1999), 4.

47. Nancy Fraser, "Rethinking the Public Sphere: A Contribution to the Critique of Actually Existing Democracy," in *Habermas and the Public Sphere*, ed. Craig Calhoun, 109–142 (Cambridge, Mass.: MIT Press, 1992).

48. Geoff Eley, "Nations, Publics and Political Cultures: Placing Habermas in the Nineteenth Century," in Calhoun, ed., *Habermas and the Public Sphere*, 289–339, cited in Fraser, "Rethinking," 116.

49. I use the term "bourgeois" here to mean the equivalent of the Chinese term *zichan jieji* (literally, "the class with capital assets" as a noun and those who identify with the interests of this class as an adjective, as in "bourgeois intellectuals," as opposed to "proletariat intellectuals"), which is the equivalent of the term "capitalist class" in English. However, Ellen Meiksins Wood has pointed out that "the conventional identification of *bourgeois* with *capitalist* and both with *modernity*" in English contributes to the naturalization of capitalism and prevents any imagination about noncapitalist modernities. See Ellen Meiksins Wood, *The Origin of Capitalism: A Longer View* (London: Verso, 2002), 183.

50. The "three represents" gave a revisionist interpretation of the party's history by stating that the party has always represented the developmental requirements of China's advanced productive force, represented the developing orientation of China's advanced culture, and represented the fundamental interests of the overwhelming majority of the Chinese people. See, Fewsmith, *China since Tiananmen*; Gang Lin, "Ideology and Political Institutions for a New Era," in *China After Jiang*, ed. Gang Lin and Xiaobo Hu, 39-68 (Stanford, Calif.: Stanford University Press, 2003).

1

Reconfiguring
Party-State Power

*Market Reforms, Communication,
and Control in the Digital Age*

The post-Mao Chinese state, as Wang Hui has observed, installed the
economic reforms and reinserted itself into the capitalist world system
through acts of physical violence—domestic repression of popular protest
and an external war against Vietnam in 1979, which "became China's entrance ticket to the world system."[1] The state's deployment of symbolic
violence is no less significant. Domestically, the reform program was
launched through a massive propaganda campaign against the "ultra-
leftism" of the "Gang of Four" who were ousted through a coup shortly
after Mao's death in 1976. This was soon followed by the suppression of
the "Democracy Wall" movement and the fledgling independent press
between 1978 and 1979. In 1980 the "four great freedoms" (*sida ziyou*)—
the right of the people to "speak out freely, air views freely, hold great debates, and write big-character posters" (*daming, dafang, da bianlun, daz-
ibao*)—which were entrenched in the Chinese Constitution in 1975 and
invoked by Democracy Wall activist Wei Jingsheng in self-defense at his
trial in 1979, were deleted from the Chinese Constitution. A constitutional
clause granting workers the right to strike was simultaneously removed.[2]

Internationally, media portrayal of the border war with Vietnam as a
"self-defensive" patriotic war and popular culture representation of the
war in the early 1980s, epitomized by the hit film *Wreaths under the High
Mountains* and its patriotic theme song, served to unify a national population struggling to recover from the divisive "class struggles" of the Cultural Revolution and inaugurated the reform era's nationalistic orientation. Media representations of a war with China's former socialist ally and
an enemy of the United States also reinforced disillusionment with

"socialist internationalism" and post-Mao China's pragmatic accommodation of the United States as the world's anticommunist hegemonic power at the onset of the "neoliberal revolution" launched by the electoral victories of Margaret Thatcher in 1979 and Ronald Reagan in 1980.

Just as the suppression of the Democracy Wall movement denied popular participation in China's initial transformation from state socialism, so did the state's violent suppression in 1989. Consequently, "price reform introduced at gunpoint became a success,"[3] and neoliberal-oriented economic reforms were implemented system-wide, from the overt and covert privatization of state-owned enterprises to the progressive commercialization of mass media, health care, education, housing, and other social services. Although the traces of physical violence from June 4, 1989, have long been erased from Tiananmen Square, the state's symbolic violence continues: June 4 remains at the top of the state's list of forbidden topics, not only in the media, but also in academic publications. Predictably, strict censorship rules were applied to the media's handling of the January 17, 2005, death of former party general secretary Zhao Ziyang, who had been under house arrest since 1989 due to his opposition of the military crackdown in 1989.[4] The elimination of Zhao Ziyang from public discourse and his death during house arrest underscored the fact that China's post-1989 market reforms were sustained by political and symbolic violence of the highest order.

If China boasts one of the fastest-growing economies since the 1990s, it also has one of the most oppressive regimes in using coercive state powers to control public communication. The Falun Gong movement was suppressed as a heretical religious cult. Individuals who dare to communicate unsanctioned information and promote dissenting ideas are prosecuted under the criminal offences of "disclosing state secrets," "inciting to subvert state power," and "endangering national security." On the ground, the police and, increasingly, thugs hired by local authorities detain and obstruct reporters, confiscate their audio- and videotapes, and harass or even beat them when they try to interview protesters. In "virtual China," cyber police squads, as many as 30,000 in one estimate,[5] are patrolling Chinese cyberspace, deleting politically incorrect content in real time, blocking websites, monitoring networking activities of citizens, and tracking down and arresting offending individuals. Between May 2003 and June 2004, as many as 17 Internet activists were tried in China, which resulted in jail sentences as long as 14 years, making China the top country for jailing Internet activists.[6]

Of course, the jailing of journalists and Internet writers is only a small component of a pervasive regime of coercive, regulatory, bureaucratic, technological, and normative power that penetrates every facet of Chinese public communication, from the physical design of China's Internet to the choice of words by anybody who wishes to publish in China. In October 2007, Reporters without Borders and Chinese Human Rights Defenders released an investigative report on the party-state's regime of Internet control. Written by a Chinese technician working for an Internet company under the pen name Mr. Tao, the report claims that the Chinese government "monitors the Internet by means of a skilful mix of filtering technologies, cyberpolice surveillance and propaganda" and that "[d]raconian censorship hunts down anything to do with human rights, democracy and freedom of belief. It nips free expression in the bud."[7]

Rather than focusing on one particular medium, this chapter maps some of this regime's key dimensions throughout the entire Chinese media system and highlights both the continuities and changes, including its expansion in depth and scope, as well as its growth in sophistication since the early 1990s. The chapter then contextualizes this regime within the broad contours of ideological, political, and social struggles during a period of accelerated capitalistic development, intensified social contestation, and rapid advance in digital technologies. Complementary to the existing literature's focus on the suppression of negative news in general and liberal voices in particular, I foreground the suppression of popular social protests and leftist perspectives as a key dimension of this regime.[8] Moreover, I move beyond a moralistic and anticommunistic condemnation— all too often expressed in Western media reports and in the writings of native informants/dissidents outside China—to locate party-state power in the context of the profound contradictions of "socialism with Chinese characteristics." Central to this analysis is the party-state's highly contested construction of a "revolutionary authoritarianism"[9] through both the resuscitation and modernization of its ruling technologies and the articulation and rearticulation of its revolutionary hegemony as it manages the increasingly conflictual class relations of a rapidly emerging market society. Finally, although I won't go so far as to say that "tales of China's political repression and terror have more to do with the political, ideological, and commercial objectives of Western media (with their national interests lurking behind them) than with what really happens in China today,"[10] jailed Chinese journalists and Internet writers have indeed occasionally served as bargaining chips between Western and Chinese governments in foreign policy. Consequently, it is necessary to examine the *politics* of what the *Wall Street Journal* has called the "censorship debate" in China.[11]

MAPPING POST-1989 PARTY-STATE POWER IN MEDIA AND COMMUNICATION

Based on lessons learned from the outbreak of the pro-democracy movement in 1989 in China and the collapse of Eastern European communism and the Soviet Union, wherein the political liberalization of the media was believed to be a major contributing factor,[12] the party set out to reassert media control and upgrade its ruling technologies in the post-1989 era. As part of this development, it fortified the state's entire propaganda apparatus and elevated the propaganda and ideology portfolio within the party leadership.[13] During Jiang Zemin's reign as party general secretary, Ding Guan'gen, head of the party Central Committee's Propaganda Department (PD), was simultaneously the Politburo Standing Committee member in charge of ideology and culture. Although the concentration of power under Ding in Jiang Zemin's leadership has not been repeated under the Hu Jintao leadership, the renewed emphasis on ideology and the upward flow of power in the ideological field is evident both in the leadership's consecutive ideological education campaigns among youths, party members, journalists, university professors in the social sciences (particularly those in the journalism and communication fields), and in the prominent hands-on role of Li Changchun, the Politburo Standing Committee member in charge of ideology and culture.

At the same time, the role of the government in macromanaging media structure and disciplining the media has been significantly expanded, along with the role of repressive state apparatuses such as the police and the courts in the prosecution of dissent. Thus, though the reform period has generally been characterized as an era of neoliberal downsizing of the government, captured in the "small government, big society" slogan, the same period has seen a steady increase in the number of government departments and bureaus in the communication field. In fact, the media, communication, and culture sector has been an "anomaly" considering the merger and reduction of specialized government departments, especially those in the industrial and commercial sectors.[14] In 1982 the party's broadcasting bureau was transformed into the Ministry of Radio and Television under the State Council, which evolved into the current State Administration for Radio, Film, and Television (SARFT). In 1987 the State Council created the State Press and Publications Administration (SPPA), responsible for licensing, overall planning, regulation, and market discipline of print media and audiovisual publications, including newspapers, periodicals, books, and audio and video records.

The 1990s saw the further expansion and strengthening of government agencies responsible for both communication content and the structure of rapidly expanding information, media, and cultural systems. The State Council Information Office (SCIO), modeled after the press offices of Western governments, manages government communication with the outside world. This office also doubles as the external arm of the party's PD.[15] In 1998, in the midst of major bureaucratic streamlining that witnessed the reduction in the number of government ministries from 40 to

29, the government not only strengthened the SPPA with added personnel and established the Culture Industry Bureau under the Ministry of Culture, but also established the Ministry of Information Industry (MII) to promote, coordinate, and regulate the development of China's information sector. However, the MII, created through a merger of the Ministry of Posts and Telecommunications and the Ministry of Electronic Industry, quickly proved to be inadequate and ineffectual in macromanaging a rapidly converging and globalizing information and communication sector. Consequently, in December 2001, the Chinese leadership strengthened a previously existing supraministerial coordinating body around information to formally establish the State Leadership Group on Informatization, with then premier Zhu Rongji as its leader. As of 2006, this supraministerial body was headed by Premier Wen Jiabao, with Huang Ju, Politburo Standing Committee member and deputy premier; Liu Yunshan, head of the party's PD; Zeng Peiyan, head of the State Development and Reform Commission; and Zhou Yongkang, minister of Public Security, as the group's deputy leaders, and the heads of other relevant state commissions, ministries, party departments, and government agencies responsible for various sectors of the communication and information industries as its members. This effectively created a de facto "information cabinet" above the State Council, to ensure the highest and broadest possible state stewardship over China's rapidly expanding information and communication fields. The objective is twofold: "to further strengthen leadership over the promotion of our country's informatization buildup and over the maintenance of the state's information security."[16]

The explosion of the Internet and mobile technologies and the imperative to control these highly dispersed and versatile new media have further extended the depth and scope of the Chinese state's role in the communication field. In addition to the MII, which regulates both the technological and industrial structures of China's Internet system and is responsible for licensing Internet service and content providers, a new unit, the Internet Information Management Bureau, was added to the SCIO in early 2000. This unit is charged with the responsibilities of monitoring Internet news and Bulletin Board Services (BBS) and directing party-state propaganda on the Internet.[17] Other state agencies, from the Ministry of Culture to the State Industry and Commerce Administration to the Ministry of Public Security and the Chinese military, all have jurisdiction over the Internet. In 2000 the SPPA was renamed the General Agency of Press and Publication (GAPP), and its status was upgraded from a deputy ministry–level agency to full ministry level. In addition to strengthening its enforcing capacities to combat illegal and pornographic publications and expanding its regulative capacities in publication- and copyright-related issues, an important reason for this upgrade was the agency's added responsibility for approving web-based publishing applications and monitoring web-publishing content. When the leadership orchestrated a campaign against pornographic websites in summer 2004, it mobilized as many as 14 party-state agencies in the endeavor.[18]

An apparent division of labor has emerged between the party and the government, whereby the party focuses on designing overall policy and enforcing and promoting the party line in propaganda while government departments are charged with the regulation of the structural and industrial aspects of communication industries. This division ensures that the party can legitimate its will through laws and regulations and employ state apparatuses to implement its policies. The media are still defined as the mouthpieces of the party and academic attempts at defining the media as "society's public instruments" (*shehui gongqi*) have been strictly prohibited. As "the party takes care of the media" (*dangguan meiti*), state agencies expand their role in managing communication structures and policing communication flows, serving as the judicial and executive arms of the party.

Party Propaganda Disciplines

The party's overarching power is also felt in the media's everyday practices. The party's central Propaganda Department (PD) is the omnipresent body, exerting its formidable power in sustaining the party's dominance in the area of ideology and culture.[19] Jiao Guobiao, a former journalism professor at Peking University, accused it of being "the largest and most powerful protective umbrella for the forces of evil and corruption in China" in a widely circulated 2004 Internet essay. In Jiao's polemical view, the PD operates its arbitrary and unaccountable power as if it were witchcraft, and it is as "powerful and self-righteous as the Roman Catholic Church in the Middle Ages in Europe."[20] Like the Roman Catholic Church, the PD combines traditional means with advanced communication technologies in the delivery of its messages. For example, the belief is widely circulated among China's journalistic community that the PD often issues its propaganda disciplines (*xuanchuan jilü*) through word of mouth and telephone calls made by nameless operatives. Not only is the phone number concealed, no telephone record is allowed.

As Judy Polumbaum notes, the party exercises its authority in the news media in a "directive mode,"[21] primarily accomplished through the establishment of propaganda disciplines, a set of implicit and explicit policy statements, and instructions governing the operation of the news media. This includes long-established rules, annual conferences of the heads of PDs, and periodic propaganda guidelines transmitted through various "red-headed" documents such as speeches by leaders, "urgent announcements," "minutes" of conferences, "opinions," and the articulation of an official line and exact formulation, or "the size of the mouth" (*koujing*) and wording (*tifa*) on a particular issue.[22] For example, a crucial 1953 rule that forbids party organs from criticizing the party committee with which they are affiliated remains a key instrument that keeps the media under the control of party committees at various levels. This rule is so hegemonic that it has become common sense, deeply ingrained in the collective consciousness of the entire media system. Similarly, the December 1984 "Regulations Governing the Publication of Books about the 'Great Cultural Revolution'" remains instrumental for the party in controlling media discourse on this key historical event.[23] Another long-established rule is the authority of Xinhua News Agency in enforcing a unified propaganda line. On certain events, Xinhua is the only authorized reporting agent. Media outlets have no choice but to carry the Xinhua copy, known as "general copy" (*tonggao*). Although the number of media outlets has proliferated, the role of Xinhua "general copy" has been consolidated.

The most common face-to-face form of media discipline is the brief meeting (*tongqihui*), a meeting in which key media gatekeepers are summoned to the party's PD to receive instructions. During these meetings strengths and weaknesses in media work are identified, relevant media outlets are censured, and sensitive topics are defined while the nature of their treatment/nontreatment is delineated: some are to be completely avoided, some are to be reported but without extensive treatment, and some are to be reported with Xinhua "general copy" only. Contrary to liberal expectations that the Hu Jintao leadership may loosen up propaganda control, the PD under Hu's leadership has strengthened the micromanagement of propaganda.

Some topics are either completely forbidden or to be reported under strict control—typically in the form of Xinhua "general copies" in local newspapers—when the explosive nature of an event and the ensuing international media coverage make complete domestic news blackout an unviable option. These include news reporting of ongoing social conflicts, particularly "mass events" such as workers' and farmers' protests, ethnic conflicts, and other forms of grassroots social contestation. Other taboo topics are of a more transient nature and are "defined situationally."[24] Thus, in the words of one cyber essayist, the party line is "not a straight line, but an ever-changing and hard-to-grasp curve."[25] A range of factors, including the shifting focus of the party's policy priorities at a given period, intra-elite power struggles, domestic and international political climates, and, indeed, changes in political season—for example, whether a sensitive political date or an important political event is approaching—are all possible variables. Rather than undermining the effectiveness of party control, however, the ever-shifting and unpredictable nature of the party line ensures its continuing relevance and its disciplinary power. As Zhou Yongming wrote in the context of Internet censorship, "Like a sword of Damocles hanging over editors' heads, the ambiguity of government policy in this area has turned out to be very effective."[26]

Government Regulations

The commercialization and rapid expansion of the communication industries, particularly the involvement in media production and distribution by nonparty entities, have led the party to strengthen the structural management of the media through specialized government agencies. China's global reintegration, especially the pressure of transnational capital entering the Chinese market, has made government regulation of media industries a further necessity. That is, with the development of a market-oriented media economy and globalization, the postrevolutionary Chinese state is rapidly modernizing itself, assuming the regulatory role that a modern capitalist state plays in a market economy, and turning itself into "a machine capable of mediating the contradictions of capital."[27] "Such a macroeconomic stewardship," Jing Wang has observed, "may not be a contemporary manifestation of the tyrannical impulse of the state. . . . On the contrary . . . the state sit[s] at the wheel to temper the excesses of the market and 'save capitalism from itself.'"[28] However, in contrast to communication regulatory agencies in the West, which typically operate at arm's length from the government, China's GAPP, SARFT, MII, and the Ministry of Culture are government departments subject to PD directives. In the case of the SARFT, it still has direct editorial responsibilities over China Central Television (CCTV), China National Radio, and China Radio International. Moreover, instead of passing legislation about the media, which would inevitably invoke debates over the meaning of the constitutional guarantee of press freedom at the National People's Congress (NPC), the party has opted to authorize relevant government departments to legitimate its preferred media structure by administrative "regulations" (*tiaoli*), which only require approval by the State Council. This explains why the work to draft a press law, which proceeded with considerable speed and energy in the late 1980s and invoked debates on the meaning of press freedom, was suspended immediately after 1989.[29] Since then, the call for a press law has been dropped in Chinese communication policy discourse. As of 2006, the only communication-related legislation approved by the NPC is the least controversial "Advertising Code of the People's Republic of China."

The most comprehensive government regulations in media are issued by the GAPP and the SARFT. The GAPP is responsible for the implementation of basic regulations covering four industrial sections in the printing and electronic publications field: "Regulations on Newspaper Management," "Regulations on Periodical Management," "Regulations on Publishing Management," and "Regulations on Electronic Publications." The SARFT administers the "Regulations on Film Management," "Regulations on Radio and Television Management," and "Regulations on the Management of Satellite Ground Reception Facilities." These sector-specific regulations institutionalize and legitimate the basic structure of the existing Chinese media production, circulation, and reception system: no private or foreign ownership of print and broadcasting media, state licensing of print and broadcast media organizations, the need for print media organizations to have an official sponsor at and above county-level standing and state monopoly of broadcasting, and the permit system for film and television content production, distribution, and satellite television reception. These regulations also typically contain sweeping lists of forbidden content categories. The 1997 "Regulations on Radio and Television Management," for example, contain seven forbidden content categories.[30] The "Regulations on Film Management" establish the censorship system and contain detailed procedures for its implementation.

With these administrative regulations serving as the basic framework, each government agency makes a whole range of administrative and normative orders, in the form of "stipulations" (*guiding*), "management measures" (*guanli banfa*), "notices" (*tongzhi*), and "censure notices" (*tongbao*). These instruments concretize and improvise procedures and normative guidelines for managing specific subsectors of the media industry, addressing new problems as they arise.[31] These highly arbitrary and piecemeal responses to the party's new policy initiatives and rising problems are not always enforced; nevertheless, they represent an effort to make media control more acceptable by virtue of its predictability and more legitimate within the framework of building a "socialist legal system" and establishing the "rule of law." WTO membership and related changes in the media and culture industries led to the establishment and revision of a whole series of rules and regulations since 2001, in areas ranging from copyright to foreign investment and web publishing.

Formal bureaucratic procedures and impromptu rules on "special cases" are combined to maximize disciplinary power. The SARFT's "Stipulations on TV Drama Censorship and Management," for example, is a subsector administrative order deriving its authority from the 1997 "Regulations on Radio and Television Management." It establishes two crucial mechanisms of state control in this important area of media and culture: preproduction topic approval and postproduction censorship. To begin with, no television drama will be allowed to be produced without prior topic approval; second, a topic must go through a two-tier approval system—preliminary approval by provincial broadcast bureaus and final approval by the SARFT; third, topics related to "important political, military, foreign policy, united front, nationality, religion, law and order cases, and well-known personalities" must obtain rewritten approval/clearance from relevant government authorities. This, in effect, diffuses censorship power by turning each government department into de facto gatekeepers of television drama production. After a television drama is made, it must pass censorship to obtain a distribution permit.[32] Significantly, and indicative of the progressively restrictive environment of media production, the 2004 departmental regulation has 10, rather than 7, forbidden content categories, some of which are even more comprehensive and broader than the "Regulations on Radio and Television Management."[33] Furthermore, as I will discuss in chapter 4, the SARFT can issue specific notices that impose more restrictive preapproval and censorship procedures on certain topics. Additionally, both the GAPP and the SARFT maintain the annual review system for newspaper, broadcast, and film and television program production license holders.

In contrast to print and broadcast media, the versatile and dispersed nature of the Internet has led to the state's total mobilization in a regulatory frenzy. By September 2005, the website of the China Internet Information Center had listed as many as 43 relevant laws and regulations relating to different aspects of Internet operation, with many focusing on the Internet's news and informational provision functionalities.[34] Some of these earlier regulations extended the basic principles of control over print and broadcasting media to the Internet, including mandatory permits for commercial websites providing news and BBS and provisions forbidding commercial websites to publish news reports of their own or information from overseas sources, thus ensuring the dominant status of traditional party and government media over the Internet. "Regulations on the Management of Internet News and Information Services," issued by the SCIO and MII in September 2005, consolidated and refined this regime of government power over Internet news and informational and BBS content. "No-news organizations" are only allowed to redistribute officially published news. The forbidden content categories, totaling 11, are longer than the list for broadcast and television series production, with special categories such as "spreading rumors, disturbing social order, and undermining social stability," "agitating illegal gathering, association, demonstrations, protests, and the gathering of masses to disturb social order," and "engaging in activities in the name of illegal civil organizations."[35]

Personnel Control and Certification

Personnel control, supported by state ownership of major media organizations, is a key component of the party-state's power over the media. As

Judy Polumbaum writes, "No chief editor could ignore the power of political authorities to appoint and remove leading personnel at news organizations."[36] The party's disciplining power has been most visible throughout the 1990s and early 2000s in the dismissal of chief editorial personnel at liberal-oriented newspapers such as *Beijing Youth Daily* (*Beijing qingnian bao*), *Nangfang Weekend* (*Nanfang zhoumo*), *China Youth News* (*Zhongguo qiannian bao*), *Nangfang Metropolitan News* (*Nanfang dushi bao*), and *Beijing News* (*Xinjing bao*). The disciplining and containment of *Southern Weekend* in the early 2000s, for example, was accomplished primarily through the consecutive replacements of its chief editor, until the newspaper was brought under the control of a party functionary.[37]

A less visible but no less significant development in personnel control, however, has been the formalization of government certification of journalists, chief editors, and broadcast hosts, making China the only state in the world to formally license journalists. Ironically, this system was simultaneously a response to the corrosive impact of the market forces on news organizations and the journalistic profession. First, journalism education was not able to meet personnel demands created by the sudden expansion of the media industry. As a result, many "unqualified" journalists had entered the field. Second, some news organizations issued press cards to their advertising and business personnel, who in turn invoked the journalistic authority to solicit advertising contracts. Third, and perhaps most worrisome for authorities, some news organizations, especially newly established and smaller commercially oriented ones, set up local news bureaus, issuing and even selling press cards to individuals who abused journalistic privileges for private gains. Consequently, as part of the restructuring of the press system since the 1990s, state authorities centralized the issuance of press cards, with the GAPP, Xinhua, and the SARFT as the administering agencies.

By the early 2000s, the government had stepped up efforts to certify journalists. In 2003 the PD, the GAPP, and the SARFT launched a nationwide compulsory training program for journalists. With the exception of journalists who already had high professional rank (in China, journalists, like university professors, are on a professional ranking system), all other journalists, regardless of whether they had a journalism degree, were required to take a training program in official ideology, media policies and regulations, journalism ethics, communication theory, and related topics. In January 2004, journalists who had successfully completed the training program were issued new nationally registered press cards.[38]

The Chinese state is thus subjecting journalists to a system of professional certification and self-regulation in a way that has some superficial resemblance to the self-regulation of the legal, medical, and accounting professions in the West. Of course, the fact that the state, rather than the professional associations, issues the licenses makes the Chinese system fundamentally different. The SARFT's "Provisional Regulations on the Management of Qualifications for Broadcast Editors, Reporters, Announcers, and Hosts," issued on June 18, 2004, provided a glimpse of this system—no doubt another institutional innovation with Chinese characteristics. According to the regulation, editors, reporters, announcers, and hosts who have worked in broadcasting institutions for over one year are required to pass an annually held national exam administered by the SARFT and to obtain an operating license. In addition to a university degree, qualifications include "supporting the basic theories, lines, and policies of the Chinese Communist Party." The licenses are renewable for a two-year term. Disqualifying conditions not only include criminal records and records of party and administrative dismissal, but also "personal mistakes causing a major accident in propaganda" and "violation of professional disciplines and ethics." Moreover, license holders are obligated to "uphold correct guidance of opinion."[39]

Prepublication Review and Censorship

Though there are formal censorship systems for film and television drama production, as Judy Polumbaum notes, "there is no formal, institutionalized, and universalized pre-publication censorship apparatus" in the Chinese news media.[40] In routine news production, news organizations are expected to submit material to the party's PD or relevant authorities for clearance on matters of importance, while the party has powers to intervene at every step of the news process. This gives considerable leeway to local party committees and news organizations themselves. The operational effectiveness of the system lies both in its paradoxical combination of rigidity and flexibility and its rule-bound and ad hoc nature.

Hai Ming's description of the workings of the control regime in news organizations is illustrative of the party's directive control and its prepublication censorship system.[41] While the news department chief typically exercises final censorship authority, depending on the nature of a topic, this authority can shift upward all the way to a deputy editor-in-chief/deputy director of editorial or the chief editor in a news organization, beyond the news outlet to the highest local party authority, or further to a member of the central Politburo Standing Committee. Sometimes, all it takes to censor or change a news story is a telephone call from above. Inside the media organization, the office of the editor-in-chief serves as the transmission belt of official propaganda guidelines by issuing daily "propaganda notices" or "propaganda requirements" to each editorial department. The main content consists of "Notice from the PD," "Notice from the Municipal Propaganda Department," "No reporting on such and such event," "All must use Xinhua general copy," and so on. The following record of propaganda guidelines received by a Beijing newspaper between 2003 and 2004 on the topic of Sino-Japanese relations reveals the scope, intensity, as well as the level of specificity of prepublication media control: "The topic of constructing the Beijing-Shanghai high speed railway [by Japanese companies] . . . is very sensitive; no autonomous self-initiated reporting is allowed" (PD, September 27, 2003); "Do not report Northwest University student protests against obscene dances by Japanese students" (PD, October 31, 2003); "Nongovernmental organizations will leave for Diaoyu Islands in a few days [to protest against Japan's territorial claims over the disputed islands]: media are not allowed to follow the groups; downplay relevant reports, control the use of reports supplied by these organizations; no commentary, no feature report and interviews, only simple and objective reporting" (PD, March 23, 2004); "Downplay Sino-Japanese disputes over the East China Sea; no spin, no in-depth analysis or interviews . . . must prevent reports that provoke extreme emotional reactions" (Press Bureau of the Ministry of Foreign Affairs, July 1, 2004).[42]

Postpublication Monitoring and Censure

Although postpublication media monitoring has always been an important weapon in the party's arsenal of media control, this system has been systematically strengthened since the late 1990s. In addition to the party's PD, which has its long-established media monitoring system, the GAPP, SARFT, and their local counterparts have also established permanent staff in media monitoring. The SARFT, for example, implemented a media monitoring system in 1999, with personnel under the SARFT's General Editorial Office. By 2000, all CCTV programming, the programming of China National Radio, as well as all the provincial satellite channels had been under systematic monitoring. Media monitors are required to lodge daily reports and provide periodical evaluations of media programs in terms of their overall political orientation and their adherence to the party's propaganda disciplines and the state's broadcasting rules and regulations. In addition to full-time media monitors, part-time monitors are drawn from the ranks of senior propaganda officials, media workers, journalism professors, and retired party officials. A typical press monitor (*shendu yuan*) reads a dozen or more newspapers on a daily basis and is paid with a stipend. Because these individuals wield considerable power in media evaluation, media outlets are eager to cultivate good relationships with them. Significantly, the logic of the "doubled up" or "cross-checking" system of press monitoring by both party and government organs works to make monitors in each system more stringent than the others, so as to avoid reprimand for failing to spot problems.[43]

National and local reports of press monitoring activities provide a glimpse of the nature and scope of media monitoring work. The primary purpose of press monitoring, according to Shi Feng, a deputy director of the GAPP, is to maintain "tight gate-keeping in three areas" (*yanba sanguan*): the political gate, the opinion orientation gate, and the quality gate. Shi further specified that media monitoring involves the following functions: to identify a problem immediately, to make immediate judgments about its nature, to address it in accordance with laws and regulations, and to issue a timely censuring notice, thus providing a warning to the entire system.[44]

The scope of media monitoring is expansive. In 2003 the Shenzhen press monitoring system alone, for example, sifted through a total of 230 newspapers and periodicals and examined as many as 150 books and more than 200 audiovisual publications. Press monitors were also said to have published four issues of *Shenzhen Publishing Monitor* and two issues of internal newsletters, with a total of more than 50 articles.[45] More significantly, the Shenzhen press and publications bureau adopted a policy that systematically incorporated press monitoring into the system of control. Under this policy, a publication that receives two warnings from the press monitoring unit for political deviation will be censured internally; three warnings in a year will result in reprimands and even dismissal of responsible individuals.[46]

Because the Internet evolved during the post-1989 period of tightened media control and due to the technological features of the Internet, the traditional media's prepublication preview and postpublication monitoring systems are collapsing into an elaborate process of manually operated and automated censorship, which has received much outside journalistic and scholarly attention.[47] With the increasing sophistication of firewalls and filtering software, the survival time for offensive content in cyberspace has been progressively reduced. A March 2005 report, for example, noted that lag time had been reduced from "up to 30 minutes" to "less than a few minutes" within 18 months.[48] In December 2004, the GAPP announced the establishment of a "24-Hour Real Time Web-Publishing Content Reading and Monitoring Mechanism." In addition to serving the censorship function, this system is also charged with the responsibility of gathering and analyzing intelligence regarding the general ideological and content orientation of web publishing.[49]

NEW FEATURES IN THE REGIME OF PARTY-STATE POWER

The Dispersion of Control Responsibilities

Recognizing the weakness of a top-down disciplinary regime in which lower-level functionaries failed to internalize the party's censorship imperative and were prone to wait and act on instructions from above, the party-state's post-1989 disciplinary power has become much more dispersed, localized, and internalized by each level of the propaganda hierarchy. This new localized and dispersed responsibility system is best captured by the principle, widely understood within the media system, that "each has responsibility for the defence of [its] own territory" (*shoutu youze*). At the central level, this means that the PD must take responsibility in matters of ideological control, so as to ensure that the party's grip on power is not undermined from the ideological front. With regard to each media outlet, this translates into a mode of editorial self-discipline in which each organization is "focusing on the 'territory' underneath the tip of its own feet, trying to eliminate every possible 'mistake.'"[50]

This new mode of discipline has been most explicitly operationalized in the newest medium, the Internet. As Lokman Tsui writes,

> Of particular importance is the directive that specifies that every individual and company is responsible for what is published on its part of the network, thereby effectively creating a situation where everybody is his [*sic*] own self-censor. For example, a person who has created a personal homepage deemed offensive can be held liable, as well as the ISP hosting the homepage, who should have been able to spot the offending content in the first place. This directive creates a situation where content is not censored merely once or twice but multiple times. Automated screening goes hand in hand with human moderators. . . . The result is a disciplinary power that is dispersed and operates recursively throughout each node of the network.[51]

Thus, the party's answer to the poststructuralist question of "how control exists after decentralization"[52] is the decentralization of control. Chinese press scholar Yu Guoming has even gone so far as to note that under this regime, the practice of newspapers checking with each other for the layout of important stories and the phenomenon of "one thousand papers with one face," typical of the Cultural Revolution era, are not uncommon.[53] A GAPP official agreed. He noted how this system compels media gatekeepers, in an attempt to keep their jobs and outperform each other, to sometimes end up being more draconian and cautious than higher-level propaganda officials.[54]

Meanwhile, technological convergence and the development of the Internet and new media have turned telecommunication carriers and Internet service providers into content controllers. In new media areas such as short message services (SMS), the obligation to maintain "information security," that is, the state's political imperative of controlling content, was enforced through business contracts between Internet service providers (ISPs) and state-controlled mobile phone operators China Mobile and China Unicom. Because the very survival of their business depends on these contracts, SMS service providers exercise extreme forms of self-regulation.

As Wei Gao writes, "Licensed SPs [SMS service providers] would set up standard procedures to avoid 'illegal content' even if they knew communications administration or mobile carriers did not keep an eye on them everyday," and they are wary of causing troubles even in apparently apolitical services such as mobile chattering/dating programs, because the company has to assume responsibility for any subversive messages it carries.[55] With their stocks carefully watched in global capital markets, China's telecommunication and information businesses, from partially privatized state telephone carriers to ISPs, not only cannot afford to ignore the state's control orders, but also have themselves become part of the state's control regime. In this and other ways, the state has been able to construct a "wireless leash," turning mobile messaging into a means of control.[56]

The creation of the national "Illegal and Unsavory Information Report Center" (net.china.cn) on June 10, 2004, at the demand of the SCIO turned every Internet user into a potential postpublication censor.[57] Any individual, upon spotting an illegal and unsavory webpage, is invited to report the website to the center. The News and Information Services Working Committee of the China Internet Association, an industry association, became the implementation body of the SCIO's order.[58] In establishing these kinds of societal surveillance mechanisms, the party establishes a panoptic power in which "surveillance is no longer solely a matter practiced by the government but instead flows through social conduits on all levels, resulting in a dispersion of disciplinary power that conveniently runs along the very same grid of decentralized structure that is characteristic of the Internet."[59]

Passive Censorship and the Minimization of Political Costs

As the party decentralizes control to maximize its effectiveness, it has also tried to minimize its political costs. In an era of media explosion, "passive censorship," which aims at limiting the impact of oppositional ideas by neglect within a small elite circle, has been adopted as a more practical form of control. In the past, due in part to its self-righteous impulse as a holder of truth and its mission of politically educating the masses and transforming their consciousness, the party would typically organize a public critique of ideas deemed "incorrect." As part of Deng's "no debate" decree and perhaps the party leadership's own increasing cynicism over its "truth," the party has more or less given up its mission of political indoctrination to simply concentrate on the management of its own publicity,[60] realizing that public criticism of oppositional and deviant ideas often has the reverse impact of increasing publicity of these ideas and creating high-profile dissidents and symbols of public opposition. The necessity of maintaining China's international image in an era of increasing economic interdependence has added further pressure for the leadership to minimize the repercussions of heavy-handed censorship. Nowadays, when a problematic publication evades the censorship system and appears in the market, authorities quickly and quietly try to stop the publication or the distribution of the work. Depending on the severity of the problem, the stage at which the problem was discovered, and, no doubt, negotiation among censors and publishers, a publication receives different types of postpublication censure, ranging from closure, recall, a ban on further sales at the retail stage, an end to further printing and distribution while allowing existing stocks to be sold, and prohibition of media publicity of a work while allowing its circulation in the market. In official media management terminology, this is called "cold treatment" (*leng chuli*). For example, an issue of *Strategy and Management* (*Zhanlue yu guanli*), which contained a critical article about North Korea, was recalled through mail in 2004. The journal was subsequently quietly shut down. The book *A Survey of Chinese Peasants* (*Zhongguo nongmin diaocha*), which provided a devastating portrait of the plight of Chinese farmers, was banned at the retail level in March 2004 after it had sold more than 150,000 copies. The book *Past Events Are Not Like Clouds* (*Wangshi bingbu ruyan*), about the life stories of leading rightists, received "cool treatment": its remaining stocks were allowed to be sold in bookstores, but further printing was halted and the media were banned from giving publicity to the book. Consequently, although controversial books have been published, their reception is often limited to a small urban, intellectual, elite circle.[61] Falun Gong was an exception that proves the rule: it operates at the level of popular beliefs and Li Hongzhi, unlike elite intellectuals, had mass followers who took organized actions. Consequently, the party retreated to its "propaganda state" past using both old and new techniques in combating the group and its ideas. Similarly, when a writer is deemed politically subversive, the party will issue an internal media ban, prohibiting the publication of his or her ideas in the media.[62]

From Totalizing Control to Domination

The party now aims at effective domination rather than total control of media messages. As Ji Bingxuan, the executive deputy director of the PD said at the Central Party School, "It is impossible to have no errors in our propaganda, given the current tremendous size of the media industry and the huge content of newspapers, but we must try our best to avoid big errors, particularly to avoid errors concerning politics, policy, and public opinion guidance."[63] Underscoring this strategy is the notion of "correct guidance of public opinion," or the short form "correct guidance" (*zhengque daoxiang*) in the Chinese media, which means to promote a dominant interpretation of social reality and ensure coordinated articulation and promotion of a politically correct "main melody" (*zhu xuanlü*) in the cacophony of media voices. This in turn implies two changes. First, in cases relating to the elite political debates and intellectual discourses, the technologies of censorship have undergone a process of refinement, and as a result, censorship is increasingly "more a matter of negotiation than negation."[64] Regarding elite intellectual websites, for example, "the process of government censorship has evolved from the old totalitarian control mechanism to a new, looser system with some room for manoeuvring," resulting in a situation of "expanded space under more refined control."[65] Second, this implies a strategy of differentiated control across media outlets and types of media content: television, which has the broadest audience reach, is most tightly controlled. The print media, in turn, are more tightly controlled than the Internet, which is limited to a smaller audience. Within the mass media sector, influential national media outlets and leading regional media outlets are the focal targets of control. Obscure niche market journals targeting an elite academic audience, on the other hand, are given more leeway. The Internet, because of its more limited mass audiences and the technical challenges of control, has been most open in relative terms. The operation of this regime of "multiple layers of censorship"[66] reveals an apparently paradoxical situation in the Chinese communication field since the early 1990s. On the one hand, there has been the widely shared observation that media control has been tightened; on the other hand, there has been growing space for expression. The following words of a Shanghai writer of politically iconoclastic stories perhaps best capture the party's new paradigm of domination: "As long as no one reads them, they don't care."[67]

In short, by confining certain ideas to cyberspace and niche publications, the party has minimized the reach of these ideas, thus limiting their impact. Similarly, by driving dissenting writers abroad, the party severs the organic linkages between potential intellectual leaders and social movements. As Lokman Tsui observes, "The government, after all, is less interested in containing the elite, than in making sure that the vast majority do not get unfiltered access."[68] Communication has never simply been an issue of "free" expression. It has always been an integral part of political organization and social mobilization.

The Rearticulation of Ruling Ideologies and Proactive Media Management

While steadfast in practicing censorship, the party-state has also been compelled to become more proactive in rearticulating the terms of its ideological hegemony and in proactively managing the symbolic environment. Notwithstanding Bruce Gilley's cynical claims that the current Chinese regime "advocates nothing at all," with its legitimacy "based wholly on performance,"[69] the party came to power through leading an anticapitalistic and anti-imperialistic social revolution, and it launched its reform program on the promise of developing, not abandoning, socialism. "An essential feature of Chinese alternative modernity," Liu Kang has observed, "is revolutionary hegemony, or the primacy of culture and ideology, not just in legitimating the modern nation-state but also in constituting the basic and core components of the new socialist country."[70] Despite the reform era's shift of focus from ideological revolution to economic development, the party continues to derive at least part of its political and ideological legitimacy from the Maoist revolutionary hegemony. Ideology, which in post-Mao China can be conceived of "in terms of the ways in which the meaning mobilized by symbolic forms serves to establish and sustain relations of domination,"[71] remains indispensable for the party's rule.[72]

Although Western media and academic discourses tend to ignore official discourses, "ideological considerations played a significant role in determining the acceptability of certain policies over others" in China,[73] and continuous reinvention and rearticulation of its ruling doctrines has been an integral part of the party's project of pursuing neoliberal developments in the name of socialism. Deng first stabilized and rationalized the political and ideological fields for market-oriented developments by imposing the "Four Cardinal Principles"—upholding the socialist road, the dictatorship of the proletariat, the leadership of the Communist Party, and Marxism–Leninism–Mao Zedong Thought—and by endorsing concepts such as "the primary stage of socialism" and "socialism with Chinese characteristics." He then glossed over the ideological and social contradictions of the post-1989 reforms with the "no debate" decree and the developmentalist dictum that "development is a hard truth." In this way, Deng left his successors to address the profound political, ideological, and social contradictions of the economic reforms, including the fact that the Communist Party, the self-proclaimed vanguard of the working class, had engendered capitalists, while laying off state enterprise workers en masse and creating a massive new "proletariat" in the form of migrant workers without citizenship rights in the urban areas. The Jiang Zemin leadership dealt with this political and ideological challenge by inventing the "three represents" thesis.

Since coming to power in late 2002, the Hu Jintao leadership has tried to address the excesses of capitalistic development in the 1990s through a combination of ideological and social policy initiatives. The leadership has not only launched "new deal"–type redistributive policies—referred to in some media outlets as the "Hu-Wen New Deal"—such as abolishing the agricultural taxes to relieve the burden for farmers and expanding social security but also, perhaps more importantly, articulated a whole series of new political doctrines and launched a massive ideological education campaign that aims to "preserve the advanced nature of Communist Party members." In 2003 the so-called scientific concept of development—"sustainable development" in the language of "scientific socialism"—was propagated in the aftermath of the SARS (severe acute respiratory syndrome) epidemic to correct the single-minded pursuit of neoliberal economic growth at the cost of social development and environmental sustainability. In 2004, among other initiatives that I will discuss later on, the leadership attempted to strengthen official ideology by launching a massive "Basic Research and Construction Project in Marxism" as a means to fend off the creeping impact of neoliberalism as an ideological force. Simultaneously, it attempted to address mounting social conflicts and ensure social control by articulating the slogan "constructing a socialist harmonious society," a society, according to Hu himself, that "should feature democracy, the rule of law, equity, justice, sincerity, amity and vitality."[74] In late 2005 and early 2006, in response to economic depression and social disintegration in the rural areas, the party leadership recycled a key slogan of socialist idealism in the 1950s, that is, "to construct a new socialist countryside." Perhaps epitomizing the party's reclaiming of revolutionary symbolism to justify its rule, CCTV's prime-time national news program now includes the nightly recounting of a pre-1949 revolutionary story under the headline "Red Memories."

Thus, instead of bidding "farewell to revolution," the party, while embracing market reforms on the one hand, continues to draw upon its revolutionary legacies to sustain its rule at both the tactical and normative levels on the other.[75] In particular, although there are continuities between the Jiang Zemin and Hu Jintao leaderships, the Hu Jintao leadership has distinguished itself not only by articulating a new concept of development, but also by intensifying the reappropriation of the revolutionary legacy and the rearticulation of socialist slogans. Whether these new developments represent power shifts within the reformist elite or whether they reflect a more structural challenge to the neoliberal-oriented development path and a renewed commitment to socialism is a topic of contention inside China, and I will revisit this topic in the conclusion. At this point, I will simply argue that although these doctrines should not be taken at face value and their efficacy must be empirically analyzed, they should not be dismissed as completely empty expressions in the party's already overflowing ideological dustbin. As the social contradictions of China's capitalistic development become more acute, the party is more and more compelled to elaborate its ruling ideology in a way that may still have some appeal to the vast majority of the population. Thus, even if such regime ideology is "a living lie,"[76] it nevertheless sets the basic terms of the party's ideological hegemony and thus serves as symbolic resources for social contestation—as Feng Xiujü's invocation of socialism testifies. Moreover, the very acts of its elaboration and dissemination—from Jiang Zemin's maneuvers to encode the "three represents" in the party's constitution to the Hu Jintao leadership's imposition of massive ideological education campaigns on party members, journalists, and academics in the social sciences and humanities—are essential dimensions in the exercise of power. To stay in power, the party must continue to articulate and rearticulate its communistic pretensions—otherwise, as I will show shortly, communism threatens to once again become a powerful subversive ideology against party-led capitalistic developments in China.

At the operational level, the party, while continuing to rejuvenate the ranks of its Leninist propaganda structure and make instrumental use of traditional Maoist propaganda campaign methods, has also incorporated Western-style media management techniques. The art of public relations and image making, imported from the West and first adopted by businesses, is now serving the party's propaganda objectives. "Leadership image design" has become a new topic for applied communication research and everyday media management practices. From Hu Jintao making dumplings in a rural household to celebrate the Chinese New Year to Wen Jiabao helping rural woman Xiong Deming to collect her husband's unpaid wage, the mainstream media are inundated with carefully scripted images designed to project a "pro-people" popular leadership. Similarly, public opinion polls, once condemned as a "bourgeois" practice, have been used and abused both in state-organized media campaigns and in everyday media reporting. Proactive news reporting of negative events aims to turn the party-state into the primary definer in a media world where simple suppression no longer works.[77] All these contributed to the cultivation of more "sophisticated propaganda" in the post-1989 era.[78]

The outbreak of SARS in 2003 and domestic and international backlashes against the media's initial cover-up have provided further impetus for the leadership to take a proactive approach to negative news and to improve its crisis management in an increasingly fragile and crises-laden social and ecological system. As part of a statewide building up of the mechanisms for the management of public emergencies (*tufa gonggong shijian yingji jizhi*), which encompass environmental disasters, major accidents, and social crises, the implementation of the news spokesperson system, first introduced in 1983 in an attempt to use Western governmental techniques to coordinate the state's external propaganda, has been deemed an urgent task since 2003.[79] By late 2004, a three-tiered news spokesperson system, consisting of the State Council Information Office, various central government departments, and provincial-level governments, has been enacted.[80] Many lower-level governments, especially municipal governments and their functionary departments, have also rushed to appoint their own news spokespeople as a way of modernizing governance.[81] In 2004 the SCIO held 14 training classes for news spokespeople and trained more than 2,000 local officials in news management techniques.[82] A State Council regulation aimed at increasing access to government information will be implemented by May 2008.[83]

The party-state's proactive role in creating domestic propaganda and in projecting China's "soft power" abroad—that is, the power of ideological influence and persuasion, a term borrowed from the lexicon of the ruling elite in the United States—is most evident regarding the Internet. Special funds have been allocated to five official websites—*People's Daily*, Xinhua News Agency, China International Radio, and the China.org and *China Daily* websites. Official Internet discussion forums, such as the "Strengthening the Nation Forum" (*Qiangguo luntan*) at the *People's Daily* website, were launched to harness new communication forms and genres.[84] The government has also been proactive in using the Internet to disseminate its views on sensitive issues, thus "deliberately taking the initiative to occupy cyberspace."[85] Other analysts have also written about the government's use of misinformation as an instrument of control, including the use of fake proxy servers as "honey pots," that is, as a means to monitor the activity of Internet users who try to break through government censorship by using proxy servers.[86] A plan to send a thousand net soldiers to the Internet front, to participate in BBS discussions and thus "guide" web opinion, was disclosed in early 2005.[87]

A propaganda official I interviewed observed the development of a number of proactive strategies in the party's media management. First, the party is strengthening the role of the PD as a proactive organizer of propaganda campaigns, outlining specific requirements for the treatment of a story—for example, front-page treatment or leading item treatment. Second, the party is strengthening the role of official news at both the national (i.e., Xinhua "general copy") and local levels (written by provincial or municipal party organs). Third, propaganda officials are facilitating the routine distribution of official news through the press spokesperson system. Fourth, there has been a renewed attempt at shaping the ideological orientation of Chinese journalists, as exemplified by the 2004 campaign of educating journalists in the party's media theory and propaganda disciplines. Fifth, the party has renovated its traditional *nomenklatura* system of personnel management by stepping up the training of future propaganda officials and media managers through the more conscious deployment of the "revolving door" strategy. The Guangzhou municipal PD, for example, sends senior journalists and editors with the potential to become media managers to work in the PD, that is, to role-play as propaganda officials. The advantage of such an exercise is considerable: the media professional not only brings intimate knowledge of the "other side" to the PD, but also facilitates the communication and implementation of the PD's orders in media outlets, where such a person typically has an extensive interpersonal network and significant credibility. Moreover, in the long term, such an experience will inevitably embed the perspective of a propaganda official in the mindset of a promising senior media manager. Finally, contrary to the popular image of PDs populated by the old and ideologically ossified, young individuals with master's, and even doctoral, degrees and foreign experiences now form the backbone.

Perhaps the party's instrumental uses of old campaign methods and proactive media management techniques are best illustrated by its handling of SARS in 2003. Initially, officials forced the media to cover up news about the epidemic's spread. However, such a strategy backfired and provoked a political crisis as the news blackout "hampered the spread of information and efforts to curtail the disease."[88] It also sparked the spread of rumors through word of mouth and mobile phones and Dr. Jiang Yanyong's exposure of the epidemic to the international media. Consequently, the party not only allowed the media to report the SARS crisis but also turned the fight against SARS into a traditional mass mobilization campaign.[89] During the process, the party retained tight control of *how* the crisis was to be reported, including details regarding the scope of the epidemic and the number of cases. In particular, the "SARS party line" emphasized the leadership's care for the people and the sacrifice of party members, medical doctors, and ordinary people alike, with the patriotic theme of building national solidarity in a "people's war" against a common enemy. As Fewsmith observed, this more proactive propaganda approach was largely successful.[90] The leadership has certainly drawn a lesson from this experience. For example, the "Decision of the CCP Central Committee on the Enhancement of the Party's Governance Capability," passed at the 4th Plenum of the 16th Party Congress in September 2004, explicitly states the need to "strengthen the abilities to guide public opinion and assume preemptive power in public opinion work."[91]

The Privatization and Localization of Media Control

Although ideological continuity and policy differences still matter a great deal, and the central leadership's imperative to maintain ideological and political unity has become stronger as debates over the directions of China's reforms have heated up in recent years, the multifaceted nature of party-state power and "the simultaneously centralized and decentered nature of state politics"[92] have also meant that censorship can be driven by the politics of naked power and the blunt self-interest of individual officials. This has a number of implications. First, censorship is often deeply implicated in intraparty power struggles, and the publication of certain news and views can serve as an effective bargaining chip in such struggles. Initial censorship and subsequent openness in media reporting of the spread of SARS in 2003, for example, are linked to power struggles inside the party, more specifically the intricate politics and protracted process of power transition between the so-called Third Generation and Fourth Generation leaderships centered around Jiang Zemin and Hu Jintao, respectively. As well, because power abuse is pandemic in China, propaganda officials, like officials in other party-state branches, may abuse their censorship power for private financial gains.[93]

Second, just as the party-state now prosecutes dissenting individuals by charging them with crimes such as "disclosing state secrets" and "subverting state power," individual power holders are privatizing the power of media control through the legal system. Jiang Weiping, the Dalian-based Hong Kong *Wenhui Daily* correspondent, was sentenced to eight years in prison in 2002 because his investigations revealed the wrongdoings of powerful Liaoning provincial officials.[94] Although international pressures led to Jiang's early release in January 2006, another journalist, Li Chanqing of the *Fuzhou Daily* in Fujian Province, was standing trial in a Fuzhou court in the same month and thus became another casualty of official retaliation against critical reporting.[95] Journalists are harassed, attacked, and even jailed, not because their reporting violates the central party leadership's propaganda disciplines, but because such reporting exposes the wrongdoings of individual power holders and threatens their positions. In a case that shocked the Chinese journalistic community, on October 20, 2005, more than 40 traffic police officers, under the leadership of police captain Li Xiangguo, stormed the editorial office of *Taizhou Evening News* (*Taizhou wanbao*) in Taizhou City, Zhejiang Province, and beat up the paper's deputy editor-in-chief, Wu Xianghu, because the paper had published a report criticizing high license fees the traffic police had imposed on electric bicycles. This happened *despite* the fact that the newspaper conducted the investigation at the invitation and in the company of relevant Taizhou City authorities and that the Taizhou City Party Disciplinary Committee had previewed and approved the report.[96] On February 2, 2006, the 41-year-old Wu Xianghu died in a Hangzhou hospital. It is also common for local officials to block the distribution of magazines and newspapers that contain reports critical of them. The power of media control at both the production and distribution ends, in other words, has been partially de-ideologized and practiced in an increasingly diffused manner to serve the interests of power holders. Perhaps the most extreme example involved a massive recall campaign of a book that contained nothing but official government documents. In 2000 a party-affiliated magazine publisher in Nanchang, Jiangxi Province, compiled a book of various official policies banning illegal fees levied against farmers and calling for alleviating the financial burden of farmers. However, fearing that such documents, once in the hands of farmers, could become a weapon in their struggle against illegal taxation, local officials ordered the police to perform a door-to-door search, retrieving about 11,000 of the 12,000 copies that had been sold.[97]

The confrontation between officials and journalists at *China Youth News*, the organ of the Communist Youth League, is illustrative of not only the instrumentalization of media by officials, but also of its potential fascist-style implementation through business management mechanisms. *China Youth News* is the only outspoken central-level official paper in the country, managing this feat by maintaining a certain degree of autonomy from officials at the Communist Youth League. However, this relative autonomy has weakened in the past few years. In June 2004, the confrontation between the paper's professional culture and the instrumentalism of Communist Youth League secretary Zhao Yong reached such a level that Lu Yuegang, a nationally renowned journalist at the paper, posted an open letter denouncing Zhao on the Internet.[98] Then, in August 2005, the announcement of a new bonus system for journalists at the paper led to the Internet circulation of a protest letter by Li Datong, another well-known liberal-minded journalist and the editor of the paper's flagship investigative weekly *Freezing Point* (*Bingdian*). The letter denounced the paper's new editor-in-chief, Li Erliang, who was appointed by the Communist Youth League in December 2004 in a reshuffle widely regarded as part of the Hu Jintao leadership's tightened control over media. Li Erliang attempted to change the paper's journalistic culture to make it more responsive to propaganda officials by devising an appraisal system that linked bonuses to praise from party leaders. Under the system, an article praised by a Chinese Communist Youth League Central Committee official earned the author 80 points; praise by a national government department or a provincial party committee earned 100 points; an article praised by a PD official received 120 points; and praise by members of the Politburo was worth 300 points.[99] In this context, the observation of Li Fang, a former editor at the paper, that "the dynamics inside party media were changing from professional ideas about proper content to a cliquish loyalty based on pleasing the party" is highly relevant. One does not have to project a golden past of professional journalism to recognize the intensification of media instrumentalism.

In yet another development that underscores the seizure of media control by local party bosses and their power in muffling media criticisms, propaganda officials from 17 provinces and metropolitan areas, including those from Guangdong, Hebei, Henan, and Shanxi provinces, sent a joint petition to the Party Central Committee in 2005, demanding the central leadership step up control of central-level media outlets and to stop the media's practice of "[public opinion] supervision in a different jurisdiction" (*yidi jiandu*),[100] that is, media outlets from one province reporting critically on another province and central-level media outlets reporting critically on local issues, typically power abuses by officials below county levels. Because media outlets cannot possibly expose power abuse at higher levels and criticize the party committees with which they are affiliated, the practice of *yidi jiandu* had been widely recognized as a positive step toward a more critical media in China. However, this development infuriated local officials. To appease them, the General Office of the CCP Central Committee issued a directive calling for a halt to *yidi jiandu*, with a new rule requiring reporters from central-level media outlets to clear with local authorities critical reports written about them. Furthermore, the PD in its detailed guidelines on the implementation of this new directive proposed two "whenevers": "whenever issuing a critical story about a different jurisdiction, permission must be sought from that jurisdiction's party Propaganda Department; whenever issuing a critical media report involves a leading official, permission must be sought from that official's superior."[101] This has effectively undermined the relative autonomy and authority of central-level media vis-à-vis local officials, not to mention the ability of media outlets from one province to report critically on another.[102]

Normalizing, Synergizing, and Rationalizing Control

While the party-state has the strongest imperative to control the media, societal pressures, especially "moral panics" created by the media themselves among cultural elites, moral conservatives, and worried parents and teachers within the urban social strata can also strengthen and legitimate the state's regime of control. In June 2002, an unregistered Internet café in Beijing caught fire and killed 25 people. This led to the creation of a moral panic in the official media about the hazardous nature of unregistered Internet cafés. Immediately, the state launched a major crackdown on them nationwide. Moral panic over pornography and Internet gambling has provided another powerful rationale for state control—the archetypal victim is the Internet-addicted teenage boy who misses classes and plays in the Internet cafés for days and nights on end. In July 2004, the state launched the "people's war" against pornographic content in cyberspace, with individuals reporting pornographic websites receiving cash rewards. By October 2004, some 445 people had been arrested and 1,125 websites shut down with the help of tips.[103] Since then, the normalizing impulse of Internet regulation has been further internalized and entrenched in industry self-regulation and in a language that transforms the objective of control into a matter of civilization and, indeed, a matter of hygiene for the Chinese body politic. On April 9, 2006, the first day of Hu Jintao's visit to the United States, Sina, Sohu, Netease, and 11 other influential Chinese websites collectively issued the "Proclamation to Run Websites in a Civilized Way." The next day, the "civilized Internet" (*wenming wangluo*) campaign was launched with the slogan "run websites in a civilized way, surf online in a civilized way."[104] On April 12, the Internet Society of China called on its 2,600-plus members and businesses to promote the "healthy" development of Internet businesses, with "concerted efforts to supervise content, delete 'unhealthy' information and oppose acts that undermine 'Internet civilization,' harm social stability and hamper development of Internet businesses."[105]

Though the explicitly stated purpose of these campaigns was to protect juniors and uphold social morality, political control was an underlying motive, or at least a calculated synergetic objective. Spelling out "the real danger of the state that now markets itself as a benevolent regulator" on the one hand,[106] and in a playing out of a Polanyian double movement that now requires the state to provide protection against a destructive market that threatens to destroy the social fabric on the other, state regulation of the media and cyberspace has acquired a new social and moral imperative, while offering a cover for political control. One media regulator, for example, readily admitted that rooting out politically subversive material in the guise of fighting pornography wins the approval of society and is less controversial in the eyes of foreign critics. Once again, although the market mechanism opens up opportunities for media organizations and individuals to pursue economic interests and thus provides an incentive to potentially challenge party control, the excesses of the market provide the moral ground for the party-state to expand its regime of disciplinary power.

Meanwhile, if ideological work was once carried out in the name of a revolutionary mission by ideologically committed individuals such as Deng Tuo,[107] it is now increasingly implemented by individuals who have come to regard their job as an occupation, just like any other occupation in modern society. The plight of former communist officials in Russia and Eastern Europe serves as a powerful reminder of what may happen, resulting in these propaganda officials' overriding objective of maintaining social stability and sustaining the current regime. The imperative of climbing up the bureaucratic ladder or simply the need to keep one's job become the operational motives for media censorship and self-censorship. For some, the state objective of sustaining social stability has become an internalized, normative goal in everyday practices. As one former journalist put it, the notion of "stability above everything" had such a hegemonic power over him that whenever he encountered a sensitive topic, the first thing that came to his mind was whether reporting it would undermine stability, not whether he would lose his job.[108] For others, a job is just a job. "Doing labor for the Communist Party" (*wei gongchandang dagong*) is how a middle-rank official at a state media control agency characterized his work. What is significant about this expression is that instead of using the term "work" (*gongzuo*), which implies agency and connotes a sense of collective ownership in the job to be done, the speaker uses the colloquial term "doing labor" (*dagong*), which is typically applied to migrant and temporary workers in the private economy and to stress the hired nature of the work as well as the workers' powerlessness and insecurity. In this discourse, the speaker distances himself/herself from the party, while simultaneously equating it as a "boss" or a private capitalist employer. Thus, the authoritarian logic of the private market, in which one must obey the boss, is being imported into the realm of media and party propaganda. In a different context, Zhongdang Pan quoted a senior editor from a major Beijing daily as saying, "This paper belongs to the Party, it's not yours, nor is it mine. The Party is the boss and I'm just an employee. Submitting to the boss's leadership is only logical."[109] A journalist professor similarly notes how media censors in party PDs and government press offices keep a clear division between their personal life and their work. They go to the office to work as censors and propagandists for the state and come home as private individuals in the realm of leisure and consumption.[110]

The sense of a job to be done, of not getting into trouble, was conveyed to me by a Beijing "responsible editor" when my article on international communication, which contains an analysis of the increasing role of global civil society in the democratization of media systems elsewhere in the world, became an offending piece. Note how personal responsibility is dissolved in a discourse of "national conditions," "the basic requirements of our profession," and the imperative of "reducing trouble" in the following editorial correspondence:

> As you are aware, due to the national conditions of our country, the party central puts a very high political demand on press and publication work. To maintain a high level of unity with the party central is the most basic requirement for our profession. Therefore, we are very cautious in dealing with articles addressing important political issues, trying our best to be accurate and to minimize trouble.[111]

When the choice is between publishing and not publishing at all, one is often compelled to comply with censorship, thus helping to sustain the "logic of the system." When an editor says that although she is willing to risk her own job to publish your article, she cannot face her employees if the article leads to the publication's termination, thus endangering the livelihood of those employees, how many authors would feel justified in further pressuring the editor? The alternative of not having the article published at all means an even greater concession to the censorship system. As another editor told me, to publish my essay on media democratization as the leading article in her journal was already a bold move. Although to "revalorize the conceptual category of complicity" is not necessary, surely "domination is not total; resistance is never complete."[112]

However, not all individuals operate by "coping" or compromising. Because the party is the only political game in town, an individual with the career ambition to climb up the bureaucratic ladder must perform well and with ingenuity in a censorship post. Li Datong's letter to his editor-in-chief is poignant:

> We are not naive enough to think that this was the product of you personally. It goes without saying that you were merely the executor. Yet you have no psychological inhibition, you were creative and you were proactive. The goal is to transform the *China Youth News* quickly into a party organ that the League Central Secretariat had in mind. This type of "party organ" has one characteristic: it must unconditionally help one to "get the right conditions for a promotion" and everything else that gets in one's way must be destroyed.[113]

CONTEXTUALIZING CONTROL: WHAT IS AT STAKE AND WHO IS THE PARTY MOST AFRAID OF?

Censorship and Capitalistic Development: China in a World Historical Context

Samir Amin has written about how the unequal development imminent in capitalist expansion put the anticapitalist revolutions not by specific classes, but by "the peoples of the periphery," on the agenda of history. Therefore, "the three tendencies of socialism, capitalism and statism combine and conflict" in postcapitalist regimes, resulting from social movements that "feed on the spontaneous popular revolt against the unacceptable conditions created by peripheral capitalism" on the one hand, and fall short of "making the demand for the double revolution by which modernization and popular enfranchisement must come together" on the other hand.[114] As the product of one of these major anticapitalist and anti-imperialist revolutions in the periphery of global capitalism in the first half of the 20th century, the Chinese party-state embodies all the tendencies and tensions that Amin has described from the beginning of its formation.[115] This legacy continues to shape China's deeply conflicted social transformation. Although this process is often viewed in the "transition literature" as a single, linear though disjunctive one, with political democratization "lagging behind" economic development,[116] a crucial analytical distinction must be made between two transitions—an industrial and economic transition (the transition from a planned economy to a market economy) and a democratic political transition (the transition from a postrevolutionary vanguardist political system to a democratic political order).[117] A market economy may well be a necessary precondition for a liberal democratic political order, which is perhaps even feasible in China in the near future, although as I will discuss in the conclusion, the prospects for such an order continue to be frustrated by China's revolutionary legacy and its class-based definition of "people's democracy." Moreover, the historical fact remains that the Chinese state's sustained suppression of popular demands for political participation created the repressive political conditions for the establishment of a market-based economic order.

This is not to justify state repression but to ground the current regime of party-state power in Chinese communication in concrete political economic and world historical contexts. Nor do I suggest that the party played out a capitalist vanguard role in accordance with some teleology. The indeterminate nature of this process is evidenced in the elite divisions before and during 1989, which led to the demise of two party general secretaries, the intensive struggles between competing discourses of reform throughout the 1990s and 2000s, as well as ongoing challenges against further neoliberal developments both within and outside the party.

Moreover, the repression that has been part and parcel of China's reestablishment of a market economic order and its reincorporation into the global market system, while no doubt horrendous, is by no means unique. One need not accept a radical functionalist position that capitalism and democracy are inherently antithetical to each other to recognize their uneasy historical accommodation and that at particular historical junctures, they sometimes are in tension.[118] Even in the British context, the suppression of radical ideas through either state censorship or economic marginalization was integral to the consolidation of a liberal democratic social order.[119] Advanced capitalist market economies (Italy, Germany, and Greece) have reverted to dictatorial rule, and the introduction of market reforms in Asia (Indonesia) and Latin America (Brazil, Chile, Argentina, and other countries) was sometimes preceded and sustained by harsh military dictatorships.[120] In the contemporary context, theorists who have followed a Polanyian analysis of the contemporary "neoliberal revolution" have noted how neoconservatism has become a concomitant development with or an inevitable response to the suppression of oppositions against neoliberalism. As David Harvey writes, Polanyi's fear is precisely that "the liberal (and by extension the neoliberal) utopian project could only ultimately be sustained by resort to authoritarianism. The freedom of the masses would be restricted in favour of the freedoms of the few."[121]

Whether China's reform program constitutes a full-scale "capitalist restoration" and the resultant Chinese society a fully reconstituted capitalist social formation with reestablished capitalistic class power is debatable.[122] After all, the Chinese state still claims the mantle of "socialism," and the censorship regime disallows any description of current Chinese development as being "capitalist." Although strong arguments have been made that "market socialism" is a "contradiction in terms,"[123] China's search for a socialist alternative to capitalist modernity has a historical legacy. Moreover, as Arif Dirlik has argued, whether to call the current Chinese system capitalist or socialist is not just a matter of description. Rather, it is a matter of prescription in the sense that such a representation is intended to shape the reality that it pretends to describe, thus constituting part of "an intense struggle between two discourses that seek to appropriate its future for two alternative visions of history."[124] As Dirlik notes, within the history of Chinese socialism, there has been a "perennial contradiction" between "an idea of socialism that derives its language from a universal ideal of an egalitarian and democratic society, and one that renders socialism into an instrument of parochial pragmatic goals of national development."[125] This, in a sense, can be seen as the Chinese manifestation of the same world historical tension between democracy and capitalism.

As the post-1989 Chinese leadership unleashed the power of the market and entrenched a pragmatic notion of socialism as economic development, they further reinforced their coercive and discursive disciplinary powers in the political, ideological, and cultural spheres. Instead of viewing this regime of state power as an orientalist despotic or communistic totalitarian deviation from some transcendental liberal democratic "norm," I argue that its reconfiguration has been part and parcel of the forging of the Chinese "market state" to articulate with neoliberal development in an era of globalization and information technology–driven accumulation. More importantly, the heightening of state censorship and control of communication since the early 1990s is as much a cause for as a response to deepening social tensions and intensifying political, ideological, social, and cultural struggles resulting from accelerated market reforms and global reintegration. For example, if the post-1989 political repression and the sociocultural dislocation resulting from these processes had produced Falun Gong as a powerful backlash in the first place, the movement's militant strategies of media hacking have played an instrumental role in the party's fortification of its regime of control since 1999. Once such a regime is in place, of course, it facilitates control over communication by other disenfranchised social groups. Similarly, it was precisely the tactical resistance of media gatekeepers in giving prominent play to official news stories and ideological directives in their everyday practices that has led party propaganda officials to issue ever more detailed guidelines with regard to the treatment of these stories and the implementation of the party's propaganda initiatives.

"Guard against the Right, but Guard Primarily against the Left"

On the one hand, liberal and neoliberal advocates of the end of one-party rule and more radical forms of neoliberal development such as the complete privatization of state-owned enterprises continue to be targeted by the party,[126] and as I will demonstrate in chapter 6, by 2004, the neoliberal program of accelerated privatization had been challenged by societal forces from below as well. This attempt to "guard against the right," which, together with limits on private media ownership (discussed in chapters 3 and 4), can be seen as the party-state's most visible efforts in frustrating capitalist class formation, has been loudly resisted domestically and well documented abroad. On the other hand, although there is a potential gap between the Jiang Zemin and Hu Jintao leaderships when the latter succeeded the former and needed to mobilize popular support to consolidate its power, a point I will elaborate in more detail in the conclusion, the party-state's regime of control has also been aimed at the communicative activities of mass social movements such as independent newsletters and websites by labor activists, leftist charges against "capitalist restoration," and most importantly, the forging of a counterhegemonic alliance between the "masses" of disenfranchised workers and farmers and their organic intellectuals. Rather than aiming at regime change or toppling the state, such protests would aim to "make the central state to live up to its revolutionary mandate against foreign capitalists, private interests, and local authorities"[127] or "to shame the party-state into living up to the promises of its own 'revolutionary tradition.'"[128] Because the party's repression of the communicative activities of the left and grassroots social movements is less adequately documented and contextualized, the following discussion focuses on this plank of the regime of control.[129] I revisit and update this discussion in the conclusion, as I discuss intensive and complicated communication politics leading to the 17th Party Congress in October 2007.

Gang Lin has noted that a significant trend characterizing the theoretical and ideological confrontations of the post-Mao era is that "leftists . . . dramatically lost their offensive momentum and became a small group of hapless defenders of the dogmatic socialism."[130] The story, however, is more complicated. Although the excesses of the Cultural Revolution contributed to the demise of many party leftists and remaining aging leftists within the party have had little access to the mass media, let alone political power since the mid-1990s, leftist critiques of the reform program have normative appeal and popular resonance. Moreover, these leftists did not lose their ideological and discursive spaces within the official and market-oriented media "naturally." Among other factors, coercive state power, in the form of censorship and party propaganda disciplining—the same force that liberal and neoliberal intellectuals have fought against—had been systematically used to suppress leftist critiques of the party's betrayal of the lower social classes. This was no better articulated than by Deng's famous instruction to the party that it must "guard against the right, but guard primarily against the left" during his southern tour of 1992.[131] On this fundamental issue, the party line has been quite straightforward, not an "ever-changing and hard-to-grasp curve."

As well, it seems unfair to dismiss the leftists as simply defending some bygone form of "dogmatic socialism," or worse, as harboring "totalitarian nostalgia."[132] The complicated political and social history of the Chinese communist revolution as well as the lived experience of Chinese socialism by different social classes under Mao has meant that the collective, and no doubt selective, memories of the bygone era are necessarily multidimensional and inflected with contested understandings. As I demonstrate in greater detail in chapters 5, 6, and the conclusion, behind the leftists' critiques of the reform program are concrete political economic interests and fundamental unanswered questions about the past, present, and future path of Chinese development.

Although the acceleration of market reforms after 1992 produced extraordinary economic growth and dramatically reduced poverty, its negative consequences have posed profound challenges to the party's professed socialist goals and provided the background for the resurgence of leftist critiques of reform.[133] Partially because of the party's disjunctive political and ideological strategy of "signaling left, turning right" and partially because of the neoliberal ideological hegemony in the Western media and the influence of neoliberal ideas inside China,[134]

> the one thing you rarely see discussed is just how right-wing China is. Not just right-wing for a communist country, with an injection of American investment here and there, but full of gut-instinct right-wingery; right-wingery of the sort that regards China's newly enormous disparity of wealth as perhaps natural, at worst a necessary evil; right-wingery that regards authoritarian, paternalistic control, particularly of the poor, as a duty of government; right-wingery of the sort that elsewhere has student radicals marching in the street crying fascist.[135]

As a result, the "left," as a (re)emerging and potentially counterhegemonic discursive formation, encompasses a wide range of political and ideological positions defined by their critique of the negative social consequences of neoliberal developments, their opposition to the imposition of more radical measures of capitalistic reconstruction, and most importantly, their common overriding concern for social justice and equality. More specifically, the critiques of "old leftists" (in rhetoric, in their party elder status as revolutionaries, as well as in terms of their age) or party elite leftists have been joined and consecutively overwhelmed by those of a younger generation of "new left" intellectuals and, more importantly, by those of a much larger, more heterogeneous, and more vocal group of grassroots critics of market reforms.[136] Such discourses not only resonate with counterneoliberal global intellectual currents and social justice movements, but also reflect residual socialist norms and emergent popular consciousnesses within Chinese society. In short, the communist revolutionary legacy, which reform-era liberal and neoliberal intellectuals have tried so hard to elide, suppress, and even repudiate, "not only haunts the social consciousness like a specter of the past but also lives in the present."[137] Thus, the resurgence and reformulation of leftist discourses have proceeded at both the elite and popular levels. On the one hand, "new left" intellectuals well tuned to the neo-Marxist, postmodernist, and postcolonial literature have developed critical analyses of global capitalism and China's role in it. On the other hand, perhaps as the ultimate "dialectic" of the Chinese revolution, the lived experience of global capitalism and American imperialism has led some Chinese intellectuals, workers, and farmers to reclaim as their own the anticapitalist and anti-imperialist themes of the Communist Party.[138]

These leftist discourses, existing both in tandem and in tension with the official ideology of "socialism with Chinese characteristics," and as I will discuss in chapter 3, articulating with various strands of popular nationalistic critiques, have gained influence in various forums at and beyond the margins of a market-driven media system dominated by a peculiar combination of official political doctrines and neoliberal market economics. These have included long underground essays—the so-called ten-thousand-character essays (*Wanyanshu*) from the early to mid-1990s—"old" leftist political and literary periodicals such as *The Pursuit of Truth* (*Zhenli de zhuiqiu*), *Midstream* (*Zhongliu*) (until their suspension in 2001), and *Contemporary Currents of Thought* (*Dangdai sichao*); academic journals such as *Reading* (*Dushu*) (in July 2007, *Reading*'s two "new left" executive editors were replaced, creating a major controversy—I will discuss this important development and its significance in the conclusion); slogans at workers' and farmers' protests; on-the-street "small-character posters" and leaflets; as well as various open letters and political appeals to the party leadership. Since the early 2000s, these outlets have been joined and boosted by leftist websites hosted both inside and outside China, includ-

 dissent

ing China and the World, Huayue Forum, Mao Zedong Study, Peasant-Worker World and its discussion site Protagonist Forum, Utopia, and Mao Zedong Flag.[139]

A wall poster I serendipitously discovered on August 18, 1999, captures the tenor of grassroots leftist critique of market reforms in the most straightforward form. The one-page poster, entitled "Communism Manifesto" (*Gongchan zhuyi xuanyan*), was posted on an official newspaper reading window hosting the Beijing party organ *Beijing Daily* (*Beijing ribao*) nearby the Central People's Radio tower in central Beijing. It is not the famous pamphlet by Marx and Engels; rather it is a critique against market fundamentalism and an argument about the continuing relevance of communist ideals. Its main points are: (1) workers are unemployed, and there is a crisis of overproduction and a blind worship of the market; (2) the "plan" versus the "market" is a false dichotomy that can be dispelled by a simple acknowledgment of the interventionist policies of the U.S. state, which bullied China to hold its own global hegemony; and (3) the capitalist road has reached a dead end; communism is not obsolete. At the bottom, an added-on handwritten line—the handwriting betrayed the non-elite status of the writer—declared, "Practice is the sole criterion of truth. There is no unchallengeable doctrine. Compatriots, this is meant to stimulate debate. Please pass it around."

The irony is hard to miss. Against the backdrop of the party's broadcast and print mouthpieces, this poster sent two powerful messages at once. Communism has gone underground (again) in China, and China's market reforms—viewed by Deng Xiaoping as the "second revolution"—have generated its antithesis. If the party leadership launched the market reforms in 1978 by debunking the "truth" of the "plan" through the "truth debate," the very same language has been reappropriated by grassroots leftists to challenge the "truth" of the "market" 20 years later.

Various strands of leftist critiques not only presented a daunting challenge against the party's ideological pretensions, but also exposed the narrow liberal market agenda of a broad coalition of liberal and neoliberal intellectuals. This coalition had existed both in collaboration and in tension with the party-state. On the one hand, they are supportive of the party-state's market reforms. On the other hand, they have been either critical of the party-state's political repression or its blockage against the implementation of more radical neoliberal policies—in Zhu Xueqin's famous metaphor, the "visible foot" of the state had stamped on the "invisible hand" of the market in China.[140] Until the mid-1990s, this coalition had been assumed to be the sole alternative to the party in an intellectual environment where they have the discursive power to label their opponents as old or new "leftists," while their self-chosen political identification, "liberals" (as opposed to "rightists"), "came to enjoy an inviolable,

[Handwritten margin note: What? I thought the just spent pages stating that leftist counter-culture is a threat to the party-state's power?]

even sanctified aura."[141] Although leftist critics of the party's reform program are marginal, by insisting on the relevance of the "socialist" versus "capitalist" debate or by simply insisting on the values of economic justice and social equity, they forced the party and liberal and neoliberal intellectuals to confront the political, ideological, and social contradictions of market reforms. Since the reform was carried out in the name of socialism, leftists were "justified" in criticizing pro-capitalist theories and policies.[142] The political damage of the leftist critiques, if published and legitimated in the mainstream media, would have been devastating. They would have reflected serious divisions inside the party and triggered a national debate about the direction of the reform process. Thus, one witnesses the most peculiar phenomenon in Chinese communication. On the one hand, there has been an explosion of media outlets and an increasingly competitive media market. On the other hand, the most profound political and ideological debate about the direction of China's social transformation—dubbed by Taiwan journalist Shen Hongfei as "a great communist debate at the end of the 20th century,"[143] with reference to the debates trigged by the "ten-thousand-character essays" in the mid-1990s—was carried out without the mass media, which suppressed any public reference to these essays. The party's new strategy of censorship by neglect found its calculated application in this case.

Despite repeated defeats and the passing away of "old leftists" within the party, leftist opposition to the further consolidation of capitalistic social relations continued to gain strength in the 2000s, threatening to reach disenfranchised workers. For example, as soon as Jiang Zemin officially sanctioned the incorporation of capitalists into the party in his July 1, 2001, speech, "old leftists," through two signed letters and articles in *Pursuit of Truth* and *Midstream*, launched an attack. They not only attacked Jiang for his theoretical and logical inconsistency, his dishonesty, and his abandonment of class analysis, but also for his violation of basic party discipline and democratic procedure by unilaterally proclaiming a position on such an important issue without discussion and approval by a party congress.[144] Confrontation between the central leadership and marginalized "old leftists" within the party, together with fear that their writings could inflame Chinese workers, led to the suspension of *Pursuit of Truth* and *Midstream* in the summer of 2001. By the time of their closure, these "old leftist" critics had begun to "gain adherents among millions of disenfranchised workers and farmers,"[145] and their journals had already become "vital to the labor activists' propaganda efforts."[146] Although most analysts and dissident activists have either focused on the liberal or the so-called freedom faction within the party[147] or advocated the creation of bourgeois liberal democratic political parties as a way to end the Communist Party's political monopoly in China,[148] given that the party itself seemed to have completed a de facto shift from "being a dictatorship of the left to a dictatorship from the right"[149] toward the end of the Jiang Zemin leadership, the possibility of leftists splitting the Communist Party and gaining popular support was real. The stakes were so high that according to a *South China Morning Post* report on August 23, 2001, "President Jiang Zemin has ordered the anti-reform leftist forces to be 'exterminated at the budding stage.'"[150] As a party that came to power as much through the power of the pen as through the barrel of the gun, the leaders know all too well the importance of counterhegemonic ideological formation and how communication can mobilize social movements.[151]

Contrary to Jiang's wish, however, elite and popular leftist discourses have continued to gain momentum since 2001. Because the official regime of censorship, together with the forces of commodification and market recentralization (discussed in chapter 2) and the concerted marginalization efforts on the part of neoliberal intellectuals (discussed in chapter 6), left no space for "old" and popular leftist discourses in the print media (while the more academic-oriented "new left" intellectuals are debating their liberal and neoliberal counterparts in scholarly journals that have limited popular reach and thus little social mobilization impact), "old leftists"— some of them in their nineties—discovered the Internet, which had just taken off as a new medium in the early 2000s. In this way, "old leftists" unwillingly coalesced with and strengthened a multiplicity of online popular leftist discourses, which, unlike the "old leftists," have never had print media access to begin with. Specifically, in 2003, when editors of *The Pursuit of Truth*, seeing little hope in resuming the journal's publication, collaborated with nearly a hundred retired party members in launching the website Mao Zedong Flag (*Mao Zedong qizhi*), it quickly prompted a rapid alliance of existing leftist forums and became a major source site for online leftist discourses, turning leftists into the dominant voices in Chinese Internet chat rooms.[152] Even the *People's Daily's* "Strengthen the Nation Forum," which was launched in 1999 in the aftermath of the NATO bombing of the Chinese Embassy in Belgrade so that Chinese netizens could vent their nationalistic anger against the United States in an officially contained forum, had been dominated by left-leaning participants.[153] Precisely because "old leftists" are retired revolutionaries and as such are "still located at the periphery of the party-state's center of *political* influence,"[154] they function as the living embodiments and the speaking subjects, not the empty signs, symbols, and caricatured images, of the revolutionary legacy that the party invokes through Mao and must rely upon for its continuing legitimacy. Their regained leadership in a broad leftist discursive formation is thus particularly threatening to a neoliberal market authoritarian agenda. As I have mentioned in the introduction and will discuss in chapter 6, by late 2004, a large-scale debate on the future of the reform—the "third debate on reform"—had broken out.

To be sure, many "old leftists" within the party share with the party leadership its insistence on party monopoly of power, its elitist and paternalist orientations, and its commitment to top-down and technology-driven modernization. After all, they were the political and ideological allies of Deng when he ousted the more radical Maoist Cultural Revolution leftists in the party after the death of Mao. As the subject of abuse by their right-wing opponents—for example, they have been called the "red fundamentalists"—and as a result of the painstaking ideological work on the part of liberal and neoliberal intellectuals who enjoy considerable access to market-oriented media outlets and university classrooms, "the left" as a political label has ironically had a strong negative connotation in China, where the Communist Party rules and the ruling ideology is said to be Marxism. More specifically, "leftism" has been identified with the disasters of the Great Leap Forward and the Cultural Revolution, while being disarticulated with anything that is positive in the history of Chinese socialism or with any position that favors the interests of the lower social classes. This ideological work has been crucial for the conditional triumph of the market reform agenda and the implementation of "neoliberalism with Chinese characteristics." Within this ideological process, the trope of "leftism" in general (not just "ultra-leftism") and the specter of the Cultural Revolution have played the same and perhaps a more effective role as the ideology of anticommunism in the United States[155] or the "evil of communism" in right-wing propaganda in Third World authoritarian regimes during the Cold War era.

The Hu Jintao leadership, which has tried to address the social deficits of neoliberal development by turning the language of socialism into a form of reformist populism, has had a more ambivalent relationship with "old leftists" and grassroots leftists, and I revisit this issue in more detail in chapter 6 and in the conclusion. On the one hand, the leaders' wariness of complete capitalistic reintegration and their renewed commitment to the rhetoric of socialism have provided a discursive space for leftists to legitimate their voices.[156] On the other hand, the leaders have also clearly demonstrated their hostility toward more militant grassroots leftists. In a case that underscores the party's persistent suppression of leftist critiques, especially grassroots leftist critiques on behalf of Chinese workers, on September 9, 2004, the 28th anniversary of Mao's death, Zhang Zhengyao, a Maoist, was arrested in a public square in Zhengzhou, a hinterland city known for its militant labor protests, for distributing a leaflet entitled "Mao Forever Our Leader." The next day, Zhengzhou police raided Zhang's apartment, taking away his computer, the remaining leaflets, and other documents. Three others connected with Zhang were also arrested. The four were charged with "deliberately spreading falsehoods to damage other's reputation, and undermining social order and national interests,"[157] with two of them—Zhang Zhengyao and Zhang Ruquan—found guilty of libel and given three-year prison sentences.

Between a Communist Youth League Mouthpiece and the Communists Net: The Politics of Two Censorship Tales

Two censorship tales in early 2006 dramatized the political economic and ideological parameters that define the regime of party-state power in communication, its "structured asymmetries"[158] vis-à-vis different ideological positions and social forces in its actual application, as well as the uneven nature of the resistance to it. On January 25, 2006, *China Youth News's Freezing Point* weekly, whose liberal-minded editors have engaged in protracted struggles against the increasing instrumentalism of the Communist Youth League Central Committee, was suspended because of its publication of a lengthy article by Professor Yuan Weishi on January 11, 2006. In his article, Yuan, a Sun Yat-sen University philosophy professor, repudiated official history in middle school textbooks for its one-sided nationalistic and anti-imperialist narrative. In particular, Yuan faulted the official depiction of the armed resistance of the Taiping rebels and the Boxers against foreign invaders in the 19th century as patriotic and heroic precursors of the party's own anti-imperialist struggles. Yuan also criticized the official narrative's failure to condemn the violence of the rebels and their backward and antiforeign views, as well as its unwillingness to hold the Qing government responsible for violating international laws and committing other obstinate and criminal acts. Most provocatively, Yuan depicted Chinese culture as not only backward, but also violent, claiming that just as the Cultural Revolution–generation youths committed their violent excesses because they "grew up drinking the wolf's milk," today's youth in China, being educated by the official textbooks, "are continuing to drink the wolf's milk!"[159] In language reminiscent of what left-leaning, popular nationalist writer Wang Xiaodong has named as "reverse-racism"[160] and what Paul Pickowicz has described as "reverse Orientalism"[161]—an influential discourse that has long permeated pro-Western Chinese liberal intellectual writings and cultural productions— Yuan seems to have effectively inverted the discourse of anti-imperialism. He interpreted the Boxer Rebellion of 1900 as "against civilization and humanity" (*fan wenming, fan renlei*), maintaining that the Boxers' "evil deeds" (*zui'e xingjing*) "brought greatest tragedy to the country and the people" (*gei guojia he renmin dailai moda de zainan*). When the PD's postpublication review system identified the article as problematic, the PD of the Communist Youth League Central Committee issued an order to suspend the paper's publication and force a "rectification." Formal charges against the article include "attempted to vindicate the criminal acts by the imperialist powers in invading China," "seriously distorted historical facts," "seriously contradicted news propaganda discipline," "seriously damaged the national feelings of the Chinese people," "seriously damaged the image of *China Youth News*," and "created bad social influence."[162] Of course, consistent with the reform-era practice of not provoking debates and minimizing negative political impacts, the authorities banned news reports of the very act of censorship itself.[163]

Nevertheless, the suspension gained broad publicity on the Internet and in the international media and was widely resisted and protested both within and outside *China Youth News*. Li Datong, *Freezing Point*'s editor, posted an open letter on the Internet condemning the "unconstitutional" and "illegal" suspension of the paper. An influential group of 13 liberal-minded and retired high-ranking party officials, academics, as well as former media and propaganda chiefs also issued an open letter to condemn the censorship acts as "ridiculous and rude and totally beyond the boundaries of law."[164]

What was lost in the ensuing domestic and international drumbeat against censorship and the seemingly universalistic defense of press freedom is the fact that the *China Youth News*, the official Communist Youth League organ, should have been able to publish a piece that so explicitly challenged official party view in the first place. Moreover, in the absence of American-style journalistic conventions of "objectivity" and "balance," the official-organ nature of the paper had meant that such a view would have gained the status of an officially sanctioned view without rebuttal. Behind the apparently universalistic condemnation of censorship and the liberal invocation of the authority of the law, then, is the struggle between the political/bureaucratic and liberal intellectual segments of the ruling bloc over historical truths and the control of an official party organ—as Yuan Weishi said explicitly, he wrote the article to "tell the true history to our youths."[165]

In late February 2006, as the party-state's censorship regime capitulated and as liberal forces celebrated their partial victory over the party's decision to allow *Freezing Point* to resume publication on March 1, 2006 (with the removal of Li Datong as its chief editor, but not his dismissal from the paper), this same multifaceted regime issued a censorship order of a very different nature. On February 22, 2006, the Internet Propaganda Management Division of the Beijing Government Information Office ordered the closure of two prominent grassroots leftist websites, China Workers Net (*Zhongguo gongren wang*, established on May 1, 2005) and Communists Net (*Gongchandang ren wang*, established on December 26, 2005), and the latter's bulletin board, Worker-Peasant-Soldier BBS (established on January 20, 2006). The reason was that these websites did not have a registered capital of 10 million yuan (US$1.2 million) and thus were illegal in a state that is ruled by a Communist Party. According to the September 2005 "Regulation on Internet News and Information Service Management," an organization that is eligible to register as a news and information service on the Internet must be a legal entity that has provided such a service for more than two years and without any record of violating relevant laws and regulations; moreover, when such an organization is a business entity, its registered capital should not be less than 10 million yuan.[166] To be sure, these websites had all passed Recordation (*bei'an*) as Internet service providers with the MII when they were first established. However, they were now deemed as corporate entities engaging in the provision of news and informational services and thus were subjected to the minimum requirement of 10 million yuan in registered capitalization.

The party had shut down many websites before on political grounds, and many existing ones continue to operate without the required amount of capitalization. However, this was the first time the authorities invoked this requirement to shut down grassroots and autonomous workers and communist websites. What had made these websites so dangerous to the party was that they provided "uncensored news about worker unrest"[167] and had gained influence as leftist websites and as the "opinion forums of workers and farmers."[168] Even more threatening to the party, these websites dared to claim to be "communist" outside the party; that is, they are autonomous workers' and communist communication channels, and they have attempted to mobilize and organize themselves as such. As Andy Hu wrote,

> Inasmuch as "there are too many fake Communists within the Party," the senior administrator [of Communists Net] explicitly stated the new site's aim was to stand against the fake (*chang duitaixi*). It was also determined that the site should serve the purposes of uniting "true Party Communists" and the masses external to the Party. Contrary to conventional partisan distinctions, anyone equipped with a communist consciousness (*gongchanzhuyi juewu*) is considered "communist" (*Gongchandang ren*)—thus the website's name, which is intended to "draw a clear, outright line of demarcation with revisionism" (*qizhi xianming de he xiuzhengzhuyi huaqing jiexian*).[169]

Yan Yuanzhang, who is not a party member, but was a contributor to the Protagonist website before becoming an administrator of China Workers Net, has not only developed an acute Marxist analysis about how the Chinese working class has been "stripped of" the economic conditions for its self-organization, "with its class consciousness blurred and political quests manipulated," but also had this to say in an interview in the aftermath of his website's shutdown:

> If you want to prevent attacks on the Communist Party, it's best you do the right thing in the first place. So, if you're going to violate the rights of workers,

how do you get off complaining about attacks on your Communist Party? If you claim you're the leader of the working class and then you turn around and lay off a huge mass of state-owned enterprise workers, without doing anything to protect the power or interests of the workers' unions, of course you're going to face an angry response from workers. . . . China today is basically controlled by a new capitalist class. . . . The shutting down of a website like ours is, in effect, the silencing of workers who face hardships in today's China. We can't rely on intellectuals to accurately express the terms of those hardships. Nor can we expect them to lead the struggles to resolve the class conflicts that cause their pain . . . for us, *the* issue at hand is the right of Chinese workers to run their own web discussion lists to express themselves without having to encounter obstacles in their own country.[170]

That Yuan's article appeared in an official newspaper, while leftist websites could only carve out an existence at the margins of the Chinese cyberspace—with highly unstable severs that are often hacked—is itself highly indicative of the asymmetric access to venues of public discourse by proponents of "antigovernment" views of the right and the left. Moreover, contrary to the outburst of anger and protest by leading party editors and intellectuals, who defended *their* right to present *their* views as the official view in a party organ as a *constitutional* right and condemn the party's censorship as being ridiculous, editors at these marginal websites could only express a sigh of resignation in the face of legalized repression. In announcing their closure, the sites' voluntary operators stated that "we are a bunch of volunteers serving the workers and peasants, and also a bunch of paupers without 10 million. Therefore, [we] can only accept the finale of the website being declared illegal."[171] When a left-oriented university student posted a notice on his own marginal Revolutionary Marxism website to protest the closure of the China Workers Net, his site was immediately shut down, while he was "summoned to hear a dozen officials threaten him with expulsion from his university for backing Mr. Yan."[172]

More significantly, although liberal intellectuals decried the party's censorship of their views and used their domestic and international social networks to fight against it, and did so by invoking constitutionalism and speaking a universalizing discourse of press freedom, none of them rose to defend these websites on constitutional grounds, let alone condemn the blunt capitalistic bias of the government regulation and the power of economic censorship as perhaps also "rude," and in violation of the Chinese Constitution, which after all affirms equal citizenship rights for all, regardless of whether one can come up with 10 million yuan or not.

Finally, and perhaps most reflective of what truly matters in the struggle over control in Chinese communication, while *Freezing Point* is a Communist Youth League official organ and thus the party, in principle, has the "right to censorship," including the power to close a media outlet it owns, the leftist websites are not party organs, and thus, from the liberal perspective, for the government to order their closure should, in principle, have been more outrageous. Liberal intellectuals, who have long advocated a private media sector, turned out to have no interest in defending truly independent and non-party-state-owned and -operated Internet websites as a matter of principle. Instead, they rushed to defend a party organ that happened to publish *their* point of view. Before I turn to discuss economic marginalization as a means of political control in the next chapter, I would like to note that leftist views on the web have been a target of party censorship from the very beginning of the Internet's history in China. A Maoist website, for example, was among the first three Internet websites blocked by the Chinese government in the Chinese Internet's infancy.[173]

CONCLUSION

China's elaborate regime of party-state power in public communication has few parallels in the contemporary world. What is apparent is the party's determination to sustain this regime at all costs and by all means, its ability to constantly revamp and perfect this regime, and its progressive amplification and modernization since the early 1990s. The old practice of the official press "publishing the same photographs of the nation's new leaders in the same order and in the same place on every front page"[174] remains intact. Similarly, the state's campaigns against Falun Gong believers and its use of old-style mass mobilization, ideological rectification, and media propaganda techniques caution against any premature announcements about the state's retreat from private life and traditional propaganda.

Moreover, contrary to wishful thinkers on the ideological right who had hoped for a more liberal regime under the leadership of Hu Jintao, the past few years have not only witnessed the leadership's intensifying rearticulation of the official discourse on socialism, but also an amplification of coercive power, including the closure and major reorganization of a number of outspoken publications, the removal of the chief editors at various newspapers, not to mention a (widely felt) tightened grip on the Internet, leading foreign observers to believe that the leadership has launched "a campaign of media repression unprecedented for nearly 20 years."[175]

Despite the new leadership's "pro-people" image and its avowed concern for the well-being of the presumed masters of the "People's Republic" who have now been officially designated as China's "vulnerable social groups" (*ruoshi qunti*), for the news media to report on the numerous incidents of protests by expropriated farmers, laid-off state enterprise workers, and uncompensated pensioners, as well as other disenfranchised and dispossessed groups, is almost impossible. Media outlets and Internet websites that braved censorship orders to report these events have invariably been punished. Since political stability has been the overriding concern of the central leadership, and the potential of intellectual criticisms reaching the disenfranchised farmers and workers to form a formidable political and ideological opposition remains, the party-state's continuing ability to suppress oppositional ideas and prevent the formation of counterhegemonic alliances between various protesting social forces is no small accomplishment. As Perry and Selden observed,

> What is striking is that for all the popular anguish and the variety and depth of contemporary protests, to date no significant organizational focus, whether enshrined in a political party or social movement, has emerged at the regional, national or even local level effectively to challenge the Communist party.[176]

As they concluded, Chinese resistance movements are for the most part small, local, and isolated from one another, lacking interconnected ideological and organizational bonds. Diverse social groups face different dilemmas and thus "frame their grievances and demands in distinctive terms that do not easily transcend the barriers of class, region, gender, religion, nationality, or educational level."[177] Apart from other structural and contingent reasons, including the party's adept deployment of the divide and rule strategy,[178] the fragmented and uncoordinated form of many Chinese resistance movements, I argue, is also partly the result of the party-state's continuing ability to control information flows and block popular access to autonomous and effective means of communication, on the one hand, and to monopolize the discourse of socialism as an alternative to capitalism, on the other. Precisely within this context the dominant forces within the party-state have found a regenerated alliance between "old leftist" and autonomous grassroots leftist discourses most threatening.

Although one cannot overstate the pervasiveness and draconian nature of this regime, nor its efficacy in social control, as a way to set up the next chapter, I must emphasize that what is also significant and perhaps most striking today is the persistence, and indeed the accelerated velocity and expanded scope, of resistance against it and the ever more thunderous drumbeat of opposition to it. There are negotiations and tactical contestations at every step of media production, distribution, and consumption, and the growing sophistication and militancy of the protests match that of the regime itself. Just as Internet users have long learned to find cracks in the firewalls and devise alternative symbols to communicate censored words, journalists and even media managers are developing increasingly sophisticated techniques to evade and resist propaganda orders. For example, a high-level Shanghai broadcast official, after instructing the broadcast outlets under his control to defy propaganda disciplines in reporting a major international breaking event, deliberately turned off his cell phone, making himself inaccessible to the party PD for a while.[179] Wang Keqing, perhaps China's bravest investigative reporter, went undercover to investigate the June 11, 2005, "Dingzhou Incident" in Hebei Province, where local authorities used violent force to seize land from farmers for the construction of a power plant. A home video recording of the murderous demolition attack on villagers protesting the project was smuggled out of a police barricade and ended up in the possession of the *Washington Post*.

The weights and impacts of these acts of resistance are significant. Internet postings about a Jiangxi school explosion accident forced former premier Zhu Rongji to retract the official version of the story. Military doctor Jiang Yanyong's exposure of the government's SARS cover-up through the foreign media forced the government to change its media strategy. Massive civil society mobilization in Hong Kong led to the halt of attempts at imposing a mainland-style antisedition regime against the press. Just as Jiao Guobiao's open crusade against the PD was unprecedented, so were the protests at the *Beijing News* in December 2005, which involved a walkout by about 100 journalists protesting the firing of the paper's top editors,[180] as well as the campaigns inside and outside the *China Youth News*, which first led the newspaper's leadership to abandon the appraisal system,[181] and then the republication of *Freezing Point*. Although the Dingzhou video by local villagers did not make it into the domestic media, its release to the international media helped to highlight a struggle that has been waged by Chinese farmers all over the country. As UK journalist David McNeill puts it, with the video, "the world got a rare glimpse of the deadly, mostly unseen war between Chinese developers and the poor who stand in their way," and it "brings more unwelcome attention for Beijing on the enormous social tensions created by China's explosive economic growth."[182]

However, not all measures of repression and all victories of resistance are equal in scope and similar in nature. For Zhu Rongji to change his explanation of the cause of the Jiangxi school explosion is one thing, for domestic news media to be silent about protests by workers and farmers, or to refrain from reporting ongoing elite debates about the fundamental directions of the reforms, is quite another. As the cases of *China Youth News* and the grassroots leftist websites demonstrate, the ideological parameters are asymmetric, the terrains of contestation uneven, and the party regime of power profoundly class biased. All these beg further questions: How much longer can the party sustain a regime of power defined primarily by political and bureaucratic control? Must it survive indefinitely? Are there other means to ensure that the ruling ideas remain those of the rulers or at least that other discourses get marginalized? Will there be a point at which the party-state no longer needs to resort to the imposition of control as an arbitrary measure but will be able to achieve control less visibly and yet perhaps more efficaciously and even seemingly naturally? More importantly, how will such a change affect the substance of the ruling ideas and redefine the party's political nature? These questions inform the discussions about the economic transformation of the party-state's media and cultural institutions in the next chapter.

NOTES

1. Wang Hui, *China's New Order*, ed. Theodore Hunters (Cambridge, Mass.: Harvard University Press, 2003), 65.

2. Maurice Meisner, *The Deng Xiaoping Era: An Inquiry into the Fate of Chinese Socialism, 1978–1994* (New York: Hill and Wang, 1996), 118, 122–123.

3. Wang, *China's New Order*, 65.

4. Lindsay Beck, "Zhao's Death Shows Limits of China's Media Freedom," Reuters, 27 Jan. 2005, story.news.yahoo.com/news?tmpl=story&u=/nm/media_china_dc (accessed 27 Jan. 2005).

5. Yi Lan, "*Zhongguo wangluo he meiti de kongzhi he fankongzhi*" (Control and Counter-Control inside China's Internet and Media), www.peacehall.com/news/gb/china/2004/06/200406280843.shtml (accessed 16 Oct. 2004).

6. Hai Tao, "*Zhongguo jiajin kongzhi hulianwang*" (China Tightens Control of Internet), www.peacehall.com/news/gb/china/2004/06/2004/06231340.shtml (accessed 16 Oct. 2004).

7. Reporters without Borders and China Human Rights Defenders, *Journey to the Heart of Internet Censorship*, Oct. 2007, www.rsf.org/IMG/pdf/Voyage_au_coeur_de_la_censure_GB.pdf (accessed 23 Oct. 2007).

8. He Qinglian provides perhaps the most detailed description of the Chinese government's suppression of negative news and liberal voices. See He Qinglian, "*Zhongguo zhengfu ruhe kongzhi meiti*" (How the Chinese Government Controls the Media), *Dangdai Zhongguo yanjiu* 11, no. 3 (2004): 36–55; 11, no. 4 (2004): 78; 12, no. 1 (2005): 14–48; 12, no. 2 (2005): 18–80; for other accounts of the party's propaganda system and media control, see Jiao Guobiao, "*Zhongguo you wuqianwan dangweishuji*" (China Has 5 Million Party Secretaries), *Kaifang* (Nov. 2005): 65–69; Jiao Guobiao, "*Zhongguo you sibaiwan ge xuanchunbu*" (China Has 4 Million Propaganda Departments), *Kaifang* (Dec. 2005): 26–30; David Shambaugh, "China's Propaganda System: Institutions, Processes and Efficacy," *China Journal* 57 (Jan. 2007): 25–58.

9. Elizabeth J. Perry, "Studying Chinese Politics: Farewell to Revolution?" *China Journal* 57 (Jan. 2007).

10. Liu Kang, *Globalization and Cultural Trends in China* (Honolulu: University of Hawai'i Press, 2004), 82.

11. This point was driven home in March 2006 when some well-known bloggers in China voluntarily closed their sites. After the closures predictably led to Western media reports of yet another act of government censorship, and even a statement of condemnation by the French group Reporters without Borders, the bloggers came out to say that they purposely shut down the sites to make a point about freedom of speech, to expose Western media "irresponsibility," and most specifically, "to give foreign media a lesson that Chinese affairs are not always the way you think." Geoffrey A. Fowler and Juying Qin, "Chinese Bloggers Stage Hoax Aimed at Censorship Debate," *Wall Street Journal*, 14 Mar. 2006, B3.

12. Guoguang Wu, "The Birth of Sophisticated Propaganda: The Party-State and the Chinese Media in Post-Reform Politics," paper manuscript made available to the author.

13. For a detailed description, see Shambaugh, "China's Propaganda System."

14. Dali L. Yang, "Rationalizing the Chinese State: The Political Economy of Government Reform," in *Remaking the Chinese State: Strategies, Society and Security*, ed. Chien-min Chao and Bruce J. Dickson, 19–45 (London and New York: Routledge, 2001).

15. The website of the "International Communication Office of the CCP Central Committee," for example, leads to the SCIO's www.china.org.cn website.

16. "*Zhu Rongji zhuchi guojiaxinxihua lingdaoxiaozu diyici huiyi*" (Zhu Rongji Chaired the First Meeting of the State Informatization Leading Group), Xinhua, 27 Dec. 2002.

17. "*Zhongguo sheli wangluo xuanchuan guanlijiu*" (China Establishes Internet Propaganda Management Bureau), *Qiao bao*, 7 Apr. 2000, A2.

18. Some of these are the Central PD, the External PD of the CCP, the Ministry of Public Security, the Ministry of Education, the MII, the Ministry of Culture, the SARFT, the GAPP, the State Industry and Commercial Administration, and the State Council Legal Office.

19. The party has renamed it officially as the Department of Publicity in English, after learning that the term "propaganda" has a negative connotation.

20. Jiao Guobiao, "*Taofa Zhongxuanbu*" (Declaration of the Campaign against the Central PD), msittig.freeshell.org/docs/ jian_guobio_essay_utf8.html (accessed 16 Oct. 2004).

21. Jane L. Curry, "Media Management and Political Systems," in *Press Control around the World*, ed. Jane L. Curry and Joan R. Dassin (New York: Praeger, 1982), 105, cited in Judy Polumbaum, "The Tribulations of Chinese Journalists after a Decade of Reform," in *Voices of China: The Interplay of Politics and Journalism*, ed. Chin-Chuan Lee (New York: Guilford Press, 1990), 53.

22. Shambaugh, "China's Propaganda System," 53.

23. For an English version, see Michael Schoenhals, ed., *China's Cultural Revolution, 1966–1969: Not a Dinner Party* (Armonk: M. E. Sharpe, 1996), 310–312.

24. Polumbaum, "The Tribulations," 54.

25. Xiao De, "*2003 Zhongguo meiti shida shijian*" (Ten Big Events about the Chinese Media in 2003), www.jsw.com.cn/zk/gb/content/2003-12/11/content_483563.htm (accessed 14 Oct. 2004).

26. Zhou Yongming, *Historicizing Online Politics: Telegraphy, the Internet, and Political Participation in China* (Stanford, Calif.: Stanford University Press, 2006), 179.

27. Jing Wang, "Culture as Leisure and Culture as Capital," *Positions* 9, no. 1 (Spring 2001): 93.

28. Wang, "Culture as Leisure," 92–93.

29. Yuezhi Zhao, *Media, Market, and Democracy in China: Between the Party Line and the Bottom Line* (Urbana: University of Illinois Press, 1998), chapter 2.

30. These include harmful to national unity, sovereignty, and territorial integrity; harmful to national security, honor, and interest; inciting national division and damaging national unity; disclosing state secrets; slandering and libel; promotion of obscenity, superstition, and violence; and other content prohibited by laws and administrative orders.

31. The SARFT, for example, issued so many administrative orders over the broadcasting and audiovisual industries in 2004 that it became a topic of derision for many scholars.

32. At this stage, there is limited decentralization of power. Provincial broadcast authorities have final censorship authority on domestic television dramas produced within their jurisdiction, but they can forgo this authority and defer authority to the SARFT.

33. New additions include content that "opposes the basic principles of the Constitution," promotes religious sects, "disturbs social order and undermines social stability," "undermines the lawful interest of others," and content deemed "harmful to societal virtue and the superior traditions of national culture." SARFT, "*Dianshiju shencha guanli guiding*" (Regulations on Censorship and Management of Television Drama), 20 Sept. 2004, www.sarft.gov.cn/manage/publishfile/20/2206.html (accessed 22 Oct. 2004).

34. See the website www.cnnic.net.cn/index/0F/index.htm.

35. SCIO, the MII, "*Hulianwang xinwenxinxi fuwu wangle guiding*" (Regulations on the Management of Internet News and Information Services), 5 Sept. 2005, www.cnnic.net.cn/html/Dir/2005/09/27/3184.htm (accessed 5 Nov. 2005).

36. Polumbaum, "The Tribulations," 52–53.

37. In a major clampdown in January 2000, Jiang Yiping, its editor-in-chief and an award-winning journalist, was sacked for her handling of several stories. Qian Gang, a prominent Beijing-based journalist, was assigned as the acting editor-in-chief. Instead of containing the investigative edge of the paper, as the party's propaganda officials had hoped, Qian sustained the paper's outspoken legacy. By late May 2001, the party had ousted Qian and the paper's front-page editor for their exposure of the social ills behind a major criminal case.

38. The system is administered by the GAPP's official website, www.gapp.gov.cn, and journalists must go online to activate their press cards. The general public, in turn, presumably can verify the authenticity of a journalist's card, thus preventing possible fraud and abuse of journalistic privileges. Wang Bo, "*Zhubu jianli xinwen congye renyuan zige zhunru zhidu*" (Gradually Establishing the System of Certifying Journalists), www.gappedu.cn/xw/djzw.htm (accessed 14 Oct. 2004).

39. SARFT, Order No. 26, "*Guangbo dianshi bianji jizhe, boyinyuan zhuchiren zige guanli zanxing guiding*" (Provisional Regulations on the Management of Qualifica-

tions for Broadcast Editors, Reporters, Announcers and Hosts), 18 Jun. 2004, www.sarft.gov.cn/manage/publishfile/20/1931.html (accessed 14 Oct. 2004).

40. However, special "work teams" sent by the party to particular news outlets to investigate political transgressions do act as censorship boards. Polumbaum, "The Tribulations," 52.

41. Hai Ming, "*Xinwen shengchan guocheng zhong de quanli shijian xingtai yanjiu*" (A Study of the Practical Forms of Power in News Production), academic.media china.net/academic_xsjd_view.jsp?id=1180 (accessed 24 Mar. 2006).

42. Notes provided by an individual who worked at this media outlet.

43. He, "*Zhongguo zhengfu ruhe kongzhi meiti*" (part 2), 47.

44. "*Quanguo baokan shendu gongzuo huiyi qiangdiao baokan shendu yao 'yanba san-guan'*" (National Press Monitoring Work Conference Emphasizes Tight Gatekeeping in Three Areas), www.xwcbj.gd.gov.cn/xwfb/ news_brow.asp?id=4980 (accessed 11 Oct. 2004).

45. Shenzhen Press and Publications Bureau, "*Guifan guanli, cujin fazhan, tuidong Shenzhen xinwen chubanye quanmian fanrong*" (Normalizing Management, Spurring Development, and Promoting the Full-Scale Prosperity of the Shenzhen Publishing Industry), www.szwen.gov.cn/NEWSWEB/hygk/hygk_ztbd_02.htm (accessed 11 Oct. 2004).

46. He Qinglian, "*2003 nian Zhongguo 'xinwen meiti gaige' gaile shenme?*" (What Did Chinese Media Reform Accomplish in 2003?), www.zhongguohun.com/data/2003-9-12029.html (accessed 11 Oct. 2004).

47. Jack Linchuan Qiu, "Virtual Censorship in China: Keeping the Gates between the Cyberspaces," *International Journal of Communications Law and Policy* 4 (1999): 1–25; Lokman Tsui, "The Panopticon as the Antithesis of a Space of Freedom: Control and Regulation of the Internet in China," *China Information* 17, no. 2 (2003): 65–82. He, "*Zhongguo zhengfu ruhe kongzhi meiti*" (part 4), 38–80.

48. Mark Ward, "China's Tight Rein on Online Growth," BBC News, news.bbc .co.uk/1/hi/technology/4327067.stm (accessed 5 Nov. 2005).

49. "*Xinwen chuban zongshu chuanda zhongyang 'guanyu jin yibu jiaqiang hulianwang guanli gongzuo de yijian' jingshen*" (GAPP Transmitted the Party Central Committee's Ideas on Strengthening the Management of the Internet), 8 Dec. 2004, www.bnup.com.cn/mainnewsdetails.cfm?iCntno=1301 (accessed 27 Jan. 2005).

50. Yu Guoming, "*Shishui fang'ai le Zhongguo chuanmeiye de fazhan?*" (Who Hinders the Development of China's Media Industry?), in *Zhongguo meiti fazhan yanjiu baogao 2002* (China Media Development Report 2002), ed. Luo Yicheng, Zhang Jinhai, and Shan Bo (Wuhan: Wuhan chubanshe, 2003), 31.

51. Tsui, "The Panopticon," 70.

52. Alexander Golloway, "Protocol, or, How Control Exists after Decentralization," *Rethinking Marxism* 13, nos. 3–4 (2001): 81–88.

53. Yu, "*Shishui fang'ai le Zhongguo chuanmeiye de fazhan?*" 31.

54. Interview, 12 Aug. 2004, Vancouver.

55. Wei Gao, Staging the "Mobile Phone Carnival": A Political Economy of the SMS Culture in China (master's thesis, School of Communication, Simon Fraser University, 2005), 82.

56. Jack Linchuan Qiu, "The Wireless Leash: Mobile Messages Serve as a Means of Control," *International Journal of Communication* 1 (2007): 74–91. Electronic version, ijoc.org/ojs/index.php/ijoc/article/view/15/19 (accessed 15 Apr. 2007).

57. *"Guowuyuan xinwenbangongshi fuzhuren Cai Mingzhao zai hulianwang xin-wenxinxi fuwu gongzuo weiyuanhui di'er ci huiyi shang de jianghua"* (Speech by SICO Deputy Director Cao Mingzhao at the Second Meeting of the News and Information Services Working Committee), net.chian.com.cn/Chinese/ic/426451.htm (accessed 27 Jan. 2005).

58. According to the center's own figures, by noon of August 23, 2004, www.china.cn had received 54,763 reports. Min Dahong, *"2004 Nian de Zhongguo wangluo meiti"* (China's Internet Media in 2004), 22 Dec. 2004, www.blogchina.com/new/display/60621.html (accessed 27 Jan. 2005).

59. Tsui, "The Panopticon," 72.

60. Wu, "The Birth of Sophisticated Propaganda"; Zhou He, "Chinese Communist Party Press in a Tug of War: A Political Economy Analysis of the Shenzhen Special Zone Daily," in *Power, Money, and Media: Communication Patterns and Bureaucratic Control in Cultural China,* ed. Chin-Chuan Lee, 112–151 (Evanston, Ill.: Northwestern University Press, 2000).

61. Geremie Barmé, "Spring Clamor and Autumnal Silence: Cultural Control in China," *Current History* (Sept. 1998): 257–262.

62. Hu Jiwei, former editor-in-chief of *People's Daily* and arguably the most outspoken crusader for greater media freedom within the party-state establishment, has been one such silenced voice. In an account published in a Hong Kong magazine, Hu described in great detail his experience as a nonexistent person in the post-1989 Chinese media scene. Editors who violated the publication ban and published Hu's articles were punished. Hu's attempts at self-publishing without public distribution were also frustrated. Four printers declined to take Hu's business. A fifth agreed to do so, but when he discovered that Hu's two volumes on democracy contained content calling for a reversal of the party's June 4 verdict, fearing that his business would be shut down, he quietly destroyed the books that had already been printed without giving Hu a single copy. Hu Jiwei, *"Zhongguo xinwen gaige de quzhe licheng"* (The Zigzag Path of Journalism Reform in China), *Kaifang* (Sept. 2003): 26–29.

63. Ji Bingxuan, *"Zai xinwei meiti gugan xuexi sange daibiao zhongyao sixiang jinxing Makesi zhuyi xinwenguan jiaoyu peixunban kaiban shi de jianghua,"* *Zhongyang dangxiao baogao xuan* 237, no. 9 (2003): 13, cited in Wu, "The Birth of Sophisticated Propaganda," 9.

64. Geremie Barmé, *In the Red: On Contemporary Chinese Culture* (New York: Columbia University Press, 1999), 258.

65. Zhou, *Historicizing,* 170, 180.

66. Zhou, *Historicizing,* 173.

67. Orville Schell, "A Lonely Voice in China Is Critical on Rights and Reform," *New York Times,* 24 Jan. 2004, E45.

68. Tsui, "The Panopticon," 76.

69. Bruce Gilley, *China's Democratic Future: How It Will Happen and Where It Will Lead* (New York: Columbia University Press, 2004), 33.

70. Liu, *Globalization,* 50.

71. John B. Thompson, *Ideology and Modern Culture* (Stanford, Calif.: Stanford University Press, 1990), 19.

72. Liu Kang, who defined ideology as "a system of meaning and values that help to legitimate a dominant political power," made a similar point. See *Globalization*, 53.

73. Kalpana Misra, *From Post-Maoism to Post-Marxism: The Erosion of Official Ideology in Deng's China* (New York and London: Routledge, 1998), 8.

74. "Hu: Harmonious Society Crucial for Progress," Xinhua, www.chinadaily.com.cn/english/doc/2005-06/28/content_455332.htm (accessed 1 Aug. 2005).

75. Perry, "Studying Chinese Politics," 16.

76. Gilley, *China's Democratic Future*, 33.

77. For example, when an explosion occurred in Tiananmen Square on February 15, 2000, the state media and the state-controlled website www.china.org.cn quickly reported the incident and described the perpetrator as a "mentally ill" individual to deflect foreign media reports about the politically motivated nature of the suicide explosion. Wang Xi'ai and Zhang Ximing, "*Wangluo xinwen chuanbo: Xinshiqi yulun daoxiang de yige zhongyao zhigaodian*" (Internet News Transmission: An Important New Command Height in Directing Public Opinion in the New Era), *Gaige* 4 (2000): 27–28.

78. Wu, "The Birth of Sophisticated Propaganda."

79. "*Tufa gonggong shijian yingji jizhi*" (Mechanisms for Responding to Public Emergencies), news.xinhuanet.com/ziliao/2006-01/17/content_4062615.htm (accessed 13 May 2006).

80. "*Zhongguo zhengfu sange cengci de xinwen fabu tizhi jiben jianli*" (The Chinese Government's Three Levels of News Release System Has Been Basically Established), www.china.org.cn/Chinese/zhuanti/fyr/74316.htm (accessed 24 Jan. 2005).

81. The Shanghai government, for example, justifies the establishment of this system as part of its attempt to "adopt more international ways of doing things" and to better serve the citizens and ensure the citizen's right to know. "*Shanghai shizhengfu qidong xinwenfayanren zhidu*" (Shanghai Government Started the News Spokesperson System), www.people.com.cn/GB/shizheng/1920030603/1007470.html (accessed 24 Jan. 2005).

82. "*Dangguan yao xuehui jieshou caifang*" (Being an Official Involves Learning to be Interviewed), *Dushi kuaibao* (30 Dec. 2004): 17.

83. The regulation was released on April 5, 2007. For the text of the regulation, see www.gov.cn/zwgk/2007-04/24/content_592937.htm (accessed 31 Dec. 2007).

84. Zhou, *Historicizing*, 141–154.

85. Zhou, *Historicizing*, 146.

86. Tsui, "The Panopticon," 74.

87. Personal correspondence with an Internet researcher in Beijing, 25 Jan. 2005.

88. Joseph Fewsmith, "China and the Politics of SARS," *Current History* (Sept. 2003): 250.

89. Perry, "Studying Chinese Politics," 15–16.

90. Fewsmith, "China and the Politics of SARS," 254.

91. CCP Central Committee, "*Zhonggongzhongyang guanyu jiaqiang dangde zhizheng nengli jianshe de jueding*" (Central Committee of Chinese Communist Party Decision on Strengthening the Party's Governance Capabilities), www.china.org.cn/chinese/2004/Sep/668376.htm (accessed 2 Oct. 2004).

92. Lisa Rofel, *Other Modernities: Gendered Yearnings in China after Socialism* (Berkeley: University of California Press, 1999), 36, cited in Lin Chun, *The Transformation of Chinese Socialism* (Durham, N.C.: Duke University Press, 2006), 176.

93. In one case, the Putuo District of Ningbo City paid 800,000 yuan to ask the Central PD to stop a CCTV special feature; in another case, the principal in a public health accident paid several hundred thousand yuan to spike a CCTV report. Jiao, *"Taofa Zhongxuanbu."*

94. For more examples, see He Qinglian, *"Zhongguo zhengfu ruhe kongzhi meiti"* (part 3), 14–41.

95. Edward Cody, "Backing Whistle-Blower Lands Journalists in Jail," *Vancouver Sun*, 25 Jan. 2006, A12.

96. Liu Binlu, *"Jiaojing duizhang buman piping baodao, shuaizhong baoshe zishi bei tingzhi"* (Traffic Police Chief Unhappy with Critical News Report, Led an Attack at a Newspaper Office, and Was Suspended), china.ynet.com/view.jsp?oid= 6600000 (accessed 2 Feb. 2006).

97. For more details, see He Qinglian, *"Zhongguo zhengfu ruhe kongzhi meiti"* (part 3).

98. Lu Yuegang, *"Zhi Zhongguo gongchanzhuyi qingniantuan zhongyang shujichu shuji Zhao Yong de gongkaixin"* (An Open Letter to Executive Secretary Zhao Yong of the Central Committee of the Chinese Communist Youth League), 13 Jun. 2004, www.huanghuagang.org/library/open_letter_to_Zhao_Yong.htm (accessed 1 Nov. 2005).

99. Li Datong, *"Jiu Zhongguo Qingnianbao xinde kaopingbanfa zhi Li Erliang zongbianji de xin"* (A Letter to *China Youth News*'s New Editor-in-Chief Li Erliang), www.zonaeuropa.com/20050817_2.htm (accessed 5 Nov. 2005).

100. Ji Shuoming, *"Xia jingji yi zizhong, difang xiang zhongyang shuobu"* (Localities Say No to the Center, Asserting Economic Prowess), www.chinatopnews .com/gb/MainNews/Forums/BackStage/2005_9_17_9_6_14_730.html (accessed 24 Jan. 2005). Interviews with media insiders in Beijing confirmed the existence of new guidelines aiming at curbing the media's practice of *yidi jiandu.*

101. Ji, *"Xia jingji yi zizhong."*

102. Yuezhi Zhao and Sun Wusan, "'Public Opinion Supervision': Potentials and Limits of the Media in Constraining Local Officials," in *Grassroots Political Reform in Contemporary China*, ed. Elizabeth Perry and Merle Goldman, 300–324 (Cambridge, Mass.: Harvard University Press, 2007).

103. Edward Cody, "China Declares a People's War against Porn," *Vancouver Sun*, 21 Aug. 2004, A13; "China Pays Cash for Reporting Porn," *South China Morning Post*, 11 Oct. 2004, www.asiamedia.ucla.edu/article.asp?parentid=15723 (accessed 11 Oct. 2004).

104. Andy Hu, "Swimming against the Tide: Tracing and Locating Chinese Leftism Online" (master's thesis, School of Communication, Simon Fraser University, 2006), 122.

105. Xinhua Net, "Internet Society Calls for 'Healthy' Development," news.xin huanet.com/english/2006-04/13/content_4417421.htm (accessed 27 Apr. 2006), cited in Hu, "Swimming against the Tide," 149.

106. Wang, "Culture as Leisure," 93.

107. Timothy Cheek, *Propaganda and Culture in Mao's China: Deng Tuo and the Intelligentsia* (Oxford: Clarendon Press, 1997).

108. Interview, 4 Jun. 2004, Wuhan.

109. Zhongdang Pan, "Media Change through Bounded Innovations: Journalism in China's Media Reforms" (paper presented at the International Communication Association Convention, New York City, 26–30 May 2005), 7.

110. Interview, 6 Jun. 2004, Wuhan.

111. Personal editorial correspondence, 28 Apr. 2003.

112. Wang, "Culture as Leisure," 99.

113. Li, "*Jiu Zhongguo qingnianbao.*"

114. Samir Amin, "Social Movements in the Periphery," in *New Social Movements in the South: Empowering the People*, ed. Ponna Wignaraja (London: Zed Books, 1993), 95.

115. In a different framework, Lin Chun has analyzed the Chinese state in terms of "the triad of nationalism, socialism and developmentalism." See *The Transformation of Chinese Socialism*.

116. For a critique of this literature, see Perry, "Studying Chinese Politics."

117. As I will argue in chapter 2, there is an intertwined cultural transition as well—the reorientation of a whole range of institutions, processes, values, and experiences in the broadly defined realm of communication and culture that is irreducible to either politics or economics.

118. Ellen Meiksins Wood, *Democracy against Capitalism: Renewing Historical Materialism* (New York: Cambridge University Press, 1995).

119. Christopher Hill, *The World Turned Upside Down: Radical Ideas during the English Revolution* (London: Temple Smith, 1972).

120. James Petras and Henry Veltmeyer, *Globalization Unmasked: Imperialism in the 21st Century* (London and New York: Zed Books, 2001), 108.

121. David Harvey, *A Brief History of Neoliberalism* (Oxford: Oxford University Press, 2005), 70.

122. For relevant discussion, see Meisner, *The Deng Xiaoping Era*; Arif Dirlik, *Marxism in the Chinese Revolution* (Lanham, Md.: Rowman & Littlefield, 2005); see also Martin Hart-Landsberg and Paul Burkett, "China and Socialism: Market Reforms and Class Struggle," *Monthly Review*, Jul.–Aug. 2004; Yiching Wu, "Rethinking 'Capitalist Restoration' in China," *Monthly Review*, Nov. 2005, 44–63; Lin, *The Transformation of Chinese Socialism*.

123. Ellen Meiksins Wood, *The Origin of Capitalism* (New York: Monthly Review Press, 1999), 196.

124. Dirlik, *Marxism in the Chinese Revolution*, 229.

125. Dirlik, *Marxism in the Chinese Revolution*, 151–152. See also Lin, *The Transformation of Chinese Socialism*.

126. While the term "liberal" is often defiantly invoked by Chinese intellectuals to describe their own political position, virtually no Chinese intellectuals are identifying themselves as "neoliberals." Although it is not easy to make a clear distinction between a "liberal" and a "neoliberal" position in the Chinese intellectual spectrum, a "liberal" position tends to focus on the advocacy of political and civil liberties and Western-style liberal democracy, whereas a "neoliberal" position emphasizes radical market reforms, while either remaining silent or expressing open fear of democracy and popular political participation. As Liu Kang has observed, insofar as Chinese neoliberals refrain from publicly calling for the party to give up its monopoly of power and do not press their issues too hard and too

straightforwardly, their voices are not only tolerated, but also often promoted by the media. They pose a threat to the party when their advocacy for the open embrace of capitalism and free elections threatens to collapse "socialism" as an ideological icon, ultimately undermining the party's political legitimacy. See Liu, *Globalization*, 74.

127. Harvey, *A Brief History*, 150.

128. Perry, "Studying Chinese Politics," 17.

129. The Falun Gong movement had a more complicated articulation of identity and class politics. However, it has assumed an unequivocal right-wing political position with its publication of the Nine Commentaries in 2004. See Yuezhi Zhao, "Falun Gong, Identity, and the Struggle for Meaning Inside and Outside China," in *Contesting Media Power: Alternative Media in a Networked World*, ed. Nick Couldry and James Curran, 209–224 (Lanham, Md.: Rowman & Littlefield, 2003).

130. Gang Lin, "Ideology and Political Institutions for a New Era," in *China After Jiang*, ed. Gang Lin and Xiaobo Hu, 39–68 (Stanford, Calif.: Stanford University Press, 2003), 42.

131. Joseph Fewsmith, *China since Tiananmen: The Politics of Transition* (Cambridge: Cambridge University Press, 2001), 192.

132. Barmé, *In the Red*, 316–344.

133. Feng Chen, "An Unfinished Battle in China: The Leftist Criticism of the Reform and the Third Thought Emancipation," *China Quarterly* 158 (Jun. 1999): 447–467.

134. Interview, 8 Jan. 2005, Beijing.

135. Richard Spencer, "Tiananmen: Victory for Capitalism," *Spectator*, 12 Jun. 2004.

136. For a more detailed analysis of the various leftist discourses, their different intellectual and social compositions, as well as their main online and offline forums, see Hu, "Swimming against the Tide," 69–119.

137. Liu, *Globalization*, 47.

138. Perry, "Studying Chinese Politics," 17. See also Yuezhi Zhao, "The Media Matrix: China's Integration into Global Capitalism," in *Socialist Register 2005: The Empire Reloaded*, ed. Leo Panitch and Colin Leys, 65–84 (London: Merlin Press, 2004).

139. Hu, "Swimming against the Tide," 120–158.

140. Zhu Xueqin, "1998: Ziyouzhuyi de yanshuo" (1998: The Discourse of Liberalism), books.tianya.cn/zuanglan/infoview.asp?id=760 (accessed 18 Mar. 2007).

141. Xu Jilin, Liu Qing, Luo Gang, and Xue Yi, "In Search of a 'Third Way': A Conversation regarding 'Liberalism' and the 'New Left Wing,'" trans. Geremie R. Barmé, in *Voicing Concerns: Contemporary Chinese Critical Inquiry*, ed. Gloria Davies (Lanham, Md.: Rowman & Littlefield, 2001), 199.

142. Chen, "An Unfinished Battle," 459.

143. Shen Hongfei, "*Ershi shiji mo gongchanzhuyi dalunzhan*" (The Great Communist Debate at the End of the 20th Century), in *Beijing dixia "wanyanshu"* (The Ten-Thousand-Word and Other Underground Writings in Beijing), ed. Shi Ziliu, 1–24 (Hong Kong: Mingjing chubanshe, 1997).

144. See "Letter of the Fourteen" and "Letter of Ma Bin and Han Xiya," *Monthly Review*, May 2002, www.monthlyreview.org/0502cpc2.htm (accessed 16 Jul. 2004).

145. Bruce Gilley, "Jiang's Turn Tempts Fate," *Far Eastern Economic Review*, 30 Aug. 2001, 18.

146. Jiang Xueqin, "Fighting to Organise," *Far Eastern Economic Review*, 6 Sept. 2001, 74.

147. Gilley, *China's Democratic Future*, 88.

148. See, for example, Teresa Wright, "Intellectuals and the Politics of Protest: The Case of the China Democracy Party," in *Chinese Intellectuals between State and Market*, ed. Edward Gu and Merle Goldman, 158–180 (London and New York: RoutledgeCurzon, 2004).

149. Gilley, *China's Democratic Future*, 25.

150. Cited in "A Struggle within the Chinese Communist Party: An Introduction," *Monthly Review*, May 2002, www.monthlyreview.org/0502cpc.htm (accessed 4 May 2006).

151. Yuezhi Zhao and Dan Schiller, "Dances with Wolves? China's Integration into Digital Capitalism," *Info* 3, no. 2 (Apr. 2001): 137–151; see also Elizabeth J. Perry and Mark Selden, "Introduction: Reform and Resistance in Contemporary China," in *Chinese Society: Change, Conflict and Resistance*, 2nd ed., ed. Elizabeth J. Perry and Mark Selden, 1–22 (London: RoutledgeCurzon, 2003), 18.

152. Hu, "Swimming against the Tide," 87–88.

153. Hu, "Swimming against the Tide," 132–135.

154. Hu, "Swimming against the Tide," 80.

155. Edward S. Herman and Noam Chomsky, *Manufacturing Consent: The Political Economy of the Mass Media* (New York: Pantheon, 2002).

156. "Old leftists," for example, named their website Mao Zedong Flag and appropriated Hu Jintao's rhetoric of "always hold high the great banner of Mao Zedong Thought at any time under any instance" as its motto (*zhan xun*). This way, they carved out a surviving space by presenting their website as essentially supportive of the current leadership. Hu, "Swimming against the Tide," 87.

157. The China Study Group, "The Case of the Zhengzhou Four," www.chianstudygroup.org/article/103 (accessed 5 Sept. 2004).

158. I borrowed this term from Peter Golding and Graham Murdoch, who invoked it to describe power relations in the capitalist social formation. Peter Golding and Graham Murdock, "Culture, Communication, and Political Economy," in *Mass Media and Society*, ed. James Curran and Michael Gurevitch (London: Edward Arnold, 1991), 18.

159. Yuan Weishi, "*Xiandaihua yu lishi jiaokeshu*" (Modernization and History Textbooks), www.zonaeuropa.com/20060126_2.htm; for an English translation, see www.zonaeuropa.com/20060126_1.htm (accessed 11 May 2006).

160. Wang Xiaodong, "*Minzuzhuyi he Zhongguo de weilai*" (Nationalism and the Future of China), www.usc.cuhk.edu.hk/wk_wzdetails.asp?id=116 (accessed 11 May 2006).

161. Paul G. Pickowicz, "Velvet Prisons and the Political Economy of Chinese Filmmaking," in *Urban Spaces in Contemporary China: The Potential for Autonomy and Community in Post-Mao China*, ed. Deborah S. Davis, Richard Krause, Barry Naughton, and Elizabeth J. Perry (Cambridge: Woodrow Wilson Center Press and Cambridge University Press, 1995), 213.

162. Yuan, "*Xiandaihua yu lishi jiaokeshu*."

163. Philip P. Pan, "Leading Publication Shut Down in China, Party's Move Is Part of Wider Crackdown," *Washington Post*, 25 Jan. 2006, A15.

164. The Associated Press, "Communist Party Elders Slam Media Controls," *Vancouver Sun*, 16 Feb. 2006, A11.

165. Yuan, "*Xiandaihua yu lishi jiaokeshu.*"

166. SCIO and MII, "*Hulianwang xinxi fuwu guanli guiding*" (Regulations on the Management of Internet News and Information Services), news.xinhuanet.com/politics/2005-09/25/content_3538899.htm (accessed 11 May 2006).

167. "China and the Net: The Party, the People and the Power of Cyber-Talk," *Economist*, www.ebusinessforum.com/index.asp?layout=rich_story&doc_id=8481&categoryid=&channelid=&search= (accessed 11 May 2006).

168. "'*Lianghui' qianxi Beijing guan san zhuopai wangzhan*" (Beijing Shut Down Three Leftist Websites on the Eve of the "Two Meetings"), DWNEWS.Com, www5.chinesenewsnet.com/MainNews/SinoNews/Mainland/2006_2_21_17_2_53_132.html (accessed 11 May 2006).

169. Hu, "Swimming against the Tide," 139, emphasis in original.

170. Stephen Philion, "An Interview with Yan Yuanzhang," *Monthly Review*, mrzine.monthlyreview.org/philion130306.html (accessed 11 May 2006).

171. "*Zhongguo gongren wang, Gongchandang ren wang, gongnongbing BBS jijiang guanbi (Beijing shijian 2 yue 22 ri shangwu 9 dian)*" (China Workers Net, Communists Net, and Worker-Peasant-Solider BBS on the Point of Closure, 9 a.m., February 22, Beijing Time), Protagonist Forum, host378.ipowerweb.com/~gongnong/bbs/read.php?f=3&i=149033&t=149033 (accessed 21 Feb. 2006).

172. "China and the Net." The asymmetric nature of the Chinese symbolic community's responses to these two instances was also reflected in my own personal communication networks with China. Four colleagues e-mailed me Li Datong's letter and related material. However, none of my Chinese colleagues was aware of the case with the leftist websites.

173. Ethan Gutmann, *Losing the New China: A Story of American Commerce, Desire and Betrayal* (San Francisco: Encounter Books, 2004), 171.

174. John Gittings, "New China Uses Old Tactics," *Observer*, 17 Nov. 2002, observer.guardian.co.uk/worldview/story/0,11581,841806,00.html (accessed 12 Nov. 2005).

175. Jonathan Manthorpe, "Communist Party Divided on Dealing with Dissidents," *Vancouver Sun*, 30 Jan. 2006, E3.

176. Perry and Selden, "Introduction," 16.

177. Perry and Selden, "Introduction," 17.

178. Perry, "Studying Chinese Politics."

179. Interview with a media insider, 18 May 2004.

180. "Walkout Protest Hits China Paper," BBC News, news.bbc.co.uk/1/hi/world/asia-pacific/4568512.stm (accessed 4 Feb. 2006).

181. Robert Marquand, "Chinese Media Resisting Party Control," *Christian Science Monitor*, 26 Aug. 2005, www.csmonitor.com/2005/0826/p01s04-woap.html (accessed 5 Nov. 2005).

182. David McNeill, "Video Gives Rare Glimpse of Bitter War between Developers and China's Poor," news.independent.co.uk/world/asia/story.jsp?story=647367 (accessed 15 Oct. 2005).

2

Securing the "Commanding Heights"

Class, Power, and the Transformation of the Party-State's Media and Culture Sector

A s the party-state reconfigures its regime of control in the communication system, it has also progressively embraced and promoted market forces and transformed its economic basis, while turning and elevating it into a new site of market expansion. In this chapter, I examine commercialization and market-oriented industrial restructuring in the media, communication, and broad cultural sector as an integral part and, more importantly, the new frontier and central locus of the ongoing processes of state-led development and social transformation in China. This entails not only an examination of the party-state's role in engendering market relations and securing the "commanding heights" of a rapidly expanding and transforming media and cultural economy, but also a discussion of the necessarily conflicted, contradictory, incomplete, and indeed, nonlinear nature of these processes, as well as an explication of their political, ideological, and social implications. Such an explication, in turn, involves an examination of how the processes of commercialization, capital formation, and industrial restructuring in the sector are simultaneously mediated by and (re)constitutive of class and other forms of power relations in Chinese society.

As a point of departure and by way of conceptual clarification, I adopt E. P. Thompson's well-known understanding of class as "a historical phenomenon" and as a social cultural formation constituted from dimensions that start with, but move well beyond, social relations at the point of production.[1] Ironically, the suppression of the concept of "class" as part of the leftist discourse at the onset of the reform process paved the way for its

regained relevance both as something that in fact happens in human relationships and as a critical analytical category in China. First, class power
in China is best understood as being constituted politically, economically,
and culturally through a plurality of productive and administrative relations, lived experiences, social histories, and dynamic subjectivities that
have arisen or been transformed in relation to the ongoing political economic and social restructuring in the era of neoliberal globalization. The
prominent role of corruption and the currency of terms such as "the capitalization of power," "official-entrepreneurs," and "knowledge capitalists" testify to the multifaceted nature of class formation and reformation
in China. Second, because the Chinese economy is largely bifurcated
along the rural-urban divide, the most significant social division is still
one between the rural and urban populations. This division is further
compounded by income gaps within the rural economy, profound ethnic
and regional differences, and gender inequality. Third, within urban
China, there are sharp divisions among different economic sectors and
forms of ownership. Fourth, as the Chinese economy shifts from a pro-
duction-driven to consumption-driven model, bureaucratically privileged access to prime consumer goods such as urban housing has played
a formative role in the pattern of class reconstitution.[2] Finally, because "reform" is linked to "openness," that is, reintegrating the Chinese economy
with the global market system, the processes of class formation entail an
important transnational dimension. The media and cultural sector assumes a double role in these processes: it affects class structure not only
as an increasingly central vector of production and economic exchange,
but also as the means of social organization and site of subjectivity formation. From the emergence of private media capitalists to the "embour-
geoisement" of media professionals to the diffusion of consumerist values
and cultivation of "petit bourgeois" identities, processes of media commercialization, economic concentration, and the party-state's recent project of "cultural system reform" are the pivotal sites whereby a society dis-
tributes and redistributes its political power, as well as economic and
symbolic values, and constitutes and reconstitutes its class and other social relations of power both objectively and subjectively.

CARRYING THE COMMERCIAL REVOLUTION
TO THE END: NEWS CREATES VALUES

The commercial revolution in the Chinese media system started at the
very top of the party press structure with the implementation of a business-oriented cost-accounting system in several central party organs, including the *People's Daily*.[3] This change in accounting methods inaugu-

rated a dual-track system, the practice of "cause-oriented undertakings managed as business-oriented enterprises" (*shiye danwei, qiye guanli*). The term *shiye* refers to enterprises that concentrate on the production and provision of public goods and services and as a result traditionally require preferential tax treatments and subsidies. The term *qiye*, on the other hand, refers to enterprises that provide private goods and services and are not in a position to receive tax breaks and subsidies.[4] Under this system, media and cultural institutions had been, until the 2003 "cultural system reform" pilot program, defined as undertakings that provide public goods and were thus eligible for subsidies and tax breaks. However, they were to be operated as businesses, raising revenue through market-oriented activities. This initial step toward commercializing media was quickly followed by the introduction of advertising in broadcasting in 1979 and waves of market-driven business expansion in print and broad-casting media. In the press, this included the explosion of lifestyle news–oriented afternoon tabloids throughout the 1980s, the addition of market-oriented sections and "weekend editions" to existing party and government organs in the first half of the 1990s, and the proliferation of metropolitan dailies and the business papers of the late 1990s and early 2000s. In broadcasting, there has been a proliferation of specialty channels focusing on business, entertainment, and lifestyle topics. By the end of 2005, the Chinese advertising industry, which fuels the growth of the Chinese media market, comprised as many as 125,394 businesses and employed as many as 940,415 people. With total revenue of 141.63 billion yuan, advertising revenue accounted for 0.78 percent of China's total GDP, compared with 0.04 percent in 1983.[5]

Market-oriented development was initially pursued with hesitations and anxieties and introduced under the modality of "neoliberalism as exception," and it was contested by "old leftists" concerned about the erosion of the party's professed socialist values and the socialist nature of the media system. The energy for media commercialization came as much from calculated neoliberal state policy initiatives from above as from the structural pressures of a developing market economy and the imperative for the modernization of the media system, the economic self-interest of media organizations and state media managers, as well as the state's desire to divest itself of the burden of financial subsidies. But since 1992, with the marginalization of leftist resistance within the party, media commercialization has became a more explicit party-state policy, promoted as a "law of motion" under the market economy, and enforced through "thought liberation" drives and media restructuring campaigns organized from above.[6] Not only was the commercial and industrial nature of media and cultural undertakings acknowledged and endorsed, specific commercialization targets and industrial growth goals were set by state media administrations.[7] For example, the GAPP, in its "Plans for the Development of the Press and Publication Industries in Year 2000 and Year 2010," specifically mandated that "newspapers must raise the percentage of advertisement revenue in their total revenue from an average of 60 percent in 1996 to 70 percent by 2000 and 80 percent by 2010."[8] As one press administrator put it, market-oriented development has been equated with "reform" in media policy making, and the discourse has acquired such hegemonic power that to critique and resist it is to be anti-reform.[9] In the context of the post-1992 neoliberal ideological ascendancy, to be "anti-reform" ensures the marginalization, if not the end, of one's bureaucratic or academic career. In practical terms, with the decline and withdrawal of state subsidies and the increasing inability of the state to pay its media workers a decent wage in a rapidly expanding urban consumer economy, the captains of the party-state's media industry were compelled to turn media organizations into profit-making operations, conservatively to make ends meet, and more actively to ensure business expansion and profit making, which have become important evaluative criteria for their career advancement under the hegemony of a neoliberal governmentality that prioritizes economic performance. Rather than being the exception, neoliberal calculations have become the norm in the Chinese media industry, epitomized in the broadcasting industry by audience ratings.

The progressive "intensification of commodification"[10] in the Chinese media is perhaps best captured by a play on the word "values" in association with news. In the early 1980s, journalism scholars were carefully introducing the Western concept of "news values," understood to be the "intrinsic" newsworthy characteristics of an event, as a way to assert journalistic autonomy and to challenge the party's definition of what qualifies as news. By the early 2000s, the official slogan of *21st-Century Business Herald* (21 *shiji jingji baodao*), a weekly business subsidiary of the Guangdong provincial party organ *Nanfang Daily* (*Nanfang ribao*), was "news creates values," presumably both societal and monetary values, but with an emphasis on the latter in the context of the paper's explicit business orientation. This slogan has become the mantra of the Chinese media industry. With almost all other Chinese economic and public service sectors—from education to health care—being incorporated into the orbit of capitalistic development and turning into sites of profit making, and even privatized capital accumulation, media scholars and stock market analysts spoke of the media as the "last" most lucrative industry to be exploited for financial gains, and the media themselves endlessly recycled this notion in self-promotion. CCTV carried this objective of capital accumulation to the extreme during the school hostage crisis in Russia in September 2004. While reporting on the tragedy, CCTV4 concurrently flashed a multiple-choice question at the bottom of the television screen, asking its viewers to guess the correct death toll and to send in their answers through text messages on their mobile phones. Three leading state communication companies, CCTV, China Mobile, and China Unicom, shared the profit collected from mobile phone customers in this business scheme. Not surprisingly, this case of shameless exploitation of human tragedy for profit by state-owned communication companies provoked media scholars, officials, and audiences to ask: Where are CCTV's social values? What are the limits of neoliberal market rationality in state media?

The commercial revolution in the Chinese press peaked with the publication of market-driven urban subsidiaries by central party organs. In 2001 the *People's Daily* took the lead in practicing the party's newly formulated capital friendly policy in the media by raising 50 million yuan in investment capital from Beida Qingniao, a state enterprise, to launch its subsidiary *Jinghua Times* (*Jinghua shibao*) for the Beijing urban market. This created a new round of competition in an already highly competitive local press market. Before this, the *People's Daily* had tried other commercialized ventures by publishing market-oriented subsidiaries such as the popular international affairs–oriented tabloid *Global Times* (*Huanqiu shibao*). But *Jinghua Times* gave the central party organ the first truly commercialized mass appeal urban daily. In November 2003, *Guangming Daily*, another nationally distributed central party organ, teamed up with the *Nanfang Daily* Group to launch its subsidiary for the Beijing market, the *Beijing News* (*Xinjing bao*).[11] As a result, the Beijing urban market boasts seven general interest dailies, in addition to numerous national papers and specialized business and trade papers. Starting on July 1, 2004, the *People's Daily* itself, together with other central, regional, and municipal party organs, literally "entered the market" by announcing availability through newspaper vendors on the streets.[12] To be sure, this move is more symbolic than substantive because street vendors rarely carry these party organs. Compulsory subscription by public offices remains the dominant form of distribution for central and provincial party organs, just as official financial subsidies, as the applications of "exceptions to neoliberalism," have been continuously made available to central party organs during the period of rapid commercialization. Nevertheless, the announcement symbolizes the central party organ's final debut as a commodity on the streets. From the paper's accounting system reform in 1978 to its decision to "get on the newsstand" in 2004, the press of the Chinese Communist Party completed its "commercial revolution" within the time span of a quarter century.

The uniqueness of the Chinese media transformation is that rather than privatizing existing party-state media outlets or liberalizing entry by private media firms from the outset, party-state organs themselves have spearheaded the process of commercialization, adopting and containing the market mechanisms within the existing structure.[13] As I will demonstrate in the next two chapters, foreign and domestic media capital have each played important roles in propelling and deepening the processes of commercialization and market-oriented restructuring, but by and large, their operations have been *limited to* the peripheries of the media system, and more importantly, their inputs—from management expertise to media content—are *absorbed by* and *channeled through* major party-state media as they expand and metamorphose into the primary agents of the Chinese media market (*shichang zhuti*). In the press sector, the licensing system and the sponsor unit system ensured the party-state's control over the fundamental industrial structure during the processes of commercialization and market-driven expansion. No newspaper can be set up as an independent business. All must be registered under a recognized institutional publisher or sponsor, which includes party committees, government bureaucracies, mass organizations, and other institutions of official standing above the county level. Among these authorized publishers, only party committees, presumably capable of standing above special interests and representing the "general interest" of the population, can publish mass appeal papers. In this way, party committees and party organs have been "structured in dominance," with a policy-ensured advantage in "conquering" the mass market.

Consequently, although market-oriented developments seem to have created clear "winners and losers"[14] at the level of individual papers and broadcast channels, the rise of business and mass appeal media outlets and the decline of traditional national and provincial party organs have not been a zero-sum game as far as the party is concerned. Rather, it is part and parcel of the *transformation* of the party and its communicative relationships with Chinese society. Just as the party has incorporated the business strata into its ranks without overtly abandoning its traditional constituents, it has engendered market-driven and urban middle-class-oriented press without transcending the party organ structure. This has been most obvious in the daily newspaper sector. China's market-based mass appeal newspapers have three different institutional origins. Some of the most successful mass appeal papers are themselves transformed "organ papers." The *Guangzhou Daily* (*Guangzhou ribao*) and the *Beijing Youth Daily* (*Beijing qingnian bao*), discussed later in this chapter, are such examples. While their marginality in the traditional party press structure afforded them the political space to undertake the commercial revolution ahead of more central party organs, they continue to operate within the orbit of the party-state. Their spectacular growth is thus a "net gain" for a party that has itself simultaneously undergone a process of redefining its ideological orientations and reconstituting its social bases.

The core of China's mass appeal newspapers, the "evening papers" and the "metro papers," is directly affiliated with party committees or existing party organs. The "evening papers," or the general interest social- and entertainment-oriented afternoon daily tabloids, were mostly revived or newly published in the 1980s and early 1990s by major provincial and municipal party committees as second papers intended for the urban family, or by provincial and municipal party organs as their urban subsidiaries. The second category of urban mass appeal papers, the so-called metro papers, or the urban omnibus morning dailies, which emerged in the mid-1990s, are subsidiaries of provincial and national party organs. Since the first "metro paper" was launched by the *Sichuan Daily* (*Sichuan ribao*) in Chengdu in 1995, this new institutional innovation was quickly copied by other provincial party organs in the late 1990s. These papers became a perfect vehicle for provincial party organs to apply market calculations and to "conquer" the mass appeal market in core Chinese urban centers, because the political mandate of traditional organs to serve party officials of urban and rural areas alike within the provincial geographical boundary had become a disadvantage in an advertising-driven newspaper market. At the same time, because these papers are affiliated with provincial party organs and are thus above the political jurisdiction of municipal party authorities, they are able to write critical reports on municipal affairs. Again, the resulting institutional arrangement turns out to be a winning formula for the party-state. These papers operate as semi-autonomous business units of the traditional provincial party organs, serving as the perfect media for the party to reach the rising urban consumer strata, thus reconstituting them as the new power base, while simultaneously functioning as "cash cows" that cross-subsidize and sustain the traditional party organs. This strategy is clearly reflected in the GAPP's license allocation policy since the mid-1990s. On the one hand, the GAPP stopped issuing new licenses in an attempt to control the number of newspaper titles and create scale economy in the industry. On the other hand, provincial and central party organs were given the exclusive opportunity to take over existing licenses from marginal bureaucratic and trade papers and turn them into mass appeal urban papers. This licensing policy was a key component of a much larger media restructuring campaign that I will discuss later in this chapter. Consequently, despite the emergence of these mass appeal papers, the overall number of newspapers dropped from 2,202 in 1996 to 2,119 in 2003. Thus, through its licensing power, the GAPP has managed to contain the commercial revolution in the Chinese press within the orbit of the party-state. Similarly, the basic system of state monopoly in broadcasting remains intact through the entire process of commercialization and market-oriented expansion.

RECONSTITUTING CLASS POWER
THROUGH MEDIA COMMERCIALIZATION

Commercialization created new patterns of inclusion and exclusion in accessing the media as a source of political, economic, social, and symbolic power and led to a substantive reconfiguration of social relations within and around the Chinese media. This involves two processes—the (re)enfranchisement of the media elite as the cultural component of the ruling bloc and, through their work, the rearticulation of ruling ideas, the reformation of social consciousnesses, and the reconstitution of the population's subjectivities as part of the reconfiguration of structural power relations in society at large.

State monopolistic operation and the increased operational and financial autonomy of media organizations turned the party-state's media organizations and their managers—if not all rank-and-file workers—into a vested interest group. At a time when other state enterprises were undergoing bankruptcies and laying off workers at a massive scale, the party-state's media organizations, thanks to financial decentralization and incentive-based profit retaining and bonus schemes, offered not only employment opportunities, but also some of the best incomes, not to mention glamour and social status. It has often been noted that commercialization turned media organizations into self-interested economic entities, and this in turn allowed media to challenge party control. However, commercialization works as a double-edged sword. On the one hand, it has provided the necessary institutional imperatives for the media to pursue innovations, sometimes even to offer challenging content. On the other hand, media organizations and media managers developed a vested interest in sustaining the current political economic order by following the party line while pursuing financial gains. The media, in short, trade political obedience for the state's sustenance of their monopolistic operations.[15] Although there are exceptions and some liberal-minded elite journalists continue to challenge such a form of clientism and collusion, by and large, media commercialization has contributed to the entrenchment of state control in the media. In their study of the Shenzhen Press Group, Lee, He, and Huang have offered the most devastating critique of the fusion of party control and market rationality in the Chinese media.[16]

Corruption in journalism, that is, journalists receiving cash and bribes in exchange for favorable media reports, has been a systemic problem in the Chinese media since the early 1990s.[17] Although there have been persistent anticorruption campaigns and attempts to strengthen media ethics and professionalism, as market relations in the media intensify, the scope and depth of clientist and predatory practices may have actually broadened and deepened. As sociologist Sun Liping has pointed out, corruption is a systemic means of redistribution and a significant contributing factor to the extremely uneven distribution of wealth in China since the mid-1990s.[18] Thus, corruption is not a simple ethical issue. Rather, it is a predatory form of market relations in which public and private agents define the terms of market transactions at the expense of both the agenda of the state and the more generalized norms of the market. Moreover, although corruption undermines effectiveness of state policies and erodes state legitimacy on the one hand, on the other hand corruption plays a key role in the formation of the ruling political class and paradoxically contributes to the consolidation of class rule under the one-party structure. As stated by a corrupt official in the popular fiction *Wrath of Heaven* (*Tiannu*), which was based on the true story of the exposed former Beijing mayor Chen Xitong, corruption has made the regime more stable.[19] That is, although corruption engenders resistance from below and thus becomes a source of instability, it also serves to cement and constitute the ruling bloc as a class-for-itself. Wen Tiejun, a well-known rural expert, provided a lucid explication of this revealing truth when he stated that there is a lack of a "healthy social force" among the "middle class"—the political, economic, and cultural elites—to push for American-style liberal democratic politics, because a majority among them have problems with illegal income. That is, if liberal democracy entails a relatively open system of intra-elite bargaining, the common fear is that the implementation of such a system necessarily involves the exposure of systematic corruption among the elites. The strengthening of one-party rule thus becomes the only self-serving option for the alliance of political, economic, and cultural elites.[20] In the media and culture sector, publicly exposed media executives such as Zhao An, a former programming director at CCTV's Literature and Art Department (*wenyi bu*), symbolize the nexus of ideological promotion for one-party rule and illegal personal wealth accumulation in the most excessive form and at the highest echelon of the media system. Before he was sentenced to a 10-year jail term in 2003 for taking bribes, Zhao was China's most powerful art-programming director. His extravagant productions included nationally televised gala performances for the most important political and cultural occasions of the era, from the party's 70th anniversary to the single most important entertainment show in the nation, CCTV's Spring Festival Gala. His style of fusing political propaganda and spectacular televisual festivity—no doubt the most extravagant form of "indoctritainment," that is, indoctrination and entertainment in a single package[21]—so appealed to the central leadership that he was personally praised by party general secretary Jiang Zemin.[22]

The Chinese media and cultural sector had 1.23 million people on the state's official payroll in 2003, or 1.7 percent of the total workforce of 744 million.[23] As with the overall Chinese economy, this sector is highly stratified and the employment structure is shaped by evolving personnel policies under state socialism and at different stages of the reform process. CCTV, with its five classes of permanent employees and flexible casual workers with staggeringly different job security and welfare entitlements well into the early 2000s, epitomized the hierarchical, highly exploitative, and almost feudal labor structure in the Chinese media industry.[24] Reflecting the highly patriarchal nature of Chinese power relations, the extent of male domination in CCTV's top management structure is stunning. In 2003, CCTV's seven directors and deputy directors were all men, and there was not a single woman on its 23-member editorial board. Of the 56 individuals on its editorial, technical, and administrative management boards, only 5 were women, accounting for less than 10 percent of CCTV's entire top management echelon.[25] As these captains of the Chinese media industry set out to conquer the market on behalf of the party-state, they exercise highly concentrated managerial power over vast financial and human resources. The media provide the very means by which political power and economic, social, and cultural privileges are acquired. Far from being innocent sites of party-state domination, as the standard liberal outcry against party censorship would imply, the media help to constitute the political, economic, and cultural powers of China's ruling bloc. Within this context, ongoing contestation between a few highly visible liberal members of the Chinese media elite and the party's propaganda authorities, dramatized in the *China Youth News* case, is very much a conflict within a hierarchical management structure, as well as an intra-elite conflict between the dominant political class and a small yet vocal liberal faction of the dominant intellectual strata, or what Pierre Bourdieu called "the dominated among the dominant,"[26] over the political terms of elite rule.[27]

While party-state officials provide the media with monopolistic operating licenses, advertisers provide the media with their lifeblood. In 2004 government subsidies only contributed 8.858 billion yuan, or 10.7 percent, of the Chinese broadcasting industry's total revenue of 82.472 billion yuan, with advertising and other commercial income accounting for the lion's share.[28] The Chinese press is also heavily dependent on advertising revenue. For example, the *Guangzhou Daily* received 74 percent of its revenue from advertising in 2002.[29] In 2003 the newly established *Shanghai Morning Post* (*Shanghai xinwen chenbao*) received 87 percent of its revenue from advertising, with a mere 13 percent from circulation. Moreover, the cost of advertising in the Chinese media has been extremely high by international standards.[30] Because the Chinese press has been heavily dependent on a particular kind of advertising—national advertisers and large corporations—a small number of major transnational and domestic businesses have wielded substantive power over media content.

The replacement of state subsidies with advertisement revenues, of course, is not simply a business matter. Advertisement is itself a form of propaganda for the market system, and it rivals, if not replaces, political propaganda as the dominant form of mobilization speech and subjectivity making. The appropriation of Maoist political slogans by the advertisement industry, demonstrated vividly by Barmé, is perhaps not surprising.[31] Though Maoist political propaganda and current commercial propaganda differ in content, there are similarities in the structure and ideological consequences of both discourses. Maoist political propaganda promotes the cult of political personality; commercial speech cultivates commodity fetishism. Maoism instructs the politicized subjects of a socialist state to dedicate their transient life to the transcendental cause of "serving the people" and building a communist society, while commercial speech directs the all-consuming subjects to devote their limited life to the unlimited world of wealth accumulation and personal consumption in a consumer society. In an era of state-mandated consumerism, to consume is to be politically correct. After all, to cultivate the entrepreneurial self and the consumer subject is precisely the essence of neoliberal governmentality. Just as revolutionary virtues such as hard struggle, bravery, and the will to triumph have been remobilized in television series such as the *Long March* (*Changzheng*) to inspire the formation of neoliberal subjectivities that will "conquer" the market, communist symbols and icons such as "East Is Red" and "Red Flag" have all become brand names for consumer products, and the Cultural Revolution has become just another decorative motif in dining and entertainment establishments. Even Mao's famous slogan "To Carry the Revolution to the End" has been appropriated by consumer magazines to promote new lines of jeans or cosmetics. Observations about the tendency of "demobilized liberalization,"[32] which describes the transformation of the Chinese media from being an instrument of political mobilization during the Maoist era to one of economic modernization and image management in the reform era, must not only be qualified by arguments about the continuing relevance of Maoist mobilization methods in media and propaganda, but also be complemented with an understanding of the new role of advertising in the intensified mobilization of consumerist desires and impulses.

Advertising-based financing and accelerated commercialization have also led to a drastic reorientation in the content of Chinese media, with profound political and ideological implications. The media's pursuit of mass audiences—whose vast numbers compensate for affluence for brand-name mass advertisers, especially in the case of television as the most popular medium—facilitates the promotion of official nationalism and leads to the rise of mass entertainment. First, the pursuit of mass audiences assumes a mutually reinforcing relationship with the promotion of official nationalism, which aims to reconstitute individuals in an increasingly stratified Chinese society as members of a national family unified in the pursuit of wealth, power, and national dignity.[33] Within this discourse, everybody, regardless of his or her social economic status and locality, is first and foremost hailed as a Chinese (and simultaneously, as a consumer). Second, Chinese media, especially television, which had played an instrumental role in the pre-1989 political and cultural ferment with the politically and intellectually challenging documentary *River Elegy* (*Heshang*), turned to mass entertainment.[34] Although Chinese television has always contained "entertainment," as Ruoyun Bai noted, there has been a qualitative difference. Before the early 1990s, the term "entertainment" (*yule*) was not much in use. Instead, "literature and art" (*wenyi*), with all the state socialist high culture connotations of uplifting the people's aesthetic sensibilities, was the name of the game (this state socialist legacy remains in the naming of television's entertainment programming division as the "literature and art department").[35] Concomitantly, the related term "culture" (*wenhua*) was stripped of both its elitist connotation and Marxist baggage as belonging to the "superstructure" and turned into a site of capital accumulation and symbolic consumption by the citizen-consumers.[36]

The culture industry formally arrived in China in 1990 with CCTV's broadcast of *Aspirations* (*Kewang*), a 51-episode drama series, considered Chinese television's first major successful soap opera. As Yin Hong describes the show, "it was a genuine industrial product: it was made with financial support with non-state sources, and shot in a studio, utilizing artificial indoor scenes, multicamera shots, simultaneous voice recording and post-production techniques."[37] Effectively imitating the story format and conventions of indoor dramatic shows from Asia and Latin America, which in turn borrowed from the American cultural industry, *Aspirations* is the first Chinese drama series that embraced ideological conformism and took popular entertainment, rather than didactic political propaganda, as its explicit aim. The wide popularity of the show marked an ideological breakthrough in the party's approach to media: for the first time, the party's highest ideological establishment not only accepted but praised a show centering on human interests and morality play. With this show, television's conservative role of creating a morality play of unity and stability through entertainment was officially legitimated and celebrated in China.[38] Finally, it seems, Chinese television had caught up with mainstream American television both in form and in its ideological and cultural role in society. As Barmé wrote,

> The success of *Aspirations* was a victory for one of the most representative paradigms of American popular culture. With this medium, the message of

peaceful evolution—the primacy of economics over politics, consumption in place of contention—continued to insinuate itself into the living rooms of millions of mainland TV viewers. It was a development that increasingly served the needs of the Communist authorities while also preparing China's artistic soil for the germination of global culture.[39]

By the late 1990s, intensive competition between proliferating television channels, accelerated efforts on the part of the Chinese state to deepen the market logic, and a vibrant private and quasi-private entertainment production industry (discussed in chapter 4) had fully developed television's entertainment role, ensuring the irreversible institutionalization and "the final triumph of entertainment."[40] Hunan Satellite Television, an upstart provincial satellite channel that has led a relentless quest for a national audience since its inception in 1997, carried this entertainment wave to a new high. By 2004 its quest for commercial success had led it to eliminate a number of other programs that did not fit in with entertainment, including its *Findings in the Countryside* news magazine program, *despite* its popularity among rural audiences and its winning of many national journalism and Ministry of Agriculture awards.[41] The rise of Hunan Satellite Television as the leading provincial satellite channel confirmed a simple truth for the Chinese television industry: uplifting light entertainment is the safest and fastest means to popularity and capital accumulation. If the "vulgar" was once denounced by both state socialist and liberal cultural elites, "kowtowing to the vulgar" is now the mantra of the Chinese media industry.[42] In contrast to any Frankfurt School–inspired condemnation of popular culture, I argue that pleasure seeking, the affirmation of mundane and commonplace emotions, the engagement with popular concerns, and even the single-minded imperative to delight can be seen as a double liberation in post-1989 China, from both the traditional socialist didactic approach to culture *and* the intellectual elitist and vanguard position of the 1980s as expressed in *River Elegy*.[43]

However, such a position does not mean that one should simply celebrate the liberalizing impulses of commercialized entertainment or embrace active "audience power" from a market populist perspective.[44] Rather than undermine the party, commercialized entertainment has a complicated relationship with the party's hegemonic project in Chinese society. In fact, the impact of the media's commercialization on social integration and the shift to the intertwined nationalistic and pleasure-seeking orientations—culminating annually with CCTV's Spring Festival Gala—has been profound since the 1990s.[45] If advertising aims to mobilize the audience to pursue happiness through the consumption of material goods, entertainment shows mobilize the audience to pursue happiness and Chinese identity affirmation through the consumption of television discourses—even for the rural and urban poor who may not be able to partake in other forms of state-promoted "leisure culture" (*xiuxian wenhua*).[46] Not surprisingly, one of Hunan Satellite TV's flagship shows, *Kuaile dabenying* (*The Citadel of Happiness*), modeled after a Hong Kong television show entitled *Huanle zongdongyuan* (*All Out Mobilization for Joyfulness*), has been extensively cloned by television channels all over the country. CCTV, in an effort to maintain its dominant market position, offers a *Happy Dictionary* (*Kaixin cidian*). Since summer 2005, the spectacular market success of Hunan Satellite TV's *Super Girls* reality show and the program's synergistic exploitation of the mobile phone and short message services for maximizing audience appeal and profits have started a new round of competition for the production of similar types of programming in the national television market. As Arif Dirlik observed before the popularity of mobile phone ownership, "The explosion of TV ownership means that culture, as it is peddled by TV programming, may be one of the cheaper and more universal items of consumption."[47]

Of course, this does not in any way imply a conceptualization of the Chinese public as dupes. As the more detailed case studies in chapters 5 and 6 will show, China's different social classes continue to resist beyond their roles as active media consumers, and many have vigorously contested the terms of market reforms *despite* the mass entertainment industry. Nevertheless, we must examine how commercialization has engendered a *general* structural bias toward the value orientations and tastes of advertisers' most sought-after affluent urban consumers and the business strata in the coastal areas, to the neglect of workers, farmers, low-income women, and other marginalized social groups and regions. This tendency was already apparent in the early 1990s,[48] but it has intensified as the media market grew more competitive and advertisers learned to reach their most desirable audiences more effectively. The broadcasting media's social biases reveal themselves in the lack of attention to rural topics in programming content (rural topics accounted for an average of 1.69 percent of total drama series broadcasting by provincial-level television stations in 2002),[49] the absence of specialty channels dedicated to the needs of socially identifiable groups such as workers and women, and the proliferation of speciality channels catering to the lifestyle needs of urban consumers. Urban bias is pronounced even in *Focus Interviews* (*Jiaodian fangtan*), CCTV's most celebrated investigative show and arguably the most celebrated fruit of media commercialization and the highest embodiment of the Chinese media's social conscience. For example, of the show's 396 critical reporting topics between 1994 and 1998, 190, or 48.0 percent, focused exclusively on urban settings. A total of 119 cases, or 30.1, percent were concerned with issues in villages and townships.[50] Such a ratio is, of course, highly disproportionate to China's actual ratio of urban to rural residency. Even more significantly, *Focus Interviews'* more articulate urban audience members have already complained about its "disproportionate" focus on rural issues.[51] Consequently, the program faces the challenge of accommodating the viewing preference of this core audience in its future evolution. Similarly, in 2003, CCTV found it necessary to eliminate its *Agriculture News* (*Nongye xinwen*) program from CCTV7, one of the network's 14 channels at the time.[52] The program was a causality of CCTV's intensified commercialization and its newly introduced ratings-based programming elimination policy[53]—a typical case of resource allocation on the basis of neoliberal market-based truths and calculations. Then, in December 2004, CCTV12, originally launched in May 2002 and promising to dedicate itself to the economically less-developed western region, was relaunched to occupy the more profitable market niche of *Society and Law*.[54] CCTV had required the western channel to "break even within the first three years, and generate profit in the next three years."[55] Of course, this turned out to be impossible. Instead of using its monopoly profits to cross-subsidize less profitable programming production, CCTV decided to flaunt its financial prowess by erecting a 5.7 billion–yuan CCTV tower in central Beijing in 2004—the largest and most expensive skyscraper in China.[56] This project, of course, is presented as a matter of necessity and an overriding nationalistic objective—to better stage the 2008 Beijing Olympics.

The bias toward affluent urban consumers and the male-dominated political and business elite is more pronounced in the press, where literacy is a prerequisite and access is increasingly based on private family subscriptions. As well, despite waves of commercial expansion, the Chinese press is still small in relation to the population size. For example, in Beijing, one of the most developed newspaper markets in China, the combined daily circulation of seven urban dailies was estimated at 2 million copies in 2003. This was not a high figure for a capital city that boasts 8.6 million literate readers above the age of 14.[57] Instead of expanding the readership downward on China's social ladder, intensive competition among the subsidiaries of various levels of party organs has led to the publication of newspapers catering to a more upscale urban readership. While the evening papers of the 1980s and early 1990s typically appealed to the middle-to-low social economic strata and an older population, the metro papers of the late 1990s generally tended to target the urban, white collar, younger, and more affluent population. Business papers appearing in the 2000s, such as Guangzhou's *21st-Century Business Herald*, Beijing's *Economic Observer* (*Jingji guancha bao*), and Shanghai's *First Finance Daily* (*Diyi caijing ribao*), furthered the upmarket development of the Chinese press by explicitly targeting the business elite. In Guangzhou, *Information Times* (*Xinxi shibao*), a newly launched subsidiary of the *Guangzhou Daily*

Group, was disliked by party authorities and advertisers alike—party officials, still harboring cultural elitist sensitivities, viewed it as "vulgar," while
major advertisers, especially automobile and real estate advertisers, viewed
its lower-middle-class readership as irrelevant. As of late 2004, it was
widely viewed by Guangzhou media insiders as an unviable business in its
own right, and going upmarket was seen as the only sensible response to
political and market pressures.[58] In fact, party-state authorities, in an attempt to curb what they saw as the self-destructive logic of press market
competition, prevented newspapers from dropping their cover prices. For
example, during the intensive price war among rivalry subsidiaries of party
organs in the late 1990s and early 2000s,[59] the Jiangsu provincial party committee intervened and set a minimum newspaper cover price in Nanjing
City.[60] Regardless of the authorities' rationale, one of the objective consequences of such a policy has been to prevent the press from constituting the
vast majority of urban, low social classes as its readers.

Although papers such as *Workers' Daily* (*Gongren ribao*), *Farmers' Daily*
(*Nongmin ribao*), *China Women's News* (*Zhongguo funübao*), and *China Youth
News* remain as part of the state socialist legacy of the prereform period
and the fruits of the general process of societal democratization in the
1980s (*Farmers' Daily* and *China Women's News* were both set up in the
1980s), they have declined in circulation and relative institutional power
and thus have been further marginalized as commercialization has intensified since the 1990s. To be sure, these papers have never had the autonomy to speak freely, but they have tried to speak out for their respective
proclaimed constituents, and they can be more courageous than strict
party and government organs in voicing different opinions.[61] Apart from
political repression, to the extent that these papers try to address issues of
concern to workers, farmers, and women as social groups, they do not
serve as desirable advertisement vehicles.[62] Moreover, unlike party organs, efforts by these papers to create and sustain market-oriented general interest subsidiaries have been frustrated by political suppression.
Workers' Daily's mass appeal subsidiary, a later starter in the crowded Beijing urban market entitled the *Beijing New Journal* (*Beijing xinbao*), was
banned in June 2003 after it published an article criticizing the dark aspects of Chinese politics, economy, and society, including the rubber
stamp nature of China's National People's Congress (NPC).[63] *China Youth
News*, despite and perhaps precisely because of its editors' refusal to ca-
pitulate to market pressures by cultivating a consumer market niche, has
not been commercially as successful as the more explicitly urban con-
sumer-oriented mass appeal papers. While its *Freezing Point* supplement
has been socially influential, its controversial nature means that it is not
necessarily an attractive advertising venue. *China Women's News*, a national newspaper under the sponsorship of the official women's federa-

tion, created a *Weekly Review* (*Meizhou pinglun*) supplement in November 1998 in an attempt to overcome financial difficulties. The first few trial issues of the paper took a bold approach in covering hot domestic and international issues. The front-page headline of the very first issue on November 18, 1998, for example, highlighted the news story that "More Than 100 Displaced Ping'an Street Households Intended to Sue Housing and Land Bureau." The larger issue was then discussed with two experts on the legal rights of home owners and the need for proper compensation. A "This Paper's View" commentary on the same page took a critical stand on the Indonesian government's inquiry report into the May 1998 riots, which saw many women of Chinese origin gang-raped. The front page of the second issue, published on December 2, featured "A Memorandum on 20 Years of Reform," an overview of China's two decades of economic reform, with its "This Paper's View" column focusing on Beijing's 2008 Olympics bid. Not surprisingly, the weekly supplement infuriated the party's propaganda department, which quickly ordered its closure. In the party's patriarchal frame of reference, the category of general interest news and commentary about domestic and global affairs is coded as male and a women's paper had no claim to publish such content.[64] Thus, unlike *China Youth News's Freezing Point*, the *Weekly Review* hardly had the chance to establish its influence before it was banned by the party, and of course, its fate did not register with China's liberal (and mostly male) intellectual establishment, not to mention the international media. However, the party, perhaps not yet prepared to let the *China Women's News* die in the brave new marketplace, did give the paper the opportunity to take over and publish *Info-Morning* (*Xinxi zhaobao*), a paper dedicated to stock market reporting, an area that is not only fully served by existing papers, but also tends to be dominated by male readers. The paper described its readership profile in this seemingly gender-neutral way: "45 percent of the readership between the ages of 20–40, 37 percent with college education, with management personnel as the dominant group, 36 percent with a monthly income of 2,000 yuan and above—all indicators that the readership belongs to 'the urban resident strata of relatively high consuming power.'"[65] Under a press regime constituted by patriarchal party power and the power of advertisers, only by printing a paper like this can the *China Women's News* publishing house, which also publishes the *Women of China* (*Zhongguo funü*) journal, as well as other publications, hope to cross-subsidize its flagship newspaper. Thus, the system of "structured asymmetries" in the relations of power in Chinese communications is not simply constituted by political control. It is the result of the intersecting dynamics of political control and carefully managed market liberalization, the twin processes of economic enfranchisement/dispossession and social inclusion/exclusion.

Again, it would be too deterministic to suggest that commercialization and the structural transformation of the Chinese media ensure the promotion of market authoritarian values and a neoliberal governmentality in the service of a reconstituted party, business, and urban "middle-class" elite. As I will demonstrate in chapters 5 and 6, the ideological orientations of the Chinese media are highly complex, and they need to be assessed in specific contexts. However, there is no doubt that commercialization engenders new patterns of inclusion and exclusion in Chinese social communication. The following description by Liu Yong, a reporter at the *Yangcheng Evening News*, captured the new pattern of inclusion and exclusion in media representation:

> Like other sectors, mass media organizations entered a rapid process of commercialization in the 1990s. The hottest topics are no longer the sentiments of young poets and would-be young poets, nor layoffs, unemployment, rural migrants, and other mundane stories. The protagonists of the stories have shifted to big shots and bosses, getting rich and gold rush. With commercialization and the shift toward business, literature and the masses have become rapidly marginalized.[66]

The journalist narrator in *Na'er*, a 2004 novel by Shenzhen University professor Cao Zhenglu about the struggles of a working-class community against the privatization of their factory, dramatizes the class bias of the Chinese press:

> I wrote several short feature stories for the newspaper, all about laid-off workers' difficulty in paying for medical care and children's education. Of course, [they] are all shot down. In fact, I did not expect them to be published to begin with, because I know they do not fit in with the editor-in-chief's orientation. All that concerns our editor-in-chief are postmodern problems: how many people in our city own a second house and a second car, why it is more expensive to have wild greens than vegetables, more nurturing to consume bones than meats, more humanistic to die at home than in hospital, and who has the nerve to confront beggars, etc.[67]

In the story, the narrator was compelled to write what he wrote at the risk of infuriating his editor-in-chief and not having his job contract renewed because his uncle was leading the workers' struggle against privatization and for self-management. In reality, however, media gatekeepers are often economically and socially isolated from the lower social classes, their perspectives and concerns, not to mention their survival struggles. Not surprisingly, in my detailed study of nearly 500 newspaper articles in the Chinese press on China's WTO accession agreement with the United States, party organs and market-oriented papers alike, I found not a single piece that bothered to even ceremonially interview one single worker or one single farmer on the implications of China's WTO membership.[68] Even more revealing and illustrative of the ascendancy of new sources and modes of symbolic power in Chinese society, the opinions of a narrow range of elite economists and business leaders dominate press interpretation of the implications of China's WTO accession, complemented by the results of overwhelmingly positive quasi-scientific telephone-based opinion polls conducted in major urban centers, thus excluding not only the vast rural population, but also low income, urban, working-class families and migrant workers without residential telephones. Thus, if the party-state sets the tone, it is the press, especially its market-oriented sector, that actively orchestrates the discourse through authoritative international sources, expert analysis, citizen hotlines, quizzes, and statistical surveys. While the official nationalistic discourse of building a wealthy and strong China through party leadership and global integration plays a definitive role, the transnational corporatist discourse, the expert discourse of economists from elite institutions, and the consumerist discourse of "the ordinary folks" dominate the Chinese press. These discourses feed into each other to form the hegemonic voice of the reformed Chinese press on globalization. Under the guise of a universalizing language and a "larger rationality," elite interest is presented as the general interest, while "the ordinary folks" the press claims to speak for turn out to be stock owners, professionals, and privileged urban consumers. The dream of a powerful nation concretizes as a consumerist paradise for the affluent urban strata. If the parade of workers and farmers in traditional party propaganda was hollow and manipulative, the press discourse's virtual elimination of these majority social groups as discursive objects, not to mention speaking subjects, is also shocking and highly hegemonic. While the commercialized media discourse is more diverse and less manipulative, we must recognize its new mobilizing and disciplinary role and the new relations of power it serves to establish and legitimize.[69] Although market-oriented street tabloids targeting a lowbrow readership sometimes do violate the party's propaganda disciplines by covering social issues and sensitive topics such as the suicide of a laidoff worker, the neoliberal, social Darwinian, survival of the fittest logic also figured prominently as a framing ideology.[70]

The following observation, made by an editor with the now banned China Workers Net, on *Nanfang Weekend*'s ideological framing in reporting an antiprivatization struggle in a factory is perhaps most revealing of the class bias of the market-oriented media. As an outspoken liberal paper that has been the subject of the party's repeated "surgical" censorship operations, the paper enjoys domestic and international status as a "beacon" of what can be accomplished under the party's censorship regime.

Nevertheless, while the paper's more liberal ideological orientation enables it to report an event such as a struggle in a factory, it frames the struggle from the perspective of the capitalists:

> Those who didn't know thought the paper was speaking on behalf of the workers, but essentially, it was completely rejecting the workers' actual claim, which is to self-manage their own factories. What kind of image was [the newspaper] portraying to the reader in an "objective" manner? [An image] that workers are engaged in internal conflicts, disinterested in solidarity, incapable of managing collective enterprises, and that enterprises should be left for the capitalist to be of any value.[71]

OVERCOME THE PARTY-STATE ITSELF? MARKET CONSOLIDATION AND TENSIONS BETWEEN THE TERRITORIAL AND CAPITAL LOGICS OF PARTY-STATE MEDIA

Just as intercapitalist rivalry remains a key feature of the world capitalist economy and the interstate system both enables and imposes spatial limits on the operation of transnational corporations on a global scale, the expansion of market relations in the Chinese media and cultural sector has been enabled by the party-state on the one hand, and constrained by it on the other. The nature of Chinese media operations as organs of the party-state, in particular, has turned out to be an extremely acute double-edged sword as far as the media system's neoliberal reorganization is concerned. Because commercial revolution and market liberalization occurred primarily within the party-state organ structure in the press and within the framework of the administrative monopoly in broadcasting, by the mid-1990s, the decentralization and fragmentation of the media structure had become a major concern for central party-state authorities aiming to further the market-oriented development of the Chinese media.[72]

In the press, bureaucratic and trade papers continued to function as propaganda outlets for their sponsoring bodies and as a means by which government bureaucracies extracted subscription fees from subordinate units. These papers were the quintessential manifestations of "socialism with Chinese characteristics" or, perhaps more appropriately, "bureaucratic capitalism," a particular form of state capitalism that involves use of political power and official influence for pecuniary gain by bureaucratic units through capitalist or quasi-capitalist economic activities.[73] Bureaucratically enforced newspaper subscriptions added enormous financial burdens to rural townships, village governments, and schools, which then passed on the burden to the already suffering and overtaxed farmers. The bifurcated political economy of China's media system is thus fundamentally unfair: while commercial advertisers supported market-oriented newspapers and subsidized newspaper consumption by urban consumers, Chinese farmers were forced to subsidize newspapers produced by various government bureaucracies and consumed mostly by local officials. Newspapers produced by various government bureaucracies undermined the subscription base of central and provincial party organs by competing for the limited newspaper subscription budget of grassroots public institutions. Furthermore, these papers were not favored by central party-state authorities because they broke political and moral codes or contracted out editorial spaces and sold press cards to unauthorized groups and individuals operating outside the orbit of the party-state. Finally, some of these papers continued to rely on their sponsoring government departments for partial financial subsidies, a situation that was considered, by neoliberal-minded media regulators and media scholars, to be no longer compatible with market economic principles. Specifically, two kinds of newspapers were considered economically inefficient and politically problematic by central party-state authorities: those at the horizontal margins of the existing party-state sector (newspapers run by various government departments, trade associations, and mass organizations) and those at its bottom (party organs run by county-level party committees).

Similar structural issues in the broadcasting sector had also become apparent by the mid-1990s. As with the press, the problems existed at both the vertical and horizontal levels. On the eve of the economic reforms in the late 1970s, broadcasting provision was centralized at the national and provincial levels. Municipal/prefectural and county-level governments primarily provided transmission services, relaying provincial and central programming with little self-programming capacities. In a crucial 1983 policy, the central state, incapable of providing the huge financial investments necessary for increased national television coverage, allowed municipal and county governments to mobilize their own resources to build full-scale radio and television stations. This policy allowed the establishment of broadcasting stations at four levels of government—central, provincial, municipal/prefectural, and county—leading to the entrenchment of a four-tiered broadcasting structure and a proliferation of television stations at the municipal/prefectural and county levels.[74] Simultaneously, provincial stations began to set up market-oriented specialty channels in the late 1980s to capitalize on an expanding urban advertisement market and an increasing television audience base. The spread of cable technology in the late 1980s and early 1990s created yet another wave of television channel multiplication at both the provincial and municipal/prefectural levels. By 1996, there were 944 over-the-air television channels, 1,258 cable channels, as well as 1,005 "education stations" that had also gone commercial.[75] Although all these channels were affiliated with government authorities at various levels, they were operated as financially independent units. As profit-oriented operations, these stations were often in direct and increasingly ferocious competition with each other for programming and advertisements. Moreover, because neither CCTV nor provincial stations provided any financial compensation for county-level stations to transmit their programming, some county-level stations either refused to carry these programs or inserted their own advertising during transmission. In an increasingly commercialized media environment, higher-level media authorities could no longer use administrative means to enforce "must carry" obligations. In another important development, all the provinces had sent their main television channel through satellite-cable to a national audience by 1998. The availability of nearly 30 provincial satellite channels and a whole range of local channels in urban cable households completely changed the Chinese television scene and challenged the monopoly of CCTV in the national television market.

In short, by the mid-1990s, market fragmentation along territorial and sectoral boundaries and intense competition between media outlets owned by various levels of the party-state bureaucracy had undermined core central and provincial media outlets and overrode the market rationality of the central party-state planners. There was a lack of scale economy and, in the words of one central broadcasting official, "too much duplication of efforts at the local level. When a tree fell on the bank of the West Lake, six television crews would show up and shoot the same scene. What a waste of resources!"[76] In response, the central party-state adopted a two-pronged strategy to rationalize and consolidate the media market: administrative campaigns aiming at media recentralization, and the creation of conglomerates to achieve the optimal integration of political control and market efficiency.[77] In this way, the central state set out not only to further market-oriented development, but also to save bureaucratic capitalism from its self-destructive logic—from imposing extra financial burdens on farmers to subsidize official press subscription at the local levels, from marginal media outlets failing to stick to central propaganda disciplines, as well as from the destructive impacts of excessive intrabureaucratic competition with core central-party organs and broadcasting channels. Media market consolidation and restructuring assumed a further sense of urgency in the context of several broader concurrent developments in the larger media political economy in the late 1990s, including an unprecedented slowdown in the growth rate of advertising revenue in the aftermath of the Asian financial crisis in 1997, the tidal wave of global media consolidation, and the intensifying pressure of transnational media corporations to enter the Chinese market in the context of China's WTO accession. For the broadcasting sector, increased domestic competition posed by a capital-rich, more commercialized, more expansion-driven, and more aggressive telecommunications industry encroaching into its territory of cable television programming, backbone network construction, as well as residential cable service provision provided a further rationale for system reintegration and market consolidation.[78]

The top-down media restructuring campaign was officially inaugurated in 1996 with the Central Party Committee and State Council's issuance of the "Circular on the Administration of Press, Publishing, Radio, and Television Industries." In the press sector, central authorities subsequently carried out three consecutive administrative campaigns from 1996 to 2003 to eliminate, merge, and transform newspapers published by government departments, trade associations, and county-level party committees.[79] Commercially viable and politically reliable newspapers were granted operational autonomy from their affiliated government departments. Commercially unviable papers published by central and provincial-level government departments and other official organizations were either shut down or taken over by central and provincial party organs. As a result of this policy, central and provincial party organs were provided with an unprecedented opportunity to take over newspaper licenses and absorb press assets from the bureaucratic sector and to expand their market reach in the mass appeal, business, and lifestyle niche markets. Liu Bo, director of the GAPP's newspaper bureau, expressed explicitly the political control objective of building party organs into press conglomerates. He said that one of the original purposes of conglomeration was to encourage a strong paper to merge with smaller ones. However, because strong papers were not keen on taking over unprofitable operations, the alternative was to liberalize their operational conditions, including more autonomy in middle-level management and editorial personnel appointments, flexibility in wage policies, freedom to add more pages, and easy access to permits for publishing subsidiary newspapers and magazines. Liu hoped that with their financial, personnel, technological, and distributing strengths, party-controlled press groups would increase their market share and eventually drive marginal papers to bankruptcy.[80]

Furthermore, in 2003 the central party-state, in an attempt to eliminate local press subsidies, to reduce farmers' tax burdens, as well as to secure the official subscription market for central and provincial party organs, ordered the closure of most county-level party organs. The capitalist process of "accumulation by dispossession"—in this case, the dispossession of newspaper registration numbers (*kanhao*) held by county-level party organs—was thus imposed through administrative campaigns within the party-state press sector itself. Exceptions were made on political, cultural, and economic grounds. County-level newspapers set up by the party before 1949 and papers published by county-level autonomous ethnic minority administrations or in ethnic minority languages were allowed to continue. Economically, counties with a population of half a million, a GDP of 10 billion yuan, a volume of consumer goods sales of 3 billion yuan and over, and where the advertising revenue of the party organ was in excess of 4 million yuan were allowed to continue to publish the party organ. Not surprisingly, this led officials in economically less developed areas to complain about the state's blatant economic bias. Apparently, not all party committees were treated equally in the allocation of media power. Only those that had achieved certain levels of market success were allowed to have mouthpieces.

Meanwhile, the *Guangzhou Daily* (*GD*), the Guangzhou Municipal Party Committee organ that has managed to successfully expand into the urban consumer market, was selected by the Central Party Propaganda Department as a pilot press conglomerate in January 1996. The group streamlined its organizational structure, strengthened editorial control, upgraded facilities, and built an extensive distribution system both inside and outside the Guangzhou area. It took over other smaller publications and quickly increased the number of subsidiaries, boosted the circulation of the flagship paper, and increased its overall profitability and financial strength. By 1998, with revenue at 1.72 billion yuan (US$207 million) and a profit of 349 million yuan (US$42 million), the group had become one of Guangzhou's top 10 state-owned enterprises and a major economic powerhouse in the region.[81] Officially under the control of the Guangzhou Municipal Party Committee, the group competed vigorously with two other local press conglomerates, the *Nanfang Daily* Group and the *Yangcheng Evening News* Group, both under the control of the Guangdong Provincial Party Committee. Together, these three press conglomerates have dominated the Guangzhou press market with a whole range of general interest and specialized niche publications.

The *GD* Group became a model party-organ-turned-newspaper-conglomerate. Its experience was analyzed by the central authorities and widely promoted in other parts of the country from the mid- to late 1990s. The principal purpose of press conglomeration, agreed upon by the GAPP and the China Newspaper Association, was to "enable party organs to consolidate a powerful economic base through the market mechanism and ensure the better fulfillment of the party's propaganda objectives."[82] In Shanghai, the municipal government single-handedly arranged the merger of two long-established news organizations, the lucrative mass appeal afternoon tabloid *Xinmin Evening News* and the more upscale and less profitable *Wenhui News*, to form the *Wenhui-Xinmin* Group in 1998. This created a duopoly in China's biggest metropolis: while political and business-related newspapers were consolidated under the *Liberation Daily*

Group, which is the official municipal party organ, culture and lifestyle publications were grouped under the *Wenhui-Xinmin* folder.

Concomitantly, the broadcasting sector also launched consecutive re-centralization campaigns since 1996 in an attempt to rein in local broadcasting and to build national and provincial-level conglomerates, thus reverting the existing four-tiered structure to the prereform two-tiered structure. Specifically, central state planners hoped to consolidate radio, over-the-air television, and cable operations—encompassing program production, broadcast, and distribution over different technological platforms, and other related business areas—under one organizational structure at the central and provincial levels and to downsize municipal and county-level broadcasting operations. In particular, the ambitious 1999 State Council "Circular on Strengthening the Construction and Management of Cable Networks" (Document No. 82) called for the elimination of autonomous municipal and county-level cable television networks, the spin-off of cable network assets from local cable television stations, and their integration into a province-wide cable network. All of a sudden, "make it bigger and stronger" (*zuoda zuoqiang*) became the mantra of the Chinese media industry. County-level television stations were no longer permitted to self-program entertainment content. Instead, they were allowed to broadcast two hours of locally produced news and feature programs per day, with their primary function redefined as transmission stations for higher-level broadcasting authorities. To accommodate this transformation, a "common channel" was established at each of the provincial levels in 2002, allowing county-level authorities to broadcast self-produced news and feature programs at given time slots.

In December 2000, the first provincial-level broadcasting conglomerate was launched in Hunan Province, which had created the most successful commercial broadcasting system through a single-minded pursuit of entertainment programming. The seven channels operated by three separate television stations, Hunan Television, Hunan Economic Television, and Hunan Cable Television, were brought together under the single entity of Hunan Television. Major operational decisions—from the reporting of major news stories to programming, budgeting, capital investments, and personnel management—were recentralized under the "five unifications" scheme.[83] Then, in January 2001, Zhejiang Province announced the merger of three previously separated television stations, Zhejiang Television, Zhejiang Cable Television, and Zhejiang Educational Television. The conglomerate ran one comprehensive satellite channel and five other channels specializing in urban life, business, science and education, film and television entertainment, and health and sports.[84] The "station" as an organizational entity was eliminated. Different channels became operational entities responsible for meeting revenue creation and propaganda objectives set by the "group" or conglomerate level, while overall financial and personnel management power resided with the "group." In April 2001, Shanghai announced the formation of the Shanghai Media Group (SMG), a massive conglomerate monopolizing Shanghai's broadcasting, film, and cultural operations. Other provinces soon followed suit, making 2001 the year of state-engineered recentralization in Chinese broadcasting. As the year drew to an end, the wave of conglomeration reached its climax when, on December 6, 2001, just a week before China officially joined the WTO, the SARFT announced the establishment of the China Radio, Film, and Television Group, a national-level media conglomerate that aimed to combine the resources of China Central Television, China National Radio, China Radio International, the China Film Group Corporation, and related Internet and broadcasting production and distribution operations. With more than 20,000 employees and total fixed assets of 21.4 billion yuan, the entity was widely saluted by state officials and the media alike as a national industry champion ready to face the challenges of post-WTO international competition.[85]

By the end of 2003, the GAPP and the SARFT had established 39 newspaper groups, 18 broadcasting groups, 14 publishing groups, 8 distribution groups, and 6 film groups.[86] However, to the extent that it is easy to issue administrative orders and declare the formation of media groups on paper, central party-state planners and market enthusiasts were unable to realize their recentralization and market consolidation objectives as effectively as they had hoped. In fact, the sector-specific nature of the groups reveals the limits of centralized party-state power in overcoming vested bureaucrat interests and in implementing any abstract and idealized market rationality. To be sure, the GAPP was able to close, merge, or relicense most bureaucratic and county-level newspapers, thanks to an all-out political and bureaucratic mobilization, appeals for reducing the financial burdens of the already highly exploited farmers, and by granting politically and culturally based exceptions as well as making significant concessions to economically more powerful localities.[87] The SARFT, however, has not been able to fully carry out its plan to transform the functions of county-level television stations and to reintegrate cable networks at the provincial level. To be sure, the number of broadcasting stations, especially television stations, has been significantly reduced. By the end of 2002, official statistics counted 303 radio stations, 358 television stations at the central, provincial, and municipal levels, and 37 integrated radio and television stations at the municipal/prefectural levels, offering 1,882 and 2,080 radio and television channels, respectively.[88] On paper, the more than 1,375 county-level television stations had been officially relicensed, with restricted programming power and their primarily role as transmission stations. However, unlike county-level newspapers, county-level television operations, especially those in the economically developed regions, involved considerable infrastructure investments by local governments, tens of millions in advertising revenue, and substantive jobs, not to mention their propaganda function for local authorities. Even in economically underdeveloped areas, local officials are willing to maintain stations with financial subsidies because television is such an effective means to project political power. In fact, the struggle over control of television broadcasting within the state hierarchy has been extremely intense and ongoing local resistance against central state planners' "accumulation by dispossession" strategy has been formidable. As Sun Wusan has demonstrated in her case study in Hebei Province, the intricate web of vertical and horizontal administrative power relationships, especially the horizontal power of the local party-state in overriding the vertical power of the broadcasting administration, has meant that even a township was able to not only establish a television station in 1996, but also sustain its operation during a time when the central authorities had decided to deprive county-level television stations of their full programming capacity.[89] Not surprisingly, the SARFT found itself unable to persuade county-level authorities with its recentralization policy, which favored central and provincial broadcasters. In fact, one of the unintended consequences of the recentralization campaign was further fragmentation: provincial broadcasters now had an extra channel—the "common channel"—to compete with existing channels. Meanwhile, many county-level broadcasting authorities kept their existing television channels and claimed access on the "common channel." Similarly, the media conglomerates have been fraught with profound conceptual, structural, and operational challenges. The first issue concerns these conglomerates' ambiguous, hybrid, and indeterminate corporate identity. The national-level China Radio, Television, and Film Group, for example, exists only on paper. Unlike provincial broadcast groups such as those in Guangdong and Zhejiang, or Shanghai's SMG, there has not been any integration of the group's affiliated broadcast operations.

Nevertheless, the party-state is poised to not only deepen the market logic and nurture media conglomerates, but also to maintain and secure the "commanding heights" of the transformed media economy by claiming "exceptions to neoliberalism." A secretive document issued by the General Office of the CCP Central Committee on August 20, 2001, laid out the guiding principles for the restructuring and further development of the Chinese media, with its scope and implications going further beyond the promotion of media conglomeration. Known as "Document No. 17," it was only distributed to officials at the provincial and above levels of power (*shengjun ji*).[90] On January 15, 2002, the Xinhua News Agency disclosed partial content of this document in the form of a "press interview."

The Xinhua story stated the overall objectives of media reform: establishing macromanagement and micro-operational systems that ensure party leadership and "correct" opinion orientation; establishing a policy and regulatory framework appropriate to the media as propaganda and culture institutions; and promoting a market environment that facilitates "the superior allocation of resources, competition, and order," "absorbing excellent foreign culture and advanced technology," and "resisting decadent culture." More specifically, the Xinhua story set out five near-term objectives for "deepening" reform in the media sector: using the conglomerate as an organizational form to build national and regional production, distribution, and film exhibition entities and networks; rationalizing media structure and improving efficiency; promoting digitalization and network technologies; transforming the operational mechanisms of media organizations and strengthening their "capacity for self-development," which implies overcoming barriers for cross-region and cross-media expansion; and further capitalization. At the same time, the story stated, "Whatever the circumstances, the nature [of the media] as the mouthpieces of the party cannot be changed."[91] This point had previously been disclosed in a September 2001 editorial issued by the *Chinese Journalist* (*Zhongguo jizhe*), an authoritative trade journal affiliated with the Xinhua News Agency. This editorial clearly articulated the "four no changes"—the party's bottom line and its claim to exceptions to market calculations—in the market-oriented restructuring of the media system: "Whatever the changes, the [media's] nature as party and people's mouthpieces must not be changed; the party's control of media must not be changed; the party's control of cadre must not be changed; and correct opinion guidance must not be changed." The article continued on to say that the party must "always command major decision-making power, the controlling power over the allocation of capital, the censorship right over propaganda, and the right to the appointment of leading officials."[92]

To ensure these "four no changes," as an article in the 2004 volume of *China Journalism Yearbook* stated, the media conglomerates must adopt the institutional identity of "state-owned, cause-oriented undertakings" (*guoyou shiye tizhi*), meaning that they would continue the dual-track system of "course-oriented undertakings managed as business enterprises."[93] However, while these conglomerates are no longer considered party-state departments, they are not registered with the state's industrial and commercial administration as independent businesses. Rather than creating a special institutional category to accommodate such a hybrid entity, for example by enacting legislation that allows for their establishment as "public media institutions," in the form of Western-style public broadcasting corporations, or the party's "crown corporations," the party-state let these media groups exist in this institutional limbo. As the party leadership knows all too well, to open up public discussions about the nature of these media groups is to open an invitation to debate media institutional reform alongside the agenda for political liberalization. Underscoring the fusion of party-state and market power, each media conglomerate has a bureaucratic rank within the party-state power hierarchy. The Zhejiang Broadcasting Group, for example, is a bureau-level media conglomerate, meaning that its officials enjoy the bureaucratic status and privileges of a provincial government bureau. Similarly, party-state officials (typically a deputy director of PDs or government broadcasting bureaus) assume the chair and CEO positions of broadcasting conglomerates.

There is also ambiguity over property rights. Although the party-state's media assets are considered "media capital," they do not have clearly delineated property rights and the legal status as free-flowing "capital." That is, just as these groups have no corporate status, they have no legal status to conduct business transactions involving the transfer of property rights. In fact, who is the exact legal owner of the Chinese media is not even clear: the Communist Party or the Chinese state, and thus potentially the Chinese people? This is not a hypothetical question. According to one well-established Chinese media scholar, Document No. 17 was so secretive because it contained an explosive assertion by the party—that the party, not the Chinese state, is the owner of these media conglomerates. Through this document, the party has "privatized" core Chinese media organizations and claimed them as party property (*dangchan*). As this source confirmed, the document stated that China's media conglomerates "belong to" the party's PDs (*xuanchuanbu suoyou*).[94]

Given its sensitive nature, it is not surprising that this topic has only come up in private conversations with Chinese officials and media researchers. Although the media's role as the party's mouthpiece is often taken for granted and although the party dominates the Chinese state, most Chinese media managers, journalists, and media scholars tend to assume that the Chinese state, not the Communist Party, is the owner of state-controlled media. For example, to talk about "state-owned property" in reference to party-state media is common. After all, although the party press originated historically as the property of the Communist Party vis-à-vis the Chinese nationalist state, once the party took over state power, state subsidies, not party membership dues, funded the Chinese media. Even if some party organs can be traced back to the party before it came to power, few doubt that China's broadcasting media, which had a pre-1949 history but developed primarily since 1949 through state subsidies and then primarily through advertising-based self-accumulation under favorable tax policies, belong to the Chinese state.

The delineation of the party's proprietary ownership of the media is a politically awkward issue for an organization that calls itself communist and dedicates itself to the proposition of abolishing all forms of private property. Moreover, the concept of "party property" invokes the unflattering image of the Chinese Nationalist Party in Taiwan, whose "party property" became a subject of disgrace after it lost state power. Still, there is no question that the party's PD has used the process of media conglomeration to consolidate and strengthen its control of core media institutions in the country. The press conglomerates built around party organs are said to be "affiliated" with party PDs. In broadcasting, party PDs traditionally assume ideological leadership, while the SARFT and its provincial and local counterparts claim "administrative affiliation" relationships over broadcasting operations, effectively exercising ownership power. However, as a result of conglomeration, the party PD has claimed an "affiliation" relationship over broadcasting operations in some cases, while the role of the SARFT and its local counterparts has been limited to that of a regulator. To be sure, there are intra-elite and regional differences over the issue, which have been reflected in the institutional setup of the still rapidly evolving broadcasting structure. An article in the 2004 volume of *China Journalism Yearbook*, for example, described three kinds of "affiliation" relationships in broadcasting: some groups are affiliated with provincial and municipal governments; others are affiliated with provincial and municipal "party committees and governments"; and still others are affiliated with provincial party PDs.[95]

The delineation of property rights has direct implications for these media conglomerates as full-fledged business agents in the market. If these media assets are assumed to be state assets, then they should be registered with the State Assets Management Bureau, and their boards should be delegated to manage these assets. However, as the *China Journalism Yearbook* article puts it, "With one or two exceptions, most of the broadcast groups have not been entrusted with the right to manage, operate, and invest these state assets by provincial and municipal governments. The status of these groups as the holders and managers of state assets has not been established. Consequently, these groups have not become concrete [corporate] entities."[96] This means that media groups could not deepen the market logic by conducting property right–based business transactions such as mergers and takeovers.

Although the party-state has been able to absorb the force of media commercialization so far, the further territorial expansion of market logic, that is, the formation of a national media market for regional and industrial sector–based media conglomerates, has been hindered by these conglomerates' party and state organ status and existing administrative boundaries. Can Guangzhou-based press conglomerates operate a newspaper in Beijing? Can the Xinhua News Agency operate a television network? The party-state's desire to make its media operations "bigger and stronger" has inevitably generated these questions. Under the current structure, a party organ such as the *GD* serves as the mouthpiece of the Guangzhou Municipal Party Committee. All its subsidiaries are politically and administratively accountable to the Guangzhou Municipal Party Committee. If the *GD* Group publishes a paper in Xi'an, which party committee will be the political master of this paper? No matter how commercialized the *GD* Group is, it has no legitimate political and administrative grounds to expand beyond its political boundaries. As Joseph Chan observes, "Such an expansion can be interpreted as trespassing on the Chinese administrative system."[97] The expansion of one province's media outlets into another province would inevitably mean the expansion of one province's political power into another, thus undermining "the political power balance between the central authorities and local authorities and among central authorities."[98] But if media conglomerates based in the economically developed regions were not allowed to expand geographically, how could they become "bigger and stronger"? Where could their capital find new media markets to invest in? Thus, the current structure of media as affiliates of the party-state has become an institutional barrier for the territorial expansion of media conglomerates.[99]

Another hurdle that has blocked the business expansion of media conglomerates is cross-media operations. Theoretically, this shouldn't be a problem since media conglomerates are owned by the party-state: the party-state can use its administrative power to break sectoral boundaries and create a unified national market for the operation of media conglomerates. However, sectoral boundaries have been, in fact, extremely difficult to cross, and any change in the current division of media markets could undermine deep-rooted bureaucratic interests. This is particularly the case with broadcasting. Currently, broadcasting bureaus at various levels serve as the monopoly operators of lucrative regional and local broadcasting markets, while SARFT and its directly affiliated broadcasters dominate the national market. With the exception of some government education departments, no other government departments, including party organs, have been allowed to enter the broadcasting market. Xinhua News Agency, which has operated a Film and Video Department that sells programming to local television stations, for example, has lobbied hard to run a national television channel. But these efforts have led nowhere, and this has little to do with Xinhua's political credentials, nor with current state restrictions against vertical integration or any rule that prohibits a news agency from directly operating media outlets. In fact, Xinhua has already published numerous newspapers and periodicals. Vested bureaucratic interests are the major barrier. When Tian Congming, former chief of SARFT, was appointed as the director of the Xinhua News Agency, he attempted to use his personal connections at the SARFT to secure Xinhua a broadcasting license. However, Xu Guangchun, then the SARFT director, simply responded to the Xinhua application by referring to the SARFT's previous negative reply to Xinhua, which was issued by none other than Tian himself when he was the SARFT director. While the state can afford to lay off industrial workers, it is not prepared to undermine the existing interests of its media bureaucrats and media managers, who are the primary beneficiaries of a commercialized and monopolistic broadcasting system. Although they are not the legal owners of the media system, these individuals derive their political economic power and social and cultural privileges from their operational access to the media. As I argued earlier, the central leadership must ensure the bureaucratic interests of media officials and managers in exchange for their complicity in delivering the "right" kind of media content.

In short, the processes of industry expansion, market consolidation, and state capital formation in the media have brought into sharp focus not only the potentially conflictual relationship between the party and the state, but also the complicated ways in which the "territorial" and "capitalist" logics of power overlap, intertwine, and tug against each other at the central and local levels of the Chinese state.[100] Not surprisingly, progress toward cross-media and cross-regional operation has been slow. Current steps have been undertaken in the form of collaborative operations, but without the merging of existing media assets. One example is the establishment of the above-mentioned Beijing-based *Guangming Daily* Group and *Nanfang Daily* Group joint venture, the *Beijing News*, whereby the *Guangming Daily*, with its geographic base in Beijing and central party organ political status, provided the newspaper license and its political prestige, and the *Nanfang Metropolitan News*, the *Nanfang Daily* Group's successful urban subsidiary, provided capital and the bulk of the management and editorial personnel. This was hailed as a breakthrough in cross-region media operations.[101] An example in both "cross-media" and "cross-region" media operation is the establishment of the Shanghai-based financial paper *First Finance Daily* (*Diyi caijing ribao*) in 2004, a joint venture between Shanghai's broadcasting conglomerate SMG, the *Guangzhou Daily* (GD) Group, and the *Beijing Youth Daily* (BYD) Group.

As the party's media managers were struggling to find the necessary "institutional innovations" to grow media conglomerates without infringing upon administrative boundaries and challenging the existing party organ structure, they also encountered problems in integrating the different media entities within these groups themselves. In Shanghai there have been persistent conflicts of interest and business cultures within the *Wenhui-Xinmin* Group. In Beijing many believed that the central party authorities' firing of top editors at the *Beijing News* in late 2005 was as much a straightforward censorship exercise in response to its aggressive news reporting as a successful attempt on the part of the *Guang-ming Daily* to wrest editorial control of the paper from its joint-venture partner, *Nanfang Metropolitan News*.[102] Similarly, in the broadcasting sector, conglomeration has been blamed for failing to create synergy, efficiency, or a more rationalized allocation of resources. With the Hunan broadcasting authority, recentralization was blamed for undermining organizational dynamism, resulting in declined audience ratings and increased financial losses. Consequently, in September 2002, less than two years after the initial introduction of the recentralization scheme, the "reforms" were reversed. Hunan Economic Television Station was resuscitated, and the group's eight channels were once again operated by three separate corporate entities.[103] This means, among other things, the reestablishment of more senior management positions for broadcasting officials and regained financial autonomy for senior broadcasting managers. In Zhejiang a dual-track management structure at the top, an editorial board and a business management board, opened up enough senior positions to accommodate previous broadcast officials in the new corporate structure, while a less drastic recentralization scheme left enough relative autonomy to different channels. The conglomerate structure has been held together, but middle-level managers complained about declining efficiency in decision making, lack of autonomy in accessing technical facilities and personnel resources, and unfulfilled promises of resource sharing between channels.[104] Moreover, economically more successful units, especially television channels specializing in entertainment programming, are clearly unwilling to cross-subsidize less profitable operations under the recentralization scheme. As the director of a Zhejiang provincial television channel put it, "The socialist big family is very warm; unfortunately, there is no shared common interest."[105] A station director in Guangdong summarized the dilemma of the conglomeration campaign this way: "The direction sounds clear in theory, but we do not know how to get there in practice."[106] At stake are the vested interests of media officials and managers whose incomes under decentralized media commercialization are directly linked to revenue-generating abilities of a particular media channel and programming units. Consequently, there are tremendous income differentials within and between different media organizations, and there is no political will on the part of the central party-state to equalize income, not to mention initiate any substantial cross-subsidy schemes that would allow the significant redistribution of media profits to correct the inherent social biases of a market-driven media system. The media are simultaneously mouthpieces of the party and sources of bureaucratic power and personal wealth. Just as party officials at all levels are not willing to give up their control of the media, the beneficiaries of decentralized media commercialization are reluctant to give up their vested interests in the current media structure. If there is "feu-dalization" in party officials' control of media content to the extent that party officials become local "lords" in the disposal of media control power, there is also "feudalization" in the business operation of the media. In fact, such a form of "feudalization" is in many cases physically embodied in the spatial configuration of the buildings that host the different subsidiaries and operational units of newspaper and broadcasting conglomerates within the parameters of walls patrolled by armed guards.

THE REFORM'S "CULTURAL TURN":
"CULTURAL SYSTEM REFORM" AND CULTURE
AS A NEW SITE FOR CAPITALISTIC DEVELOPMENT

By 2003, conglomeration through administrative fiat had reached an institutional and operational impasse, and central state authorities had called for a halt in the rush to approve more conglomerates. Unhappy with the pace of marketization and frustrated with the inability of a bureaucratically conflicted media sector to realize the promise of Document No. 17, state planners devised a more sweeping program, under the name of "cultural system reform" (*wenhua tizhi gaige*) to provide the new conceptual and policy framework for accelerating the restructuring and development of the media and culture sector. The dual objectives expressed in Document No. 17—strengthening party control and accelerating market-oriented development—were thus recast in the new discourse on "cultural system reform." This discourse traces its origins to the "Report of the Party's 16th National Congress" in October 2002, which marked two important changes in the party's discourse on media and culture and its developmental strategies for this sector. First, it subsumed the news media, which have always had a special political significance, under the rubric of the broader realm of "culture." There was no mention of the news media in any substantial way, apart from the reiteration of the demand for the media to maintain "correct orientation to public opinion." Instead, under the section entitled "Cultural Construction and Cultural System Reform," the report gave unprecedented attention to the strategic role of culture and for the first time officially articulated a need to develop a systemic program for "cultural system reform." The report stated that politics, economics, and culture are mutually interpenetrating in the contemporary world and that the "status and functions" of culture "are becoming more and more outstanding in the competition in comprehensive national strength."[107] In this way, the party effectively displaced media reform as a key component of *political* reform with the broad agenda of cultural system reform. In doing so, the report also called for an official expansion of the party's economic reform program to the media and cultural sector and recognized this as the new focal point for capitalistic development and a strategic site for the development of "comprehensive national strength" (*zonghe guoli*)—that is, both economic power and cultural or "soft power" (*ruan shili*) in a competitive global context.

Second, and key to the newly elevated status of media and culture as a realm for systematic state-led neoliberal development, the party replaced the long-held pragmatic policy of "cause-oriented undertakings managed as business enterprise" with an official acknowledgment of a market-driven culture industry and a new distinction between "cause-oriented culture undertaking" (*wenhua shiye*), or "public interest–oriented cultural undertaking" (*wenhua gongyi shiye*), and "culture industry" (*wenhua chanye*). On the one hand, the report promises that the party supports "public interest–oriented" cultural undertakings, that is, cultural undertakings that are deemed to provide basic cultural products and services to the public and are not necessarily profitable in the market. "Important news media of the party and the state" are included in these "public interest–oriented" cultural undertakings. On the other hand, the report stated that the development of a market-oriented culture industry is an important means to satisfy the masses' spiritual and cultural needs under the market economy. As I suggested previously, the "culture industry" arrived in China with CCTV's broadcasting of *Aspirations* in 1990 (although the exact term "culture industry" was not yet in official use at the time). Since then, the conceptual development of the "culture industry" accelerated in official discourses along with the intensifying commodification of communication and culture. Landmarks have included the establishment of the Culture Industry Bureau within the Ministry of Culture in 1998, the first use of the term "culture industry" in an official party document in the party's proposal for the "10th Five-Year Plan" in October 2000, the addition of the categories of "communication and culture industry" and "information communication service" to the Chinese Securities Regulatory Commission's industry classification in 2001, and the State Statistics Bureau's issuance of "Classification of Culture and Related Industries" in April 2004.[108] The 16th Party Congress report in October 2002, by officially endorsing the "culture industry" and championing its development, marked the summation of the culture industry's ascending status. It not only ended much of the lingering leftist hesitation and anxiety about the commodification of culture, but also elevated the status of the culture industry and its development to a new political economic plateau. In fact, the report promised to "improve policies toward the culture industry, support its development, and enhance its overall strength and competitiveness."[109] Thus, if the first discursive objective of the report was to dissolve the political dimension of the media into the less politicized area of "culture," its second discursive objective was to define the party's political interest as the "public interest."

The party's "cultural turn" in its reform program was further elaborated and strengthened in subsequent party-state resolutions. In particular, "Decision on the Strengthening of the Party's Governance Capabilities," the resolution of the 4th Plenary of the 16th CCP Central Committee on September 19, 2004, put forward the proposition that the party must "deepen reforms in the cultural system, liberate and develop the cultural productive force" (*wenhua shengchanli*).[110] This is considered necessary in order to construct an "advanced socialist culture," which is one of the five capabilities the party aims to develop. Though the resolution does not define the term "cultural productive force," the discourse underscores the party's emphasis on the economic value of culture and culture as a site for capital valorization. The words of two Xinhua journalists summarize the main thrust of the cultural system reform program: "Development wants to eat off culture; culture wants to eat off the market."[111] The party, in short, has repositioned itself as the captain of the Chinese culture industry.

The party's new position has been developed under the tautology of well-trained communication scholars and the most astute global media barons. Cited as an important historical event in media trade journals and widely circulated among China's media scholars, Zhang Ximing of the Chinese Academy of Social Sciences and Xiong Chengyu of Tsinghua University were invited to a Politburo study session to give seminars on developments in the Chinese culture industry in August 2003.[112] In October 2003, Rupert Murdoch became a guest lecturer at the Central Party School, with Vice President Zeng Qinghong and other high-level officials as his audience.[113] Articulating the party's determination to implement the spirit of its 16th Congress and to become the vanguard of "advanced culture," and implicitly addressing the lasting impact of the party's traditional state socialist and moral conservatist view against a market-driven culture industry, Li Changchun told the party's cultural captains in April 2003,

> [We] must liberate [ourselves] from the shackles of out-of-date beliefs, practices, systems, and from incorrect and dogmatic understandings of Marxism. All thoughts and beliefs that impede the development of advanced culture must be decisively overcome; all practices and rules that hinder the development of advanced culture must be decisively changed; all systemic flaws that thwart the development of advanced culture must be decisively removed.[114]

Then, in January 2004, Li articulated the party's new theoretical understanding of the regime-enhancing impact of the market-driven culture industry as follows: "Under the conditions of a socialist market economy, a market orientation is consistent with the double objectives of serving socialism and serving the people." Moreover, he said, "The more our cultural products conquer the market, the more fortified our ideological front will be, the better the social benefits."[115] With these words, the party's most powerful propaganda official has not only absolved the party's once-held suspicion toward the ideological reliability of a commodified culture, believing that the market could propagate ruling ideas, but also seemed to have embraced the doctrine of "consumer sovereignty," one of the key ideological justifications of a market-driven media system. The bottom line seems to have indeed become the party line. "Serving the people" in the People's Republic means serving consumers in the market. "What makes possible the contemporary revival of 'serving the people,'" Jing Wang observed, "is the equation, contradictory or not, between socialism and democratic consumerism."[116] While it would be naive to take Li's pronouncements at face value and to underestimate either the continued ideologically based suspicion against market-driven popular culture within certain quarters of the party establishment or its moral conservatist–driven impulse to rein in the popular cultural market with heavy-handed interventionist measures, equally problematic would be any analyst not taking Li's ideas and the party program behind them seriously.

In June 2003, the party-state officially launched a nationwide pilot reform program in the media and cultural sector. Thirty-five media and cultural units, ranging from press and broadcasting groups to performance troupes, were identified as pilots for market-oriented restructuring and development. Based on the conceptual distinction between a public interest cultural undertaking and the market-oriented culture industry, Li Changchun articulated different reform principles. For the "public interest cultural enterprises," the goals are to "increase investment, transform operating mechanisms, increase dynamism, and improve services." For the "culture industry," the reform slogan is to "innovate the system, transform operating mechanisms, pursue market orientation, and increase dynamism."[117] The key difference between these sloganlike policy objectives, of course, is that while there will be changes at the operational level in the "public interest" sector, there will be changes at the systemic level in the market-oriented sector—including expanded scope for capitalization and ownership transformation. Although the central state has increased its investment in various "cultural undertakings" since 2004, the emphasis is no doubt on the market-oriented sector.[118] At a more concrete level, the guiding principles include (1) separating the regulatory and operational functions of the party-state's current cultural undertakings; (2) separating public interest–oriented and market-oriented media and cultural enterprises and separating editorial operations and business operations of a media organization; (3) spinning off and corporatizing the market-oriented cultural enterprises and the business operations of media organizations, turning these enterprises and operations into shareholding companies, and diversifying the sources of capital by absorbing foreign and domestic private capital; (4) capitalizing the media and culture industry through the stock market; and (5) nurturing a significant number of state-dominated cultural enterprises as key players in the market.

In short, if state-engineered recentralization and conglomeration did not quite achieve the goals of deepening market relations and accelerating commodification, the new project of "cultural system reform" aimed to achieve them through divestment, that is, by spinning off market-oriented operations from existing party-state media conglomerates and turning these operations into relatively autonomous market entities that are free to absorb outside capital and pursue market-oriented expansion. First, with the exception of core party organs—for example, the *People's Daily* and the People's Publishing House at the central level—which would continue to be defined as "cause-oriented undertakings" and thus be eligible for state subsidies, all other party-state media operations, including the market-oriented subsidiaries of party organs, would become business corporations. Second, within an existing media organization, for example, a newspaper conglomerate, the business side of the operation, such as advertising, printing, and distribution, would be separated from the editorial department, and the business assets would be incorporated as (party?) state capital. In turn, some of these corporate entities would be partially privatized through the stock market. Thus, in the case of an existing broadcast group, while the group would remain a "cause-oriented" entity and the holder of broadcasting licenses, all its business operations, from program transmission, program production, advertising, and program purchasing, would be spun off and incorporated as business entities.[119] Since these entities do not hold broadcasting licenses, which are held at the "cause-oriented" group level, they can be contracted out to private capital and listed on the stock market. In short, "by allowing the media to internally differentiate into editorial, non-business section and business section, it emboldens the media to pursue profits in a more unabashed and effective manner."[120] A new wave of market-driven expansion and capitalization, spearheaded by ambitious provincial and regional governments and centered on already established media conglomerates, has been unleashed. The state's relentless promotion of digital technologies and new media, from animation, online gaming, and IPTV (Internet Protocol Television) to the digitalization and integration of the country's cable television networks, which served 126 million households by the mid-2000s, has unleashed further impetus for the mind-boggling processes of system transformation and service expansion. By mid-2006, the integration of cable networks at the provincial level, no doubt the most highly resisted recentralization plan in the entire media restructuring campaign, has been either fully or partially achieved in 18 provinces through three means: shareholding, bank-financed buyout, or outright dispossession of local cable properties from the hands of municipal and county-level governments.[121] To demonstrate the determination to do away with old concepts and combat entrenched bureaucratic interests against the development of the media industry, Shanghai's party-state authorities took the bold step of enthroning Li Ruigang, a 33-year-old young executive with a master's degree from Fudan University and one year of training in media management at Columbia University, at the helm of the SMG in October 2002. Li has since unleashed a whole range of ambitious business moves in an attempt to establish the SMG as a national and global media powerhouse.[122]

However, just as the initial drive toward conglomeration turned out to be difficult to operationalize, the implementation of the party's cultural system reform principles will also pose practical challenges. Already, claims to special cultural status by a wide range of publishers, from ethnic minority–language presses to university presses, as well as potential layoffs and the loss of welfare entitlements as a result of corporatization have significantly compromised the central planners' ambitious restructuring program in the publishing sector.[123] Similarly, the stripping of "business assets" from existing media conglomerates will be extremely complicated and will involve intense bargaining and juggling for power among middle- and senior-level managers. Given the lack of transparency in the process, there are also signs that this process may result in the de facto plundering of media assets by well-positioned individuals, thus continuing the process of capitalist class formation that started with the privatization of state-owned enterprises in other economic sectors.

Nevertheless, the main thrust of the party's media and cultural reform program is clear. First, although the party may not make an open claim to property rights over China's core media and cultural operations, it will assume complete control of these institutions along the lines of the "four no changes." In addition to continued and even increasing financial subsidies to central party organs such as the People's Daily and the Xinhua News Agency, personnel control will be a key dimension. In a typical corporatized media group, the party committee, the board, and the management team will consist of the same individuals. Second, while ordinary state cultural sector workers may face the fate of layoffs, many of the party-state's media and cultural bureaucrats and managers, like the managers of other state enterprises, may have unprecedented opportunities to enrich themselves through the corporatization and de facto privatization of state media and cultural assets. To take advantage of these opportunities and to keep themselves in the game, however, they will need to maintain their political loyalty to party bosses. Finally, with political and economic recentralization and a general trend toward deepened commodification, China's major media organizations will become more closely integrated with the country's dominant political economic forces, thus furthering the inherent social biases of a market-driven media system. Two cases, the demise of Li Yuanjiang, the former director of the *Guangzhou Daily* (*GD*) Group, the party's largest and model press conglomerate, and the case of the *Beijing Youth Daily* (*BYD*), China's second most successful newspaper group, further reveal the intricacies of the operation of political and economic power in the media and culture sector, the ways in which class relations within and around the media are constituted, and the powerful, creative, and yet corrosive market logic that has been unleashed by media commercialization and further entrenched in the cultural system reform project.

ANTINOMIES OF POLITICAL AND ECONOMIC POWER INSIDE PARTY-STATE MEDIA: TWO CASE STUDIES

On September 10, 2004, Li Yuanjiang, the party's number one press baron, was sentenced to a 12-year jail term for corruption. At the height of his career, Li was the editor-in-chief, publisher, and board chair of the *GD* Group. He was also the head of the Guangzhou party PD and a member of the standing committee of the Guangzhou City Communist Party Committee. Li personified the fusion of political, media, and business power in China.

Li had climbed up the party's power ladder on the basis of his capabilities. He holds a Ph.D. in the history of the international communist movement and was a talented publisher and a charismatic leader. When the less than 40-year-old Li was appointed the editor-in-chief of the *GD* in 1991, he was the youngest editor-in-chief of a party organ. Li single-handedly turned the *GD*, a small, banal, and money-losing party organ, into a "model socialist press group," earning a reputation as the most famous and most innovative reformer of the party's media system and contributing theoretical justifications, management expertise, and hands-on journalistic experience to the party's cause. Positioning himself as a captain of the party's media industry, Li, for example, was a leading voice in the party's media recentralization campaign, explicitly viewing conglomeration as a means of press control and minimizing the impact of "small publications rather lacking in social and economic benefits."[124]

Li engaged in a wide range of corruption activities. He received cash and other forms of bribes from his subordinates and through business transactions; he was involved in capital flight by allowing the company's Hong Kong branch to hold more than 80 million Hong Kong dollars in advertising revenue, turning it into a de facto private bank account for himself and his accomplices; he and his accomplices led lavish lifestyles, entertaining themselves in the "presidential suite" of a luxurious hotel built by the newspaper group. Also typical of Chinese officialdom, Li fused political power with patriarchal power through sexual exploitation of women in subordinate positions—he had sexual relationships with more than half a dozen women within his newspaper empire. Finally and most importantly, the case involved a closely knit "common interest community" of individuals in critical positions in the newspaper's power structure. Thus, if there is no "community of common interest" in the Chinese media industry in the public sense, there are certainly "common interest communities" in private, operating the party's media businesses as feudal empires. Inside the *GD* Group, Li's exposed accomplices included his deputy editor-in-chief, his deputy director, the head of the group's advertising division, the general manager of the paper's printing factory, and Li's assistant, the director of the group's general office. Outside the group and beyond the light of official exposure were individuals at the top of the party's propaganda hierarchy in Beijing.[125] Interviews with Guangzhou media insiders confirmed Li's close ties with officials at the central PD.[126]

Li's private "common interest community," however, was missing one important bloc—local officials in Guangzhou City and Guangdong Province. This—rather than his corruption behaviors per se—proved to be fatal for him. Li was not an ideologically committed liberal. He was first and foremost a businessman, a press baron whose primary concern was his paper's financial success. Although the *GD* was innovative and popular among readers, it was never as politically liberal and socially committed as the *Nanfang Weekend* and the *Nanfang Metropolitan News*. The paper's core readership was Guangzhou's white-collar middle class.[127] Still, perhaps as the inevitable political price Li had to pay to become the party's most famous press baron, Li ruffled some political feathers in Guangdong. For example, in order to attract readers in the nearby Pearl River delta area, *GD* started to publish a daily section called "Pearl River Delta News" in 1996. And no news story was more appealing to readers than critical news about local officials. However, these municipalities are not subordinate units of Guangzhou City. Thus, by expanding *GD* into the Pearl River delta through critical reporting on local affairs, Li antagonized officials in those areas. Even worse, Li defied the orders of Guangzhou municipal party officials, who, in response to complaints by officials in neighboring municipalities, had pressured him to back off. Partly due to his arrogant and flamboyant personality, partly due to his political miscalculation—that is, he had banked his political capital in the central PD in Beijing but neglected to cultivate good relationships with his more immediate party bosses in Guangzhou—Li had demonstrated disobedience to the very party committee he answered to. Thus, he had violated the basic rule of the game: no matter how successful he had become as a press baron of national status, he remained a functionary of the local party committee he belonged to.

Within the *GD* Group, Li's power abuses created discontent among ordinary employees, who appealed to local authorities to investigate. Not surprisingly, the official account about Li's downfall began with "people power" in the fight against corruption: a letter from "a senior worker" complaining about the group's unaccounted financial assets in Hong Kong that caught the attention of the Guangzhou and Guangdong party authorities.[128] At his sentencing, Li, ever the entrepreneur, mobilized his expertise in the world communist movement to bargain for a better prison deal: "China does not have many people with this field of specialization, I am currently writing the third volume of *400 Years of Socialism*. This volume is more important than the previous two volumes, please give me a lenient punishment." [129] One wonders how Li would represent his own rise and fall as a Chinese Communist Party press baron as a footnote to the history of world socialism.

Until Li's demise, the *GD* Group was posited to be China's first newspaper to expand capitalization through a stock market listing. Instead, on December 22, 2004, *Beijing Youth Daily (BYD)*, the country's second-largest newspaper in terms of advertising revenue, became the first to sell shares on the Hong Kong stock market. Although the party-state media's primary economic base had moved from state subsidies to advertising financing, the party-state for a long time prevented the media from becoming sites of accumulation of capital for those outside the media industry. Party-state media organizations, for their part, have long been eager to turn themselves into sites of accumulation of capital in general through the stock markets. While some, including CCTV and the Shanghai broadcasting authority, have managed to list their peripheral operations in the stock markets, the Hunan provincial broadcasting authority managed to list its programming and cable transmission assets under a subsidiary in the Shenzhen Stock Exchange in 1999 without the approval of central authorities, leading the SARFT to issue an order to prevent imitation by others. In the newspaper sector, like the *GD*, the *BYD* had been in preparation for stock market listing as early as 2001. In the aftermath of Document No. 17, which finally permitted major state media organizations to raise capital from state-owned enterprises operating in other economic sectors, and in the context of a concerted push for media capitalization through the stock market by government officials, media organizations, capital markets, media scholars, as well as other elites,[130] the *BYD*, as one of the 35 pilot units in the cultural system reform program, was granted the historic opportunity to offer the first officially approved newspaper stock.

Under the principle of spinning off the business operations of a media outlet, the advertising, printing, and other business-related departments of the *BYD* were incorporated into the corporate entity "Beijing Media Corp.," with the Beijing municipal government as the sole shareholder. This corporate entity then began selling 25 percent of its shares to outside investors. The paper's editorial department and circulation arm were formally excluded from the listing entity, which has no control over editorial content but will pay a flat rate of 16.5 percent of its revenue as the paper's editorial expenses.[131] Although the term "privatization" was never used in domestic media reporting of this development, this is the "system innovation" that the party-state may apply to other media outlets. As expected, the listing was a stunning success.[132] Domestic and international media alike celebrated it as a major step in China's media and cultural system reform. Cultural system reform is a new political initiative and officials need to show positive results to accumulate the most political capital. The listing was scheduled to be an end-of-the-year achievement in 2004, and it went ahead although not all the financial statements were in order.

Still, what made the *BYD* the chosen paper of both the party and capital? The paper, which had a humble and tortured origin within the party-state media system, took advantage of its marginal position to focus on in-depth reporting of sensitive social issues and pioneered a style of journalism that fused the party line with popular journalism by addressing popular concerns, especially the concerns of ordinary Beijing citizens in the early 1990s.[133] Two of its readership-oriented supplements—*Newsweek* (*Xinwen zhoukan*) and the weekend supplement *Youth Weekend* (*Qingnian zhoumo*)—launched the paper's commercial revolution. By the mid-1990s, the paper had not only become a hot item on Beijing newsstands, but also provided a successful journalistic model for the newly emerging urban mass appeal "metro" papers.

However, political and advertising power soon changed the paper's orientation. On the one hand, the *BYD* was punished politically for its aggressive reporting, and it lost its politically bold leadership. Meanwhile, advertisers were beginning to transform the paper. In the late 1990s, the *BYD* started to publish three new supplements—*Computer Times* (*Jisuanji shidai*), *Grand Home Times* (*Guangsha shidai*), and *Automobile Times* (*Qiche shidai*). As former publisher Cui Enqing put it frankly, "These are not newspapers. They are co-published by advertising companies that wanted to borrow the newspaper as the hen to lay eggs." Cui noted that in the case of *Computer Times*, "information about computers made up 50 percent of the content, advertising made up the other 50 percent."[134] In the words of Zhang Yanping, the current publisher, the paper made a conscious business decision to capitalize on the rise of these new industries and became dependent on these advertising markets.[135]

Such a move engendered contestation. The central PD, still harboring residual state socialist values, didn't like the automobile supplement and issued a closure order. Promoting the automobile was seen as promoting "conspicuous consumption," which, under the old ideological framework, was to be avoided. However, this position no longer had any purchase in other branches of the party-state. Moreover, unlike *China Women's News*, the *BYD* had a power base in the powerful Beijing Municipal Party Committee. The paper's leadership was able to win the argument in resisting the PD's antiquated ideological control against the promotion of consumerism. After all, by the mid-1990s, the auto industry had been identified as a pillar industry by the state, consumerism the engine of economic growth, and, as Cui recalled, the state advocated "cars for the family." Moreover, Cui rationalized that even though luxury goods can only be consumed by a minority, they express the desires of the masses: "The automobile represents advanced productive force. To suppress propaganda about it and regard such propaganda as promoting conspicuous consumption is an odd and wrong-headed way of thinking and it has no place in guiding our reform."[136]

The paper subsequently undertook more conscious efforts to move upmarket in readership composition and in catering to elite interests in editorial orientation. It changed from a readers' newspaper to an advertisers' newspaper. It no longer emphasizes street sales and charges a higher cover price than its competitors. Instead, it relies on household subscriptions by its targeted readership—the successful, young, urban, white-collar strata, the kind of reader that car, information technology, and, most importantly, real estate advertisers are interested in reaching. Consequently, the paper obtained the highest subscription versus street sale ratio among all the urban dailies in Beijing. In 2001 the paper made a further upmarket move by eliminating an advertising section that was considered "low quality"—that is, advertising content about goods and services that appeal to lower social classes. As Zhang Yanping puts it, the *BYD* "occupies the most valuable audience market niche among Beijing's urban papers. Although its circulation figure is lower than that of the *Beijing Evening News*, it has consistently earned the highest advertising revenue in the Beijing newspaper market since 2000 and ranks itself among the top three newspaper advertising revenue generators in the country."[137] For example, in 2003 its daily circulation was only about 400,000 copies, and yet it raked in 900 million yuan in advertising revenue, with a profit of 240 million yuan.[138]

Although more critical readers and media experts expressed dissatisfaction with the paper's transformation from in-depth reporting of social issues into a blunt advertising vehicle, luxurious goods advertisers support the paper because of the paper's readership profile.[139] At the same time, unlike Li Yuanjiang, the *BYD*'s leadership maintains a cosy relationship with the Beijing municipal authorities. These officials, in turn, through their powers over personnel appointments and their position as official news sources, promote the business growth of the paper over other papers in the capital city. A stock market listing was therefore not only the desire of the newspaper itself, but also the "demand of the responsible departments," which aimed to set up the paper as a model for press reform. In light of the paper's humble origins, this is a reversal of fortunes.

Just as the *BYD* led the first wave of commercialization, turning official papers into readers' papers, it is posited to lead the current wave of capitalization by transforming the most dynamic sector of the Chinese press, the "metro dailies," from readers' papers into advertisers' papers. By 2004, the most visible self-promotional slogan for market-oriented newspapers was "going mainstream" (*zouxiang zhuliu*).[140] Thus, just as the party has redefined itself by reconstituting its power base through the "three represents," the commercial revolution of the Chinese media seems to have reached its logical conclusion by reconfiguring its most relevant constituencies. The *BYD*, the tiny paper once at the margins of the party-state media system, has become the chosen paper of party officials, major advertisers, upscale white-collar readers, and, of course, global financial capital. When asked about the paper's loyalty to its urban youth namesake, Zhang Yanping replied, "That only speaks of our institutional origin."[141]

But the *BYD* as a market-transformed phoenix failed to deliver on its promise as a model cultural institution both for the party-state and for stock investors. In August 2005, Beijing Media Corp. disappointed its investors with reported earnings of only 170,000 yuan in the first half of 2005, compared with the 66.3 million yuan it posted in the six months ending in June 2004.[142] A central government crackdown on real estate speculation had depressed advertising spending by real estate developers, and thus the paper's single-minded reliance on real estate advertising backfired. Then, on October 3, 2005, less than one year after its triumphant stock listing, the *BYD* shocked domestic and international media and its investors with news of the arrest of two vice presidents of the Beijing Media Corp., and four managers and staff members in the paper's advertising department, on charges of bribery and corruption.[143] While to say that perhaps this is the real "logical conclusion" of the party's cultural institution reform would be overstating the case, the story of the *BYD* does seem to epitomize the destructive logic of media commercialization and capitalization in China. The case, together with high-profile cases at CCTV and *GD*, seems to confirm that "corruption is not an aberration" but the "very essence and modus operandi" in the Chinese media economy.[144] Moreover, the logic of capital, pushed to its extreme by the *BYD*'s upmarket reorientation and its single-minded reliance on real estate advertising, turns out to be unstable and self-paralyzing.

CONCLUSION

On January 12, 2006, the CCP Central Committee and China's State Council issued "Several Opinions on Deepening Cultural System Reform," officially launching the wholesale program for restructuring the media and culture sector. China's post-Mao transformation, starting with the "economic" reforms, has definitely encompassed the realm of "culture," while (once again) deliberately delaying and bypassing the agenda of political reform. If Mao staged a "Cultural Revolution" in an attempt to sustain the party's social revolution and secure its revolutionary hegemony, the current party leadership launched a "cultural system reform" to sustain the economic reforms and forge a new hegemony over a fractured Chinese society. Reiterating the party's renewed emphasis on culture as a critical site of strategic national power and implicitly addressing mounting obstacles and resistance, the document calls forth an understanding of the importance and urgency of reform in this realm "from the vantage point of fully implementing the scientific concept of development, constructing a harmonious socialist society, and strengthening the guiding role of Marxism in the ideological field, and from the vantage point of strengthening the party's governance capabilities."[145]

Underscoring the party's social engineering ambition, the document posits the reform's guiding principles as "emancipating and developing cultural productive force," "developing socialist advanced culture," "meeting the growing spiritual and cultural needs of the people," "cultivating socialist citizens with ideals, ethics, culture, and discipline," and "promoting the full development of human beings." While setting industrial growth and market-oriented expansion as the goal, the document reiterates the conceptual distinction between "cause-oriented" cultural undertaking and market-oriented culture industry and calls for their coordinated development. It insists on the primacy of "social effects," while professing to strive for the unification of social effects and economic effects in an ownership structure in which public ownership dominates and coexists with other forms. Reflective of the leadership's renewed emphasis on the more proactive reconstruction of the party's ideological hegemony on the one hand and its proclaimed intention to promote more balanced development on the other, the document promises to increase public investment both in the "public interest–oriented" cultural sector and in the rural cultural infrastructure, as well as to promote the flow of cultural resources toward the rural areas and less developed regions. Finally, reinforcing the party's embrace of the concept of "soft power" and its growing imperative to project China's cultural power abroad, the document promotes a "going global" strategy of forging internationally competitive Chinese cultural enterprises through the coordinated effort of government support and cultural entrepreneurship.

Beneath the rhetoric lie the party's overriding dual objectives of sustaining economic growth and maintaining its hegemony by securing the "commanding heights" of a reconstructed communication and culture sector, while incorporating a consumerist mode of cultural citizenship enfranchisement. Zhang Xiaoming, a leading culture industry expert, translated the party's language in less didactic terms by framing the political economic significance of cultural system reform during the 11th Five-Year Plan Period (2006–2010) in terms of its "three historical missions": to spearhead the structural transformation of the Chinese economy from the provision of material goods to the provision of services and symbolic goods after China's per capita GDP reached the US$1,000 mark in 2003; to perfect the "socialist economic system" through the nationwide expansion of the reform program in the cultural sector; and finally, "to induce the deepening of political system reform and to fully construct a socialist harmonious society" through the steady growth of "advanced culture."[146] As Jing Wang has observed, not only has the Chinese state "not fallen out of the picture, but it has rejuvenated its capacity, via the market, to affect the agenda of popular culture." In this view, "the state's rediscovery of culture as a site where new ruling technologies can be deployed and converted simultaneously into economic capital constitutes one of its most innovative strategies of statecraft since the founding of the 'People's Republic.'"[147]

The British cultural theorist Raymond Williams, who envisioned the struggle for a socialist "common culture" as one in which the ordinary people participate in the making of social and cultural values, wrote that what "a socialist society" needs to do "is not to define its culture in advance, but to clear the channels, so that instead of guesses at a formula there is opportunity for a full response of the human spirit to a life continually unfolding, in all its concrete richness and variety."[148] Williams wrote,

> If it is at all true that the creation of meanings is an activity which engages all men, then one is bound to be shocked by any society which, in its most explicit culture, either suppresses the meanings and values of whole groups, or which fails to extend to these groups the possibility of articulating and communicating those meanings. This, precisely, was what one wanted to assert about contemporary Britain. . . . It was . . . perfectly clear that the majority of the people, while living as people, creating their own values, were both shut out by the nature of the educational system from access to the full range of

meanings of their predecessors in that place, and excluded by the whole structure of communications—the character of its material ownership, its limiting social assumptions—from any adequate participation in the process of changing and developing meanings which was in any case going on.[149]

Williams, who conceptualized a "cultural revolution" as "a third revolution" that intersects and extends the industrial and democratic revolutions in the British context, probably would not be surprised at the party's current "cultural turn."[150] However, he would be no doubt even more shocked by the structure of communication and culture in today's "socialist" China and the party's instrumentalist approach to constructing "advanced socialist culture." As I have demonstrated in this chapter, the bureaucratic and financial self-interests of the party-state's media and cultural bureaucracies, the growing market power of rising urban consumer strata, and the neoliberal ideology of market rationality cast as the norm or "law of motion" in media and cultural development have intersected to shape a specific process of commercialization and capital formation inside the party-state media and culture sector. This process has been both constituted by and constitutive of highly uneven class, urban/rural, gender, central and local, and other dimensions of power relations in China. Notwithstanding the newly expressed commitment to construct a "public cultural service system" (*gonggong wenhua fuwu tixi*) and to redistribute cultural resources toward underserved areas and populations, it remains to be seen whether the new document will usher in a period of media and cultural institution transformation different from what has already been piloted by the *GD* and the *BYD*, or CCTV and Hunan Satellite TV.

Before I conclude, I need to revisit the themes in the first part of this chapter and further explicate the social control implications of marketization and the political significance of the party's "democratic consumerism" and its elevation of media and culture as a new site of capital accumulation and social engineering. As a source of financing, advertising functioned as a de facto licensing authority in the sense that it has the power to decide what kind of newspaper will survive in the market.[151] Inevitably, as capitalistic developments take hold in the media, radical views and media outlets catering to the working class were being marginalized. Although this point has not registered in much of the writing on the political implications of media commercialization in China because of the continuing power of the state licensing system, this has been a world historical pattern.[152] Contrary to the liberal narrative of British press history as one in which a market-based press triumphantly challenged an authoritarian state and thus set the press free, James Curran, for example, effectively argued that the capitalist state consciously mobilized the market to achieve press control objectives. Calculated market liberalization, along with technological developments that increased the costs of production, gradually marginalized Britain's radical working-class press, leading to the realization of a political objective that the state had failed to achieve with either coercive means or stamp duties.[153] In the United States, where the "working class had barely begun to employ the press as an agency of class identity when the commercial penny papers began to enlist the interest and identification of laboring men"[154] in the 1830s, political radicals and working-class leaders soon realized how a commercial press owned and subsidized by capital ran against their interests. Thus, "by the 1880s, the class bases of commercial journalism began to be criticized quite pointedly in terms of the predisposing and prejudicial effects of capital."[155] The Canadian Royal Commission on Newspapers put the same argument more straightforwardly in reviewing Canada's press history: "It was left-wing viewpoints that tended to be under-represented as commercialism increased its hold."[156] Outside these Anglo-American countries, Armand Mattelart observed of Brazil before that country's transition to democracy: "The military did not succeed in imposing their schemes of total control of 'hearts and minds' by means of propaganda . . . and ended up relying on the mechanisms of the market."[157]

Although statements by the party's ideological and media leadership do indicate intention and careful calculation and rationalization, even though this is often done after the fact, it is not necessary to inscribe a capitalistic class intention in order to appreciate the political consequences of media commercialization and the profound ideological contradictions it has posited for the party.[158] As I argued in chapter 1, the party-state's regime of political power in media can be seen as partially aiming at frustrating capitalist class formation. Similarly, its effort at securing the "commanding heights" of the Chinese media and cultural economy and prioritizing state capital formation in this critical sector can be seen as an attempt to preserve and expand party-state power vis-à-vis encroaching foreign and domestic private capital. And yet, the regime of market power engendered by the policies of media commercialization and industry transformation has contributed to the structural marginalization of leftist perspectives to the disadvantage of China's lower social classes. Although the overwhelming evidence of the exercising and expansion of political power cautions against any premature suggestion that "postsocialist China has moved from a coercive to a systemic regulatory form of governance,"[159] the party is clearly resorting to a mixture of Orwellian and Huxleian approaches to sustain its rule.[160]

If the Orwellian approach remains a constant, even growing instead of declining, *despite* the increasing class containment power of the market on behalf of the dominant political, economic, and cultural forces, it is partly because of the following conditions. First, although there has been a shift toward a market economy, "a parallel shift in class relations, private property, and all the other institutional arrangements that typically ground a thriving capitalist economy,"[161] together with a parallel shift in the society's normative expectations and moral foundations, is not only incomplete, but also vigorously contested. The highly contested legal case involving the migrant-worker-turned-murderer Wang Binyu (discussed in chapter 5) and the highly controversial making of the Property Rights Law, passed by the NPC in March 2007 (discussed in chapter 6), underscore this point. Second, as I have already discussed elsewhere and as I explain further in chapters 5 and 6, as well as in the conclusion of this book, elite consensus regarding the legitimacy of the new social order resulting from the economic reforms remains fragile, and the task of popular containment and discursive disciplining in a highly traditional and yet postrevolutionary society—be it the suppression of the postmaterialist values of Falun Gong or the burying of the Maoist values of radical "mass democracy" or "people's democracy"[162] (however distorted and abused in practice)—remains formidable for the dominant social forces and their top-down technocratic modernizing project.[163] And yet, as I argued in chapter 1, the loud cry against political censorship, not the increasing power of the market, is itself politically significant because it has functioned to obscure the dramatic transformation in the Chinese media and cultural economy and its impact on reconfiguring class and other structural power relations in favor of the dominant political, economic, and cultural elites.

I think it worthwhile to emphasize how, in conjunction with overt censorship, nonestablishment leftist ideas (as opposed to the official doctrines or revolutionary myths in media and popular culture) have "naturally" failed to gain discursive space as the Chinese media system becomes increasingly commercialized, market driven, and, as I will show in the next two chapters, as foreign and domestic private capital is gradually incorporated into the system. The state's invocation of a regulation that imposes a minimum of 10 million yuan as a precondition to operate an informational website is no doubt extraordinary, but it does dramatize the capitalist class bias of the evolving system. Note the following comment by Zhao Renjie, a self-identified party member and a worker of the Yuanbaoshan Electricity Plant, in responding to the state's closure of China Workers Net and those who tried to deflect and justify this particular case of state censorship by claiming that, after all, many of the site's readers are not workers:

> The Communist Party is a vanguard of the working class . . . as to the point
> that the majority of the readers of China Workers Net are not workers, what
> does this say? Workers, especially some among an older generation of work-

ers whose interests have been severely undermined during the previous period of reform, could not even afford to feed themselves. Their television sets
are old, and you are thinking of them buying computers and even going online. . . . Precisely because a majority of workers are not online, you are able
to realize your objective of shutting up the website. If only the web-surfing
rate of workers were as high as those of stock holders and students, the
working class would have been more successful in fighting for their rights.
. . . It is said that you cannot operate a website without 10 million. We have
several hundred million—not money, but human beings, several hundred
million of experienced, highly conscious, and ever expanding working class.
If we each contribute 1 yuan, we can [afford to] operate scores of websites. To
those who shut down the website, will you approve [these working-class
websites]?[164]

The answer, of course, would be no—thus revealing the compounded
impact of political control and economic marginalization in the suppression of independent working-class communication, exposing the tension
between the party's professed objective of developing media and culture
to promote "the full development of human beings" and the actual practices of the media system. The statement is also significant in its reaffirmation of the Communist Party as a working-class party—if this statement had been hollow in traditional party propaganda, at a time when the
party's ruling elite has redefined the party to incorporate the propertied
class, this reaffirmation of the party's working-class nature is reflective of
an ongoing contestation *within* the party over its political nature and, by
extension, what and whose culture constitutes "advanced socialist culture."

NOTES

1. E. P. Thompson, *The Making of the English Working Class*, 2nd ed. (London:
Harmondsworth, 1968).
2. Luigi Tomba, "Creating an Urban Middle Class: Social Engineering in Beijing," *China Journal* 51 (Jan. 2004): 1–26.
3. Yuezhi Zhao, *Media, Market and Democracy in China: Between the Party Line and
the Bottom Line* (Urbana: University of Illinois Press, 1998).
4. Daniel C. Lynch, *After the Propaganda State: Media, Politics, and "Thought
Work" in Reformed China* (Stanford, Calif.: Stanford University Press, 1999), 75–78.
5. "*2005 nian Zhongguo guanggaoye tongji shuju baogao*" (A Statistical Report on
the Chinese Advertising Industry in 2005), www.chinalabs.com/view.asp?id=
0100131J (accessed 12 Jun. 2006). The 1980 figure is from Huang Shengmin and
Zhang Hao, "*2003–2004: Zhongguo guanggao shichang zhanwang*" (China Advertising Market Outlook for 2003–2004), in *2005 nian Zhongguo wenhua chanye fazhan
baogao* (Report on the Development of China's Culture Industry in 2005), ed.

Zhang Xiaoming, Hu Huilin, and Zhang Jiangang (Beijing: Shehui kexue wenxian chubanshe, 2005), 163.

6. Yuezhi Zhao, "From Commercialization to Conglomeration: The Transformation of the Chinese Press within the Orbit of the Party-State," *Journal of Communication* 50, no. 2 (Spring 2000): 3–26.

7. Zhenzhi Guo, "*WTO, meijie chanyehua yu Zhongguo dianshi*" (WTO, Media Industrialization, and Chinese Television), www.rundfunk-institut.uni-koeln .de/institut/pdfs/18904c.pdf (accessed 2 Jun. 2006).

8. GAPP, "*Xinwen chuban ye 2000 nian ji 2010 nian fazhan guihua*" (Plans for the Development of the Press and Publication Industry from Year 2000 to Year 2010), in *Zhongguo xinwen nianjian 1999* (China Journalism Yearbook 1999), ed. Editorial Board of China Journalism Yearbook (Beijing: Zhongguo xinwennianjian she, 1999), 57.

9. Interview, Jul. 2004.

10. Vincent Mosco, *The Political Economy of Communication: Rethinking and Renewal* (Thousand Oaks, Calif.: Sage, 1996).

11. The English name, the paper's own choice, is not a direct translation of the Chinese name.

12. Sun Zhengyi and Liu Tingting, "*2004: Zhongguo xinwenye huiwang (shang)*" (2004: China's News Media Industry in Retrospect), www.people.com.cn/ GB/14677/40606/3038055.html (accessed 28 Jan. 2005).

13. Zhao, "From Commercialization to Conglomeration."

14. Huailin Chen and Chin-Chuan Lee, "Press Finance and Economic Reform in China," in *China Review 1997*, ed. Joseph Y. S. Cheng, 557–609 (Hong Kong: Chinese University Press, 1997); Guoguang Wu, "One Head, Many Mouths: Diversifying Press Structures in Reformed China," in *Power, Money, and Media: Communication Patterns and Bureaucratic Control in Cultural China*, ed. Chin-Chuan Lee, 45–67 (Evanston, Ill.: Northwestern University Press, 2000).

15. Chen Lidan, "*Guanyu meijie ziben de jige wenti*," in *Xinwen yu chuanbo pinglun 2001* (Journalism and Communication Review 2001) (Wuhan: Wuhan chubanshe, 2001), 184.

16. Chin-Chuan Lee, Zhou He, and Yu Huang, "'Chinese Party Publicity Inc.' Conglomerated: The Case of the Shenzhen Press Group," *Media, Culture, and Society* 28, no. 4 (2006): 581–602.

17. Zhao, *Media, Market, and Democracy*, chapter 4.

18. Sun Liping, "*Shouru fenpei chaju shi ruhe kuangda de?*" (How Was the Gap in Income Distribution Enlarged?), *Nanfang zhoumo* (Nanfang Weekend), 10 Apr. 2003, www.nanfangdaily.com/zm/20030410/xw/sd/200304100873.asp (accessed 10 Apr. 2003).

19. Hu Ping, "*Wen Tiejun jiangchu jingying fubai xinsheng*" (Wen Tiejun Reveals the Elites' Inner Voice about Corruption), *Kaifang*, Apr. 2006, 41.

20. Hu Ping, "*Wen Tiejun jiangchu jingying fubai xinsheng*," 41.

21. Sun Wanning, *Leaving China: Media, Migration, and Transnational Imagination* (Lanham, Md.: Rowman & Littlefield, 2003).

22. Liu Chun, "*Cong Zhao An shijian kan jixing de Zhongguo dianshiwenyi wanhui*" (The Zhao An Phenomenon and the Disfigured Chinese Television Evening Parties), academic.mediachina.net/lw_view.jsp?id=599 (accessed 20 Jan. 2005). Zhao

An's official verdict charged him with accepting 610,000 yuan in bribery from one single source. However, few in China's media circles believed that this was the scope of his corruption. To minimize the scale of the corruption is a common self-serving practice of the authorities.

23. Zhang Xiaoming, Hu Huilin, and Zhang Jiangang, *"Zhuazhu gaige jiyu, jiji, wenjian, kuaisu fazhan wenhua chanye"* (Seizing the Opportunity of Reform, Proactively, Steadily, and Rapidly Develop the Culture Industry), in *2005 nian Zhongguo wenhua chanye fazhan baogao* (Report on the Development of China's Culture Industry in 2005), ed. Zhang Xiaoming, Hu Huilin, and Zhang Jiangang (Beijing: Shehui kexue wenxian chubanshe, 2005), 6.

24. CCTV began to reform this system in late 2003. See Cui Li, *"Zhongyang Dianshitai daguimo renshi gaige"* (A Large-Scale Personnel Reform at the CCTV), www.people.com.cn/BIG5/shehui/41259/43317/3119131.html (accessed 6 Dec. 2005).

25. Based on data in CCTV General Office, *Zhongguo Zhongyang Dianshitai nianbao 2003* (CCTV Annual Report, 2003), 13–20.

26. Pierre Bourdieu, *Acts of Resistance: Against the Tyranny of the Market*, trans. R. Rice (New York: New Press, 1998), 44.

27. As my discussion of CCTV's management underscores, my argument here is concerned more with the party's media managers and gatekeepers as a collective entity, not a few individual liberal editors that have posed open political challenges against the party and thus have become the analytical focus of Western liberal scholars.

28. Hu Zhengrong, Wang Wei, and Li Jidong, *"Xin de chidu xin de biange"* (New Measures and New Changes), in *2006 nian: Zhongguo wenhua chanye fazhan baogao* (Report on the Development of China's Cultural Industry in 2006), ed. Zhang Xiaoming, Hu Huilin, and Zhang Jiangang (Beijing: Shehui kexue wenxian chubanshe, 2006), 169.

29. Zhao Xiaobing, *"2003 nian Zhongguo meitishichang touzi fenxi"* (An Analysis of the Media Investment Market in China in 2003), www.tech.sina.com.cn/me/2003-04-11/2016177391.shtml (accessed 17 Apr. 2004).

30. Chen Jibing, *"Dui Ruidian baoye de guancha yu sikao"* (Observations and Reflections on the Swedish Press), www.cjr.com.cn/gb/node2/node26108/node27333/node28307/userobject15ai3050186.html (accessed 21 Feb. 2005).

31. Geremie Barmé, *In the Red: On Contemporary Chinese Culture* (New York: Columbia University Press, 1999).

32. Chin-Chuan Lee, "China's Journalism: The Emancipatory Potential of Social Theory," *Journalism Studies* 1, no. 4 (2000): 560.

33. Yuezhi Zhao and Zhenzhi Guo, "Television in China: History, Political Economy, and Ideology," in *A Companion to Television*, ed. Janet Wasko, 521–539 (Malden, Mass.: Blackwell, 2005), 531–532; see also Zhao Bin, "Popular Family Television and Party Ideology: The Spring Festival Eve Happy Gathering," *Media, Culture, and Society* 20 (1998): 43–58; Sun, *Leaving China*; Zhongdang Pan, "Enacting the Family-Nation on a Global Stage: An Analysis of the CCTV's Spring Festival Gala" (paper presented at the "Re-Orienting Global Communication: India and China Beyond Borders" conference, University of Wisconsin–Madison, 21–22 Apr. 2006); Lu Xinyu, *"Yishi, dianshi yu guojia yishixingtai"* (Ritual, Television, and

State Ideology), www.wyzxsx.com/Article/Class10/200608/8917.html (accessed 14 Apr. 2007).

34. Zhao and Guo, "Television in China"; see also Ruoyun Bai, "Media Commercialization, Entertainment, and the Party-State: The Political Economy of Contemporary Chinese Television Entertainment Culture," *Global Media Studies* 4, no. 6 (Spring 2005), lass.calumet.purdue.edu/cca/gmj/sp05/graduatesp05/gmj-sp05 gradinv-bai.htm (accessed 1 Jun. 2006).

35. Bai, "Media Commercialization."

36. Jing Wang, "Culture as Leisure and Culture as Capital," *Positions* 9, no. 1 (Spring 2001): 69–104.

37. Yin Hong, "Meaning, Production, Consumption: The History and Reality of Television Drama in China," in *Media in China: Consumption, Content, Crisis*, ed. Stephanie K. Donald, Michael Keane, and Yin Hong (London: Routledge/Curzon, 2002), 32.

38. Zhao and Guo, "Television in China," 532.

39. Barmé, *In the Red*, 107.

40. Bai, "Media Commercialization."

41. Bai, "Media Commercialization."

42. Barmé, *In the Red*, 280–315.

43. Zhao and Guo, "Television in China," 532–533.

44. For an overview of this literature, see James Curran, *Media and Power* (London: Routledge, 2002).

45. For the two different analyses, see Pan, "Enacting the Family-Nation," and Lu, "*Yishi, dianshi yu guojia yishiyingtai.*"

46. Wang, "Culture as Leisure," 71.

47. Arif Dirlik, *Marxism in the Chinese Revolution* (Lanham, Md.: Rowman & Littlefield, 2005), 263.

48. Chen Chongshan, "*Shuiwei nongmin shuohua: Nongcun shouzhong diwei fenxi*" (Who Speaks for Farmers? An Analysis of the Status of Rural Audiences), *Xiandai chuanbo* 3 (2003): 35–37.

49. Hu, Wang, and Li, "*Xin de chidu xin de biange,*" 174.

50. Guo Zhenzhi and Zhao Lifang, "*Jujiao 'Jiaodian fangtan'*" (Focusing on *Focus Interviews*) (Beijing: Qinghua daxue chubanshe, 2004), 20.

51. Guo and Zhao, "*Jujiao 'Jiaodian fangtan.'*"

52. Xue Hang and Zhu Yu, "*Yangshi dakai shajie, shige lanmu buxing 'xiagang'*" (CCTV Wielded the Butcher's Knife, Ten Programs Were Unfortunately Axed), www.hn.xinhuanet.com/cmsx/2003-04/02/content_358907.htm (accessed 24 Feb. 2005).

53. Leaving aside the extent to which the program reflected the interests of rural audiences, the most insulting aspect of CCTV's action was that CCTV7, unlike CCTV1, was not a "must carry" channel and thus was not even available to many rural viewers.

54. Fan Dongbo, "*Yangshi xibupindao 12 yue 18 ri ting bo*" (CCTV Western Channel to Stop Broadcasting on Dec. 18), *Huasheng bao*, 22 Nov. 2004, www.cddc.net/shownews.asp?newsid=7381 (accessed 3 Mar. 2005).

55. Fan, "*Yangshi xibupindao 12 yue 18 ri ting bo.*"

56. People's Daily Online, "State Broadcaster CCTV Lays Foundation of Its New Headquarters in Beijing," english1.people.com.cn/200409/22/eng20040922_157939.html (accessed 3 Mar. 2005).

57. Xin Peiyu, *"Zhengduo Beijing: Beijing baoyeshichang jiexi"* (Fighting for Beijing: A Brief Analysis of the Beijing Press Market), 203.192.6.68/20031/12-44.htm (accessed 20 Jan. 2005).

58. Interview, 23 Dec. 2004, Guangzhou.

59. Sun Yanjun, *Baoye Zhongguo* (The Press Industry in China) (Beijing: Zhongguo sanxia chubanshe, 2002), 189.

60. Zhou Wei, *Meiti qianyan baogao* (A Frontline Report on the Media) (Beijing: Guangming ribao chubanshe, 2002), 172–175.

61. Wu, "One Head, Many Mouths," 54.

62. Yuezhi Zhao, "The State, the Market, and Media Control in China," in *Who Owns the Media: Global Trends and Local Resistances*, ed. Pradip N. Thomas and Zaharom Nain (New York: Zed Books, 2002), 189.

63. *"Kandeng 'Zhongguo qida exin' Beijing xinbao zao chafeng"* (Beijing New Journal Closed for Publishing "China's Seven Aversions"), secretchina.com/news/gb/articles/3/6/18/44934.html (accessed 20 May 2006).

64. Interview with Wang Xiuling, Aug. 1999, Beijing.

65. *"Xinxi zaobao baozhi jianjie"* (A Brief Introduction to *Information Morning*), www.infomorning.com/Resume.htm (accessed 2 Feb. 2005).

66. Liu Yong, *Meiti Zhongguo* (Media China) (Chengdu: Sichuan renmin chubanshe, 2000), 302.

67. Cao Zhenglu, "Na'er," *Dangdai* 5 (2004), www.eduww.com/bbs/dispbbs.asp?boardID=44&ID=13741&page=1 (accessed 19 May 2006).

68. Yuezhi Zhao, "'Enter the World': Neo-Liberalism, the Dream for a Strong Nation, and Chinese Press Discourse on the WTO," in *Chinese Media, Global Contexts*, ed. Chin-Chuan Lee, 32–56 (London: RoutledgeCurzon, 2003), 44–47.

69. Zhao, "'Enter the World,'" 51.

70. Yuezhi Zhao, "The Rich, the Laid-off, and the Criminal in Tabloid Tales: Read All about It!" in *Popular China: Unofficial Culture in a Globalizing Society*, ed. Perry Link, Richard Madsen, and Paul Pickowicz, 111–135 (Lanham, Md.: Rowman & Littlefield, 2002).

71. *"Gui dajia neng youzhu yu Zhongguo yanlun ziyou"* (Will Ghost Fighting Assist China's Freedom of Speech?), blog.yam.com/torrent/archives/1158068.html-Torrent (accessed 19 May 2006), translation by Andy Hu.

72. Wu, "One Head, Many Mouths."

73. Maurice Meisner, *The Deng Xiaoping Era: An Inquiry into the Fate of Chinese Socialism, 1978–1994* (New York: Hill and Wang, 1996), 301.

74. Guo Zhenzhi, *Zhongguo dianshi shi* (A History of Chinese Television) (Beijing: Zhongguo renmin daxue chubanshe, 1991), 186–194.

75. Zhenzhi Guo, "Playing the Games by the Rules? Television Regulation around China's Entry into WTO," *Javnost/The Public* 10, no. 4 (2003): 8.

76. Interview, 12 Dec. 2000, Beijing.

77. This, of course, does not mean that the state calculated this at the very beginning of the reform process. In fact, press conglomerates grew out of strict

economic concerns in the late 1980s. In order to help major newspapers achieve financial independence, the party allowed them to publish market-oriented subsidiaries and turn their noneditorial supporting departments into profit-making businesses. By the mid-1990s, however, media mergers and conglomeration were pursued as a state policy, with both political and market considerations.

78. Yuezhi Zhao, "Caught in the Web: The Public Interest and the Battle for Control of China's Information Superhighway," *Info* 2, no.1 (Feb. 2000): 41–65.

79. For an overview of these campaigns, "*Baokan zhili: Zhizhi sanluan, tanpai guji*" (Governing the Press: Stopping Three Disorders and Curing the Disease of Imposed Subscription), 203.192.6.68/2003/09/9-48.htm (accessed 20 Jan. 2005).

80. Liu Bo, "*Guanyu baoye jituan*" (On Press Groups), *Xinwen zhanxian* 7 (1998): 25–26.

81. Zhao, "From Commercialization to Conglomeration," 16.

82. Tan Ziyi, "*Baoye jituan yantao hui zongshu*" (A Summary of the Seminar on Press Groups), in *Zhongguo xinwen nianjian 1997* (China Journalism Yearbook 1997), ed. Editorial Board of China Journalism Yearbook (Beijing: Zhongguo xinwennianjian she, 1997), 254.

83. Lu Di, "*2003 Zhongguo dianshi chanye dajiema*" (Decoding the Chinese Television Industry in 2003), *Nanfang dianshi xuekan* 12 (2003): 21.

84. Zhang Le, "*Zhejiang youxian wuxian jiaoyu santai hebing*" (Zhejiang Merged Open-Air, Cable, and Educational Television Stations), *People's Daily*, 16 Dec. 2000, 5.

85. See www.sarft.gov.cn/page/zhglxx/2001-12-06.htm (accessed 15 Jun. 2005).

86. Editorial Board of China Journalism Yearbook, *Zhongguo xinwen nianjian 2004* (China Journalism Yearbook 2004), ed. Editorial Board of China Journalism Yearbook (Beijing: Zhongguo xinwennianjian she, 2004), 110–111.

87. A total of 709 newspapers were closed, and 325 papers were relicensed to press or publishing groups. See Han Yongjin, "*Wenhua chuangxin de jiaobu*" (The Footsteps of Cultural Innovation), in *2006 nian: Zhongguo wenhua chanye fangzhan baogao* (Report on the Development of China's Cultural Industry: 2006), ed. Zhang Xiaoming, Hu Huilin, and Zhang Jiangang (Beijing: Social Sciences Academic Press, 2006), 42.

88. "*Quanguo guangbo dianshi gaikuang*" (An Overview of Radio and Broadcasting), in *Zhongguo guangbo dianshi nianjian 2003* (China Broadcasting Yearbook 2003), ed. Editorial Board of China Broadcasting Yearbook (Beijing: Zhongguo guangbo dianshi nianjianshe, 2003), 38. By October 2004, there were 278 radio stations, 315 television stations, 62 education television stations, and 1,311 integrated radio and television stations (mostly at county levels). Hu, Wang, and Li, "*Xin de chidu xin de biange*," 173.

89. Sun Wusan, "A Small Chinese Town Television Station's Struggle for Survival: How a New Institutional Arrangement Came into Being," *Westminster Papers in Communication and Culture* 3, no. 1 (2006): 42–57.

90. My knowledge of the document was based on my interview with a well-placed media scholar who had the chance to read the document through a personal connection.

91. Xinhua News Agency, *"Jiji zhudong shenru chuangxin, shenhua xinwen chuban guangbo yingshi ye gaige"* (Innovate Proactively and Rigorously, Deepening Reforms in the Press, Publication, Broadcasting, and Film Industries), www.people.com.cn/GB/shizheng/19/20020115/648902.html (accessed 15 Jan. 2002).

92. *"Bawozhu shenhua gaige de lishi jiwu"* (Mastering the Historical Opportunity of Deepening the Reform), *Zhongguo jizhe* 9 (2001): 1.

93. Editorial Board of China Journalism Yearbook, *"Zhongguo guangdian jituan fazhan gaishu"* (An Overview of the Development of Chinese Broadcasting Groups), in *Zhongguo xinwen nianjian 2004* (China Journalism Yearbook 2004), ed. Editorial Board of China Journalism Yearbook (Beijing: Zhongguo xinwen nianjian she, 2004), 104.

94. The confidential source confirmed that this was the exact wording in Document No. 17.

95. Editorial Board of China Journalism Yearbook, *"Zhongguo guangdian jituan fazhan gaishu,"* 104–105.

96. Editorial Board of China Journalism Yearbook, *"Zhongguo guangdian jituan fazhan gaishu,"* 106.

97. Joseph M. Chan, "Administrative Boundaries and Media Marketization: A Comparative Analysis of the Newspaper, TV and Internet Markets in China," in *Chinese Media, Global Contexts*, ed. Chin-Chuan Lee, 159–176 (New York: Routledge, 2003), 162.

98. Sun Chuanwei, *"Guangdong baoye jituan ke yi dao Beijing fazhan ma?"* (Can Guangdong Press Groups Develop in Beijing?), Chinese.mediachina.net/index-news-view/ap?ID=55005 (accessed 15. Oct. 2004).

99. Chen Changfeng, *"Zhongguo chuanmei jituan fazhan de zhidu zhang'ai fenxi"* (An Institutional Analysis of the Barriers to the Development of China's Media Groups), *Xinwen yu chuanbo pinglun 2003* (Journalism and Communication Review 2003) (Wuhan: Wuhan chubanshe, 2004): 77–85.

100. I borrowed this conceptual distinction from David Harvey, who has written about the overlapping and conflictual relationship between "the logic of territory" and the "logic of capital" in the operation of imperial power in the global context. See his *The New Imperialism* (Oxford: Oxford University Press, 2005).

101. However, the joint venture was subtly resisted in various forms by local interests within the Beijing party and government apparatuses from the very beginning. The Beijing press bureau, for example, refused to register the paper under its originally proposed and advertised name, *Jing Bao*. It argued that papers under the *Beijing Daily* Group had the generic claim to be *jingbao*—"papers of Beijing." Interview, 20 Sept. 2004.

102. Based on various confidential correspondences and interviews with Beijing and Guangzhou press insiders from January to May 2006.

103. Lu, *"2003 Zhongguo dianshi chanye da jiema."*

104. As an example of the lack of cooperation among different channels operating under one corporate logo, one specialty channel found itself "pirating" a news feed from the general interest provincial satellite channel, which is delegated to receive outside news feeds. Apparently, the satellite channel has no incentive to make its news available to the other channel, and when the other

channel requested the news feed, the reply was "Come to record tomorrow!" Interview, 29 Dec. 2004, Hangzhou.

105. Interview, 29 Dec. 2004.

106. Interview, 23 Dec. 2004.

107. "Full Text of Jiang Zemin's Report at the 16th Party Congress," www.china.org.cn/english/2002/Nov/49107.htm#6 (accessed 6 Dec. 2005).

108. See also Bai, "Media Commercialization."

109. "Full Text of Jiang Zemin's Report."

110. "*Zhonggong zhongyang guanyu jiaqiang dangde zhizheng nengli de jueding*" (The Central Committee of the CCP Decision on Strengthening the Governing Capabilities of the Party), 19 Sept. 2004, www.china.org.cn/chinese/2004/Sep/668376.htm (accessed 25 Sept. 2004).

111. Que Zhihong and Qiu Hongjie, "*Qianfan jinfa, fengpeng zhengjü—2004 tisu wenhua tizhi gaige* (Accelerating Cultural System Reform in 2004), *People's Daily*, 4 Jan. 2005, 2.

112. "*2003 nian shangban nian Zhongguo xinwenye huiwang*" (A Retrospective View of China's News Media in the First Half of 2003), www.tech.sina.com.cn/me/media/gc/2003-12-02/1632262938 (accessed 28 Jan. 2005).

113. "Murdoch's Appeal to Chinese Leaders," afr.com/articles/2003/10/09/1065601940384.html (accessed 10 Oct. 2003).

114. Liu Kang and Tian Shubin, "*Li Changchun: Weirao 'santiejin' jiaqiang he gaijin xuanchuan sixiang gongzuo*" (Li Changchun: Strengthening and Improving Propaganda Work by Focusing on "Three-Getting Close"), news.xinhuanet.com/newscenter/2003-04/15/content_833798.htm (accessed 5 Jun. 2006).

115. Sun Zhengyi and Liu Tingting, "*2004: Zhongguo Xinwenye huiwang (shang)*" (A Retrospective View of China's News Media in 2004, Part I), www.people.com.cn/GB/14677/40606/3038055.html (accessed 28 Jan. 2005).

116. Wang, "Culture as Leisure," 95.

117. "*Li Changchun: Guanche shiliuda jingshen cujin wenhua shiye he chanye fazhan*" (Li Changchun: Carrying out the Spirit of the 16th Party Congress, Promoting the Development of Cultural Undertakings and Industries), www.china.org.cn/chinese/2003/Jun/355762.htm (accessed 24 Nov. 2005).

118. Li Jianjun, "*2004 nian Zhongguo wenhua fazhan gaishu*" (An Overview of Cultural Developments in China in 2004), in *2006 nian: Zhongguo wenhua chanye fazhan baogao* (Report on the Development of China's Cultural Industry in 2006), ed. Zhang Xiaoming, Hu Huilin, and Zhang Jiangang, 148–152 (Beijing: Shehui kexue wenxian chubanshe, 2006).

119. Research Center for Development and Reform, SARFT, *2006 nian Zhongguo guangbo yingshi fanzhan baogao* (Report on the Development of China's Radio, Film, and Television in 2006) (Beijing: Shehui kexue wenxian chubanshe, 2006), 4–5; Hu, Wang, and Li, "*Xin de chidu xin de biange*," 164–165.

120. Bai, "Media Commercialization."

121. Research Center for Development and Reform, SARFT, 287–298; interview with a deputy director of a provincial cable network corporation, 1 Jun. 2006, Vancouver.

122. Bai, "Media Commercialization."

123. Hao Zhensheng and Xu Shengguo, *"Shenru tuijin chuban gaige, chujin chuban fazhan"* (Deepening Reform in Publishing, Promoting the Development of Publishing), in *2006 nian: Zhongguo wenhua chanye fazhan baogao* (Report on the Development of China's Cultural Industry in 2006), ed. Zhang Xiaoming, Hu Huilin, and Zhang Jiangang (Beijing: Shehui kexue wenxian chubanshe, 2006).

124. *"Tansuo yitiao Zhongguo xinwen gaige yu fazhan de xinlu"* (Exploring a New Road for Reform and Development of the Chinese Press), *Zhonguo jizhe* 4 (1996): 16.

125. Ding Guan'gen, then a Political Bureau Standing Committee member in charge of ideology and the head of central PD, and Xu Guangchun, then the head of SARFT and a deputy director of the central PD, were both reportedly strong backers of Li. Chen Jingsong, *"Li Yuanjiang qiren yu Guangzhou ribao da'an"* (Li Yuanjiang as a Person and the Guangzhou Daily Case), www.epochtimes.com/gb/2/6/13/n196194.htm (accessed 18 Feb. 2005).

126. One piece of information, provided by one Guangzhou media insider, was that when the Guangzhou press monitoring system presented negative opinions about *GD's* editorial performance, Li was able to obtain a favorable reading report on exactly the same content from the central PD. Another piece of information was that Li tried to bribe central PD officials and appeal them to intervene on his behalf when he was already under investigation by Guangdong and Guangzhou authorities.

127. Interview, 5 Aug. 1998, Guangzhou.

128. *"Yuan Guangzhou shiwei xuanchuanbuzhang Li Yuanjiang tanwu fubai'an zhenpo shimo"* (An Account of the Investigation into the Corruption Case of Former Guangzhou Party PD Director Li Yuanjiang), www.people.com.cn/GB/14677/14737/22036/2150285.html (accessed 6 Oct. 2005).

129. *"Yuan Guangzhou shiwei xuanchuanbuzhang."*

130. Hu Zhengrong, "The Post-WTO Restructuring of the Chinese Media Industries and the Consequences of Capitalization," *Public* 10, no. 4 (2003): 31–34.

131. Interview, 8 Jan. 2005, Beijing.

132. Mark Lee and Lee Yuk-kei, "Arrests Maul Beijing Media," www.thestandard.com.hk/news_detail.asp?pp_cat=1&art_id=2774&sid=4862323&con_type=1 (accessed 7 Nov. 2005).

133. Zhao, *Media, Market, and Democracy,* 141.

134. Cui Enqing, *"Zhongguo baoye jingying linian yu chuangxin siwei"* (Management Ideas and Innovative Thinking in the Chinese Press), in *Zhongguo chuanmei shichang yunying* (Capital Market Operation in the Chinese Media), ed. Stan China and the Academic Committee of China Media Forum, 82–112 (Guangzhou: Nanfang ribao chubanshe, 2003).

135. Interview, 8 Jan. 2005, Beijing.

136. Cui, *"Zhongguo baoye,"* 93.

137. Li Ying, *"Beiqing chuanmei guapai gang gu"* (Beijing Youth Media Listed at the Hong Kong Stock Market), *Nanfang dushi bao,* 23 Dec. 2004, C65.

138. Liu Xing, Ma Li, and Liu Wei, *"Beijing qingnian bao tanlu chuanmei shangshi"* (*Beijing Youth Daily* Explores the Road to Stock Market Listing), medianet.qianlong.com/7692/2004/08/16/33@2220170.htm (accessed 1 Mar. 2005). The official

circulation figure of the paper for 2003 was 600,000. However, most Chinese newspapers inflated circulation figures. The number 400,000 was based on interviews with newspaper industry insiders.

139. See Liu Hong, *"Beijing qingnian bao zenme le"* (What's Wrong with the *Beijing Youth Daily?*), www.academic.mediachina.net/lw_view.jsp?id=297 (accessed 20 Jan. 2005).

140. Sun Wei, *"Lun dushibao de fenhua"* (On the Fragmentation of Metropolitan Newspapers), xwjz.eastday.com/eastday/xwjd/node41637/node41639/userobjectla (accessed 14 Feb. 2005).

141. Interview, 8 Jan. 2005, Beijing.

142. "Beijing Media: 6 Employees Detained for Questioning," www.chinadaily .com.cn/english/doc/2005-10/04/content_482613.htm (accessed 6 Nov. 2005).

143. "Beijing Media."

144. Michael Hardt and Antonio Negri, *Empire* (Cambridge, Mass.: Harvard University Press, 2000), 202.

145. Xinhua Net, *"Zhonggong Zhongyang Guowuyuan fachu shenhua wenhua tizhi gaige ruogan yijian"* (CCP Central Committee and the State Council Issued Several Opinions on Deepening Cultural System Reform), news.xinhuanet.com/politics/ 2006-01/12/content_4044535.htm (accessed 19 Apr. 2006).

146. Hao Linlin, *"'Shiwu' qijian Zhongguo wenhua chanye fazhan de sanchong lishi shiming"* (The Three Historical Tasks for the Development of China's Culture Industry during the 11th Five-Year Plan Period), news.xinhuanet.com/politics/ 2006-01/11/content_4038285.htm (accessed 4 Jun. 2006).

147. Wang, "Culture as Leisure," 71–72.

148. Raymond Williams, "Working Class Culture," *Universities and Left Review* 1, no. 2 (Summer 1957): 30, cited in Dan Schiller, *Theorizing Communication: A History* (New York: Oxford University Press, 1996), 107.

149. Raymond Williams, "Culture and Revolution: A Comment," in *From Culture to Revolution: The Slant Symposium 1967*, ed. Terry Eagleton and Brian Wicker, 24–34 (London and Sydney: Sheed and Ward, 1968), 29, cited in Schiller, *Theorizing Communication*, 127.

150. Raymond Williams, *The Long Revolution* (New York: Columbia University Press, 1961).

151. James Curran, "The Impact of Advertising on the British Mass Media," *Media, Culture, and Society* 1, no. 1 (1981): 43–69.

152. Zhao, "From Commercialization to Conglomeration."

153. James Curran, "The Press as an Agency of Social Control: A Historical Perspective," in *Newspaper History: From the Seventeenth Century to the Present Day*, ed. George Boyce, James Curran, and Pauline Wingate, 51–75 (London: Constable, 1978).

154. Dan Schiller, *Objectivity and the News: The Public and the Rise of Commercial Journalism* (Philadelphia: University of Pennsylvania Press, 1981), 74–75.

155. Schiller, *Theorizing Communication*, 6.

156. Canada, Royal Commission on Newspapers, *Report* (Ottawa: Supply and Services Canada, 1980), 15.

157. Armand Mattelart, *Mapping World Communication: War, Progress, Culture*, trans. S. Emanuel and J. A. Cohen (Minneapolis: University of Minnesota Press, 1994), 107.

158. See also Guoguang Wu, "The Birth of Sophisticated Propaganda: The Party-State and the Chinese Media in Post-Reform Politics," paper manuscript made available to the author.

159. Wang, "Culture as Leisure," 92.

160. For a related discussion, see Bai, "Media Commercialization."

161. David Harvey, *A Brief History of Neoliberalism* (Oxford: Oxford University Press, 2005), 122.

162. For a discussion of their legacies, see Lin Chun, *The Transformation of Chinese Socialism* (Durham, N.C.: Duke University Press, 2006).

163. See Yuezhi Zhao, "Falun Gong, Identity, and the Struggle for Meaning inside and outside China," in *Contesting Media Power: Alternative Media in a Networked Society*, ed. Nick Couldry and James Curran, 209–224 (Lanham, Md.: Rowman & Littlefield, 2003); Yuezhi Zhao, "Underdogs, Lapdogs and Watchdogs: Journalists and the Public Sphere Problematic in China," in *Chinese Intellectuals between State and Market*, ed. Edward Gu and Merle Goldman, 43–74 (London and New York: RoutledgeCurzon, 2004).

164. Zhao Renjie, "*Dianchang gongren jiu Zhongguo Gongren Wang beifeng fabiao shuoming wenzhang: Gongping le, ziran jiu wending le*" (Electrical Factory Worker Penned Article Regarding the Closure of China Workers Net: With Justice, Naturally There Will be Stability), www.utopia.e-channel.info/index.php?job=art& articleid=a_20060322_124358 (accessed 15 May 2006).

3

Dancing with Wolves?

Transnational Capital, Nationalism, and the Terms of Global Reintegration

In his October 8, 2003, lecture at the Central Party School in Beijing, Rupert Murdoch, the transnational media baron who once famously proclaimed that satellite television would bring an end to authoritarian regimes everywhere, cajoled top Chinese leaders to liberalize China's media market. Murdoch not only assured them of the compatibility between market liberalization and the maintenance of political power, but also claimed that "China has the potential not only to follow the examples of the US and the UK, but to improve upon those examples to achieve a level of success all its own."[1] However, by September 2005, Murdoch's unauthorized venture to take control of Qinghai provincial satellite television to broadcast his Channel V and Star TV to a Chinese national audience had been nixed by the SARFT. In response, Murdoch accused the Chinese government of "being paranoid," claiming that his plan to expand in China had "hit a brick wall."[2] Did Murdoch go too far in pandering to Chinese ears in 2003? How plausible is a Chinese success "all its own" in this critical area of global power? If China can achieve a level of success "all its own," what role will there be for the sort of transnational capital symbolized by Murdoch? More importantly, has the Chinese state changed its policies toward transnational media capital since 2005? What are the terms and implications of China's engagement with global capitalism within and around its communication system?

With the rise of global informationalized capitalism, the famous supposition of the 19th-century British industrialists that a one-inch increase to the length of the shirts Chinese men wear would keep the mills in Manchester running for years has been updated by the captains of the global communication industries. Meanwhile, the Chinese state is set not only to create a strong national media and cultural sector, but also to project China's "soft power" abroad. China's accession to the WTO in 2001 has significantly expanded the terms of China's global reintegration within and around the communication system. This chapter assesses the nature and dynamics of this reintegration, its political and social implications, as well as elite and popular contestations over it terms. First, I assess two prevailing analytical frameworks. Second, I examine this reintegration from a transcultural political economic perspective. This entails discussing the specific ways in which transnational capital and domestic Chinese social forces have intersected to reshape Chinese communication, contributing to the intensification of particular patterns of inclusion and exclusion in social communication, analyzed in chapter 2, and the ongoing process of class formation within and beyond Chinese borders. Third, I discuss the contradictions and tensions of this process, focusing particularly on the crucial role of a rapidly globalizing communication system in mediating and containing popular nationalistic discourses.

MAKING SENSE OF THE REINTEGRATION:
TWO PREVAILING PERSPECTIVES

Two broad frameworks have underscored much of the academic and journalistic literature on this reintegration, which for most analysts has meant the expansion of transnational corporations into China. Although there are internal variations, they can be broadly called the Chinese nationalist and culturalist framework, and the liberal democratization framework.

The Chinese Nationalist and Culturalist Perspective

The Chinese nationalist and culturalist framework is a conglomeration of various positions. First, throughout the mainstream Chinese press and academic literature, a strong national industry perspective exists, which invokes specters of the "Chinese media industry under siege." Symbolized by the widely invoked "wolves are coming" metaphor around China's WTO accession in 2001, such analysis focuses on the struggle between transnational corporations—the strong intruder in the figure of the foreign "wolf"[3]—versus the Chinese industry—the weaker "lamb" figure. The archetypal article is "Challenges of Foreign Media Entry and Our Strategies," a cliché in Chinese academic and journalistic literature that continues to exist well into the new century. Shunning any broad political and ideological debates, this dominant perspective is anchored in the pragmatic question of "how to"—that is, how to connect the Chinese media and culture industry with the global tracks; how to effectively absorb foreign capital and expertise; and most important of all, how to strengthen the domestic industries' global market position. This is precisely the framework within which the accelerated marketization, recentralization, and capitalization of the state-owned media and culture, analyzed in chapter 2, has been justified. "Beginning with Adorno's critique . . . debates about the rights and wrongs of the culture industry have been long lasting . . . but the grand wheels of social development do not permit us to talk on paper too much,"[4] wrote Li Xiangmin, a professor of economics in the preface to the *2004 Annual Report on the Development of the Chinese Culture Industry*. Li then declared, "The development of the culture industry is yet another Long March under the new era. The day China's cultural industry takes off is the day the Chinese nation rises!"[5] Yu Guoming, a journalism professor and a leading industry strategist, wrote in the normalizing language of Chinese neoliberalism, with a peculiar invocation of the residual "scientific socialist" notion of "the law of motion":

> In the face of the entry of transnational media corporations, our responding strategy should be to employ heightened 'wisdom + anxiety,' learn to *use the perspective of the market, the perspective of capital, and the perspective of the laws of motion in communication industry development to reintegrate our media resources*, steadfastly make [the industry] big on the basis of making it strong.[6]

The national industry perspective is also the framework in which domestic private capital has tried to secure a stake in the post-WTO Chinese media and cultural market. The rationale is that China needs to mobilize all its capital and resources—be they state or private—to compete with foreign capital. As I will discuss in chapter 4, "forging China's Time Warner" was a common ambition of domestic private media owners.

There is also a culturalist component to this perspective, concerned with the survival of "Chinese culture" in the face of foreign media entry. The pro-integration version is cautiously optimistic about the prospects for the Chinese cultural industry in the global marketplace. Rejecting a dehistoricized and misconstrued notion of "cultural imperialism" as a simple imbalance in global cultural trade, this perspective emphasizes the creative energy of Chinese cultural entrepreneurs, the resilience of Chinese culture, and the fact that local audiences, given a choice, prefer domestic production and are more receptive to "Chinese cultural values." Echoing Murdoch at the Central Party School, Western media scholars have also joined Chinese natives in reaffirming China's substantial potential to cultivate its own globalization by exporting its cultural products.[7] Whether articulated by domestic or Western scholars, this perspective avoids the political and ideological dimensions of culture and implicitly accepts the commercial logic of media and cultural production. Meanwhile, the anti-integration perspective, a legacy of the party's anti-imperialist ideological orientation and an expression of wariness against perceived Western influences, especially American efforts at "Westernizing" (*xihua*) and "disintegrating" (*fenhua*) China, opposes "Western cultural invasion." Although less visible in mainstream Chinese publications partly because it contradicts the neoliberal embrace of global capitalism and is thus being considered as part of the unfashionable "old leftist" discourse, this sentiment is nevertheless very strong in certain quarters. At a 2002 international conference in Beijing, for example, a senior Chinese academic delivered an angry diatribe against Hollywood domination and attacked the "decadent" cultural values and marketing gimmicks of the Harry Potter franchise.[8] Glaring inequalities between Chinese and American cultural power and the party's occasional invocation of the need to guard against "Westernizing" and "disintegrating" efforts ensure that such a perspective retains some space within media and academic discourses.

Notwithstanding their differences, these two perspectives share a number of assumptions. First, they hold an essentialist notion of Chinese culture and a nation state–centered frame of analysis, viewing the domestic media and culture industry as the carrier of China's economic and cultural power. These discourses invariably assume a unified "Chinese national interest" and a (self)-orientalizing "dehistoricized and desocialized"[9] understanding of "Chinese culture." What is lost here is any discussion about the domestic class, regional, gender, and ethnic politics of "Chinese culture," exactly what it means, and who can be its legitimate representatives. Typically, these "legitimate" representatives of Chinese culture are in state-organized and market-oriented media and cultural production; grassroots practices and vernacular cultural initiatives, meanwhile, are not legitimate representatives, especially if they are not easily subjected to commercial exploitations or political manipulations. Thus, what is missed in such a perspective is a notion of culture as "a field of change and contest, and an arena in which opposing interests make conflicting claims."[10]

Second, by invoking the image of invading wolves and emphasizing the "push" of transnational corporations, this framework underplays the active role of various domestic agents in China's reintegration. To begin with, Chinese policy makers have opened the domestic communication and culture market with the objective of gaining "more advanced" management and production expertise and as part of a broader political economic strategy of reintegrating with global capitalism.[11] Also, there were the captains of China's state-owned communication industries, eager to absorb foreign capital and collaborate with transnational media corporations and become local joint-venture partners, suppliers, and distributors. Similarly, fledgling and insecure domestic private media producers are eager to collaborate with, or even be absorbed by, transnational corporations, thereby expanding their power base vis-à-vis state controllers and state-owned firms. Nor should one ignore the global ambitions and initiatives of the Chinese state or private capital.[12] In fact, the political and market imperatives of Chinese global expansion have become increasingly acute in light of global success stories like Al Jazeera or *Crouching Tiger, Hidden Dragon*. As discussed in chapter 2, global expansion has become a key plank of the party's cultural system reform project. For example, notwithstanding the Chinese state's opposition to the American invasion of Iraq, CCTV apparently hoped to exploit the commercial potential of war coverage to become "China's CNN."[13] A final blind spot of this nationalist framework is the agency of Chinese audiences. Who is to say that readers of Chinese editions of foreign magazines are victims of external cultural imposition? Who is to say that those who prefer Hollywood blockbusters to domestic productions are not exercising their freedom of choice in the marketplace? Who is to question the sincerity of former premier Zhu Rongji when he acknowledged at a news conference that he was a fan of Phoenix TV's star current affairs host Wu Xiaoli?[14] Who is to deny that the Hong Kong–based and Rupert Murdoch–supported Phoenix TV meets the informational and cultural needs of China's globally integrated political and economic elites better than CCTV does?

Third, the culturalist perspective presupposes a problematic dichotomy between the global and the national, equating the penetration of transnational corporations with cultural assimilation and homogenization. As Dan Schiller and I have argued elsewhere, the transnational media industry is willing to "parasitize," rather than flatten, cultural differences—whenever such variations promise profitability.[15] Although American media culture has not straightforwardly homogenized the world, national media systems have increasingly been remade in the American model.[16] With the diffusion of capitalistic relations of cultural production and a series of cultural "formats" based on which various differences can be expressed and elucidated in many parts of the world, one witnesses, as Stuart Hall has observed, a "peculiar form of homogenization" that does not destroy but rather "recognize[s] and absorb[s] those differences within the larger, overarching framework of what is essentially an American conception of the world."[17] In fact, Leslie Sklair has gone so far as to argue that to see globalization and localization as mutually exclusive processes is a misconception:

> The global capitalist system is predicated on the accumulation of private profits on a global scale and the leading actors in the system have no particular

interest in destroying or sustaining local cultures apart from the drive for increased profitability. Where local or national agents threaten profitability,
capitalists certainly destroy them, as colonial powers have done in the past
wherever local enterprise interfered with their expansionist plans. Economic
globalization has changed this to some extent by making it easier for globalizing corporations to integrate local partners into their cross-border networks
and to take advantage of local partners and resources, an advantage that can
be shared with local elites. Always to see opposition between the local and
the global is the result of a rather static view of traditional practices and cultures.[18]

As Dan Schiller explicates, the critique of "cultural imperialism," advanced in the context of the decolonizing struggles and socialist experiments in the Third World in the post–World War II period, is "not only,
nor even principally, about the purported homogenization of interpretation, nor even about cultural consumption more generally"; rather, "it
centered on how structural inequality in international cultural production
and distribution embodied, pervaded, and reinforced a new style of
supranational domination."[19] More importantly, it is about culture as "an
emergent site—perhaps even *the* emergent site of struggle"[20] between
supranational capitalist domination and national self-determination centered on the possibility of "imagining outsides to a globalized capitalism,"[21] that is, alternatives *to*, not *within*, the "cultures of capitalism."[22] In
China, this struggle for an alternative to capitalist modernity culminated
with a socialist revolution and ended with the disaster of, perhaps not in-
cidentally, "the Great Proletariat *Cultural* Revolution," which, as Arif Dirlik argued, can be seen as representing the "dying gasps" of this earlier
form of resistance to capital.[23] Once this history is repudiated and once it
is assumed that capitalism and markets "have been the fates of humanity
all along," with culture essentialized as national or civilizational values or
commodified products, the "homogenization/heterogenization" question
becomes a "non-problem."[24] Within this more radical perspective, the
statements of Professors Li and Yu, which brushed aside debates about
"the rights and wrongs" of the capitalist culture industry and urged the
adoption of "the perspective of capital" in developing media and culture,
can be seen as manifestations of "cultural imperialism" in China. They ex-
emplify the fact that local elites—the dominant national agents of social
transformation—have not only conveniently "forgotten" the history of
China's struggle for an alternative or, perhaps more appropriately, intentionally refused "to engage with the recent revolutionary history,"[25] but
also have come to naturalize the capitalist logic of cultural production in
China.

Furthermore, domestic elites have also become adept at internalizing
and exploiting orientalist conceptions of China to their own political and

economic advantages. On the one hand, a "socialist China worked over by global capitalism . . . has become a promoter of Orientalist notions of China, which have now been appropriated as the characteristics of Chinese society, often in the very language of Orientalism (including the term 'Oriental' itself)."[26] Shanghai's fully commercialized, Pudong-based, and post-1992 radio and television stations, for example, carry the *"Dongfang"* name in Chinese, with "Oriental" as the official English translation.[27] On the other hand, Chinese cultural elements are no longer the exclusive symbolic resources of China's domestic media industries. Nor does the nationality of media capitalists always matter—after all, in the battle for the Chinese-language media marketplace, the Australia-born James Murdoch was the one who ridiculed the Hong Kong native Richard Li for failing to cater to local Chinese tastes by serving an impoverished English menu in Li's programming lineup for his multimedia platform, Network of the World.[28] Perhaps the most ironic example of this reversal of nationalist and globalist orientations is that the Chinese branch of Murdoch's global satellite TV empire, in its effort to indigenize, is known in Mandarin only as *Xingkong Weishi* (Star-Sky Satellite Television). Meanwhile, China Central Television, which is supposedly the guardian of Chinese national culture, in its desire to project a modern and global image uses "CCTV"—its English acronym—in its logo, even for its domestic channels. As Wu Mei, a Macao-based communication scholar has noted, the pervasiveness of English signs in the Chinese national media and public spaces is an obvious sign of cultural subordination.[29]

The Liberal Democratization Perspective

Equally influential, though less explicitly articulated within China and now severely embattled outside China, is the liberal democratization framework—the idea that opening China's communication markets will undermine the party's authoritarian control and facilitate the emergence of a liberal democratic order in China. To be sure, this argument has become less self-evident, ever since Rupert Murdoch retracted his famous remark that satellite television would undermine authoritarian regimes. By February 15, 2006, as the captains of the U.S. Internet industry, including representatives from Microsoft, Cisco, Google and Yahoo!, were summoned to Capitol Hill to explain in front of a U.S. congressional subcommittee their well-publicized deeds of aiding the Chinese government in building its Internet censorship regime and in jailing Internet activists, the liberal democratization argument seemed to have been completely discredited. Nevertheless, "democracy" continues to frame mainstream discourse on this topic. In fact, international media and U.S. congressional outrage over U.S. Internet companies' capitulation to the Chinese government is the exception that proves the rule. After all, the target of critique is the individual deeds of U.S. corporations, not the system of capitalistic expansion that drives these companies to China or finds the Chinese market irresistible in the first place. Invariably, the underlying assumption has been the incompatibility between China's state-controlled communication system and global communication markets, and the inherently democratizing impact of communication technologies and global cultural flows. In this Chinese application of the longstanding "free flow" and its concomitant "technologies of freedom" doctrine in international communication, democracy is linked to the marketplace and a citizen's freedom of expression is conflated with the "freedom of commercial speech," while freedom itself is often equated with the free circulation of commodities.[30] In the United States, the political and ideological aspects of this "free flow" argument reached a feverish pitch in the debates leading to the ratification of the U.S.-China WTO agreement in 2000. Mainstream media commentators, Republican and Democratic politicians alike, all proclaimed the same shibboleth: opening China's communication markets "will make it virtually impossible for Beijing to control freedom of communications in China."[31] Furthermore, the negative version of this argument—the critique of Western corporate complicity, best articulated by Ethan Gutmann's "losing the new China" and, more specifically, "who lost China's Internet" thesis—is problematic.[32] It not only falls into the fallacy of viewing "the issue of the Internet in China simply from a perspective that combines ideological conviction with technological determinism," but also betrays a not-so-subtle 21st-century version of neocolonialism.[33] It reminds us of the famous "who lost China" question in the United States after the Chinese communist revolution, as if a market authoritarian China then, and a liberal democratic China now, is some sort of U.S. possession; as if the United States is by nature a beacon for and enabler of democracy in the rest of the world; and as if, more specifically, firewall technologies and electronic surveillance are not developed and deployed in the United States itself for proprietary, labor, and broad social control in the first place.[34]

Though the liberal democratization framework is less explicitly expressed inside mainland China for obvious political reasons, many liberal media scholars and commentators in Hong Kong and overseas Chinese publications have internalized this perspective. The assumption is clear: since press freedom and capitalism coexist in the West, then from the embrace of global capitalism logically flows press freedom. Sun Xupei, a liberal Chinese media scholar, for example, framed the "WTO challenge" as one of reducing the "information gap" between the outside world and China. According to him, Western countries possess a higher volume of information than China, and this huge information gap inevitably leads to debilitating effects when the Chinese system opens up. Consequently, the best way to reduce these effects in China is by internally circulating sensitive and negative information. Sun further argued that the Chinese body politic was more capable of dealing with bad news than the party leaders have allowed.[35] Sun was also among those who have argued for the replacement of the party's arbitrary control of the media by the rule of law, believing that the WTO would inevitably force the Chinese state to abide by internationally acceptable "rules of the game" in media regulation.

Though the liberal democratization argument served and will continue to serve as a powerful rhetorical device in pushing for the further opening of the Chinese media market, its usefulness as an analytical framework is dubious on a number of counts.

First, the liberal democratization framework underestimates the ability of the Chinese state to negotiate with transnational capital over the terms of entry while maintaining its regime of power in the media. For example, one of the three principles governing the accession of Chinese-language satellite channels to Time Warner and Star TV in Guangdong Province is the right of the Guangdong cable network to block sensitive information during transmission, a long-held practice of the Guangdong cable authority when importing Hong Kong channels.[36] To be sure, a set of transparent and legally binding "rules of the game" creates more predictable and stable conditions for capital accumulation and elite bargaining.[37] As Lenin pointed out long ago and as David Harvey reaffirmed recently, "The preferred condition for capitalist activity is a bourgeois state in which market institutions and rules of contract (including those of labour) are legally guaranteed, and where frameworks of regulation are constructed to contain class conflicts and to arbitrate between the claims of different factions of capital."[38] However, the state can always use draconian legislation to curtail popular expression. Moreover, as the *Wall Street Journal* stated quite frankly, not only have transnational media barons such as Rupert Murdoch realized that they have much less leverage than they thought in dealing with the Chinese government, but "when big sums of shareholders' money are involved, it can be difficult to resist the impulse to self-censor."[39] As the captains of the U.S. Internet industry put it clearly in front of U.S. congressional leaders, they either have to cooperate with the Chinese state or risk losing a foothold in the world's most promising Internet market.[40]

Second, even assuming that foreign media can enter China unfiltered, the democratization framework contradicts the well-documented double standards of the U.S.-dominated transnational media in the coverage of global affairs and their complicity in sustaining authoritarian regimes elsewhere in the world.[41] Although China is by no means a U.S. client state—not only due to its size, but also because of the anticapitalist and anti-imperialist legacy of Chinese socialism and China's potential challenge to U.S. global domination—and the discourse of human rights will continue to serve as a relevant frame in Western media coverage of China, transnational media and entertainment corporations, like firms in other sectors of transnational capitalism, have everything to gain from a stable political environment and the low labor costs secured by an authoritarian Chinese state.[42] While there will always be notable exceptions, the absorption of American news production into entertainment giants with business interests in China could further undermine the liberal democratic value orientations of mainstream American journalism. Democracy does not exist independent of class interests and conflicts, nor of the hegemonic relations among states within the broad global political economy. From the U.S. media's imperialist involvement in Latin America to their complicity in Indonesia's genocide in East Timor, their record of allegiance to democratic communication is, to say the least, mixed and highly contingent on the interests of U.S. transnational capital in any given country.[43]

Third, the liberal democratization argument takes for granted ideological conflicts between global capitalism and "socialism with Chinese characteristics." To be sure, there are substantive differences between Chinese and Western media in terms of their ideological orientations. As discussed in chapter 1, the Chinese leadership shows no sign of abandoning the socialist rhetoric. Official pronouncements continue to be wary of Western political and ideological penetration, insisting on a "socialist market" alternative to capitalist global integration and expressing "an ambition of resisting subordination to global capitalism."[44] Wu Guangguo, for example, cited a lecturer at the Central Party School as saying that "ideology is the field where China fights against the penetration from the Western countries for changing China, and the Western media is the major tool of such a penetration," aiming at China's demise.[45]

However, with China's continuing commitment to market reforms, including those in the media and culture sector, the degree of ideological convergence between global capitalism and "socialism with Chinese characteristics" is also considerable. More substantively, as Chinese society assumes the general characteristics of a capitalist social formation, the potential for ideological cross-promotion between capitalist and Chinese media does exist. For example, where does one draw the communist versus capitalist ideological line when former party general secretary Jiang Zemin admires the Hollywood blockbuster *Titanic* for its ideological work—that is, its implicit discourse on class relations—and recommends the movie to his fellow Politburo members, thereby turning himself into the highest-profile promoter of the film in China?[46] Similarly, the current leadership has such a high appreciation of the prosocial messages of Korean television series, which have swept China in the so-called Korean Wave in the early 2000s, that they encouraged domestic television producers to learn from these shows.

On the one hand, the Western news media will continue to report news that is suppressed in China, and the party-state's control regime is in place partly to prevent the reporting and circulating of the kind of political news stories—including the struggles of Chinese workers and farmers—that elite Western newspapers such as the *New York Times* and the *Guardian* are reporting. This explains why the party-state will not give Murdoch and his fellow transnational media owners a free hand in China. On the other hand, to the extent that neoliberal reorganization of the national state across the world has "flattened" the earth for capitalistic developments, cultural formulas, products, and know-how that help to sustain unequal power relations in other cultures and explore the senses and sensibilities of "becoming modern"[47] through the development of a capitalistic social formation are likely to be appropriated and interpreted to address similar social relations and cultural experiences in China. As Anthony Fung has argued in his study of Viacom's wide range of collaborative activities with the Chinese state, to conclude that "global capital kowtows to Chinese authorities; or that the state backs down to allow their entry" would be too simple; rather, "transnational media corporations and the Chinese authorities work in tandem to produce a state-global media complex."[48] This is particularly the case in entertainment and popular culture production.

To be sure, there will always be local inflections, and a given media text is always polysemic. The debate over the impact of Hunan satellite television's *Super Girls* (*Chaoji nüsheng*) is an illustrative case. A Chinese adaptation of the reality television show *American Idol*, *Super Girls* solicits audience participation in the making of pop culture stars by allowing members of the audience to vote for their favorite singers—with votes sent through SMS via state mobile phone operators at 1 yuan per message, 10 times the regular price. On the one hand, liberal media commentators celebrated the triumph of the market over the state and were eager to dramatize the political democratization implications of *Super Girls* and the undermining of CCTV's dominant market power by a provincial channel. On the other hand, critical media scholars were wary of the show's individualistic and consumerist value orientations and its cross-promotion and synergetic articulation with a whole range of sponsors and industry participants as a marketing and profiting-making machine. Moreover, they pointed out the conflation between democracy and the market, more specifically, between manifestations of an "enthusiasm for [political] democracy" and reaffirmation of "depoliticized" individual identities and cultural rituals through the consumption of the program on the part of its fans.[49] Shanghai-based media scholar Lü Xinyu, for example, has posited the question: If "democracy" can only parasitize itself under the hegemony of the market, is it still democracy?[50] Some parents and educators, meanwhile, are worried about young girls' obsession with the role models and unrealistic expectations for quick money and fame that the show sets up. What is fascinating is that all these interpretations are themselves part of Chinese cultural politics. Moreover, unless one is a shareholder of Hunan broadcasting's stock market–listed company and thus stands to benefit from its increased stock value, one should not automatically assign any democratizing value to its undermining of CCTV's market power—it all depends on how these competing state broadcasters allocate their resources and whether they have any commitment to use the profits from entertainment programming to cross-subsidize less lucrative programming that is essential for the cultivation of democratic citizenship.

Finally, the liberal democratization framework is oblivious to the profound social tensions in Chinese society and the relationship between communication and social control that I discussed in chapter 1. For example, the real issue is not just whether well-off urban elites are capable of dealing with "negative" news stories about labor strikes and farmer riots. Rather, at stake is whether such stories—even in the most "objective" form—will serve to organize these groups and amplify their demands for more say in the reform process, and whether the beneficiaries of the reforms are willing to negotiate a better deal with China's workers, farmers, and other subaltern social groups. When the urban population fears being outvoted by the larger rural population, and when private property owners fear being (re)expropriated by another radical social revolution, the social basis for political authoritarianism is deeply entrenched. As I have argued in the preceding chapters, the role of communication must be understood within this context of class relations and social conflicts. Liberal analysts seem to be oblivious to the complicated power relations between the Chinese media, Chinese state, and different social forces in a highly fractured and polarized society and the possibility that media outlets, even if they were freed from direct party censorship, may choose to suppress stories about social unrest and the voices of China's underclasses.

THE TRAJECTORY OF CHINA'S REINTEGRATION: A TRANSCULTURAL POLITICAL ECONOMY PERSPECTIVE

The trajectory of the Chinese communication industry's reintegration with the global communication system is better understood through a transcultural political economy perspective.[51] To start, China's nearly three decades of "openness" and its WTO accession must be put into a longer and broader historical context. The portrayal of this as a new beginning for the Chinese communication industry obscures the fact that the Chinese communication system had always been "open" to varying degrees even before the reform period. Though WTO entry was certainly a landmark, the Chinese system became an integral part of the global capitalist communication system at the very beginning of the reform process: from the first Chinese television advertisement in 1979 promoting a Swiss watch to the Chinese government's decision in the early 1980s to prioritize telecommunication network development in coastal China, coordinating transnational capital's need to overcome the crisis of overaccumulation and its search for cheap labor in the shift toward post-Fordist flexible accumulation and neoliberal strategies of development. While the fact that transnational communication corporations can now expand their scope of operations in China is highly significant, the most important change in the Chinese national communication system has been its commercialization and its transformation into a platform for capital accumulation—regardless of the national origins of capital. In this section, I first historicize this "openness" and then examine the patterns of reintegration in various sectors of the Chinese communication system, as well as the implications of this reintegration for the processes of class formation within and beyond Chinese borders.

Communication with the outside world is not new to China. This is the case with both traditional and state socialist culture—two analytically distinct legacies of contemporary Chinese culture. There was never an essential "Chinese culture" to begin with; foreign ideologies and communication technologies, from Buddhism to Marxism, have long shaped Chinese society, just as Chinese ideas and communication technologies have shaped the rest of the world. Nor was cultural isolationism the official policy of choice in Mao's China. Here a distinction must be made between cultural isolationism and the selective importation of foreign culture. The fact that Mao's China reestablished national control of communication and rejected capitalist culture does not mean that it was closed to foreign interaction. After all, not only was Chinese communism as a social system the hybridized product of Marxism, Leninism, and Maoism, but also China's television system was set up with technological assistance from the Soviet bloc during the Cold War era. For a whole generation of Chinese growing up in the 1950s, Soviet movies, novels, and songs were as popular as today's American pop culture. When China broke its relationship with the Soviet Union, it continued to champion internationalism and cultural exchanges with a few other favored countries. The isolationist image of a Maoist China contradicted sharply the Cold War image of a radical China bent on exporting Maoism to the Third World. Indeed, Mao's "Little Red Book" even found a market niche among the counterculture youth in the West, and Maoism, as Liu Kang reminded us, "became in the globally radicalized, 'revolutionary' decade of the 1960s an internationally influential theory of revolution, or a version of revolutionary globalism."[52] Moreover, Mao's policy of self-reliance was as much an ideological choice as a virtue made out of necessity—the West, led by the United States, was isolating China politically, economically, and culturally. This history is important to revisit because its suppression is precisely what helps to sustain a dehistoricized "isolationist" versus "openness" dichotomy. Moreover, prereform China's cultural screen against the West was never total. It had always been erected to shield ordinary people, not the ruling elite, who had access to Western media through the classified information system. At issue here is the pattern of inclusion and exclusion: who had access to what, and on what terms, not an abstract binary between inclusion and exclusion. The binary framework makes sense only if one internalizes the expansionist and profit logic of the transnational corporations: China as a media market was indeed closed to them. Party elites reading selected foreign wire stories were not targeted as consumers by multinational advertisers.

Thus, what is at issue is the nature and character of Chinese communication with the outside world. Although elements of a commercial media system coexisted with foreign media in pockets of Chinese capitalism before 1949, only the reformed communist state has succeeded in turning China into a mass consumer society, thereby creating lucrative regional and national communication markets. Instead of taking the capitalistic character of the Chinese communication system for granted, the apparently national-centric reorganization of the Chinese communication system during the reform era must be viewed as an integral part of the neoliberal-oriented global restructuring of communication and culture, leading to the formation of a truly globalized communication system and the spread of the culture-ideology of consumerism.[53] Although direct investment by transnational media corporations in China is significant, the desire for and resistance against reshaping the Chinese media system to match the commercially most advanced American model symbolized by U.S.-based transnational media corporations—from their operational principles to their organizational structures, content formats, and value orientations—to the exclusion of other Western models (e.g., the European model of public broadcasting), must be the starting point of analysis.

Consequently, one could argue that the most insidious form of capitalist cultural domination is when a national media system internalizes the logic of transnational capitalism. This kind of cultural domination does not have to involve the direct participation of American capital or American-originated media content or, for that matter, Japanese or Korean media capital or content. Rather, its most telling evidence is found in the discursive orientations of China's national news media, a realm that is still formally under the control of the Chinese state. I have already discussed how Chinese press coverage of the U.S.-China WTO agreement in 1999 ignored the perspectives of China's domestic, low social classes. Consistent with this, the coverage not only suppressed leftist antiglobalization discourses and effectively erased the postrevolutionary Chinese history of pursuing "self-reliance" and national development outside the global capitalist system, but also naturalized neoliberal globalization and internalized the imperative of U.S.-led transnational capitalism. The Chinese media not only relied on American media and the U.S. Embassy for the content and interpretation of the WTO agreement, but also served as propaganda organs for transnational corporations and their spokespersons.[54]

The Chinese media's coverage of the U.S. invasion of Iraq in 2003 is perhaps an even more telling example. Here was an event in which the Chinese state articulated its opposition to American imperialism. On the surface, the Chinese media relayed the official position, to the extent that Internet posts by American apologists inside China attacked CCTV for its anti-imperialist pronouncements. However, a deeper level of submission to American imperialist power overshadowed official antiwar pronouncements. To begin with, the Chinese state allowed no room whatsoever for popular expression of antiwar sentiments in the media, just as there was no such expression on Chinese streets. Secondly, instead of engaging with fundamental questions regarding the legitimacy of the war, the Chinese media, following the lead of the American media, focused on military strategies and tactics and the display and analysis of American weaponry. To do so, they relied heavily on Pentagon-supplied footage of the war. As a result, a brutal war was almost turned into a reality television show displaying American military might and imperial reach.[55] Here, the penetration of American "soft power" was evident in Chinese television's submission to the technological and discursive logic of American commercial television—the imperial war as an integrated global news spectacle[56]—*despite* the Chinese state's official opposition to the war. In fact, the intensive coverage of the war on Chinese television was the result of a deliberate decision on the part of state officials and CCTV top management in an attempt to make CCTV "China's CNN" and to strengthen the position of domestic media vis-à-vis transnational media following China's WTO accession. This included the launching of a CNN-style 24-hour news channel. As I will discuss later, with the entry of foreign satellite broadcasting into China, the imperative of global competition became real, and, apparently, Chinese media policy elites believed that the way to win the Chinese audience was to mimic CNN's format and style and to make transnational media footage, which mostly meant

American material in this case, available to a domestic audience who had increasingly demanded such material.

At the same time, the accelerated reorganization of the Chinese communication and cultural system in the context of global integration expanded and intensified the processes of class and other social identity formation within and beyond China's borders. Foreign direct investment affects the class structures and state formations of other countries.[57] Specifically, an argument has been made that the penetration of American capital as a social force tends to undermine the formation of "a coherent and independent national bourgeoisie," diminishing "the likelihood that domestic capital might challenge American dominance—as opposed to merely seeking to renegotiate the terms of American leadership."[58] With this in mind, the rest of this section offers an overview of the emerging patterns of production and consumption in a range of transnationally integrated telecommunication, print, and audiovisual media industries in China and their implications for transnational class and identity formation.[59]

Telecommunications and the Internet

The drastic shift from the internally oriented and heavy industry–focused development strategy of the Mao era toward the post-Mao strategy of market-oriented, information technology–driven, and exported-led development spearheaded the Chinese state's policy of systemically prioritizing telecommunication development in the coastal areas and major urban centers since the early 1980s.[60] The reorganization of China's telecommunication network to articulate with transnational capitalism's post-Fordist accumulation strategy is thus instrumental to China's "opening-up" to the global capitalist system. Thus, the scope of foreign penetration in the Chinese telecommunication markets is much broader than in the mass media sector because of its centrality as the critical infrastructure for globalized capitalist production, its role as an important site of accumulation in its own right, as well as its apparently less political nature. In addition to foreign loans and direct investment in the telecommunication equipment market, Chinese bureaucratic capital, through a covert joint-venture scheme for China Unicom, first imported foreign equity investment through the back door into the lucrative Chinese mobile phone service market.[61] China Unicom, licensed in 1993 as a second state-owned telephone service provider, chose to focus on the mobile phone market and was made a viable business from the onset with the support of foreign capital. In a short period, intensive market competition between equipment makers and between China Unicom and China Telecom, then the incumbent operator, led to the creation of the world's largest mobile phone network, turning cellular phones into an integral component of the Chinese urban "middle-class" lifestyle and a primary means of communication for a highly mobile Chinese population. Today, mobile phones are one of the most fetishized commodities in China, as well as one of the most lucrative sources of capital accumulation.

Transnational capital scored a major victory in the push for China to open up its telecommunication services market through the terms of China's WTO accession, which obligate China to allow up to 49 percent foreign ownership in basic and 50 percent in value-added telecommunication services.[62] The result has been the exacerbation of a pattern of telecommunication development that has already been highly uneven and driven by elite interests to begin with.[63] As of 2006, as the Chinese state struggled to fulfill its broken 9th Five-Year-Plan-period (1995–2000) promise of providing "universal service"—defined as two telephone connections to an administrative village—domestic and foreign equipment makers and major Chinese telecommunication service providers, which have absorbed transnational capital through the stock markets, were aggressively pushing for massive investments in 3G—third-generation mobile phones—as a new point of market growth.[64] Meanwhile, one of the new sites of foreign investment in telecommunication has been the lucrative markets of private line circuits and broadband services for transnational corporate users.[65] AT&T, for example, has set up a joint venture to provide broadband services to transnational corporations based in Shanghai's Pudong District. Time Warner, meanwhile, has allied itself with Chinese computer maker Lenovo in an attempt to enter the Chinese Internet service market. With the bursting of the global telecommunication bubble in the early 2000s, foreign capital is not likely to flood the Chinese telecommunication service market in the short term. Yet the pattern is already clear: transnational businesses and high-end domestic Chinese users are the prioritized customers being served by China's globally integrated and increasingly market-driven telecommunication systems.

Furthermore, any celebration of the spectacular explosion of telecommunication in China and its "trickle down" benefits to the low social classes must be squared with the fact that, today, the main difficulty facing China's tens of millions of laid-off and migrant workers—many working in electronic factories making the latest information gadgets—is probably not that they do not have a phone number through which prospective employers can reach them or that they cannot transmit their remittances back to the countryside quickly enough. After all, even the men and women who squat in the open-air labor market to sell their labor power usually sport a mobile phone.[66] The problem, instead, is the lack of jobs and other means of economic sustenance, low wages, and even worse, employers' delinquency in paying wages.[67] As well, because the Internet developed during the period of market liberalization and globalization, transnational integration has been the defining feature in the evolution of this new medium. China's leading commercial portals are all NASDAQ-listed companies, and the accumulation imperative of transnational capital has significantly shaped the development of new communication service markets such as short message services.[68] Apart from American companies, East Asian capital, notably South Korea companies, has also made considerable investment in China's Internet services market, including the rapidly expanding online gaming business.[69]

The Print Media Industry

Although the print media sector has the strongest state socialist legacy and the Chinese press has been tightly guarded, the first U.S.-China business joint venture was actually established in a niche market within this sector. Today, the transnational initiator of this joint venture, International Data Group (IDG), remains one of the most successful foreign investors in China.[70] IDG began its publishing business in 1967 with the launch of *Computerworld* in the United States and has since been at the forefront in the promotion of globalization through information technologies.[71] Rather than going through the propaganda department and directly entering the Chinese mass media market, IDG began targeting the niche market of information technology publications and exploited a fissure in the Chinese bureaucratic structure by finding a business partner with no apparent stake in politics and ideology—the then Fourth Ministry of Machine Building Industry, which was in charge of the electronics industry. By 1998, what was left of this planned economy–era government department had become part of the Ministry of Information Industry. Naturally, it is currently IDG's joint-venture partner.

In March 1980, IDG and its Chinese state partner signed a contract to establish *Computerworld* (*Jisuanji shijie*), a Chinese version of its flagship weekly publication. This was a highly significant contract: even by 2006, it remained the only state-approved joint venture in newspaper publishing, far exceeding the scope of foreign operation in the Chinese media outlined in the WTO accession agreements 20 years afterward. The publication, which has since become China's flagship information technology publication, was an instant success. By the late 1990s, its advertising revenues rivaled leading urban mass circulation newspapers. As the paper's website boasted in 2006:

> As one of the top 10 Chinese newspapers . . . we attract 220,000 subscriptions and a high-quality [*gao suzhi*] royal readership of 1.5 million with more than 260 pages of carefully selected information weekly. . . . [T]he recognition of manufacturers and retailers lead *Computerworld* to control a 50 percent share

of the information commodity advertising market, the sum total of all other similar media outlets [in China].[72]

As the post-Mao leadership made information technology the "key link"[73] in its development strategy, IDG publications made available up-to-date technical information and championed the ideology of globalization through information technologies. *Computerworld*, in particular, provided the right communication product for the right customers at the right time. On the one hand, it served as a perfect advertising vehicle for transnational information technology advertisers eager to sell their products in the Chinese market. On the other hand, it fit in perfectly with the information and cultural needs of a Chinese technocratic elite gearing up to constitute themselves as the party's new social basis and the embodiment of China's "advanced productive force," as Jiang Zemin would later characterize them in his "three represents" thesis. Their job, of course, was to transform the domestic economy around information networks and integrate it with globalized informational capitalism. By 2002, IDG's publishing empire in China encompassed 22 titles, including *Digital Fortune*, which boasts a readership profile of individuals between 25 and 45 years old with "an annual income above 100,000 RMB" and a "global perspective," and *Digital Power*, which again caters to "young, successful people with a higher level of education" who promise to "have considerable spending power and social status."[74] Although these publications do not command the ideological significance of, say, a Chinese version of *Reader's Digest*, their role in integrating the Chinese techno-cultural elite with global informational capitalism has nonetheless been profoundly significant.

Once IDG had established a cozy relationship with the Chinese state and helped to create an information/knowledge-economy-based Chinese "middle social strata" or "middle class" through the provision of technical know-how, consumer- and business-oriented transnational media products quickly followed up by serving this group with consumer advertising and business and lifestyle tips aiming to enfranchise them as the Chinese segment of the affluent transnational business and consumer strata. Since the Chinese state prohibits the independent operation of foreign-owned media outlets in the country and the more sensitive area of news is still off limits, the main means of foreign penetration in the Chinese print media has centered on advertising management and copyright collaborations between Chinese and foreign publishers in business and lifestyle magazines. Typically, a foreign collaborator controls and manages the advertising business of a Chinese magazine. Although this arrangement maintains the appearance of nonforeign involvement in the editorial side of a Chinese publication, the role of advertising in shaping the overall editorial orientation and readership demographics of Chinese publications is of critical importance. Copyright collaboration involves a Chinese magazine's importation of a foreign brand name and the use of foreign magazine content. Apart from IDG, which has served as an effective broker between American and Chinese publishers by collaborating with the Chinese magazine *Trends* (*Shishang*) to publish the Chinese versions of *Cosmopolitan, Esquire, Harper's Bazaar, Cosmo Girl,* and *Good Housekeeping,* France's Hachette Filipacchi Press teamed up with the Shanghai Translation Publishing House to publish the Chinese version of *Elle* as early as 1988, while Time Warner publishes a Chinese version of *Golf.* In fact by 2006, Time Warner had celebrated its flagship *Fortune* magazine's Chinese edition's 10th anniversary. While America's *Playboy* has long expressed an interest in the Chinese market,[75] its British counterparts—"lad mags" *FHM* and *Maxim*—have been just as keen in planning their own Chinese versions.[76] With a typical price of 20 yuan per issue (US$2.50, more than the daily income of an assembly line worker), these magazines, segmented by gender, age, and lifestyle choices, compete ruthlessly for transnational consumer advertising and the same affluent urban middle-class readership. For China's rising business and professional strata, publications such as the *Harvard Business Review* and *Esquire* serve both as useful sources of information and indispensable symbols of class distinction and identity formation. As one domestic journalist wrote, members of the new Chinese bourgeoisie make a fashion statement by placing a copy of the *Harvard Business Review* at their bedsides.[77]

The Chinese consumer, lifestyle, and business magazine market is thus truly transnational and transcultural—that is, transnational consumer culture embellished with various national tastes. Rather than being restricted by a tightly controlled domestic publications regime, China's consuming elites are served with the best of all possible worlds through the magazine industry's flexible cooperation with transnational publishers. *Trends Traveler* (*Shishang lüyou*), for example, has a copyright arrangement with the American-based *National Geographic Traveler* and picture and text exchange cooperation with the French magazine *Guide Moncos* and the Taiwanese magazine *To Go.* The magazine is truly transnational and yet fully localized, a feast of incredibly appealing pictures and narratives catered specifically to the university-educated, high-income, urban, white-collar traveler between 25 and 40. As these magazines help the Chinese consumer elite globalize their lifestyles and connect themselves with their counterparts in Paris, New York, and Tokyo, they also coach them to view China through the transnational tourist gaze and to construct new discursive relationships with fellow Chinese citizens.

Although hard news titles are still not welcome, the number of foreign-integrated magazines is small in comparison with domestic titles, and their circulations are kept low deliberately to maintain their upscale market appeal, these magazines nevertheless account for a lion's share of the Chinese magazine industry's circulation and advertising revenues.[78] At newsstands in major Chinese urban centers, these magazines are systemically privileged over national magazines, threatening to marginalize even the most popular domestic titles. As a Shanghai newsstand operator put it, "Every space on my newsstand means money. I have to make sure that only those magazines that are profitable are displayed on my newsstand. . . . I prefer selling these [foreign-collaborative] magazines because they go very quickly . . . these magazines are usually four or five times more expensive than the others, so I earn more profit by selling them."[79]

These remarks are indicative of the broad impact of glocalized foreign brands on the structure and orientation of the domestic magazine industry. First, domestic publishers without the organizational capital to import foreign brands quickly jumped into the newly cultivated, lucrative consumer and lifestyle magazine market by publishing second-tier imitations of transnational brands. For example, by the late 1990s, the Women of China Press, which publishes the namesake *Women of China* (*Zhongguo funü*) magazine, the organ journal of the All China Women's Federation and the flagship of the official women's liberation movement, had begun to publish the glossy, middle-class women–oriented lifestyle magazine *Hao zhufu* (the "good housewife" in literal Chinese translation, although the magazine only adopted the word "Good" for its English title on the cover). That an indigenous Chinese magazine feels compelled to have an English title on the cover is itself illustrative of the impact of foreign-imported brands and their trend-setting influence.[80] Second, instead of trying to reach potential readers in the lower social strata, domestic magazines, facing increasing competition for the same thin layer of affluent urban consumers, not to mention the allure of the foreign market itself, are attempting to globalize themselves. The popular women's magazine *Women's Friends* (*Nü you*), for example, has made significant progress in overseas expansion. Following the launch of an Australian edition in Sydney in 2001, a North American edition debuted in Vancouver in November 2003, targeting the city's growing community of Chinese-speaking professional and business-class women. The transnational mobility of its founding editor, who immigrated to Canada but returned to China once she acquired a Canadian passport, fits the globalization strategy of both her publisher and the Chinese state perfectly well. Meanwhile, China's hundreds of millions of rural women, who are worthless as consumers to both domestic and transnational capital, are served by a tiny magazine called *Rural Women Knowing All* (*Nongjianü baishitong*), edited by urban feminist Xie Lihua and partially supported by the Ford Foundation.[81] On the one hand, upwardly mobile, young, urban Chinese women, a much sought-after readership group by glocalized magazines, espoused transnational dreams of "working in big American corporations in China and shopping at French specialty stores."[82] On the other hand, some poor rural women, who stay at home to look after the young, the old, the livestock, and the crops in depressed rural villages and who have found their cries lost in a cacophony of one-way mass "communications" that seldom address their immediate needs and concerns, have found death to be their only means of social communication—suicide rates among rural Chinese women are the highest of all population groups in the world.[83] Social and cultural ramifications of uneven access to communicative and cultural resources aside, from the economic perspective, underconsumption by China's vast rural population of 900 million and the urban working class continues to exacerbate the country's crisis of overaccumulation in general, and the Chinese media and cultural market is no exception. The ability of the U.S. culture industry to develop a strong domestic market and enfranchise the diverse immigrant population was crucial to its eventual global expansion and universalistic appeal. In contrast, many branches of the Chinese culture industry have so far not been able to substantively enfranchise China's vast numbers of internal migrants, not to mention the rural population. For example, as of July 2005, cinema chains operating in major metropolitan centers generated about 90 percent of the Chinese film industry's box office revenue.[84] Under the party's new "going global" directive, many media conglomerates and cultural entrepreneurs have stepped up their efforts in reaching a global audience. The American and Chinese difference underscores the changed patterns of social integration between the Fordist and post-Fordist modes of capitalist accumulation.[85] As Arif Dirlik wrote,

> Indeed, while it may be argued that no lives, or aspects of life, remain untouched by the operations of capital, it is also the case that global capitalism no longer seeks to incorporate all within it, but proceeds rather by marginalizing the great majority of the earth's people, who have now become irrelevant to its operations either as producers or consumers.[86]

The Chinese state, while pushing for the Chinese culture industry's global expansion, continues to emphasize national integration and express its commitment to develop a nationally integrated market. For example, the state has made significant investments in communication networks in remote regions, especially in Xinjiang and Tibet. As I discussed in chapter 2, the recent "cultural system reform" program has also begun to recognize the need to increase the culture industry's reach in rural or underdeveloped areas. How this can be achieved remains an open question.

The Broadcasting Industry

Broadcasting, as a result of the state socialist legacy and sustained popularization efforts since the 1980s, is no doubt the most inclusive, though also unevenly accessed, mass media sector in China.[87] However, a similar dynamic of selected foreign entry, upmarket mobility, and outward global expansion has also been unfolding here. Most significantly, Phoenix TV, a Hong Kong–based satellite television joint venture between Murdoch's Star TV and Liu Changle, an overseas Chinese businessman with close connections to the Chinese state, has been providing information and entertainment for an elite Chinese audience since 1997. By March 1998, Phoenix TV Chinese claimed to reach 44.98 million households in China, or 15.9 percent of total Chinese television households.[88] This is no ordinary audience. Rather it is an audience constituted by political, economic, and cultural privileges. Although state regulations prohibit the reception of foreign satellite television by private households, as was the case during the prereform periods, the Chinese elite has been less constrained by such regulations. According to state regulations, Chinese hotels that rank three stars or above and luxurious apartment complexes catering to expatriates and affluent domestic residents are allowed to install dishes to receive foreign satellite transmissions. In addition, major government departments, media, academic, and financial institutions are allowed to install their own satellite dishes. Since most of these institutions have internal cable television systems that wire their offices and living quarters, residents in such exclusive neighborhoods have always been able to receive Phoenix TV and other foreign broadcasters legally. Compared with the average Chinese television audience, the Phoenix audience, as characterized by a Phoenix TV executive, is made up of "three highs and one low"—high official rank, high income, high education level, and low age.[89] As Philip Pan wrote in September 2005, "Phoenix is now the channel of choice for much of China's new elite and perhaps does more to shape its political views than the party's media outlets."[90]

On the one hand, Phoenix TV has refrained from critical reporting on domestic Chinese politics and social issues and has been highly opportunistic on several occasions—for example, by broadcasting an emotionally charged nationalistic concert immediately after NATO's bombing of the Chinese Embassy in Belgrade and by launching a propaganda campaign against Falun Gong immediately after the Chinese state banned the movement. On the other hand, unlike state-controlled media outlets, Phoenix TV can report breaking global news with more immediacy and more freedom. For example, while Chinese state television restricted reporting of the September 11, 2001, terrorist attacks on the United States, Phoenix TV broadcast the event live with its convenient access to U.S.

sources, including footage from News Corporation's Fox TV. In the context of CCTV's failure to provide timely and adequate television footage of the attacks, Phoenix TV became such an attractive alternative that some affluent Chinese booked rooms in luxury hotels in order to watch it. CCTV has to fulfill the party's propaganda orders and it has a lingering socialist obligation to appeal to a broad audience and meet the needs of different social constituents, and to reflect popular concerns by producing investigative journalism that exposes social problems, particularly regarding corrupt rural officials and the plight of Chinese farmers in the country's hinterlands.[91] By contrast, Phoenix TV, while always "walking a fine line" and recognizing that "the political risk is higher with news than with any other kind of programming,"[92] is not constrained by any "extra-market" concerns. Instead, it provides exactly what its upwardly mobile and outward-looking audience is interested in—the latest global news, the latest business, travel, and consumer information, and uplifting light entertainment to match the spirit of China's "winners" of globalization. CCTV was so humiliated and upstaged by Phoenix TV's coverage of the 9/11 terrorist attacks that it felt compelled to launch its 24-hour news channel in time to portray the spectacle of the American invasion of Iraq to win back this increasing vocal and powerful domestic audience.

Based on its initial Chinese channel's successful formula of providing tailored news and current affairs information for China's domestic elite, and attracting not only transnational but also domestic advertisers aiming at a high-end consumer base—as a domestic Chinese news headline reported as early as 1998 in "State Enterprises Rendezvous with Phoenix TV"[93]—Phoenix TV launched an even more specialized InfoNews Channel on January 1, 2001. In the words of Phoenix TV president Liu Changle, this new channel "is targeting those high-end mainland Chinese hungry for international news coverage in Putonghua," contrary to CCTV's focus "on news related to the country and government."[94] This new channel, which avoids the politically more sensitive term *"xinwen"* (news) in mainland Mandarin by using the Hong Kong Mandarin term *"zixun"* (info-news) in its title, gained limited entry into the domestic Chinese market in early 2003. Because it is "one of the few foreign-owned TV broadcasters on the mainland able to broadcast information about events not covered by government media, and because of its relatively affluent viewership and the international outlook of its programming, Phoenix TV has been able to "punch above its weight in the mainland's TV advertising market."[95] By 2004, income from China had accounted for approximately 75 to 80 percent of Phoenix TV's total advertising revenue of HK$1 billion, making it the fourth-largest Mandarin television network, just behind CCTV, Beijing TV, and Shanghai TV. Such an achievement, as Liu was quick to add, was extraordinary, given that "the other broadcasters have over 90 per cent coverage of the population, whereas Phoenix TV only has 18 per cent coverage reaching 50 million to 60 million households in China."[96] Indeed, what matters most is not the "quantity" but the "quality" of the viewers. Although not entirely by its own choice, no other media outlet has done a more spectacular cream-skimming job in the Chinese media market than Phoenix TV.

Although Phoenix TV is by far the most localized, most commercially successful, and most influential foreign-invested television operator reaching the elite Chinese news and current affairs market, other transnational broadcasters have been equally aggressive in trying to cultivate their respective Chinese audience niches. Viacom's MTV, for example, has worked very closely with leading domestic Chinese broadcasters such as CCTV and the SMG to produce youth popular culture targeting "15–34 year-olds and cater[ing] to this group with consumerist values."[97] As is the case with IDG's joint venture in China, here Chinese state authorities "seem to have selected certain national media and bureaucracies and given them special permission to trial collaborative ventures with global capital to create a new youth culture, which combines a sense of Chineseness with a Western modernity stripped of any strong political values."[98] By early 2003, the Chinese state had made available as many as 31 overseas and Hong Kong–based specialty satellite television channels to selected audience markets, including CNN, BBC World Service, HBO, CNBC Asian Pacific, Bloomberg Asian Pacific, ESPN, MTV Mandarin, and Discovery. The officially approved cable landing of Phoenix TV Chinese and InfoNews channels, Sun TV, Star TV's Mandarin entertainment channel, and Time Warner's China Entertainment Television (CETV, Time Warner later sold its controlling share to Tom.com, a Hong Kong firm controlled by billionaire Li Ka-shing) in the Pearl River delta has further expanded the access of foreign- and Hong Kong–invested television channels. Rapid urban residential developments and the unfolding process of digital cable transition may provide further opportunities for uneven access to these exclusive channels. At the same time, as is the case with domestic trade and lifestyle magazines, China's market-driven and content-starved domestic television channels have been eager to translate and repackage foreign content, from documentaries on the Discovery Channel to cartoons on Nickelodeon. Consequently, a highly commercialized domestic communication system that is already skewed toward the affluent social strata in the coastal regions is facing further upmarket pressures. Perhaps not surprisingly within this context, CCTV decided to marginalize its rural channel and abandon its western channel, as discussed in chapter 2. The pressures of global competition have forced it to prioritize services to high-end domestic audiences, such as 24-hour news and financial reports, and to overseas audiences, even if it means trading foreign access to the domestic market—for example, in 2001 China allowed Time Warner's CETV and News Corporation's *Xingkong Weishi* access to the Guangdong market in exchange for the two media conglomerates' agreement to carry CCTV's overseas English-language channel, CCTV9, in their U.S. cable systems.

The Film Industry

Hollywood had a significant presence in the Chinese film market before 1949. The Maoist regime not only ended Hollywood's fortunes in China, but also developed a strong indigenous film industry. In the early 1980s, Chinese films enjoyed enormous popularity, but as the "reform and openness" process deepened, a number of factors—political control, underinvestment, competition from commercialized state television, and drastic social stratification and audience/market fragmentation—combined to undermine the viability of the domestic film industry. By the late 1980s, the term "crisis" had entered the domestic discourse on the state of the film industry.[99] Annual attendance at theaters dropped from 21 billion in 1982 to just under 4.5 billion in 1991.[100]

Hollywood, meanwhile, tried to reenter the Chinese market as soon as U.S.-China diplomatic relations were restored in 1979. Chinese audiences, isolated from Hollywood for nearly 30 years, necessarily had some catching up to do. Hollywood's reentry into China thus began with public screenings, especially on state television, of cheap Hollywood classics, with Rupert Murdoch's 20th Century Fox playing a leading role in supplying them. By 1985, when the Hollywood blockbuster *Rambo: First Blood* was released in China and caused a sensation, China's reengagement with Hollywood had already intensified significantly. By 1994, under the double pressure of Hollywood and the distribution and exhibition arms of the domestic film industry to boost revenue, China had decided to accept an annual importation of 10 first-run international blockbusters on a box office revenue–sharing basis. Driven by profit considerations and the sensibilities of affluent urban viewers, who had come to regard seeing the latest Hollywood blockbusters as part of their global cultural citizenship entitlement, the state-controlled film distributor and cinemas, as well as the mass media, enthusiastically promoted Hollywood movies, while ignoring domestic productions. In 1995, the "most glorious year" for the Chinese film box office thanks to Hollywood imports, more than 70 domestic films were denied distribution to theaters.[101] By 1998, when the Hollywood blockbuster *Titanic* garnered a record one-quarter of the year's total Chinese box office revenue, domestic Chinese production, which had ranged between 100 to 130 films annually since the 1980s, had dropped to a record low of 37. The prestigious Xi'an Film Studio had had to lay off more than 10 percent of its workforce.[102]

In response, more entrepreneurial Chinese filmmakers, in an attempt to secure commercial success and circumvent political control, not only gradually adopted Hollywood narrative styles, formulas, and business models, but also increasingly looked to the global market. The success of filmmakers such as Chen Kaige and Zhang Yimou on the major international film awards circuits in the 1980s and early 1990s, and their inclusion in the "foreign" section of major North American video rental chains, signaled the beginning of the selective incorporation of a Chinese filmmaking elite into an American-dominated global film industry that was becoming increasingly multicultural. Over time, these filmmakers have gained at least partial autonomy from the domestic film infrastructure and garnered the support of transnational investors and distributors. In this way, they constitute themselves as the Chinese representatives of the transitionally integrated cultural elite.

One must understand the significance of China's WTO accession provisions regarding the film industry within this context. Although the audiovisual sector was excluded from the final General Agreement on Tariffs and Trade (GATT) that created the WTO, the powerful Hollywood lobby secured major gains through the bilateral U.S.-China WTO agreement that took effect in 2001. Under the agreement, China committed to quadruple film imports to 40 films per year upon accession. The number had increased to 50 by 2005, of which 20 would be first-run Hollywood blockbuster movies. It reduced tariffs on audiovisual imports, opened up its consumer market for audiovisual products to foreign distributors, and most importantly, allowed foreign investors to own up to a 49 percent share in companies that build, own, and operate cinemas in China. A full-scale restructuring of the film industry in China—from production to distribution, exhibition, and consumption—has been under way since China's entry into the WTO. Major transnational entertainment conglomerates such as News Corporation and Time Warner have teamed up with domestic Chinese partners to establish production facilities and revamp the Chinese cinema infrastructure. The interests of various players in the Chinese film industry are now increasingly linked to transnational capital. The post-WTO liberalization of film distribution and exhibition markets has also put pressure on the Chinese state to increase coproductions and import quotas. The top executive of a newly established film distribution firm, for example, called for—as early as 2003—an increase in film import quotas and the reclassification of Hong Kong and Taiwanese films as "domestic productions" so as to increase the number of Hollywood imports.[103]

The pattern of integration between the Chinese film industry and Hollywood suggests that any notion that China can achieve success "all its own" is probably far fetched. Rupert Murdoch, whose investments in China range from audiovisual production to Internet websites, in all likelihood knew this well when he lectured party leaders in Beijing. Indeed, perhaps what was most significant was not what he said, but the very fact of his lecturing to the Chinese leadership: it signified the emergence of a new form of alliance between transnational capitalists and China's ruling political economic and cultural elite.

Zhang Yimou's 2002 Hollywood-style martial arts blockbuster *Hero*, widely hailed in both Chinese and global media as China's response to American cultural imperialism, perhaps best exemplifies such a new form of globally coordinated political, ideological, and business power or, more precisely, "the spirit and structure"[104] of transnational capitalism in the post-9/11 world. The "spirit" of *Hero*—its fascist thematic and aesthetic orientations—not only pays tribute to the party's political authoritarianism,[105] but also resonates with the dominant logic of neoliberal globalization.[106] The film, which had started shooting a month before the 9/11 terrorist attacks on the United States, was opportunistically rearticulated by Zhang Yimou and his production and marketing crew to address the topic of global peace, with producer Zhang Weiping adding a personalized touch from the perspective of the globalized movie star Zhang Ziyi, who played the role of Ming Yue in the movie: "Ziyi is often in the United States. She has a unique perspective on this issue. She said that *Hero* will rally and uplift the national spirit of the American people and that the American people currently need myths about heroes."[107] In this way, Emperor Qin's notion of imperial peace achieved through war was rearticulated with the ideology of the war on terrorism,[108] and Zhang Yimou, who had previously established himself by telling national myths of a third world country, reoriented his film to promote the logic of imperial domination with the self-righteousness and hegemonic intentions of the powerful. As Chinese cultural critic Zhang Yiwu put it, with the deepening of globalization and China's rapid economic growth, parts of the Chinese imaginary have become more and more detached from the original "third world" narrative that has defined the cultural imaginaries of Chinese modernity, and this is precisely the new global dimension in the "spirit" of *Hero*.[109]

On the business side, the film is a tribute to both the globalizing strategies of Hollywood majors and the global ambitions of Chinese cultural entrepreneurs. This US$31 million project was backed by Walt Disney's Miramax Films, which purchased its distribution rights in North America, Australia, New Zealand, the United Kingdom, Italy, Latin America, and Africa in advance for US$22 million. The film was coproduced by the Beijing New Picture Film Co., a private Chinese film company, and a Hong Kong–based company led by Bill Kong, who gained global commercial success by producing *Crouching Tiger, Hidden Dragon* for Sony Pictures. The marketing machine for the film, molded after the Hollywood boilerplate, was not only unprecedented in the history of the Chinese movie industry in its scope and depth, but also in its synergistic articulation with the consuming priorities and cultural sensibilities of its targeted domestic audience—the winners, or heroes, of neoliberal globalization. A mobile phone promotional tie-in, for example, effectively flattered the targeted upscale urban filmgoers who are potential users of the Internet-enabled, super-expensive mobile phone Dopod 688, "the hero of mobile phones."[110] This crowning of film viewers/high-end mobile phone users with a heroic status overlaps nicely with the "net hero" or "knowledge hero" status of the readers of IDG's Chinese publications. Like *Hero*, which was framed as a national champion to conquer the global market, China's transnationally integrated information elite have been entrusted with a technonationalist agenda of developing China's information industries.

While the Chinese and global media celebrate the film as a "Chinese" and "Asian" success for political and marketing reasons, once again the transnational dimensions of *Hero* should be underscored. After all, it drew upon Hollywood capital, business practices, as well as managerial and star power and was created with the global market in mind. Consequently, the question "whose hero?" is indeed highly pertinent.[111] As Stanley Rosen observed in early 2003, Hollywood has accelerated its efforts to co-opt Chinese filmmakers who demonstrate commercial potential since the international success of *Crouching Tiger, Hidden Dragon*. As China's national film industry becomes increasingly transnational, purely domestic productions with no transnational appeal "may be doomed" by playing to mostly empty theatres.[112]

Thus, as "China goes Hollywood" by reshaping its film industry and incorporating Hollywood financial and cultural capital as well as its business practices and narrative styles, Hollywood incorporates China into "global Hollywood" and its new international division of cultural labor[113] for its cultural resources, cheap production costs, and potential market. Although *Hero* appears triumphant in China, it says little about the autonomy of the Chinese film industry. Instead, *Hero* testifies to the triumph of the Hollywood-style commercial mode of film production in China. In short, if one takes the commercial logic for granted and sticks to a nation-state framework of analysis, then the triumphant rise of *Hero* and subsequent big-budget, transnational capital–funded, high-tech, and intensively promoted globalized Chinese productions such as Zhang Yimou's *House of Flying Daggers* and Chen Kaige's *The Promise* is significant. But if one takes issue with the very spread of the commercial logic in cultural production, then the "Chineseness" of these films underscores the success of the capitalist culture industry on a global scale. Similarly, while *Hero* does embody one particular interpretation of Chinese history and culture, it is one viewed from the perspective of the rulers and the co-opted, and one that erases the very appearance, not to mention the perspective, of the ruled, including that of Meng Jiangnü, a legendary provincial woman who traveled a great distance to deliver warm clothing to her husband, who was drafted by Emperor Qin to build the Great Wall, and cried so hard over news about her husband's death that the Great Wall collapsed in response. By late 2005, as even the restructured Chinese film industry's narrowly focused domestic urban audience had begun to ridicule the unfulfilled promise of Chen Kaige's ambitious Warner Independent Pictures–backed film *The Promise* as an entertaining commodity—by widely circulating and cheering a 20-minute Internet video parody of the movie by self-employed multimedia editor Hu Ge, entitled *A Bloody Case That Was Started by a Steamed Bun* (*Yige mantou yingfa de xue'an*)[114]—the Chinese cultural elite's pursuit of global reintegration in the communication and culture industry seemed to have reached a critical moment: reintegration has not only failed to deliver the promise of the market but also, more importantly, has rendered itself increasingly irrelevant to internal class and cultural politics, especially the complicated intersections between class and nationalistic politics in China. I turn to these issues in the next section.

CLASS, NATION, AND THE CONTAINMENT
OF POPULAR NATIONALISTIC DISCOURSES

The Chinese communication industry's incorporation of foreign capital or the expansion of this sector as a component of the penetration of China by transnational capital mostly serves transnational class interests, which are shared by a small fraction of the Chinese population. If anything, this tends to aggravate the political economic and cultural contradictions of China's rearticulation with an American-dominated global capitalism. If the communication and culture industry has been a pivotal venue for China's global reintegration and a central axis of transnational class formation, it is also within and through this realm that the resistances to, and the political economic and cultural contradictions of, neoliberal globalization have manifested themselves in China.

On the one hand, the Chinese state expresses continued commitments to national development and resisting subordination to global capitalism. On the other hand, to create a foreign investment–friendly environment and to gain the favorable international conditions for its economic development, the Chinese state long followed Deng Xiaoping's dictum of *taoguang yanghui* in its dealings with the dominant powers in the current global order. This dictum posits that one must hide one's brightness or lay low in order to earn the time to accumulate the necessary strength for eventual greatness. In this way, the Chinese state justifies its retreat from the Maoist anti-imperialist agenda as a strategic move. During this process, however, China's political, economic, and cultural elites have developed extensive transnational linkages, potentially constituting themselves as the Chinese segment of "the transnational capitalist class."[115]

Exemplified by Zhang Yimou's reliance on the Chinese state to clear censorship for his films and to enforce an antipiracy regime and his service to the state *both* as an official propagandist (by directing the Chinese state's globalist projects such as the 2008 Beijing Olympics and Shanghai's 2010 Expo bids) and as a delegate to the National People's Political Consultative Conference (NPPCC), China's transnationally integrated elite is closely intertwined with the Chinese state, relying heavily on its integrationist strategy to sustain their privileged position within the globalizing Chinese political economy. To sustain a foreign direct investment–led and export-oriented pattern of economic growth, the Chinese state has long adopted macroeconomic policies that help sustain U.S. consumerism and militarism, including the massive purchasing of U.S. Treasury bonds.[116] At the same time, it has been slow to enact substantive social reforms to boost domestic consumption and secure social peace. Many members of the Chinese political and business elite, meanwhile, have responded to state attempts to curb their excesses (through anticorruption campaigns, for example) by voting with their feet—obtaining foreign passports and sending their wealth and families abroad. The staggering volume of capital flight and the massive exodus of private entrepreneurs, government officials, and members of their families to the United States, Canada, Australia, and other countries through immigrant and student visas, as well as the phenomenon of government officials absconding with huge amounts of financial assets to foreign countries, is thus the other side of the story of the FDI-driven and export-oriented Chinese "economic miracle."[117] The flip side of this dimension of transnational class formation is the export of Chinese workers as "indentured labor abroad" by government bureaucracies and the flight of tens of thousands of Chinese farmers to the West through dangerous international human trafficking networks and their enslavement in the sweatshops in New York, Los Angeles, and other global cities.[118]

Transnationality has thus become an increasingly important aspect of class reconstitution in a globally reintegrated China, where the most important divisions are "not those of East or West, or Chinese and foreign, but new divisions along lines of generation, class, and region, with different access to power, wealth, and knowledge, and different relationships to the forces of globalization."[119] In turn, this has led to complicated articulations of nationalist, class, regional, and generational politics. On the one hand, a hegemonic bloc consisting of transnational capitalists, foreign state managers and policy makers, globalizing Chinese political, economic, and cultural elites, and the urban-based "middle class" whose members are the preferred customers of both domestic and transnational capital is assuming a dominant position in Chinese media and culture.[120] The containment of social conflicts, the suppression of class discourse, the orchestrating of a state-centered mix of developmental and cultural nationalisms, and the cultivation of consumerism, tempered by "middle-class" reformism ("caring for the socially vulnerable") mixed with a dose of socialist rhetoric, constitute the official agenda of Chinese media and culture. As I emphasized at the beginning of chapter 1, the Chinese state and the official media actively instigated nationalism at the onset of the reform process through the border war with Vietnam. Since then, a "state-led pragmatic nationalism," which emphasizes "the instrumentality of nationalism for rallying support in the name of building a modern Chinese nation-state"[121] through strategic cooperation with the United States under the new foreign policy doctrine of "great power cooperation,"[122] has dominated elite media discussions of foreign affairs.

On the other hand, because the party has not explicitly denounced its anti-imperialist legacy, nationalism as an official discourse of domestic political legitimation and the dominant foreign policy position of accommodating American global hegemony have always coexisted in tension with a more radical discourse of nationalism as a liberational and oppositional force against an unjust global order and the party leadership's wariness against outside efforts at "Westernizing" and "disintegrating" China. Consequently, official nationalism and the party's foreign policies have been consistently contested in popular nationalistic discourses, especially leftist nationalist discourses on the Internet.

As Peter Hays Gries has noted, the mainstream Western view of Chinese nationalism as party propaganda generated by the party elite for its own instrumental purpose is not wrong, but "it is incomplete" and it risks "dangerously trivializing the roles that the Chinese people and their emotions play in Chinese nationalism."[123] In fact, nationalism in the reform era is not a uniquely top-down phenomenon. The nationalistic impulse of "saving the nation" was a pivotal motivational force of the student movement in 1989, serving as the key link connecting the anti-imperialistic May 4 Movement in 1919 and the anti-NATO protests of 1999.[124]

The rise of various strands of popular nationalistic discourses since the 1990s has both internal and external conditions, as well as historical and contemporary dimensions, which are quite different from the official rationale of ideological legitimation. As Zhou Yongming has argued, we must "pay sufficient attention to the role of human agency" and acknowledge that Chinese nationalists are not merely subjects who submit to "external" factors passively.[125] In the context of an increasingly commercialized and globalized Chinese media system and a rapidly expanding Chinese cyberspace, popular nationalistic sentiments against the perceived imperialistic behaviors of China's global and regional rivals, the United States and Japan, have erupted frequently since the late 1990s.[126]

As Dai Jinhua has observed, the pseudo-binary discourses of Sinocentrism and Americanization coexist and feed into each other in contemporary China.[127] Dai's observation cautions against any simple conclusion about the necessarily oppositional nature of popular nationalistic sentiments. Nevertheless, popular nationalism's independent existence underscores a tension between the party's anti-imperialist historical legacy and its current accommodation with U.S.-led global capitalism. Popular nationalists perceive the Chinese state to be compromising Chinese territorial sovereignty and the principle of international justice in the single-minded pursuit of economic development, and they have routinely charged the dominant foreign policy elite with being naive and soft in dealing with the United States and Japan throughout the 1980s and 1990s.[128] Moreover, contrary to the Western media image of ignorant and xenophobic young Chinese manipulated by the party, online Chinese nationalists are well informed about the outside world, and "the more informed Chinese are, the more nationalist they may be."[129]

Chinese nationalism is a complicated, fluid, and multifaceted phenomenon.[130] Some strands of Chinese nationalism likely express chauvinistic or xenophobic tendencies and reflect "an arrogant overconfidence in the overprivileged" in response to China's economic ascendancy.[131] Chinese critiques of American imperialism have often been advanced from the perspective of the "national interests" of an aspiring nation aiming to achieve more parity in global power relations, that is, within a realist, or what Zhou Yongming identified as a "de-ideologized," paradigm defined by the concepts of "comprehensive national power," "national interests," and "the rule of the game," meaning that "China has no choice but to accept the existing world system and play according to the rules, but that it can increase its status . . . try to revise the rules (because of their innate inequity), and even become one of the rule setters (for the purpose of pursuing national interests)."[132] However, there is also an internationalist critique of unequal global power relations anchored in the concerns of domestic social classes disadvantaged by neoliberal globalization.

A brief contrast between two best sellers in the late 1990s is illustrative here. Chinese nationalism was historically intertwined with the communist revolution and was expressed in the dual discourse of anticapitalism and anti-imperialism. With the party's de facto abandonment of this dual discourse, jingoistic anti-U.S. and anti-Japanese sentiments became dominant in the mid-1990s, expressed most evidently in the 1996 best seller *China Can Say No (Zhongguo keyi shuobu)*. Instead of championing the principles of global justice and equality, this nationalism, consistent with the "de-ideologized paradigm," is primarily concerned with Chinese national sovereignty and "China's acquisition of overseas markets, resources, and even survival space" in the course of the country's national development.[133] As such, it is also consistent with the right-wing ideology of neo-authoritarianism, limiting itself to championing China's national self-interests in a neoliberal global order.[134]

As China is dragged further into the global market system and as the social costs of neoliberal globalization borne by the lower social classes become increasingly evident and, moreover, as the political economic contradictions of global capitalism further unravel themselves in front of Chinese eyes—from the "Asian" financial crisis to NATO's bombing of Yugoslavia—one witnesses the rearticulation of left-wing popular nationalisms that are democratic and utopian. Drawing their intellectual inspirations from the party's anticapitalist and anti-imperialist legacy, these are popular nationalisms that "the government could neither associate with nor claim to speak for."[135]

This intellectual development can be best seen in *China's Pathway under the Shadow of Globalization* (*Quanqiuhua yinying xiade Zhongguo zhilu*), a popular book from 1999 written by some of the same young authors who had contributed to *China Can Say No*.[136] Instead of simply appealing to jingoistic anti-Americanism, *China's Pathway* contains a sophisticated critique of the international political economy from neo-Marxist and postcolonial perspectives. Appropriating Chinese neoliberals' favorite Western intellectual source, Frederic Hayek, and applying his ideas to a global context, the book argues that the domination of international capital could lead to a new authoritarian global order and a "new road to serfdom."[137] Moreover, *China's Pathway* does not shy away from class analysis, and it does not operate with a simplistic China versus the United States nationalistic framework. It points out the collusion of domestic political, economic, and intellectual elites with global capitalism. Instead of being caught in the "catching up with the West" developmental nationalist discourse, the book demonstrates a sharp understanding of the logic of uneven development within global capitalism and clearly allies itself with the global disenfranchised. Most importantly, the book attacks the false dichotomy between democracy and nationalism and argues that popular democracy must be the basis of nationalism. Operating under the premise that "a nationalism that is devoid of democracy is very likely false," the book argues, "If we have no rights to control these ['national industries'], we have no necessity to protect them. . . . If citizens have no right to contain the rights of the ruling elite, nationalism, including economic nationalism, may very well be false and a pretense for some people to pursue private interests."[138] Consequently, the book advocates a political reform program to curtail corruption and empower the democratic participation of subordinate social classes. Not surprisingly, the book, completed just as the Chinese government reopened the WTO accession negotiations with the United States in 1999, had a hard time finding a publisher and then failed to get reviews in the mainstream media.[139] In short, one must distinguish between right-wing and left-wing popular nationalistic sentiments, just as one must not "dismiss popular Chinese leftism as a mere expression of *rightwing* Chinese nationalism."[140]

As the *New York Times* had come to realize in a March 30, 2003, editorial, "If a free, uncensored press ever arrived in the Arab world, many Americans will be shocked by what it says."[141] The same may also be said about the Chinese media. Pro-U.S. intellectuals, for example, expressed dismay that the overwhelming majority of Chinese people surrounding them—from young faculty members lecturing to cheering university students to workers on the streets—were critical of American foreign policies and saw the terrorist attacks on 9/11 as a blowback from these policies.[142] If the Chinese media were truly free, presumably they would more openly reflect such a majority view. Nor should one simply assume that privately owned media would necessarily cultivate a desired pro-Western version of "individualistic libertarian nationalism" rather than "collectivistic-authoritarian nationalism."[143] Perhaps the Japanese case is comparable in historical terms. According to James Hoffman's research into the convergence of populist and nationalist discourses in the Japanese commercial press under Meiji Japan at the dawn of the 20th century, private and market-driven papers were more aggressive in stimulating imperialistic nationalism than the government was in the debates leading to the Russo-Japanese War.[144]

A similar dynamic is evolving in China, where popular nationalism contains both right-wing and left-wing tendencies. Market-oriented popular newspapers such as *Global Times* (*Huanqiu shibao*), a subsidiary of the *People's Daily*, have not only been more open than the official party organs in reporting international issues, but have also tended to foreground the conflict angle between the United States and its allies on the one side and China and other countries on the other. In the words of Tiananmen activist Liu Xiaobo, China's market-oriented media are profiting from "jingoism": "Prevented from criticizing the country's leaders and reporting fully and objectively on domestic affairs, China's media often find it expedient to turn their critical gaze outward. . . . Publishing jingoistic, anti-foreign articles played to national sensitivities that always simmer, and thus could easily be brought to a boil, with obvious benefits for the bottom line."[145] The partial nature of this explanation, of course, becomes self-evident when one realizes that the Internet—the most transnationalized, least commercialized, and freest corner of the Chinese communication system—has been the most articulative of popular nationalistic and anti-imperialist sentiments. Zhang Siqi, a Shanghai-based liberal intellectual, wrote painfully in the aftermath of the anti-Japanese protests in Shanghai in April 2005: it is simply wrong for Western observers to assume that "the masses in communist countries necessarily stand with the West in opposition against domestic tyrannical regimes. . . . Instead, the masses are the active supporters of the government's nationalistic policies."[146] Zhang further observed, "Even more difficult to accept, precisely because of its opportunistic nature, the Communist Party only makes use of nationalism [opportunistically] rather than pursue an all-out nationalist position. It thus still has the motivation to contain popular nationalism. If true nationalists were in power, China could be another Nazi Germany."[147]

Notwithstanding the equation of nationalism with right-wing nationalism in the above quote, the statement underscores the fact that the party, while continuing to champion its own version of nationalism on the one hand, faces a daunting task in containing popular nationalistic discourses on the other. Thus, while it entrusts Phoenix TV to bring international news to elite audiences and to articulate their ideological and cultural sensibilities, it relies on censorship of domestic media, including the Internet, to contain popular nationalistic discourses. Censorship not only controls extremist comments, but also news reporting of key facts that the Chinese state fears may provoke popular protests against its dealings with the United States and Japan. For example, the Chinese state censored news reporting of its $2.87 million compensation payment to the United States for damage inflicted on U.S. diplomatic property in China by anti-American demonstrations in 1999,[148] and it censored news reporting as well as Internet discussion of the "bugged plane incident"—when bugging devices were found in a Boeing 767 jet delivered from the United States and due to serve as the official aircraft of Chinese president Jiang Zemin in January 2002.[149] Similarly, the Chinese state's policy of downplaying Sino-Japanese conflicts in the media has been consistent since the mid-1990s, as noted by Suisheng Zhao,[150] and is testified to by the party's detailed censorship guidelines regarding the media's handling of issues related to Japan between 2003 and 2004, as discussed in chapter 1. In October 2004, Zhao Qizheng, head of China's State Council Information Office, openly resorted to the state's censorship power to appease Japan, promising, "There will be no anti-Japanese reporting by major news organizations."[151]

But the Chinese state risks losing its own legitimacy by censoring news about unfavorable U.S. and Japanese foreign policy developments. Moreover, growing transnational information flows have made it increasingly difficult to block Chinese nationalists from connecting up with international developments and with each other both inside and outside Chinese borders.[152] In March 2005, Chinese websites such as Sina.com started their online petition activities against the Japanese bid for a permanent UN Security Council seat by following the actions of overseas Chinese groups. Although the media were not allowed to print anti-Japanese reports at will, national media transmission of official Xinhua stories about the government's protests against Japanese textbooks and its opposition to Japanese membership in the UN Security Council, together with nationally televised news about anti-Japanese protests in Korea from April 6 to April 8, 2005, provided the official media environment for popular nationalists to take to the streets on Saturday, April 9, 2005, leading to unprecedented waves of anti-Japanese protests in nearly 40 cities. Although mainstream Western and overseas Chinese media tended to portray these protests as being manipulated by the Chinese state, and the party leadership may well have "played with fire" by manipulating popular nationalism for foreign policy objectives,[153] as Jeffery N. Wasserstrom wrote in the context of the 1999 anti-NATO protests: "The divide between 'spontaneous' and 'orchestrated' demonstrations is often fuzzy, and the two sorts of events not only can look a great deal alike to outsiders but feel very similar to those taking part."[154]

Although the banning of domestic media and Internet coverage of these protests was clear for the world to see, as *New York Times* reporter Jim Yardley wrote, "It hardly mattered. An underground conversation was raging via e-mail, text messages and instant online messaging that inflamed public opinion and served as an organizing tool for protesters. The underground noise grew so loud that . . . the Chinese government moved to silence it by banning the use of text messages or e-mail to organize protests."[155] A full-scale mobilization of state apparatuses that combined media persuasion (pleading for the channeling of such spirit into nation building, stressing the primacy of political stability, and highlighting reconciliatory remarks by the Japanese side while downplaying the Japanese demand for a Chinese apology and compensation for the violent protests) with intimidation (including a hard-line editorial from Shanghai's *Liberation Daily* condemning the law-breaking nature of the protests and warning against the potential political manipulation of the protests, nationally televised news featuring the arrests of some violent protesters, and the police raid of a leading nongovernmental nationalistic organization's headquarters), as well as the massive deployment of police forces, prevented the further outbreak of protests on the historic date of May 4—the anniversary of China's modern nationalistic movement against imperialism.

In short, commercialized media outlets, the Internet, and mobile phones—the fruits of China's market reforms and the very means of China's global reintegration—have also become the channels by which the most globalized segment of the Chinese population, namely, educated

urban youths, expresses the multifaceted discourse of Chinese nationalism. Although it may hold true that "for the government, incidents of urban students abusing foreigners are far less threatening and more con-
trollable than those of peasants beating up police in impoverished
villages,"[156] Chinese popular nationalism may potentially be a dangerous
force for China's ruling political class and for transnational capitalism,
which values the cheap labor and a stable accumulation environment
guaranteed by a repressive state. Because nationalism grows out of interactions with other nations and the global political economy, how Chinese
popular nationalism evolves will be inextricably linked to China's foreign
policy environment, especially American and Japanese policies toward
China, and these states may not be able to depend on the Chinese state's
continuing ability to suppress Chinese nationalistic sentiments in the long
term. Suisheng Zhao has gone so far as to say that "it is very possible that
if the Chinese people should repudiate the communist government of
China, it could be for nationalist reasons after a conspicuous failure of the
government's program of national construction or after the people of
China conclude that the government's foreign policies run counter to the
national interest."[157]

Yet "the Chinese people" are socially divided and "the national interest" cannot be taken for granted. The reemergence of nationalistic consciousnesses has gone hand in hand with the revival of grassroots leftist
discourses among displaced workers and farmers. Extreme forms of opposition to global capitalism have included violent attacks against Western businesspeople and even bombings of symbols of transnational capitalism such as McDonald's shortly after China's WTO entry in 2001. Jiang
Xueqin, a freelance Canadian journalist, wrote about the mixing of anti-
imperialist and anticapitalist sensibilities among some of China's disenfranchised workers:

> Contrary to Western perceptions that the common people are benefiting from
> the free market, the Chinese see their government and the nation's elite as
> conspiring to sell them out to imperialists, a.k.a. the Americans. Frustrations
> with the government's economic policies are now entwined with rapidly ex-
> panding anti-Western sentiments. . . . Once again chanting "Long Live Chair-
> man Mao," they [the workers] see foreign investors stealing China's wealth,
> China's rich mingling freely with expatriate businessmen and China's elite
> sending their children and cash to the United States.[158]

Written under the pen name of "Large Scale Unemployment," one Internet posting further articulated the nature of China's global reintegration in sharp structural terms: "The reason Chinese leaders were willing
to sacrifice China's economic future by joining the WTO was political: it
ensured the support of overseas Chinese capital, American banks, and

transnational corporations, accelerated China's transformation into capitalism, and strengthened the position of these leaders among the Chinese elites."[159]

In April 2005, nationalistic outbursts and working-class struggles were coming dangerously close to each other. As tens of thousands of Chinese students and citizens waged anti-Japanese protests in major cities, including Shenzhen, more than 10,000 workers at Uniden Electronics, a Japanese-owned factory in Shenzhen that makes cordless phones for Wal-Mart, started a strike against Japanese management for refusing to allow them to unionize, for dismissing fellow workers who had organized a strike in November 2004, and to demand improved working conditions. By April 20, 2005, the Shenzhen government, fearing the spread of the protests outside the factory walls, had to deploy a massive riot-police force to prevent the striking workers, mostly migrant women, from inspiring another wave of broader anti-Japanese protests in the city.[160] The *China Labour Bulletin* wrote,

> The present strike, following on the heels of walkouts on November 29 and December 10, 2004, contains echoes of the strikes directed at Japanese enterprises that exploded in the 1920s fuelling nationalist and revolutionary movements. It also evokes the Chinese government's worst fears during the 1989 movement upsurge: that workers might join the protests on the side of students and intellectuals.[161]

By late 2005, as part of the coalition between old communists in their eighties and nineties, middle-aged displaced workers, and youthful netizens on the Internet, leftist nationalistic oppositions against the party's accommodation with the U.S.-led neoliberal global order had reached a new height in response to a November 25, 2005, *People's Daily* Overseas Edition article by Zheng Bijian about the directions of the party in the 21st century, the tone of which was set by an essay by Han Xiya and Ma Bin, two "old leftists" within the party.[162] In his article, Zheng, the party leadership's key foreign policy strategist and director-general of the Forum on China's Reform and Opening-up, nominally a nongovernmental organization, intended to deflect U.S. right-wing fear of China's rising, reaffirm the leadership's commitment to neoliberal globalization, and accommodate, rather than challenge, the current U.S.-dominated global order. Zheng states,

> There is no doubt that economic globalization has helped China improve itself through peaceful means. The CPC has no disposition to challenge the existing international order. . . . Economic globalization has offered necessary international resources to China's modernization drive. Through the market flow elements of production making it unnecessary to seize other countries' resources by way of territorial expansion and contesting for colonies.[163]

Among other points of contention, the two leftists attack Zheng's article for capitulating to U.S. global hegemony, misrepresenting the harsh reality of neoliberal globalization for China's low social classes (rather than a China that rides triumphantly on neoliberal economic globalization, "China's vast laboring people made pitiful and painful sacrifices for this economic globalization"), naively and misleadingly glorifying the magic of the market in allocating resources ("even children know that America's invasion of Iraq has something to do with oil"), internalizing the logic of colonialism ("if neoliberal globalization fails and if the rest of the world does not embrace it, then even China will resort to colonialism to plunder resources elsewhere"), erasing history and opportunistically appealing to Chinese cultural values such as "harmony," and single-handedly changing the party's highest ideals of realizing communism to maintaining sovereignty and realizing development and modernization (if so, what distinguishes the Chinese Communist Party from bourgeois parties that share the same objectives in other countries?). In short, for the duo, Zheng's article was written "for U.S. imperialism" with the hope that American leaders would like a Communist Party of China that "is now pleased to be a responsible, interest-bound, formal member of the U.S.-dominated global system and will strive to maintain it with the United States."[164]

Han and Ma's article not only denounces the illegitimacy of Zheng as a private individual in declaring the future directions of the party (shouldn't this be done by the party's national congress?) and thus poses an implicit challenge against the undemocratic nature of the party, whose leadership may have endorsed the publication of Zheng's article, but also contends that Zheng's announcement represents a "class power" (*jieji liliang*) of vested interest groups. Also evident in Han and Ma's article is a professed solidarity with the opposition against neoliberal globalization in the Global South and a charge against the party's betrayal of its constitutionally confessed principles of opposing imperialism and "hegemony" and supporting the struggle for national independence and economic justice by developing countries. Consequently, the leftist website Mao Zedong Flag, which first published the article on February 2, 2006, and provoked wide discussion on the Internet, was temporarily shut down by the authorities between late February and March 2006, together with the closure of the three leftist websites discussed in chapter 1.

CONCLUSION

China's reintegration with global capitalism within and through the communication and culture realm has profound domestic and global implications. To be sure, the overall scope of transnational media operation in

China is rather limited as a portion of their overall business volume.[165] Moreover, the process is not a smooth one. Time Warner's divestment from the CETV venture in 2003, for example, was a sign that transnational corporations, especially some of the monoliths, had quickly realized that they had overextended themselves and that there were no quick results in China. As a Reuters report concluded in June 2006, "turning China's 1.3 billion pairs of eyes into the world's top viewing audience is proving tough work for the world's major media firms, which are finding that big numbers do not always translate into billions of dollars."[166]

The highly fluid nature of communication and cultural markets also means that companies must constantly adjust their investment strategies. In June 2006, in light of a slowdown in the growth of Phoenix TV's advertising revenue, Rupert Murdoch's Star TV sold nearly 20 percent of its 37.5 percent stakes in Phoenix TV to China Mobile. The strategic alliance, a perfect marriage between the Chinese elite's leading news and mobile phone providers, gives China Mobile "preferential access to Phoenix's news and selected programs" to develop mobile video services for 3G mobile phone users, while allowing Phoenix TV to supplement its advertising revenue with program licensing as well as "access to China Mobile's network and customer base on favorable terms."[167] In this way, Phoenix TV is posited to take the strategy of cream-skimming to a new height.

For its part, the Chinese state has also entered into a more cautious consolidation mode, after having significantly enlarged the scope of foreign penetration in the first few years of its WTO accession. Reflective of the lingering relevance of the leadership's understanding that certain forces in the West continue to be interested in subverting their rule, they articulated a new discourse, "safeguarding national cultural security," in the aftermath of Western-backed "color revolutions" that toppled governments in the former Soviet republics of Georgia, the Ukraine, and Kyrgyzstan between 2003 and 2005. On August 4, 2005, five government departments— the Ministry of Culture, the SARFT, the GAPP, the State Development and Planning Commission, and the Ministry of Commerce—jointly issued "Several Opinions Regarding the Importation of Foreign Capital in the Cultural Sector" to consolidate previous policy initiatives in this area. While reaffirming openness for full foreign investment or junior foreign partnership in areas where concessions were made in China's WTO accession agreements, the document reasserts national control of the media and cultural system's key functions. Specifically, it restricts foreign capital from investing in and operating news media, broadcasting transmission networks, broadcasting program production, film importation and distribution, book publishing, Internet audiovisual services, news websites, web publishing, and other important services.[168] Concurrently, authorities stopped issuing any new licenses for foreign satellite channels and for companies importing newspapers, magazines, electronic publications, audiovisual products, and children's cartoons; set limits on the number of foreign copyrighted products Chinese companies are allowed to publish; and limited foreign companies to one joint venture with local partners. New policy initiatives also claimed to "strengthen management of imported cultural products," including existing foreign satellite channels.[169] In this context, the SARFT nixed Murdoch's joint venture with Qinghai satellite television.

By September 2006, in conjunction with Murdoch's indictment of the Chinese state as "being paranoid," the MII's issuance of "Notice Concerning Strengthening the Administration of Foreign-Invested Value-Added Telecommunications Business Operations," the Xinhua News Agency's assertion of its monopolistic position in the distribution of foreign news and business information inside China, as well as hiccups in *Rolling Stone*'s launching of a Chinese edition, the foreign media and investment community had painted a picture of a restrictive Chinese state closing its doors to foreign capital in the Chinese media, telecommunications, and Internet industries.[170] However, what was not highlighted in these foreign media outrages was the fact that Murdoch's joint venture was unauthorized and beyond the WTO accession terms in broadcasting in the first place. Similarly, because the Chinese state has never officially permitted the kind of foreign entry that the MII's and Xinhua News Agency's respective rules aim to curb, what these two state agencies tried to do can be understood as attempts to curb what they considered to be unlawful collaborations between Chinese and foreign companies that had already taken place and on which they had previously remained silent or failed to take any action. In the *Rolling Stone* case, the problem turned out to have more to do with the technicality of its entry than an outright ban on foreign collaboration as such.[171] Specifically, disputes revolved around the magazine's failure to follow the necessary procedures and its prominent display of the English title *Rolling Stone* on the magazine's cover. Once the magazine agreed to remove the English title and retain the Chinese title of its domestic collaborator *Audiovisual World* (*Yinxiang shijie*) on the cover, the collaboration went ahead, while "the source of the content is no different [than *Rolling Stone*]."[172]

With aggressive foreign investors and willing Chinese partners viewing their collaboration as an attractive business strategy, the Chinese state must use its coercive powers to stop the encroachment of foreign capital into the core communication areas, while trying to maintain an effective mother-in-law role for itself in the marriage of domestic and foreign capital in what it perceives to be less essential areas, especially to ensure that the partners do not flaunt their relationship too much, or else the party will have to face further left-nationalistic critiques of capitulation to American imperialism, cultural or otherwise. The Chinese state's abrupt order on June 8, 2006, to immediately stop the screening of Hollywood blockbuster *The Da Vinci Code*, which was on its way to becoming one of the most successful foreign films in China, once again underscores the less-than-graceful steps of its "dances with the wolves."[173] Whether for the officially stated reason of making way for domestic films or for some other unexplained reason, the stakes are very high. Although the number of domestic feature films produced has rebounded in recent years (from 91 in 2000 to 260 in 2005), largely because of a dramatic increase in films made by the private sector (from 23 in 2000 to 172 in 2005),[174] a much smaller number of imported films still accounted for about 45 percent of total box office revenue in 2004,[175] making the state's protectionist measures essential for domestic films.

Notwithstanding both the Chinese state's commitment to national development and the American right's fear of "China's rising" and projections of China as the United States' next imperial rival, Dan Schiller concluded in his analysis of China's outward expansionary initiatives in communication hardware, content, and services that while these are significant developments, they "are best apprehended neither as a developing country's attempt to redress glaring imbalances in the global communication system . . . nor as a current threat to the global dominance of the United States."[176] Rather, Schiller pointed out, the significance of these developments lies "beyond any punitive zero-sum game between current hegemon and would be rival," but in the ways they have contributed to the "structural reconfiguration of transnational capitalism with which China's rise is so profoundly intertwined."[177] Schiller called attention to how

> [a]ssimilating the structural logic of the transnational market system requires China's policy makers to employ a conception of the national economy that hostages the social needs of the vast majority of the population to capital's demands for accumulation. This tends to undercut any prospect of national self-determination in the older sense.[178]

This perspective also underpins my analysis of the impact of global reintegration on Chinese communication, how this has contributed to reshaping the structure and value orientations of the communication system, and how it has influenced the processes of transnational class and identity formation. On the one hand, the Chinese communication industry's global reintegration has accelerated the expansion of transnational capitalism and facilitated potential transnational class formation. On the other hand, as the rise of popular nationalistic discourses and the biting "old leftist" critique against the leadership's accommodation with U.S. global hegemony have both testified, this process is profoundly conflicted both internally and externally.

By reintegrating with the global market system, the Chinese state, like other postcolonial states, has found "for the 'nation' a place in the global order of capital, while striving to keep the contradictions between capital and people in perpetual suspension."[179] Because the party-state now legitimates itself by legitimizing capital,[180] much of its friction with the outside world—from its ongoing trade disputes with the United States to Xinhua's assertion of its monopolistic news distribution power—can be interpreted as intercapitalist rivalry. However, the Chinese state's anticapitalist and anti-imperialist legacies continue to haunt it. Moreover, ascending forces of protectionism, imperialism, and the Cold War legacy of anticommunism in the United States and elsewhere in the world continue to feed Chinese forces of nationalism and anti-Americanism, if not always anti-imperialism. As Lin Chun has noted,

> As long as the global liberal ideology with an open or unspoken anticommunist (and racist) influence continued to be (perceived as) destabilizing, with the collapse of the Soviet Union in the background, official fear and public caution readily joined forces in China. If historically the weak and vaguely proposed liberal solution fell through in revolutionary China because of the liberal-colonial alliance, the constant economic and political "China bashing" at the present had a similar impact. The cold war survived in hot globalization to keep the concept of imperialism alive.[181]

Thus, "the current transformation in China is bound to be open-ended despite the mighty power of globalization that everywhere keeps driving the process toward integration."[182] Processes of transnational capitalist integration are necessarily diverse and conflicting social encounters. These "awkward encounters," producing what anthropologist Anna Lowenhaupt Tsing calls "friction," are constitutive both for China and the dominant Western political economic and cultural powers. Thus, although China's neoliberal-oriented development strategies feed into the expansionary logic of informationalized global capitalism, they also create anxieties about national identity and a place in the world both in China and elsewhere.[183] Just as documenting the expansionary logic of neoliberal capitalism and the structural implications of China's articulation with it is essential, paying attention both to the political agency of the Chinese state and its normative underpinnings within Chinese society is also necessary. This entails an analysis that foregrounds the profoundly ambiguous nature of this articulation and the ongoing struggles over its terms.[184]

The Chinese state is posited to enlarge its own place within the existing system of U.S.-led transnationalizing capitalism, perhaps even to transform it. In addition to its determination to deter Taiwanese independence by contesting U.S. military supremacy through the doctrine of "asymmetrical warfare," which was underscored in the Chinese military's launching of an antisatellite ballistic missile in January 2007, recent developments have not only included the protectionist initiatives in various communication sectors discussed above, but also broader measures in reducing reliance on foreign capital and technology, from the passage of a Corporate Income Taxation Law in March 2007 that ends preferential tax treatment for foreign firms and promises to facilitate a shift away from a foreign investment–dependent and export-driven economy,[185] to the promotion of "indigenous innovations" in technological developments, especially in the information and communication sector, and the decision to build China's own jumbo passenger jet.[186]

A *New York Times* report noted in relation to the CCTV's broadcast of a documentary series titled *The Rise of Great Powers* in November and December 2006: "With its $1 billion in foreign exchange reserves, surging military spending and diplomatic initiatives in Asia, Africa and the Middle East . . . Chinese party leaders are acting as if they intend to start exercising more power abroad rather than just protecting their political power at home."[187] Instead of merely guarding against the penetration of American "soft power" in China, official Chinese discourses have sought to strengthen China's own "soft power," emphasizing, among other things, essentialized Chinese cultural values, such as harmony and unity between humans and nature, which presumably are capable of transforming the negative dimensions of Western capitalist culture. In addition to expressing China's intention to coexist with global capitalism without being subordinated by invoking the Confucian idea of "harmony without uniformity" (*he'er butong*), official media have also welcomed the "Beijing Consensus" as formulated by former *Time* magazine editor and Goldman Sachs analyst Joshua Cooper Ramo as an alternative to the "Washington Consensus" and neoliberal globalization.[188]

Yet the Chinese state has also been extremely cautious in its global communication strategies. For example, the Hu Jintao leadership, after having used the idea of China's "peaceful rise" to describe its foreign policy goals in 2004, later opted for the "tamer-sounding" idea of China's "peaceful development," because the term "development" suggests that "China's advance can bring others along," whereas the term "rise" implies that others must decline in a relative sense, risking stoking fears of a "China threat" in Japan and the United States.[189] Similarly, Chinese media and academic discourses have not only highlighted the tentative nature of the "Beijing Consensus" but also were quick to contrast its mode of articulation and means of promotion with those of the "Washington Consensus." Wu Shuqing, a former president of Peking University, acknowledges,

Whereas "the Washington Consensus" was advanced purposefully and systematically and its subscribers truly formed a consensus on the basis of their acceptance of neoliberalism, "the Beijing Consensus" as a perspective emerged voluntarily within the global public opinion arena. . . . [I]ts content is still under discussion, and neither its proponents nor the participants of its discussion share the theoretical basis of such a "consensus."[190]

Wu concluded that there is not yet "an already formulated 'consensus.'"

This point is certainly well taken. Contradiction and contention, rather than consensus, have been the defining features of Chinese communication policies and politics. Moreover, just as the ideology of consumerism cannot serve as an adequate basis for identity formation by the winners of globalization in China, the agents of China's capitalist global reintegration project, unlike Zhang Yimou in *Hero*, cannot simply erase the vast numbers of disenfranchised workers and farmers from the domestic social picture and turn them into uniformed soldiers and palace guards—although some farmers have indeed managed to turn themselves into cheap movie extras for such roles, as I will show in the next chapter.

NOTES

1. "Murdoch's Appeal to Chinese Leaders," afr.com/articles/2003/10/09/1065601940384.html (accessed 10 Oct. 2003).

2. "Murdoch Calls Beijing Paranoid," www.newsmax.com/archives/ic/2005/9/20/201726.shtml (accessed 25 May 2006).

3. This is an interesting reversion of Yuan Weishi's use of the "wolf" metaphor as discussed in chapter 1.

4. Li Xiangmin, "*Jingshen jingji shidai de Zhongguo wenhua chanye*" (China's Culture Industry in the Era of Spiritual Economy), in *Zhongguo Wenhuachanye niandufazhan baogao* (Annual Report on the Development of China's Culture Industry), ed. Ye Lang (Changsha: Hunan renmin chubanshe, 2004), 7.

5. Li, "*Jingshen jingji*," 7.

6. Yu Guoming, *Jiexi Chuanmei bianju: Laizi Zhongguo chuanmeiye diyixianchang de baogao* (Analyzing Changes in the Media: First-Hand Reports from China's Media Industry) (Guangzhou: Nanfang ribo chubanshe, 2002), 38, my emphasis.

7. John Sinclair and Mark Harrison, "Globalization, Nation and Television in Asia: The Case of India and China," *Television and New Media* 5, no. 1 (2004): 27–40.

8. Personal observation at the "International Relations and Cultural Communication" conference, Beijing Broadcasting Institute, Beijing, 13–14 Apr. 2002.

9. Arif Dirlik, *Marxism in the Chinese Revolution* (Lanham, Md.: Rowman & Littlefield, 2005), 267.

10. E. P. Thompson, *Customs in Common* (New York: New Press, 1991), 6, cited in Dan Schiller, *Theorizing Communication: A History* (New York: Oxford University Press, 1996), 157.

11. According to one of the interpretations, culture is a concession that the Chinese state had to make to buy time to improve the competitive positions of other industries where there are more jobs at stake. See Michael Curtin, "The Future of Chinese Cinema: Some Lessons from Hong Kong and Taiwan," in *Chinese Media, Global Contexts*, ed. Chin-Chuan Lee, 237–256 (New York: Routledge, 2003), 237.

12. Dan Schiller, "Poles of Market Growth? Open Questions about China, Information and the World Economy," *Global Media and Communication* 1, no. 1 (Apr. 2005): 79–103.

13. Leslie Chang and Charles Hutzler, "CCTV Aims to Be China's CNN," *Globe and Mail*, 27 Mar. 2003, B12.

14. Mark Landler, "Entrepreneur Walking Fine Line at a News Channel for China," *New York Times*, 8 Jan. 2001, www.nytimes/com/2001/01/08/business/08CHIN.html (accessed 8 Jan. 2001).

15. Yuezhi Zhao and Dan Schiller, "Dances with Wolves? China's Integration into Digital Capitalism," *Info* 3, no. 2 (Apr. 2001): 140.

16. Edward S. Herman and Robert W. McChesney, *The Global Media: The New Missionaries of Corporate Capitalism* (London: Cassell, 1997).

17. Stuart Hall, "The Local and the Global: Globalization and Ethnicity," in *Culture, Globalization, and the World-System*, ed. Anthony D. King (London: Macmillan, 1991), 28.

18. Leslie Sklair, *The Transnational Capitalist Class* (Oxford: Blackwell, 2001), 256.

19. Schiller, *Theorizing Communication*, 89.

20. Schiller, *Theorizing Communication*, 96.

21. Dirlik, *Marxism in the Chinese Revolution*, 289.

22. Stewart R. Clegg and S. Gordon Redding, eds., *Capitalism in Contrasting Cultures* (Berlin: Walter de Gruyter, 1990), cited in Dirlik, *Marxism in the Chinese Revolution*, 265.

23. Dirlik, *Marxism in the Chinese Revolution*, 281.

24. Dirlik, *Marxism in the Chinese Revolution*, 303–309.

25. Dirlik, *Marxism in the Chinese Revolution*, 267–268.

26. Dirlik, *Marxism in the Chinese Revolution*, 268.

27. I had translated it into "East" in *Media, Market, and Democracy* without knowing the official translation.

28. Jonathan Manthorpe, "Asian Media Heirs Run into Financial Reality," *Vancouver Sun*, 23 Sept. 2000, H3.

29. Wu Mei, "Globalization and Language Sovereignty: The Use of English on China's Television and in Public Signs" (paper presented at the "Asian Culture and Media Studies" conference, Beijing Broadcasting Institute, Dec. 2003). Chinese authorities have since tried to limit this development.

30. Armand Mattelart, *Networking the World, 1794–2000*, trans. Liz Carey-Libbrecht and James A. Cohen (Minneapolis: University of Minnesota Press, 2000), 43–44.

31. Bob Davis, "Gore to Lobby for Chinese Trade Accord," *Wall Street Journal*, 15 Mar. 2000, A2.

32. Ethan Gutmann, *Losing the New China: A Story of American Commerce, Desire and Betrayal* (San Francisco: Encounter Books, 2004).

33. Zhou Yongming, *Historicizing Online Politics: Telegraphy, the Internet, and Political Participation in China* (Stanford, Calif.: Stanford University Press, 2006), 144.

34. Dan Schiller, *How to Think about Information* (Urbana: University of Illinois, 2007).

35. Sun Xupei, "'*Rushi' dui Zhongguo xinwen meiti de chongji*" (The Shocking Effects of WTO Entry on the Chinese News Media), *Ming Pao Monthly*, Mar. 2001, 34–39.

36. Sun Zhengyi and Liu Tingting, "*2002: Zhongguo xinwenye huiwang*" (*xia*) (A Retrospective View of the Chinese Media Industry in 2002, Part II), xwjz1.eastday.com/epublish/gb/paper159/200301/class015900002/hwz595963.htm (accessed 15 Oct. 2007).

37. Zhenzhi Guo, "Playing the Games by the Rules? Television Regulation around China's Entry into WTO," *Javnost/The Public* 10, no. 4 (2003): 5–18.

38. David Harvey, *The New Imperialism* (Oxford: Oxford University Press, 2005), 91.

39. "Beijing Calling," Editorial, *Wall Street Journal*, 7 Sept. 2001, A14.

40. Ann Cooper, "China's Jailed E-Journalists," *Seattle Times*, 19 Apr. 2006, seattletimes.nwsource.com/html/opinion/2002938475_anncooper19.html (accessed 5 Jun. 2006).

41. Edward S. Herman and Noam Chomsky, *Manufacturing Consent: The Political Economy of Mass Media*, 2nd ed. (New York: Pantheon, 2002).

42. Chin-Chuan Lee, "The Global and the National of the Chinese Media: Discourses, Market, Technology, and Ideology," in *Chinese Media, Global Contexts*, ed. Chin-Chuan Lee, 1–31 (New York: Routledge, 2003), 10.

43. For the most compelling argument on this point, see Herman and Chomsky, *Manufacturing Consent.*

44. Lin Chun, *The Transformation of Chinese Socialism* (Durham, N.C.: Duke University Press, 2006), 1.

45. Guoguang Wu, "The Birth of Sophisticated Propaganda: The Party-State and the Chinese Media in Post-Reform Politics" (paper manuscript made available to the author), 14.

46. Mark O'Neill, "Titanic Fever Sweeps Beijing," *South China Morning Post*, 3 Apr. 1998.

47. Koichi Iwabuchi, *Recentering Globalization: Popular Culture and Japanese Transnationalism* (Durham, N.C.: Duke University Press, 2002).

48. Anthony Fung, "'Think Globally, Act Locally': China's Rendezvous with MTV," *Global Media and Communication* 2, no. 1 (2006): 84.

49. Lu Xinyu, "*Yishi, dianshi yu guojia yishixingtai*" (Ritual, Television, and State Ideology), www.wyzxsx.com/Article/Class10/200608/8917.html (accessed 14 Apr. 2007).

50. Lu, "*Yishi.*"

51. For further elaboration, see Paula Chakravartty and Yuezhi Zhao, eds., *Global Communications: Toward a Transcultural Political Economy* (Lanham, Md.: Rowman & Littlefield, 2007).

52. Liu Kang, *Globalization and Cultural Trends in China* (Honolulu: University of Hawai'i Press, 2004), 30.

53. Sklair, *The Transnational Capitalist Class*; Herman and McChesney, *The Global Media*.

54. Yuezhi Zhao, "'Enter the World': Neo-Liberal Globalization, the Dream for a Strong Nation, and Chinese Press Discourses on the WTO," in *Chinese Media, Global Contexts*, ed. Chin-Chuan Lee, 32–56 (New York: Routledge, 2003). In the words of Wang Hui, Chinese media reports on the WTO "corresponded with the American media on the same issue" (*China's New Order*, ed. Theodore Hunters [Cambridge, Mass.: Harvard University Press, 2003], 102).

55. Guo Zhenzhi, "*Chong Yilake zhanzheng he feidian baodao kan Zhongguo xinwen meiti*" (A Perspective on the Chinese News Media Based on Their Coverage of the Iraqi War and SARS), *Chuanmei yanjiu*, www.rirt.com.cn/magazine/ml_11.asp (accessed 5 Feb. 2004).

56. James Compton, *The Integrated News Spectacle: A Political Economy of Cultural Performance* (New York: Peter Lang, 2004).

57. Leo Panitch and Sam Gindin, "Global Capitalism and American Empire," *Socialist Register 2004* (London: Merlin, 2003), 19.

58. Panitch and Gindin, "Global Capitalism," 19. For analysis of the implications of foreign investment in Chinese domestic capital and labor formations, see Yasheng Huang, *Selling China: Foreign Direct Investment during the Reform Era* (Cambridge: Cambridge University Press, 2003), and Mary Gallagher, *Contagious Capitalism: Globalization and the Politics of Labor in China* (Princeton, N.J.: Princeton University Press, 2005).

59. Space limits do not permit me to include in this discussion the advertising industry in China, which not only has the highest level of foreign penetration, but also plays an instrumental role in shaping the Chinese media system and promoting transnational consumerism. For relevant discussions, see Jian Wang, *Foreign Advertising in China: Becoming Global, Becoming Local* (Ames: Iowa State University Press, 2000); Jing Wang, *Brand New China* (Cambridge, Mass.: Harvard University Press, 2007). For a differently framed description of foreign penetration in Chinese communication industries, see John Downing and Yong Cao, "Global Media Corporations and the People's Republic of China," *Media Development* 4 (2004): 18–26.

60. Yuezhi Zhao, "Caught in the Web: The Public Interest and the Battle for Control of China's Information Superhighway," *Info* 2, no. 1 (Feb. 2000): 46.

61. For analysis of the role of foreign capital in the Chinese telecommunication industry, see Ding Lu and Chee Kong Wong, *China's Telecommunications Market: Entering a New Competitive Age* (Cheltenham, UK, and Northampton, Mass.: Edward Elgar, 2003).

62. Lu and Wong, *China's Telecommunications Market*, 69–93; Daniel Roseman, "The WTO and Telecommunications Services in China: Three Years On," *Info* 7, no. 2 (2005): 25–48; Kenneth J. DeWoskin, "The WTO and the Telecommunications Sector in China," *China Quarterly* (2001): 630–654.

63. Yuezhi Zhao, "Universal Service and China's Telecommunications Miracle: Discourses, Implementation, and Post-WTO Accession Challenges," *Info* 9, no. 2/3 (2007): 108–121. For other studies of uneven development in Chinese telecommunications, see Zhao, "Caught in the Web"; Eric Harwit, "Spreading

Telecommunications to Developing Areas in China: Telephones, the Internet and the Digital Divide," *China Quarterly* (2004): 1010–1030; Jack Linchuan Qiu, "Coming to Terms with Informational Stratification in China," *Cardozo Arts and Entertainment Law Journal* 20, no. 1 (Mar. 2002): 157–180; Carolyn Cartier, Manuel Castells, and Jack Linchuan Qiu, "The Information Have-Less: Inequality, Mobility, and Translocal Networks in Chinese Cities," *Studies in Comparative International Development* 40, no. 2 (Summer 2005): 9–34.

64. Zhao, "Universal Service."

65. See Schiller, "Poles of Market Growth?"

66. Martine Bulard, "China Breaks the Iron Rice Bowl," *Le Monde Diplomatique*, monediplo.com/2006/01/04China (accessed 8 Feb. 2006).

67. For further discussion, see Yuezhi Zhao, "After Mobile Phones, What? Re-Embedding the Social in China's 'Digital Revolution,'" *International Journal of Communication* 1, no. 1 (Jan. 2007), ijoc.org/ojs/index.php/ijoc/article/view/5/20 (accessed 5 Apr. 2007).

68. Wei Gao, "Staging the 'Mobile Phone Carnival': A Political Economy of the SMS Culture in China" (master's thesis, School of Communication, Simon Fraser University, 2005).

69. Downing and Cao, "Global Media Corporations," 21.

70. Tom Mitchell, "Mainland Ties Bind Pioneer Publisher," *South China Morning Post*, 12 Jul. 2000, www.scmp.com/News/Template/PrintArticle.asp (accessed 13 Jul. 2000).

71. Mitchell, "Mainland Ties."

72. See the website www.baibaofp.com/index-jsjsj.htm (accessed 30 May 2006).

73. Milton Mueller and Zixiang Tan, *China in the Information Age: Telecommunications and the Dilemmas of Reform* (Westport, Conn.: Praeger, 1997), 56.

74. IDG website, www.idg.com/www/idgpubs.nsf/webPubsByCountryView (accessed 16 Feb. 2004).

75. Kim Chipman, "Playboy's Interest in China Rises," *Vancouver Sun*, 22 Oct. 2002, D11.

76. "Lad Mags Go to China," *New York Times*, 18 Apr. 2004, Section 4, 12.

77. "*Mei Sanda zazhi andu chencang jin neidi*" (Three Big Name U.S. Magazines Sneak into the Mainland), www.cddc.net/shownews.asp?newsid+4069 (accessed 6 Mar. 2004).

78. Yuejue Jin, "F-Magazines in China" (master's thesis, School of Journalism, University of British Columbia, 2003).

79. Interview by Xiaojing Ma, 12 Jan. 2003, Shanghai, cited in Jin, "F-Magazines in China," 27–28.

80. From personal interviews conducted in December 2001 in Beijing, it was clear that editors at the magazine house were not unconscious of the ideological contradictions of this undertaking. Yet as they pointed out, the magazine house, which used to be profitable selling the *Women of China* alone, could now only survive by launching *Good* and using its revenue to cross-subsidize the *Women of China*, which still maintains a less consumerist and more feminist orientation.

81. For a detailed analysis of the role of this journal and potentials and limits of social communication between urban feminist activists and rural women, see Paul Pickowicz and Liping Wang, "Village Voices, Urban Activists: Women, Violence,

and Gender Inequality in Rural China," in *Popular China: Unofficial Culture in a Globalizing Society*, ed. Perry Link, Richard P. Madsen, and Paul G. Pickowicz, 57–87 (Lanham, Md.: Rowman & Littlefield, 2002).

82. China News Agency, "*Shishang bianhua: Nianqingren 'ha fa'*" (Changed Fashion: Young People Worship Anything French), *Shijie ribao* (Vancouver), 8 Mar. 2003, A9.

83. Elisabeth Rosenthal, "Women's Suicides Reveal Rural China's Bitter Roots," *New York Times*, 24 Jan. 1999, A12. See also, Sing Lee and Arthur Kleinman, "Suicide as Resistance in Chinese Society," in *Chinese Society: Change, Conflict and Resistance*, 2nd ed., ed. Elizabeth J. Perry and Mark Selden, 289–311 (London: RoutledgeCurzon, 2003).

84. Yin Hong and Zhan Qingsheng, "*2005 nian Zhongguo dianying chanye beiwanglu*" (China's Movie Industry in 2005), in *2006 nian: Zhongguo wenhua chanye fazhan baogao* (Report on the Development of China's Culture Industry in 2006), ed. Zhang Xiaoming, Hu Huilin, and Zhang Jiangang (Beijing: Shehui kexue wenxian chubanshe, 2006), 118.

85. I am grateful to Dan Schiller for pointing out the significance of this difference to me.

86. Arif Dirlik, *Marxism in the Chinese Revolution* (Lanham, Md.: Rowman & Littlefield, 2005), 311.

87. In 2005 the population coverage rate for radio and television was 94.48 percent and 95.81 percent, respectively. There were nearly 500 million radio receivers, 400 million television sets, and 126 million cable households. However, more than 81.1 percent of Chinese households could only receive 1–5 analog television channels, 22.4 percent of urban households did not have cable television access, and 9.27 percent of Chinese villages were still beyond the reach of broadcasting signals. Research Center for Reform and Development, SARFT, *2006 nian Zhongguo guangbo yingshi fanzhan baogao* (Report on the Development of China's Radio, Film, and Television) (Beijing: Shehui kexue wenxian chubanshe, 2006), 160–161, 340.

88. See website www.phoenixtv.com/info/watch.htm (accessed 28 Sept. 2000).

89. Interview, Jul. 1999, Hong Kong.

90. Philip P. Pan, "Making Waves, Carefully, on the Air in China," *Washington Post*, 19 Sept. 2005, A01.

91. For a detailed discussion of CCTV's investigative journalism, see Yuezhi Zhao, "Watchdogs on Party Leashes? Contexts and Limitations of Investigative Reporting in Post-Deng China," *Journalism Studies* 1, no. 4 (Nov. 2000): 577–597; Yuezhi Zhao and Sun Wusan, "'Public Opinion Supervision': Potentials and Limits of the Media in Constraining Local Officials," in *Grassroots Political Reform in Contemporary China*, ed. Elizabeth Perry and Merle Goldman, 300–324 (Cambridge, Mass.: Harvard University Press, 2007).

92. Landler, "Entrepreneur Walking Fine Line."

93. Xie Jinwen, "*Guoqi xiangyue Fenghuang Weishi*" (State Enterprises Rendezvous with Phoenix TV), *Zhongguo jingying bao*, 8 Dec. 1998, 2.

94. Mark Lee, "Phoenix Spreading Its Wings," www.phoenixtv.com/phoenixtv/77412215665197056/20050513/549819.shtml (accessed 30 May 2006).

95. Lee, "Phoenix Spreading Its Wings."

96. Lee, "Phoenix Spreading Its Wings."

97. Fung, "'Think Globally,'" 76.

98. Fung, "'Think Globally,'" 77.

99. Ying Zhu, *Chinese Cinema during the Era of Reform: The Ingenuity of the System* (Westport, Conn.: Praeger, 2003), 20.

100. Stanley Rosen, "China Goes Hollywood," *Foreign Policy* (Jan./Feb. 2003): 94–98.

101. Dai Jinhua, "*Zhongguo dianying: Zai huaile zhong chenmo*" (Chinese Cinema: Sinking in Happiness . . .), *Xiandan chuanbo* 2 (1999): 21.

102. Liu Xitao, "China's Film Industry Suffers a Major Blow with WTO Entry," *Qiaobao*, 24 Nov. 1999, B1.

103. Peng Jingfeng and Xu Chang, "*Dianying faxing qudao da xipai*" (An Allover Reshaping of Film Distribution Channels), *Shenzhou shibao*, 20 Jul. 2003, C3.

104. In using this expression, I am making an allusion to Robert A. Brady, *The Spirit and Structure of German Fascism* (London: V. Gollancz, 1937).

105. For the most devastating critique on this theme, see Evans Chan, "Zhang Yimou's *Hero*—The Temptations of Fascism," www.filmint.nu/netonly/eng/heroevanschan.htm (accessed 7 Dec. 2005).

106. Zhang Yiwu, "*Yingxiong: Xinshiji de yinyu*" (*Hero*: A Metaphor for the New Century), in *Wenhua yanjiu* 4 (Cultural Studies 4), ed. Tao Dongfeng, Jin Yuanpu, and Gao Bingzhong (Beijing: Zhongyang bianyi chubanshe, 2003), 131–142.

107. Yahoo! China, 4 Nov. 2002, cited in Zhang, "*Yingxiong*," 133.

108. For further discussion, see Yuezhi Zhao, "Whose *Hero*? The Spirit and Structure of a Transnationally Integrated Chinese Blockbuster in the Post 9/11 Global Order," in *Re-Orienting Global Communication: India and China Beyond Borders*, ed. Michael Curtin and Hemant Shah (Urbana and Chicago: University of Illinois Press, forthcoming).

109. Zhang, "*Yingxiong*," 135.

110. "*Nengkan dianying de shouji duopuda yanyi Yingxiong dapian*" (The Dopod Cellphone That Can Show a Movie Shows Blockbuster *Hero*), tech.sina.com.cn/it2/2002-12-17/1619156346.shtml (accessed 5 Dec. 2006).

111. Bingchun Meng, "A Hero of Whom? A Case Study of Global-Local Alliance in the Chinese Film Industry" (paper presented at the "Union for Democratic Communication" conference, St. Louis, 22–24 Apr. 2004).

112. Rosen, "China Goes Hollywood," 98.

113. Toby Miller, Nathan Govil, J. McMurria, and Richard Maxwell, *Global Hollywood* (London: British Film Institute, 2001).

114. For the video, see www.yuco.cn/wmv/1mt.wmv (accessed 12 May 2006). For a more detailed discussion, see Andy Hu, "*The Promise* and the Undelivered Promise of the Market," unpublished manuscript, Apr. 2006.

115. Leslie Sklair defines the "transnational capitalist class" as being composed of "corporate executives, globalizing bureaucratic and politicians, globalizing professionals, and consumerist elites." See his *The Transnational Capitalist Class*, 4.

116. China purchased $100 billion worth of dollars in U.S. Treasury bonds in the first 10 months of 2003 alone. See Robert Brenner, "New Boom or New Bubble? The Trajectory of the US Economy," *New Left Review* 25 (Jan.–Feb. 2004): 87.

117. Yuezhi Zhao, "The Media Matrix: China's Integration into Global Capitalism," in *Socialist Register 2005: The Empire Reloaded*, ed. Leo Panitch and Colin Leys (London: Merlin Press, 2004), 209.

118. Anita Chan, *China's Workers under Assault: The Exploitation of Labor in a Globalizing Economy* (Armonk, N.Y.: M. E. Sharpe, 2001), 172–205.

119. Dirlik, *Marxism in the Chinese Revolution*, 302–303.

120. Yuezhi Zhao, "Transnational Capital, the Chinese State, and China's Communication Industries in a Fractured Society," *Javnost/The Public* 10, no. 4 (2003): 53; Schiller, "Poles of Market Growth?" 88.

121. Suisheng Zhao, *Nation-State by Construction: Dynamics of Modern Chinese Nationalism* (Stanford, Calif.: Stanford University Press, 2004), 207.

122. Ye Zicheng, "*Zouchu jihua wuque*" (Move beyond a Polarization Perspective), *Nanfang zhoumo*, 15 Jan. 2004, www.nanfangdaily.com/cn/am/200401150698.asp (accessed 20 Jan. 2004).

123. Peter Hays Gries, *China's New Nationalism: Pride, Politics, and Diplomacy* (Berkeley: University of California Press, 2004), 18, 20.

124. Jeffrey N. Wasserstrom, "Student Protests in Fin-de-Siecle China," *New Left Review* 237 (Sept./Oct. 1999): 60.

125. Zhou, *Historicizing*, 212.

126. For a discussion of some of the earliest manifestations of online Chinese nationalism, see Sun Wanning, *Leaving China: Media, Migration, and Transnational Imagination* (Lanham, Md.: Rowman & Littlefield, 2003), 113–136; Jack Linchuan Qiu, "The Changing Web of Chinese Nationalism," *Global Media and Communication* 2, no. 1 (2006): 125–128.

127. Dai Jinhua, "Between Global Spectacle and National Image Making," *Positions* 9, no. 1 (Spring 2001): 161–186.

128. Suisheng Zhao, *Nation-State by Construction*, 162; see also Zhou, *Historicizing*, 181–195.

129. Zhou, *Historicizing*, 212.

130. See Liu, *Globalization*, 68–69, for an alphabetical soup of various kinds of Chinese nationalisms. See also Zhou, *Historicizing*, 211.

131. Sklair, *The Transnational Capitalist Class*, 29.

132. Zhou, *Historicizing*, 227.

133. Yu Bing, "*Zhishi jie de fenlie yu zhenghe*" (The Disintegration and Reintegration of the Intellectual Cirle), in *Sichao: Zhongguo "xinzuopai" jiqi yingxiang* (Trends: China's "New Left" and Its Impact), ed. Gong Yang (Beijing: Social Sciences Academic Press, 2003), 3.

134. Yu Bing, "*Zhishi jie*," 3.

135. Such a situation parallels the situation in China in the early 1920s, when diverse schools of nationalists from young Marxists to Confucian nationalists flourished in the country ruled by an allegedly nationalist but essentially comprador-oriented, right-wing regime, which could speak to the demands of neither. Andy Hu, "Swimming against the Tide: Tracing and Locating Chinese Leftism Online" (master's thesis, School of Communication, Simon Fraser University, 2006), 57–58.

136. Fang Ning, Wang Xiaodong, and Song Qiang, *Quanqiuhua yinying xia de Zhongguo zhilu* (China's Pathway under the Shadow of Globalization) (Beijing: Zhangguo shehuikexue chubanshe, 1999).

137. Fang, Wang, and Song, *Quanqiuhua*, 136.

138. Fang, Wang, and Song, *Quanqiuhua*, 37.

139. Zhou, *Historicizing*, 166.

140. Hu, "Swimming against the Tide," 75.

141. "Why Al Jazeera Matters," Editorial, *New York Times*, 30 Mar. 2003, www .nytimes.com/2003/03/30/opinion/30SUN2.html?th (accessed 30 Mar. 2003).

142. See, for example, articles by Wang Dongcheng, Yang Zizhu, Zhi Xiaomin, Yu Jie, Zhang Yuanshan, Sha Lei, and Ge Hongbing in *Dangdai Zhongguo yanjiu* 76 (Nov. 2002): 117–156.

143. Liah Greenfeld, *Nationalism: Five Roads to Modernity* (Cambridge, Mass.: Harvard University Press, 1992), 11, cited in Suisheng Zhao, "Chinese Nationalism and Authoritarianism in the 1990s," in *China and Democracy: Reconsidering the Prospects for a Democratic China*, ed. Suisheng Zhao, 253–270 (New York: Routledge, 2000), 253.

144. James L. Huffman, *Creating a Public: People and Press in Meiji Japan* (Honolulu: University of Hawai'i Press, 1997), 308–309. I am grateful to Timothy Cheek for sharing this book with me and for suggesting this comparison.

145. Liu Xiaobo, "China's Media Profits from Jingoism," *Taipei Times*, 27 May 2005, 8, www.taipeitimes.com/News/edit/archives/2005/05/27/2003256819 (accessed 1 Jun. 2005).

146. Zhang Siqi, *"Tamen weihe zheyang kuangre?"* (Why Are They So Fervent?), *Kaifang*, May 2005, 11.

147. Zhang, *"Tamen weihe,"* 11.

148. Zhao, *Nation-State by Construction*, 160.

149. Zhou, *Historicizing*, 208–209.

150. Zhao, *Nation-State by Construction*, 274.

151 "Beijing Tightens Controls on Domestic Reporting on China," *Strait Times Interactive*, www.straittimes.asia1.com.sg/home/0,1869,00.html? (accessed 4 Oct. 2004).

152. Ouyang Bin, *"Zhongguo minjian fanri shili yanshao"* (Unofficial Anti-Japanese Force in China Rages), *Fenghuang zhoukan*, www.tzsl.org/ Article_Print.asp? ArticleID=469 (accessed 19 Jun. 2006).

153. Yu Wenxue, *"Hu Jintao xue wanhou"* (Hu Jintao Learned to Play with Fire), *Kaifang*, May 2005, 10–13.

154. Wasserstrom, "Student Protests," 61.

155. Jim Yardley, "A Hundred Cellphones Bloom, and Chinese Take to the Streets," www.nytimes.com/2005/04/25/international/asia/25china.html (accessed 29 Apr. 2005).

156. Jonathan Watts, "Violence Flares as the Chinese Rage at Japan," www .observer.guardian.co.uk/international/story/0,1461648,00.html (accessed 2 May 2005).

157. Zhao, *Nation-State by Construction*, 265.

158. Jiang Xueqin, "Letter from China," *Nation* 274, no. 8 (4 Mar. 2002), www.thenation.com/doc/20020304/xueqin (accessed 12 Dec. 2005).

159. Daguimuoshiye, "*Zhongguo jingying de zhanlüe suo mianlin de sida tiaozhan*" (Four Major Challenges Face the Chinese Elite's Strategies), 69.41.161.6/ huaShan/BBS/wenzai/gbcollected/374.shtml (accessed 23 Feb. 2004).

160. "*Shenzhen rizi qiye 2 wan gongren bagong yao chengli gonghui*" (20,000 Workers in Japanese-Owned Factory in Shenzhen Strike to Demand Unionization), www7.chinesenewsnet.com/MainNews/EntDigest/Life/2005_4_21_13_30_30_9 90.html (accessed 25 Apr. 2005).

161. China Labour Bulletin, "Striking Shenzhen Workers at Japanese-Owned Wal-Mart Supplier Firm Demand Right to Unionize," www.zmag.org/ content/showarticle.cfm?SectionID=17&ItemID=7713 (accessed 25 Apr. 2005).

162. Han Xiya and Ma Bin, "*Qiwen gong xinshang, yiyi xiang yuxi—Siren jing gan xianbu Zhongguo Gongchandang zai 21 shiji de zouxiang*" (An Extraordinary Essay to be Appreciated by All, A Questionable Idea to be Analyzed by All: A Private Individual Dares to Declare the Chinese Communist Party's Directions in the 21st Century), host378.ipowerweb.com/~gongnong/bbs/read.php? f=3&i=149936&t=149936 (accessed 23 May 2006). Ma, an economist born in 1914, was a former adviser to the State Council Center for Development Research and former general manager of the Anshan Iron and Steel Company; Han, born in 1924, was former candidate secretary of All-China Federation of Trade Unions.

163. Zheng Bijian, "Way That Communist Party of China Takes in 21st Century," english.people.com.cn/200511/23/eng20051123_223414.html (accessed 23 May 2006).

164. Han and Ma, "*Qiwen gong xinshang.*"

165. Colin Sparks, "China, the WTO and the Mass Media: What Is at Stake?" *Media Development* 44, no. 3 (2003): 3–7.

166. Doug Young and Kenneth Li, "Western Media Lost Their Way," Reuters, 19 Jun. 2006, www.thestandard.com.hk/news_detail.asp?pp_cat=5&art_id=20971& sid=8449682&con_type=1 (accessed 19 Jun. 2006).

167. Mark Lee, "Phoenix TV Lands Dynamic Platform," www.thestandard .com.hk/news_detail.asp?we_cat=2&art_id=20469&sid=8332627&con_type=1&d _str=20060609 (accessed 9 Jun. 2006).

168. "*5 buwei zhiding 'guanyu wenhua lingyu yinjin waizi de ruogan yijian'*" (Five Ministries and Commissions Formed "Several Opinions on Importing Foreign Capital in the Cultural Sector"), news.xinhuanet.com/newscenter/2005-08/04/content_3309000.htm (accessed 19 Jun. 2006).

169. Joe McDonald, "China Shuts Door on New Foreign TV Channels," *Guardian*, 5 Aug. 2005, www.guardian.co.uk/china/story/0,7369,1542827,00.html (accessed 11 Nov. 2005); Elizabeth Guider and Patrick Frater, "China Pulls Rug out from Rupe, News Corp. Foiled in Boosting Penetration," *Variety*, www.variety .com/article/VR1117928147?categoryid=1442&cs=1 (accessed 11 Nov. 2005).

170. Liu Hong, "*Xinuiding—Tiyu, yule, shishang zazhi bude jin Zhongguo*" (New Regulations: Sports, Entertainment, Lifestyle Magazines Not Allowed to Enter China), lajaocity.publishhtml/4/2006-04-07/20060407155721.html (accessed 15 May 2006); Michael Chin and David Huang, "China Imposes Stricter Regulations on Foreign Invested Internet and Telecom Businesses," www.dorsey.com/publi cations/legal_detail.aspx?FlashNavID=pubs_legal&pubid=232573603 (accessed

18 Apr. 2007); "China New Media Curbs Condemned," BBC News, 12 Sept. 2006, news.bbc.co.uk/2/hi/asia-pacific/5337248.stm (accessed 18 Apr. 2007).

171. I am grateful to an interview conducted by Li Xiren with Hao Fang, the magazine's editor-in-chief, 19 Apr. 2006, on my behalf.

172. See also, Bill Savadove, "China: *Rolling Stone* Goes Audio to Pacify Authorities," www.asiamedia.ucla.edu/article.asp?parentid=43927 (accessed 25 May 2006).

173. Associated Press, "China Bans *Da Vinci Code* Movie," *Vancouver Sun*, 9 Jun. 2006, A9.

174. Research Center for Reform and Development, SARFT, 325.

175. Hu Zhengrong, Wang Wei, and Li Jidong, "*Xin de chidu xin de biange*" (New Measures and New Changes), in *2006 nian: Zhongguo wenhua chanye fazhan baogao* (Report on the Development of China's Cultural Industry in 2006), ed. Zhang Xiaoming, Hu Huilin, and Zhang Jiangang (Beijing: Shehui kexue wenxian chubanshe, 2006), 169.

176. Schiller, "Poles of Market Growth?" 79.

177. Schiller, "Poles of Market Growth?" 86.

178. Schiller, "Poles of Market Growth?" 89.

179. Partha Chatterjee, *Nationalist Thought and the Colonial World: A Derivative Discourse?* (London: Zed Books, 1986), 168.

180. Hu Zhengrong, "The Post-WTO Restructuring of the Chinese Media Industries and the Consequences of Capitalization," *Javnost/The Public* 10, no. 4 (2003): 34.

181. Lin, *The Transformation of Chinese Socialism*, 238.

182. Lin, *The Transformation of Chinese Socialism*, 12.

183. Paula Chakravartty and Yuezhi Zhao, "Toward a Transcultural Political Economy of Global Communications," in *Global Communications: Toward a Transcultural Political Economy*, ed. Paula Chakravartty and Yuezhi Zhao, 1–19 (Lanham, Md.: Rowman & Littlefield, 2008).

184. Yuezhi Zhao, "Neoliberal Strategies, Socialist Legacies: Communication and State Transformation in China," in *Global Communications: Toward a Transcultural Political Economy*, ed. Paula Chakravartty and Yuezhi Zhao, 23–50 (Lanham, Md.: Rowman & Littlefield, 2008).

185. Exceptions are made for foreign companies invested in new and high-technology areas considered to be of national importance. See Pricewaterhouse-Coopers, "Impact of New China Corporate Income Tax Law on Foreign Investors," *China Tax/Business News Flash*, Mar. 2007, www.pwccn.com/webmedia/doc/633098999748634912_chinatax_news_mar2007_6.pdf (accessed 21 Oct. 2007).

186. For a more detailed discussion, see Yuezhi Zhao, "China's Pursuits for National Sovereignty and Technological Developments in the Network Age: Hopes, Follies and Uncertainties" (paper presented at the 2007 Beijing Forum, 2–4 Nov. 2007).

187. Joseph Kahn, "China, Shy Giant, Shows Signs of Shedding Its False Modesty," *New York Times*, 9 Dec. 2006, www.nytimes.com/2006/12/09/world/asia/09china.html (accessed 11 Dec. 2006).

188. Joshua Cooper Ramo, *The Beijing Consensus* (London: Foreign Policy Centre, 2004), fpc.org.uk/fsblob/244.pdf (accessed 18 Apr. 2007).

189. Kahn, "China, Shy Giant."

190. Tian Hong, "*Zenyang kandai 'huashengtun gongshi' yu 'Beijing gongshi'*" (How to View the "Washington Consensus" and the "Beijing Consensus"), 16 Jun. 2005, theory.people.com.cn/GB/40553/3473930.html (accessed 19 Apr. 2007).

4

Entertaining the Masses

Domestic Private Capital, Popular Media, and the Role of Cultural Entrepreneurs

As the party-state has accommodated and selectively incorporated transnational capital in various media and communication sectors, thereby profoundly transforming the system, it has done the same with domestic private capital. Moreover, WTO accession has significantly changed the policy and industrial environment for domestic private media development. Although by no means equal partners, today, three distinctive and yet inextricably intertwined sectors—the party-state, transnational capital, and the domestic private sector—intertwine and jointly shape the Chinese media system and broader cultural environment. There is even a rough division of labor: party-state media inform the nation through their domination in news and informational content provision, transnational media groom the elite with exclusive international news, business information, lifestyle tips, and niche market entertainment, and domestic private media productions amuse the masses and mediate their multifaceted lived experiences with popular entertainment. This chapter analyzes the structural and ideological formation of domestic private capital in the cracks of the party-state media system and under the shadows of transnational media. In analyzing this process, I discuss the historically contingent relationships between private media and independent media, assess the status of domestic private media capital, and explore the political role of China's rising private capitalists or the "national bourgeoisie" in China's rapidly evolving media and culture industry. Differences in semantics, including "people-run media" (*minying meiti*) and "privately owned media" (*siying meiti*), and in terms of capital, "societal capital" (*shehui ziben*), "private capital" (*siying ziben*), and "nonpublic capital" (*feigongyouzhi ziben*), are key dimensions of this analysis.

I begin with a brief account of the party's historical relationship with media outside its orbit, the changing nature and composition of such media, and the shifting terrain in the struggle for press freedom. I then discuss the rise of the private sector, recent state policies that selectively legitimate private media activities, the complicated and dynamic interactions among the state and different forms of media capital, and the rapidly evolving nature of domestic private capital involvement in this sector. The second part offers two case studies: the struggles and strategies of Beijing media entrepreneur Wang Changtian and his Enlight Media, and the media operations of Guangsha and Hengdian industrial conglomerates from Zhejiang Province. These cases not only provide insights into the dynamics of interaction between state policy, state media, and private media, but also highlight the temporal and spatial dimensions of domestic private media capital formation since the late 1990s. Of particular significance is the rapid change in the type of private media players, from former journalist Wang Changtian in Beijing to industrial capitalists in Zhejiang, one of China's most developed provincial economies and the heartland of indigenous Chinese entrepreneurship.

FROM PRIVATELY OWNED MEDIA TO PEOPLE-RUN MEDIA AND BACK AGAIN: A HISTORICAL PERSPECTIVE

In liberal media theory, private ownership is inextricably linked to conceptions of media freedom and political independence from the state. In the party's traditional conception, private media ownership is the hallmark of a bourgeois political system. This is as antithetical to the party's traditional definition of "socialism" as allowing opposition parties. Although the Chinese Constitution does not explicitly prohibit private media ownership, the current licensing system explicitly prohibits the establishment of print and broadcasting media outlets by individual citizens or corporations as independent businesses. Yet the party has had to face private media throughout its pre-1949 and post-1949 history. Before 1949, when it struggled with the Chinese Nationalist Party for political power and cultural hegemony, the Communist Party not only developed its own media system, but also actively sought the collaboration of privately owned commercial media. As a reward for their support and as a defining character of the "New China," which counts the "national bourgeoisie" as one of its founding constituents, the party-state initially permitted the continued operation of a number of privately owned newspapers. However, rapid socialist transformation was quickly implemented and all private newspapers either faltered in the new political economic environment or were eventually nationalized. By 1952, no more privately owned newspapers were left in China.[1]

Various Chinese social forces, however, have never stopped the struggle for independent, if not necessarily privately owned, media. In 1957, when Mao solicited criticisms of the party during the "hundred flowers" moment, liberal intellectuals demanded private newspaper ownership as a dimension of political and ideological pluralism. Implied in the demand for "newspapers run by private individuals" (*siren banbao*) was the assumption that these papers would enjoy editorial autonomy from the party. These voices, however, were quickly suppressed during the anti-rightists campaign in the same year.[2]

The quest for autonomous communication took a completely different, and indeed opposite, turn during the Cultural Revolution, especially during its initial stage between 1966 and 1969. If the call by the "bourgeois rightists" or "capitalist roaders"—as they were then labeled—for private media ownership would constitute one of the obvious manifestations of a potential "capitalist restoration" that Mao and the Red Guards set out to prevent, Mao and the Red Guards tried to accomplish their revolutionary goals through communication channels outside the existing party-state media structure, namely, the big-character posters and Red Guard communication networks.

Red Guard media and communications, including the notorious Red Guard tabloids, were one of the main instruments of the Cultural Revolution. However, they remain perhaps the least studied phenomena in Chinese communication. Although domestic Chinese scholars have written much to reinsert the history of private media in the early years of the People's Republic, as one overseas Chinese who has a keen interest in Red Guard media put it, "virtually no one in China is doing the research, not because of material constraints, but because of political pressure and the harsh suppression of the left wing."[3] Although the fact that Mao mobilized the Red Guards to struggle against the "capitalist roaders" within the party-state apparatuses meant that Red Guard media were not autonomous, suffice it to say that they were not completely manipulated either. In fact, although there are differences in degree and in substance, the kind of anarchical "freedom" and communicative empowerment felt by the Red Guards can be seen as analogous to the brief moment of "press freedom" experienced by liberal intellectuals and party-state journalists in May 1989, when they could report on student demonstrations as a result of a paralyzing division within the party leadership before the eventual June 4 crackdown. As Michael Schoenhals, perhaps the most authoritative scholar on the communicative activities of the Red Guards, observed, the "current affairs groups" (*dongtai zu*), newsletters (*dongtai bao*), or "current intelligence reports in brief" (*dongtai jianbao*) developed by numerous Red Guard organizations between fall 1966 and September 1967 constituted "non-state-controlled current information networks" and represented an important case of state-enabled grassroots "information empowerment."[4] These information networks not only collected information and intelligence on party officials who were suspected of having taken the "capitalist road," but also served to circulate Red Guard struggles against members of the party-state bureaucracy. Indeed, these networks quickly became so powerful and so threatening to the party-state as a whole that it quickly ordered their dismantling, leading to their quick demise by September 1967.[5]

Nevertheless, a more contained form, the Red Guard tabloids, continued to flourish afterward. Again, their relationship with the party-state bureaucracy, including established party-state media, was complicated. Though it is impossible to have a complete picture of the institutional structure of these publications, let alone their numbers, the following self-description, provided by the *Weidong* tabloid, a leading Red Guard tabloid published by the "Weidong" Red Guards at Nankai University in Tianjin in 1968, offers a glimpse of its operation:

> Pioneering work is always difficult. In those early days, the only thing the handful of Weidong fighters had at their disposal was an empty room, a few tables and chairs, and a few discarded stencil-cutting tools. None of them had any experience of running a newspaper, nor had they ever watched a paper being printed. . . . A tiny handful of Party-persons in power taking the capitalist road stripped up hoodwinked representatives of the masses to steal, loot, and smash up the premises. Disaster struck as the printing plant was raided and the printing and typesetting equipment was smashed to pieces. The floor was littered with bits and pieces of lead type. The Weidong fighters set out to repair the machinery and to cast new type. As they did not know how, they humbly invited the workers to be their teachers. They learned the art of typesetting and layout from the skilled workers. On 13 February 1967, the very first issue of *Weidong* reached the broad masses of readers.[6]

The publication claimed to print not only political polemics, but also "complete, systematic, and accurate investigation reports," with a national readership and some of its articles being carried by leading party organs. Elizabeth Perry and Li Xun also shed light on the complicated relationship between the party-state, party-state media, and Red Guard publications in Shanghai. On the one hand, the Shanghai Party Committee, as part of its tradition of "offering sponsorship and direction to a mass organization under its auspices," actively supported the first Shanghai Red Guard organization, "providing its members with an office, helping them to print up a tabloid, entitled *Red Guard*, and dispatching liaison personnel to give organizational and ideological guidance."[7] On the other hand, some Red Guards, who had hoped to piggyback the established distribution network of the official party organ *Liberation Daily* to distribute their own publication called *Red Guard Battle News*, had to occupy *Liberation Daily*'s office to get the Shanghai mayor's agreement to "supply enough paper to print up some 650,000 copies of *Red Guard Battle News*— far greater than the circulation of *Liberation Daily* itself" and to approve the circulation of the tabloid to all *Liberation Daily* subscribers.[8] Much needs to be learned about Red Guard media and communication and any serious inquiry of the topic will necessarily have important theoretical and political implications. Nevertheless, suffice it to say that the relationship between the party-state and Red Guard media and communications cannot be characterized as a simple one-way street of top-down manipulation.

With the death of Mao and the end of the Cultural Revolution, the struggle for an independent press resumed in a quite different political context as part and parcel of the Democracy Wall movement in 1978–1979. An independent press and competitive elections were the two reforms Democracy Wall activists considered essential to the democratization of Chinese socialism.[9] While the official media, small in number and highly centralized in structure, plunged into the repudiation of the Cultural Revolution radical leftists and served as instruments of a "thought liberation" campaign on behalf of Deng and the reformist camp, unofficial publications, namely big and small character posters by individual citizens and unregistered mimeographed journals by small citizens' groups, served as the means of communication for the movement. The unregistered journals, numbering at least 55 in Beijing and 127 in other cities by one account (comparable to the number of official newspapers at the time), were produced with mimeograph machines and openly sold on the streets.[10] They called themselves "people's publications" (*minjian kanwu*) rather than "underground" or "dissident" publications, thus implicitly asserting a claim to political legitimacy in a country that, after all, is named the People's Republic. These publications carried political essays and poems by democracy activists while their editorial teams provided the organizational basis for emerging independent civil society organizations, a situation quite similar to the "outside the party" (*dangwai*) magazines that provided the organizational and ideological basis for an emerging political opposition against one-party rule in Taiwan in the 1970s.[11]

Editorial independence from the party was the defining feature of these publications. However, it would be odd to conceptualize them as constituting a "privately owned press," not only because their ownership status was not legally sanctioned, but also because their founders were not primarily concerned with the property rights, let alone profit making, of their publications. Rather, their primary objective was the promotion of political democracy or cultural democracy.[12] The populist and democratic orientation of these publications was perhaps best captured by the inaugural editorial statement of *Exploration* (*Tansuo*), one of the most famous publications of the era:

> The freedom of speech, press and assembly as provided in the Constitution shall be this publication's guiding principle. . . . As the spokespeople of those who suffer, and taking the search for the cause of China's social backwardness as our main aim, this publication maintains that only the majority of the population who are powerless and poor can define its cause and find a solution. This publication hopes in such a way to reach for the truth.[13]

Though Deng Xiaoping initially encouraged the Democracy Wall activists and their publications, because their critique of Mao and the Cultural Revolution was consistent with the elites' critique of ultra-leftists, the movement soon went beyond what Deng could tolerate and was quickly suppressed. If press freedom is first and foremost defined as the freedom of citizens to publish without state sanction or intervention, the brief flourishing of the people's (*minjian*) press during the Democracy Wall movement turned out to be the highest point of its realization in "socialist" China. These publications were politically, institutionally, and financially independent of the party-state. Although they were sold on the streets and thus assumed the form of a commodity, they were free of commercial advertising. In this way, the market only played a subordinate role as a mechanism in distribution and perhaps in production (to the extent that printing materials must be purchased). Furthermore, this press was owned and controlled by citizens or voluntary associations of citizens, who simultaneously assumed the identities of editor/publishers and the owners of their own means of communication.

The pro-democracy movement in 1989 was another historical moment in the struggle for autonomous communication. By then, however, press freedom mostly meant the editorial freedom of journalists in established party-state media: their freedom from political censorship, their role as watchdogs over power holders, and their freedom to speak for the "people," rather than for the party. While the right of citizens to publish newspapers—a central issue in the elite struggle over press law in the mid-1980s—was raised by a few outspoken liberal intellectuals, by the late 1980s, the rights-based discourse entered the press freedom debate predominantly in the idea of the right of the people to be informed, not to produce their own media.[14] Hu Jiwei, then editor-in-chief of the *People's Daily* and perhaps the most outspoken crusader for press freedom within the party establishment, argued, for example, "Freedom of the press for citizens is the right to be informed as masters of the country, their right of political consultation, their right of involvement in government and their right of supervision over the party and government."[15] Although Hu imagined the ideal newspaper of the future as one run by entrepreneurs who are politically committed or have the power to influence political leaders, he did not explicitly argue for the right of private capitalists to publish newspapers.[16] Hu's thoughts were representative of liberal intellectuals trying to work within the party at the time. Thus, on the one hand, as the Chinese media system began to be commercialized and as the costs for running a newspaper increased, the agents of the "free press" were no longer the grassroots editor/publishers of the Democracy Wall era. On the other hand, private media capitalists who, in the imagination of liberal intellectuals, either have liberal inclinations themselves or would allow journalists to maintain editorial autonomy both from the party-state and from themselves, had not yet become a social force. In media theory, the most elaborate thesis, advanced by journalism scholar Sun Xupei, called for a "socialist press freedom" within a broad Marxist reformist discourse.[17] Sun's proposed press structure presumed the importance of state media ownership and a dominant role for the party-controlled press. However, he argued for supplementary space for independent newspapers run by various professional and social groups.[18]

Compared to 1978, the number of official media outlets had proliferated as a result of liberalization within the party-state sector; members of the liberal intellectual elite, who were the main voices behind the movement, had more or less gained access to the official mass media either through their roles as writers and editors for established media or through de facto control of newly established media outlets loosely affiliated with party-state institutions.[19]

The drastic post-1989 changes I described in the previous chapters have not only set the new context for the struggle for autonomous communication, but also redefined the nature of domestic nonstate media and the relationship between private and independent media.

To begin with, harsh political repression and increased social division in the age of the Internet diminished the possibility of a single and well-organized social force or movement that could advocate a politically independent press as a political cause. On the one hand, politically active individuals from liberal intellectuals to workers' rights activists continued to struggle to publish independent journals and newsletters. Although their editorial scopes became much more specific, these publications were the new incarnations of the Democracy Wall era's unofficial publications, and these unregistered publications, especially working-class newsletters, invariably met harsher state repression. For example, in 1999 a group of laid-off workers in northwest China faced criminal prosecution for the "crime" of setting up a newsletter called *Chinese Work-ers' Monitor* (*Zhongguo gongren guancha*) to expose corruption among offi-cials and mismanagement of their company.[20] On the other hand, for many Chinese citizens, the rise of the Internet and their socialization in this instrumental networked means of communication have increased the opportunities for free expression and an independent press in the literal sense—that is, the ownership of media outlets—is no longer seen to be a prerequisite for "press freedom."[21] Today, the most popular activity of "free press" crusaders is to publish webzines, post their ideas on the In-ternet in various web forums, or increasingly, to blog—by 2006, approxi-mately 10 million Chinese were said to have set up their own blogs.[22] As discussed in chapter 1, this freedom, dependent upon the ownership and management of the Internet infrastructure by the state, is constrained. Nevertheless, this is currently the most feasible and effective means of in-dependent communication.

Then, in a concomitant development, with the commercialization and industrialization of the Chinese media system and the development of an increasingly complicated media structure and division of labor, pri-vate media entrepreneurs, rather than political essayists and "freedom crusaders," have become a social force with interest and capital, in op-erating the media for profit-making purposes. Private media ownership has consequently assumed a different meaning—for example, it could be in the form of sole proprietary control over a media outlet, or it can also mean owning operational right or shares of the business operations of a state-controlled media outlet. In particular, concurrent with the rise of Chinese consumer society and the cultivation of media entertain-ment, the party-state has developed a differentiated policy regarding the entry of private media capital in the rapidly expanding Chinese me-dia and cultural sectors. On the one hand, the production and distribu-tion of news and informational content are deemed "sacred" and con-tinue to be dominated, if not completely monopolized, by the state sector. On the other hand, the provision of nonnews content, from books to television entertainment, and the areas of advertising and distribu-tion have been open to the private sector. As discussed in chapter 2 and as I will detail shortly, this framework has been legitimated by the party's cultural system reform program.

In short, the history of non-party-state-owned media and the related struggle for "press freedom" in the People's Republic, which begin with the party's failed attempt to incorporate private newspapers from the old regime in the early 1950s, seem to have ended up largely with indi-viduals struggling for free expression in the state-owned media and In-ternet on the one hand and the state's selective reincorporation of do-mestic private capital in media and Internet operations on the other.

FROM UNAUTHORIZED LIBERALIZATION
TO SELECTED INCORPORATION

As part of the lexicon of "socialism with Chinese characteristics," the term "privately operated media" (*siying meiti*), often used in private conversations, has been carefully avoided in Chinese academic and policy discourses. Privately owned media in China, a phenomenon that has existed for some time without a name in public discourses, is often called "people-operated media" (*minying meiti*), while the term "non-publicly owned capital" (*feigongyouzhi ziben*) has been used in the recent policy literature, signifying the party-state's lingering hesitation to embrace the word "private." A broader term is "societal capital" (*shehui ziben*), which includes not only private capital, but also state capital outside the established media industry, that is, when public institutions or state-owned enterprises in other sectors of the economy make an investment in the media. In addition to the complications of an evolving terminology, the selective liberalization of the Chinese media market for domestic capital has been marked by many ironies and counterintuitive developments. Of particular significance have been the respective roles of state and foreign media sectors in engendering and facilitating this process.

Rental-Seeking by State Media and
the Rise of Domestic Private Media Capital

The rental-seeking and profit-making activities of state media organizations have been the primary initial mechanisms through which domestic private capital expanded its operation. The development of the private sector in book publishing, distribution, and retailing is most illustrative. Beginning from 1982, the private sector was allowed into the area of book retailing and secondary distribution. However, state publishing houses continued to monopolize book publishing. Yet, state publishing houses, which have exclusive access to ISBN codes assigned by the GAPP, ended up selling the codes (and thus the rights to publish individual books) to private book publishers in their pursuit of quick profits. Since these codes are assigned free of charge by the state, this is a business with no cost and only profit from the perspective of state publishing houses. The risk, of course, is a potential fine and even the closure of the publishing house when a book so published becomes the target of state censorship. The selling of book codes contributed directly to the formation of the so-called second channel of illegal and semilegal book publication and distribution, enabling private book retailers—"book merchants"—to expand their operations to the entire book publishing industry, thereby becoming de facto full-fledged publishers.[23]

The result has been a massive underground and semi-underground publishing industry that has significantly reshaped the Chinese book market. Private bookstores accounted for more than half of total book sales in volume and revenue in 2002 (excluding textbooks, which remain monopolized by the state-owned Xinhua bookstores). Approximately 80 percent of the best-selling books are published and promoted by private "book merchants,"[24] with the private sector employing as many as 400,000 people, doubling the state sector employment.[25] With revenue of about 200 million yuan per year, underground book publishing (and pirating) has become such a lucrative business that it has been dubbed China's "secondary mint," forming a major sector of the underground Chinese economy.[26] Moreover, this underground sector has developed a symbiotic relationship with the state sector. While underground publishers are dependent on the acquisition of official book codes, the selling of book codes enables many of the more than 500 state-owned publishing houses to sustain themselves or make profits in an increasingly commercialized and competitive market, allowing them to even cross-subsidize the publication of less lucrative and state-mandated books. Publishing houses in economically less developed areas have had a particularly dependent relationship on selling book numbers to the underground sector.

In the news media, initial rental-seeking activities by state media institutions involved the "contracting out" of editorial and advertising management functions of existing newspapers and broadcast channels to state capital outside the media sector or private business. Although such a practice was explicitly prohibited by state policies and private capital often risked being punished when the state intervened to stop such activities, the late 1990s and early 2000s have witnessed increasing state tolerance and, indeed, explicit sanction of this practice in a number of cases, including programs on CCTV and China National Radio. A more recent development of this practice has been the partial privatization of state media operations. Within the terms of such an arrangement, or "institutional innovation" in reform terminology, a formal shareholding company is set up between a state media outlet and one or more outside investors. While the investors contribute capital and management expertise, the state outlet contributes the partial operational right of the media. For example, on April 25, 2004, the *Beijing Youth Daily* reported that a shareholding company had been approved by the SARFT to "comprehensively manage the content of Guiyang Television, with the exception of news programming." The new company—with Guiyang Television owning 40 percent of shares; Jintiandi Film Television and Cultural Corp., a Beijing-based private media company, having 30 percent; and Quanlai Industrial Corp., a Shenzhen-based private business, owning the remaining shares—pays Guiyang Television "a channel use fee and operation fee," in exchange for the partial management rights to its two channels.[27] The profits of the new company are to be divided by the three partners. In addition to retaining operation over news programming, Guiyang Television retains final censorship rights and broadcast rights of all programming. The new company, meanwhile, assumes the right to "program purchase and sales, as well as editorial and broadcasting suggestions."[28] The separation of operational rights and ownership rights and the separation of routine editorial responsibility and final gatekeeping responsibility lie at the core of this "institutional innovation."

As Mike Meyer puts it in the context of the Chinese book publishing industry, "The state ostensibly controls publishing," but it relies on private publishers "to do the heavy lifting."[29] The same is the case in other media sectors. This arrangement allows the state to retain strategic control over media content and enables state media institutions and their senior management to secure income without having to be actually engaged in the mundane tasks of media production. In this way, Chinese state media operators are essentially restructuring themselves along the post-Fordist flexible accumulation strategies of capitalistic production, a development that has been characteristic of media industries all over the world.

WTO Accession and Private Capital–Friendly Policies since 2001

In media systems with well-established domestic private ownership, neoliberal globalization typically involves granting foreign capital the same investment opportunities and policy treatments that have already been enjoyed by domestic private media. In this way, foreign capital gains "national treatment." Ironically, transnational capital has been allowed more space to operate than domestic private capital in many areas of the Chinese media system. Consequently, the domestic private sector has been clamoring for "national treatment"—in other words, the privileges that the state has selectively granted to transnational media capital. Although domestic capital has the advantage of already being inside the country, and it has penetrated the domestic market through the back door, as far as the official process of media liberalization is concerned, domestic private capital has ended up riding on the back of transnational capital in China.

A number of factors, including the asymmetrical power relationship between transnational capital and domestic private capital, the party's developmental priorities, as well as its social and cultural biases, have contributed to this development. First, compared with domestic private capital, transnational capital is in a stronger position to negotiate liberalization with the Chinese state. It has the backing of powerful foreign states such as the United States and supranational institutions such as the

WTO, as well as bargaining chips such as allowing Chinese state media to gain access to foreign audiences through their cable networks or other promotional venues. Second, transnational media organizations have management expertise that is deemed essential in modernizing China's national media industry and content favored by a domestic elite audience eager to constitute themselves as the Chinese segment of the transnational consuming strata. As discussed in chapter 3, Chinese officials and media managers have been keen to localize the successful commercializing strategies and formulas of transnational media corporations, which embody modernity and "advanced productive force." In contrast, domestic private capital is not only weak and unorganized, but also seen initially as having little to offer in terms of the party's media modernization objectives. Domestic private media connoted capitalist ideological orientation within the kind of "incorrect and dogmatic understandings of Marxism"[30] that Li Changchun had come to repudiate explicitly by 2003—as I discussed in chapter 2. Meanwhile, the party leadership's lingering elitism against "vulgar" private media culture and working-class cultural establishments such as Internet cafés resonates quite well with the cultural elitism and the internationally oriented consuming priorities and cultural sensibilities of the urban "middle class."

In the print sector, as discussed in chapter 3, IDG established an equity investment joint venture with a Chinese state publisher as early as 1980. In contrast, although funds from domestic nonmedia state companies and private individuals have long been injected into the Chinese press, in a 1999 case that has broad policy implications, the state explicitly rejected the investment and propriety rights of domestic capital in the print media. The case concerned economic interests in *China Business* (*Zhongguo jingyingbao*), a Beijing-based business paper, and its subsidiary, *Lifestyle* (*Jingpin gouwu zhinan*). Although the Industrial Economy Research Institute of the Chinese Academy of Social Sciences, a state entity, has been the official publisher of this paper and its subsidiary, the parent paper's start-up capital came from a typical "contract out" agreement in which an editor secured a publishing permit through a state institution, but was responsible for the paper's finance and operations. The question of who had property rights over these financially successful newspapers soon arose: the state-authorized institutional publisher, which did not invest a single penny, or the editors who provided the initial funding? In arbitrating the case, state authorities affirmed the property rights of the state over the editors. According to the decision, state regulations do not acknowledge any entity other than the authorized publisher as the legitimate investor; consequently, private capital cannot be constituted within the framework of the state press. Instead of having the status of investors, businesses and individuals providing the initial funds are to be treated as donors or creditors.[31] In the broadcasting industry, while the state has permitted the entry of foreign satellite channels into selected markets, not a single domestic private broadcast channel has been sanctioned.[32] In fact, when the Chinese state approved the landing of foreign channels in 2002, it had not even officially acknowledged the legitimacy of domestic private television programming companies that had flourished and done much of the "heavy lifting" in entertaining the masses.

Nevertheless, as I have mentioned in chapter 2, the state has not only officially acknowledged the existence and contribution of the private media sector, but also made significant de jure openings for domestic private capital in peripheral areas of the media system since China's WTO entry in 2001, with the issuance of Document No. 17 on media reform. The party's accommodation to private capitalists at its 16th National Congress in 2002 has further entrenched a private capital–friendly media policy environment. Because the media and cultural sector is increasingly seen as economically lucrative, there has also been growing market entry pressure from domestic nonmedia state capital and private capital. As a state press regulator put it in 2004, given how far the state has gone in privatizing the overall economy and commercializing the media system, the grounds for prohibiting the entry of private capital into this sector had become increasingly shaky.[33] With the party's new focus on targeting the cultural sector as the new site of economic growth, domestic private capital is increasingly seen, and indeed called upon, as a force that can be harnessed to strengthen the national economy in general and the media and cultural sector in particular. Private media capitalists, for their part, have been eager to present themselves as champions of the Chinese nation. For example, Lu Xingdong, owner of Tanglong Media, one of the leading private television production and distribution firms, argued that the maximization of China's "national interests" required the transcendence of the state versus domestic private media dichotomy.[34] Shi Zongyuan, director of the GAPP, agreed, claiming that "the quality of publication has nothing to do with [the type of] capital, but with [state] management."[35]

Official policies issued since 2001 and speeches by media regulators have explicitly and progressively embraced domestic nonmedia state capital and domestic private capital in selected areas of media operations. The landmark Document No. 17 allowed the privatization of state media assets by listing their business sectors on the stock market. On October 27, 2002, Shi Zongyuan announced the principle of "foreign treatment for domestic private capital."[36] On December 31, 2003, the State Council issued two documents that specifically delineated the areas eligible for domestic capital investment.[37] On August 8, 2005, the State Council issued Document No. 10, entitled "Several Decisions Regarding the Entry of Nonpublic Capital into the Culture Industry," reaffirming existing practices and previous policies, while further delineating the scope of operation for "nonpublic capital" (*feigongyou ziben*) in one single document. The document aims to "fully mobilize the entire society to participate in cultural construction," to "gradually form a cultural industry structure in which public ownership is primary and multiple forms of ownership co-develop," and "to promote the overall strength and competitive power" of the country's culture industry. First, Document No. 10 encourages and supports domestic private capital in cultural performances, theater, museums and exhibitions, Internet cafés, entertainment, arts marketing, cartoons and online games, advertising, television series production and distribution, development of broadcasting technologies, movie theaters, film screens in rural areas, and the distribution of books, magazines, and audiovisual products. Second, it encourages domestic private capital in the export of cultural products and services. Third, it encourages domestic private capital to assume controlling interests in joint ventures with state cultural performance institutions and theaters. Fourth, it allows domestic private capital in the areas of printing and recordable and read-only disk reproduction. Fifth, the state allows domestic private capital to have up to a 49 percent investment in cultural enterprises in the areas of printing and distribution, the advertising and distribution areas of news media, music, science and technology, sports, and entertainment programming, and film production, distribution, and exhibition. Sixth, it allows domestic private capital to have up to a 49 percent investment in cultural enterprises involved in the building and operation of cable reception systems, as well as the digital upgrading of cable delivery networks. At the same time, the document reaffirms areas in which domestic private capital is prohibited: investment and operation of news agencies, newspaper and magazine publishing, book publishing, radio and television broadcasting and transmission stations, broadcasting satellites and related services, cable backbone networks, the provision of audio and video services on Internet and news websites, the management of newspaper sections, broadcasting channels and time blocks, the importation of books, periodicals, and audiovisual products, and involvement in state museums.[38]

According to Qi Yongfeng, a researcher at the State Development and Reform Commission who participated in the drafting of Document No. 10, the cultural industry can be divided into three subsections in terms of the extent of the "public nature" of their products, and this in turn determines the state's decision to encourage, limit, or prohibit domestic private capital. The first category is "private cultural goods," that is, those that have a low degree of "public" nature. The production and provision of these goods are to be widely open to nonpublic capital and to be regulated by the market. The second category is "pure public cultural goods," that is, "those that have a particularly high degree of public nature, directly linked to state cultural and informational security or social stability, or are directly linked to the cultural inheritance and innovation of the state and the nation." These goods are to be provided by the state exclusively. The third category, consisting of cultural products defined to be of moderate public value, is to be provided by a mixture of state and private sources.[39] Qi's three categories concretize the conceptual development that has been part of the party's cultural system reform program: the conceptual distinction between "public interest cultural undertaking" and the "cultural industry," the absorption of news media into the broader realm of culture, the deployment of the concept of the "public" and the conflation of regime interest with the "public interest," as well as the legitimacy of the state's role in the commercialized provision of media and culture. Following the issuance of the party-state's "Several Opinions on Deepening Cultural System Reform" in January 2006, government officials have announced further supports for the development of domestic private capital in selected areas of the media and cultural sector.[40]

However, central and local authorities have artificially set high barriers for business entry by private capital, raising the stakes of business and keeping the field of private media operation in the hands of established and politically well-connected capitalists. I have already discussed how the central government's exorbitant 10-million-yuan minimum capitalization requirement was used to shut down leftist websites. This is not an isolated development. For example, in a 2005 draft regulation, Guangdong's Dongguan City proposed a minimum of 1 million yuan in registered capital investment for setting up an Internet café operation. This, in the words of a former unregistered Internet café owner whose business was shut down by the government, would ensure that instead of the ordinary people, the rich people would get the licenses for Internet cafés.[41] Similarly, in Yiwu City in Zhejiang Province, a minimum of 300 computers and an operational space of 750 square meters were required for any Internet café business in 2005. A responsible official stated explicitly that the high stakes would force a business owner to ensure self-discipline in the management of Internet cafés.[42]

To be sure, actual practices often exceed what is permissible in policy. In the print media, there have been many cases of outside capital—both state and private capital—investment in newspapers since 2001. Well-known examples have included Shanghai Fuxing Group's investment in the Guangdong-based *21st-Century Business Herald* and Shandong Sanlian Group's investment in the Beijing-based business newspaper the *Economic Observer*. According to one account, more than 40 state and private businesses had made investments in over 100 print media outlets by 2004.[43] Added together, these private capital investments have ensured the emergence of a strong and vocal business and financial press, thus significantly boosting the discursive power of the rising capitalist strata. Unregistered Internet cafés, meanwhile, have continued to flourish *despite* prohibitive minimum capitalization and scale economy requirements and repeated government campaigns to clamp down on them.[44] However, if private capital has been able to expand and legitimize its ascending discursive power (if not necessarily its legal investment rights as illustrated in the *China Business* case) by sustaining or, in many cases, enabling the very publication of nominally state-owned media outlets, the party-state's stringent business regulations and market consolidation efforts, which in the Internet industry have involved the establishment of Internet café chains under the control of large businesses, have effectively served to curtail popular political communication. For example, small Internet cafés, especially those established by marginal entrepreneurs or "working-class providers"[45] of information and communication technologies (e.g., laid-off workers or veterans) who may have organic social ties to the urban working class, could potentially facilitate communication among disenchanted social strata.[46] They have the potential to function in a way that is analogous to the "reading rooms," "newsrooms," radical bookshops, cafés, and other establishments that had facilitated the development of working-class consciousness and political culture in England during the 19th century.[47] However, precisely because of their illegal status and their extremely precarious existence (due to their inability to pay high registration fees and meet prohibitive minimum capitalization requirements), their owners/operators are particularly vigilant against any subversive uses that may draw official attention.[48]

In short, rapid changes in the media industry and media technology, differences between media sectors and technological platforms and thus uneven barriers to entry, administrative fragmentation and the difference in the political cultures of various government regulatory agencies, as well as the complicated nature of China's political and cultural geography have all made the de facto and officially sanctioned processes and the scope of private capital involvement in the media extremely complex. As well, as discussed in chapters 1 and 2, because the party refuses to open up the issue of independent media ownership politically and at the legislative level, state council decisions, government agency regulations, and their various administrative orders remain the exclusive policy instruments. Throughout this process, the party-state has maintained its firm bottom line in prohibiting domestic private capital and independent media from accessing and controlling the core aspects of the communication system such as news and current affairs production and the backbone networks of broadcasting, cable, and satellite transmission.

Meanwhile, there has not been any high-profile call for "private press ownership" in the past decade. Private capital and its spokespeople seem to have been acquiescent in this regard. Just as liberal and neoliberal intellectuals have more or less been able to express themselves in existing party-state media outlets, business papers and journals funded by private capital, as well as the Internet, domestic private capital has found plenty of profit-making opportunities in the media and cultural sector. Domestic private capital, given its incorporated status and the fact that its voices have been increasingly well represented in the media system, simply appears not to have a compelling imperative to mount a frontline confrontation with the party on the issue of full private media ownership.[49]

STATE AND PRIVATE DYNAMICS IN POPULAR ENTERTAINMENT: THE CASE OF TELEVISION DRAMA

The ad hoc and legalized partial entry of domestic capital has intensified the capitalistic orientation of the media system in two ways. As noted above, private financing has led to the expansion of newspapers and magazines specializing in business and consumer information, thus boosting the discursive power of the rising business and consumer strata. In the new media sector where the financial barriers to entry are lower in the areas of website and Internet café operations, (big) capital–friendly state business regulations and recentralization campaigns have served an important social containment function. In broadcasting and audiovisual media, private capital has played a major role in the media's decisive reorientation toward entertainment, with the flourishing of various genres of television drama and syndicated television programming since the mid-1990s. This section focuses on the dynamic interaction between state policy, state media, and private television drama production, and examines how these processes shape both the structure and thematic orientations of the Chinese television drama industry, creating a highly complex and dynamic popular television culture under the party's hegemony.

Television drama is the most popular television genre in China. In 2003 television drama accounted for 28.8 percent of total viewing time of the national television audience, surpassing news (21.1 percent) and features (7.7 percent).[50] Reflective of its mass entertainment orientation, television drama generates 70 percent of the total advertising revenue of television stations, with the most lucrative prime time television drama garnering an advertising income that is 10 times the show's purchasing cost.[51] According to a CCTV-Sofres survey, the average Chinese audience spent 179 minutes watching television daily in 2002, with 52 minutes on television drama. Compared with the average audience, the audiences for television dramas tend to be older, poorer, less well educated, less likely to work in state administration, business management, and white-collar occupations, more likely to be female and rural residents, and more likely to be in central China.[52] Thus, if Phoenix TV's globally oriented news and current affairs programming targets the elites, domestically produced television dramas, the mainstay of advertising revenue for domestic television stations, constitute the main staple in the reform era "culture of the masses."[53] Starting from the broadcast of *Aspirations* in 1990, there has been a spectacular growth of the domestic television drama production industry, feeding into broadcasters' embrace of it as the most lucrative content, and intensifying the processes of commercialization in the television industry. For example, the year 2000 alone saw the broadcast of 13,621 episodes of television drama, compared with just above 12,000 episodes between 1978 and 1990 all together.[54] From 2000 to 2005, the number of domestically produced and distributed television drama episodes ranged from 9,005 to more than 11,000.[55] Unique dramatic genres for different audience niches, including imperial costume dramas, "red classic" dramas—television series based on adaptations of classics in revolutionary literature or original productions set in the party's revolutionary history—martial arts dramas, crime/anticorruption dramas, urban family dramas, and idol-of-youth dramas, have flourished, offering one hot series after another in hypercommercialized and hypercompetitive national and regional television markets. Significantly, partly because of tightened state regulation over importation, the market share and influence of imported drama has declined considerably: a 1994 SARFT policy limited the total volume of imported shows to 25 percent of total television drama broadcast on a given television channel and 15 percent between 6:00 p.m. and 10:00 p.m.; a 2000 policy further tightened this requirement, allowing only SARFT-imported shows on all television channels between 7:00 p.m. and 9:30 p.m., in effect banning the broadcast of imported shows during this period. In 2002, 18 percent of television stations did not purchase any foreign drama, and imported television drama accounted for only 14.1 percent of total purchased television drama in the same period.[56]

At the heart of this strong domestic television drama production industry are approximately 1,100 "societal" television production companies, including both private capital and nonmedia state capital but primarily private capital, with over two-thirds, or more than 700, of these companies specializing in dramatic production in 2002.[57] These companies account for 90 percent of total television production companies and a growing share of capital investment in the Chinese television production industry. In 2003 private capital accounted for as much as 80 percent of the total investment of 3 billion yuan.[58] Although many of the private television drama production companies are small in scale, a handful of companies have considerable production capacities. One of the leading private production companies, Hairun Film and Television Production Co., for example, produced over 11 television dramas with a total of 289 episodes in 2003.[59] In short, the entry of private capital has dramatically increased China's production capacity in this area, effectively making China the biggest producer of television drama in the world.[60]

Private capital operates under the state's multifaceted regime of control. Apart from content censorship rules, a television drama permit system, established in 1986, licenses the production of television drama and thus controls market entry into this area. Of the two types of licenses, type A allows the production of multiple shows and has an effective period of two years; type B allows the production of a single show, with an effective period of six months. Until August 2003, type A licenses were monopolized by state-owned television production studios. By the end of 2004, however, 24 type A permits had been issued to production companies outside the state sector. Because many smaller private companies are not able to obtain even a type B license, they end up relying on state studios to legitimate their own productions—by paying a fee to a state unit and issuing the show under its name or as a joint production. In this way, state production units become rental-seeking entities in the same manner as state book publishers.

Two other mechanisms of regulatory control involve the authorities' approval of the topic of a proposed television series and the issuing of a distribution permit. These permits constitute preproduction and postproduction censorship. A production company, even one with a type A permit, must first register and get approval of a proposed show from the SARFT and its provincial counterparts. After the show is produced, it must be previewed by these authorities and obtain a distribution permit. Both processes serve as important filtering mechanisms. For example, during one approval period in 2004, 534 shows out of the proposed 700 were approved for production.[61]

In addition, the annual "television drama topic planning" system is specifically designed to strengthen the state's guidance and coordination of television series production. At the annual national television series planning meeting, the SARFT issues guidelines regarding the dominant themes of television drama production. For example, in 2004 the SARFT required television drama production to coordinate with the celebration of many political anniversaries, including the 55th anniversary of the establishment of the People's Republic of China, the 100th anniversary of Deng Xiaoping's birth, and the 85th anniversary of the establishment of the Communist Party. While state-owned production companies are expected to follow the plan, "even private companies will voluntarily cater to the political themes in the plan"[62] to ensure a favorable spot in the broadcasting schedule.

The state also influences the direction of television drama production through administrative and financial means, effectively incorporating mechanisms of market regulation and moral sanction. One such mechanism is targeted state funding in "main melody" shows—that is, shows that are deemed by the state to promote dominant ideological themes. Another is the award system. In addition to the annual "Feitian" award for best television drama, established in 1981, the post-1989 attempt at strengthening the state's role in guiding ideological work saw the establishment of another state-level award for best cultural products, including best television drama. In less formalized forums, state leaders, propaganda officials, as well as official media outlets issue speeches that aim to shape the direction of television drama production. In unusual circumstances, authorities may even order the last minute editing and rescheduling of an ongoing television series. Finally and no less effectively, propaganda and broadcast authorities may issue ad hoc administrative orders with regard to the production and broadcast of a particular genre of shows. For example, in April 2004, the SARFT issued a special administrative order to tighten censorship over "red classics" by specifying that such topics must be approved by the SARFT itself and obtain a "Television Drama Distribution Permit" from the national-level agency, rather than simply being approved by provincial broadcasting authorities, as is the case with other topics.[63] Specifically, the order aimed to prevent television dramas that "flirt with" revolutionary classics by exploiting their fame but making excessive changes that denigrate the party's revolutionary legacy and present a less-than-dignified treatment of revolutionary heroes. Then, 10 days afterward, the SARFT issued yet another administrative order concerning television shows involving law and order issues and criminal cases (*she'an ju*). The order, entitled "Notice on Strengthening the Censorship and Broadcast Management of Case-Related Shows," effectively banned the showing of crime dramas and police-related reality shows during prime time and tightened the approval of shows on this topic. The order was implemented *despite* the fact that all the banned shows had gone through the state's topical approval and censorship procedures. The impact was immediate: ongoing popular shows in this genre were moved out of prime time overnight, television stations that defied the order were reprimanded, and less than half of the proposed crime shows were approved.[64] Because crime shows accounted for nearly one-third of total television drama shows and because prime time is 10 times more valuable in terms of advertising, one estimate had it that at least 1 billion yuan worth of investment was affected. Many small production and distribution companies suffered a fatal blow.[65]

State broadcasters themselves serve as a secondary center of power in shaping private television drama production and distribution. The power relationship between state television broadcasters and private television production companies is highly asymmetrical. First, because Chinese television broadcasting is monopolized at each level of the government, each local market is a monopoly, and private producers are at the mercy of television broadcasters, who devise and often change the rules of the game. For example, instead of paying private producers real cash, a common practice has been for television stations to "pay" private producers in advertising time. Private producers must themselves sell the advertising time to potential sponsors to realize revenue. Consequently, private producers are working with a "double jeopardy"—they have to sell programs to television stations first and then sell advertising time to advertisers. Although competition at the national level has intensified, the SARFT's push toward conglomeration and the merging of over-the-air and cable television channels in 2000 has undermined competition within provincial markets, creating an unfavorable industrial and market condition for the private drama sector at a time when state policy toward private capital investment has loosened. As well, because state television authorities have their own affiliated production studios, private production companies are in an unfavorable market position.

Yet the relationship between state regulation and private production companies is not always a one-sided dependency. After all, the SARFT's policy of limiting foreign imports has been a key enabler of the domestic private television drama industry. More importantly, the rental-seeking behaviors of state sector managers have opened up many points of entry for the private sector. Bribery is commonplace and has been formalized—it is an open secret that state television drama program purchasers normally receive a 15 percent commission for the purchasing of television drama from a private company. This mechanism is so powerful that it can at least partially undermine the structural advantage of the production arm of a state television station in the market, so that instead of buying programs from a production unit owned by the same broadcasting conglomerate, program purchasers end up buying privately produced shows and programming them at more favorable slots. Because private television production companies have a more agile institutional mechanism that allows them to respond to popular tastes and sensibilities more quickly and more effectively, they are often able to produce television shows that state television broadcasters find more attractive than their own in-house production. Coproduction arrangements between state and private production studios are also common, as both sides can exploit their respective resources.

The party, in its attempt to establish a new form of cultural hegemony, has also awarded popularity, regardless of the status of the producers.

Many award-winning television dramas have been produced by private companies. For the experienced private producer who has learned to play the game, gaining state approval on a topic and a distribution permit is often a matter of procedure. As one successful private producer stated, because it is an investment behavior and because it involves a huge amount of money, "to produce a show that cannot be exhibited is to commit suicide."[66] For this producer, even the April 2004 SARFT policy restricting crime shows at prime time is not an insurmountable barrier. The key, as he pointed out, is to gain a fine understanding of the intricacies of the party's propaganda objectives. For example, although concern about the negative impact of excessive violence and graphic depiction of crime on youths was the apparent reason behind the SARFT's "screen cleaning" order, a more political, though implicit, motive was the central authorities' concern about the excessive depiction of official corruption, including high-level corruption, on the television screen and its negative impact on the legitimacy of the party. Thus, he reasoned that so long as excessive violence and the portrayal of high-level corruption are avoided, such shows may still find a favorable place on the television screen.[67] In short, a vibrant state and private partnership has flourished in the business of entertaining the masses. By incorporating and containing private capital in cultural production, the government "has effectively ameliorated tensions and conflicts between an increasing demand and ideological control."[68]

State control, the agency of media producers, the profit imperative of private investors, and not least, an active television audience interacted to create a highly dynamic and multifaceted televisual popular culture. Official propaganda, popular concerns for hot social topics, "middle-class" social reformist sensibilities, and even traces of elite liberal intellectual discourse of the mid-1980s intertwine in complicated ways, contributing to the polysemic and hybrid nature of Chinese television discourses and their multifaceted readings, with dominant, residual, emergent, and different ideological fragments borrowing from and reinforcing each other.[69] Compared with news and current affairs programming, television drama, because of its fictional character and its more popular social basis, has been able to address popular sensibilities and social conflicts in unique ways. Rather than mere "indoctritainment" or "the opiate of the consumer,"[70] popular television, transformed by private capital and absorbing the production techniques and styles of Hong Kong, Taiwan, and international television, serves as a controlled forum for the discussion of a wide range of highly emotive issues during a period of epochal transformation, from extramarital affairs in the private domain to class, power, layoffs, and corruption in the public domain, while effectively "convert[ing] areas of contestation into spheres of co-option."[71] "Mainstream melody" dramas about law and order issues, for example, often address the topic of corruption, while packaging themselves in the form of Hollywood action adventures, replete with suspense, intrigue, love, lust, conspiracy, murder, car chases, and violence. One episode in an otherwise banal law and order series entitled *A Female Police Chief* (*Nü jingcha jüzhang*) even manages to build a plot around a standoff between the police and workers protesting against privatization in a factory, a topic that the news media are unlikely to report. Likewise, while television dramas about imperial dynasties tend to cultivate a profoundly antidemocratic political culture via the glorification of autocratic power and the naturalization of traditional values of patriarchy, submission, and social hierarchy, their narratives often smuggle in contemporary political and social critiques—for example, by presenting upright imperial officials to attack contemporary widespread corruption and express popular desires for social justice and a clean and responsible government. In this way, the production and consumption of historical dramas serve as a rich symbolic site for rhetorical contestation among various ideological forces and discursive positions in contemporary China.[72]

Perhaps the most intriguing and ideologically most productive television drama genre is the "red classics" as exemplified by *How Steel Is Tempered* (*Gangtie shi zenyang liancheng de*). Based on a novel by Soviet author Nikolai Ostrovsky, the series, which first aired in 2000 and has since served as a paradigmatic example of many more productions in this genre, tells the life story of Pavel Korchagin, a communist soldier and railway worker who devoted his life to the Russian Revolution by first fighting against the old regime and then dedicating himself to socialist construction. Popularized in the mass media and the educational system throughout the Maoist period, Pavel is a household name in China. Within the traditional communist ideology, "Pavel Spirit" stands for selfless dedication to a revolutionary cause, class struggle, and the emancipation of humanity through the creation of a communist society. Though Pavel is perhaps just another television character for a young generation fixated on celebrity and another promotional venue for advertisers, "for China's older generation, many of them Soviet-educated, veneration of the heroic Pavel is real enough and steeped in nostalgia for what they recall as a simpler time."[73] The origination and production of the show is reflective of the mutually constitutive state and market, public and private dynamics in popular television production. Rather than being initiated by old left ideologues, who neither have access to capital nor command the necessary skills, the idea for the show came from a private sector television drama producer, China Vanke Co., a property developer in Shenzhen whose audiovisual production unit decided to produce a major television series of artistic and commercial significance in celebration of the 50th anniversary of the People's Republic and the arrival of the new century. It was, in short, more an "uncertain venture capital investment" project than a preoccupation with the political and social significance of the show.[74] As Sun Jing, a Vanke executive, was quoted as saying, "The major Chinese emperors have all been done, but no one has done Pavel."[75] The idea of having yet another cultural icon "done" or commodifying yet another potentially lucrative symbol of the revolution, however, soon took on a life beyond its origin. The Shenzhen party PD loved the idea and became the show's partial investor. The Central Party PD, in turn, not only supported the Shenzhen party PD's endorsement of the show, but also gave clear guidelines about the show's production. Consequently, the show became a party-promoted propaganda project. Soon, CCTV and China International Television Corporation (CITC) joined the project, becoming partial investors and coproducers. The show was shot in the Ukraine, and CCTV, which had approved the show by the end of December 1999, decided to premiere it on February 23, 2000, at the Great Hall of the People, an unprecedented move in the history of popular television, and broadcast it on CCTV1 in prime time between February 28 and March 23, 2000, to coincide with the NPC and NPPCC meetings, thus dramatizing the political meaning of the show.[76] CCTV broadcast a rerun between April and May of the year, and the show was also broadcast on provincial networks. The show garnered an average national rating of 9–10 percent and created a national media event, with newspaper discussions, seminars, and Internet forums.

The text offered multiple readings and provided a forum for people with different ideological perspectives to converge—from anticommunists seeing Pavel as an irrelevant cultural hero of yesteryear, to "old leftists" ignoring the show's revisionist interpretation of the topic, cheering the very appearance of a communist signifier on the television screen at all, and claiming the continuing relevance of Pavel's revolutionary spirit in the fight for socialism during a period of capitalistic triumph. The most fascinating aspect of this complex dynamic of encoding and decoding, however, is the class dimension. In the original book, class conflict constituted an insurmountable barrier in Pavel's romance with Tonia, the beautiful daughter of a government official in the Russian ancien régime. Pavel, elevated by his proletarian class consciousness, joins the Bolshevik Revolution and defeats the enemies of the revolution in stirring battle scenes. In the Chinese TV version, Tonia's bourgeois class status and subjectivity were diluted to emphasize her transcendental love, with Tonia's father recast as a humanistic doctor, a "middle-class" professional—the contemporary Chinese media's favored class trope. The lovers are separated by war but meet up again at the end, with Tonia, now married to somebody else, having named her son "Pavel" in a Hollywood cliché. The subtext is clear: she has never stopped loving him, class consciousness be damned. As the director Mr. Han, who rewrote two-thirds of the original book for the TV version, said, "We are at the end of the 20th century. You can't look at things in the old narrow way."[77] Members of the show's audience, overtly sensitive to the issue of class and acutely aware of class stratification and the insurmountable class barriers in Chinese society, however, overwhelmingly reread a class-based discourse into the love story. As Yu Hongmei put it, the term "class," implicitly and explicitly, was written everywhere in media-generated popular discussions about the love story.[78] Thus, if the makers of the show, in line with the official discourse, purposely diluted the "class struggle" theme of the original text to the protest of old leftists, television audience members ended up reinjecting class back into the show, making it a cultural resource for a critique on contemporary Chinese class relations. This class theme, of course, was no longer the same as the original text, which glorified Pavel's proletarian revolutionary class consciousness, but a reversal. It glorified Tonia for her love of a person from a lower class, thus expressing an implicit critique of existing class relations in Chinese society and a popular desire to transcend them. In short, at a time when the party-state's censorship regime suppresses the autonomous rearticulation of radical discourses, a privately invested and market-driven popular television production ended up symbolically reaffirming the party's communistic ideological legacy on the one hand, while simultaneously transforming it on the other. Still, what are the trajectories and subjectivities of China's media and cultural entrepreneurs, their political and cultural orientations, as well as their specific interactions with the party-state and state sector media? I turn to this topic next.

FROM ENLIGHTENMENT TO ENTERTAINMENT: WANG CHANGTIAN AND ENLIGHT MEDIA

Wang Changtian is an indisputable leader of China's fledgling private media and entertainment industry. However, to become China's "entertainment king" was not his initial ambition. The push of the state sector and the pull of the market facilitated his astonishing rise as a successful private media entrepreneur. Born in 1965 into a poor rural family in Dalian, Liaoning Province, Wang lived in impoverished conditions during his youth. Malnutrition and exhaustion made Wang a victim of tuberculosis as he prepared for the highly competitive university entrance exam.[79] He entered the elite Fudan University in Shanghai in 1984 and received a journalism degree in 1988. He first worked in the NPC's News Bureau and as a financial reporter at *China Industrial and Commercial Times* (*Zhongguo gongshang shibao*) between 1988 and the early 1990s. In 1995,

Wang became a producer at *Beijing Express*, a popular news program on Beijing Television. He ran into political trouble in 1998, and his job was temporarily suspended after he broadcast a critical report on Falun Gong and incited a major protest by the group, which was not yet officially banned at the time. Wang was upset and quit his job.

After failed attempts to secure positions at Phoenix TV and Asia TV in Hong Kong, Wang and four other collaborators set up the Beijing Enlight Television Planning and Research Center in August 1998 and started television production "outside the system." Like many other Chinese journalists, Wang had a strong sense of social responsibility and pursued journalism for lofty political and cultural ideals. Wang's initial focus for his new business was to produce serious programming on social and cultural issues. As Li Xin puts it, even though Wang had left Beijing Television, he "still wanted to produce 'internal reference television' [i.e., critical and investigative reporting not for broadcast, but for internal policy reference by government officials], with a whole heart to use television to serve a social purpose."[80] Consequently, his initial business model was to sell program ideas and low-budget short features to state television stations. The operation was called a "center" and not a "company" for political reasons: private individuals were not allowed to engage in television production, and there was no way to register a business in this area.

The fledgling business struggled on the verge of collapse during its first year. By September 1999, all Wang's partners had quit. Eventually, sensing the transformation of Chinese television from a strong political propaganda and educational orientation to a stronger entertainment orientation, Wang abandoned his initial content plans to find a politically safe and commercially attractive market niche: news reporting in the area of entertainment, or infotainment.[81] In July 1999, Wang, with the support of a CCTV producer who was his former colleague, launched *China Entertainment Report* (*Zhongguo yule baodao*), a 30-minute program specializing in "news" about current developments in China's rapidly expanding entertainment industry. The program became an instant success with television stations across the country. More programs were launched. An extensive distribution and sales network was established. As with companies in television drama production, Wang's company exchanges television programs for advertising time.

By 2004, Wang's Enlight Media had grown into China's largest private television program producer and syndicate, with its revenue of 300 million yuan the equivalent of the combined revenue and profits of the next four largest private television content producers.[82] In addition to its flagship program, the company, within the span of four years, launched a dozen programs specializing in reporting, commenting, and promoting different sectors of the entertainment industry, with titles such as *Enter-*

tainment Center, Pepsi Music Chart, Entertainment Live Abroad, Star, Celebrity Weekly, Modern Times, Starry Tales, Sports Live, Top Chinese TV Drama, Variety Tonight, etc. These programs, totaling more than six hours per day, are carried by 300 television channels across the country, with an aggregated potential audience of 1 billion. By 2004, the company boasted a staff of 366 and had offices in media capitals such as Shanghai, Guangzhou, Hong Kong, Taipei, and elsewhere in China. As Wang's business expanded into websites, newspaper publishing, events organization, and other publicity and promotional services for the entertainment industry, Enlight Media has emerged as a powerful broker among state television stations, the entertainment industry, its audiences, and advertisers.

Symptomatic of the state's gradual opening toward the private sector since the early 2000s, Enlight Media's relationship with party-state authorities and state television stations has undergone some interesting twists. The company emerged from and has a symbiotic relationship with the state sector. When Wang first got started and operated as an unregistered business, state television's economic interests and demands for his popular programming provided him with a power base. For example, Wang was initially dependent on his former employer Beijing Television to broadcast his programs, and he used its support to expand his reach in television markets across the country. He was also dependent on the station for policy support and editorial gatekeeping. As an independent producer, Wang did not have direct access to official propaganda guidelines, including the latest PD orders that ban certain stars or content. These guidelines are instrumental in order to produce politically safe programming that ensures it will be broadcast. Consequently, Wang characterized his initial undertaking as one of "joint production," with personnel from Beijing Television assuming the roles of program producer and supervisor.[83] More recently, however, state television stations, especially resource-rich provincial stations, have increasingly seen Wang as a competitor and use him not only as a program supplier, but also as an innovator whose program content and formats they can mimic. For example, in the Beijing and Hunan markets, Wang has seen some of his programs moved to less popular channels, or dropped altogether, as Beijing Television did with his flagship program *Entertainment Live* in 2004. Thus, although the state sector can provide an initial point of entry and even a power base for private producers, its ultimate control of broadcast channels and its economic self-interest can also work to constrain private sector growth.

Meanwhile, Wang's status within the state policy establishment has improved. When he first started, he had to struggle to register his operation as a proper business. He also had to adjust to a hostile and often unstable policy environment. For example, though the company took off in the context of the reformist push for the separation of broadcasting and production in 1999, by 2000, the SARFT had put an end to discussions of this policy option; consequently, Wang felt that the policy discourse conducive to his business was receding.[84] Moreover, although the company initially had no legally sanctioned status, it had to respond to the SARFT's arbitrary interventions and containment strategies. For example, in 2000, one year after Wang gained national market success, he was in trouble with the SARFT. The problem was not so much the content of his programs, which were popular and considered politically harmless, but the names, such as *China Entertainment Report, World Entertainment Report,* and *China Network Report.* How dare a private television studio without legal status claim the name "China"? Furthermore, how dare a private television production studio use the term "report" (*baodao*) in a country where news reports are the exclusive domain of state-authorized media operations? The SARFT ordered Wang to change the names before December 5, 2000. Thus, *China Entertainment Report* became *Entertainment Live, World Entertainment Report* became *Entertainment Live Abroad,* and *China Network Report* became *Network World* (discontinued in August 2001).[85]

However, as the state moves from tolerating private television content producers to officially encouraging private capital participation and espousing the separation of broadcasting and production, it has also started to incorporate private producers into its own administrative orbit. Consequently, Wang and some of his fellow private producers have gained more legitimacy. Wang became a business partner of the SARFT in 2003 when he contracted with the SARFT-affiliated *China Radio and Television Journal* (*Zhongguo guangbo dianshi bao*) to publish *Big Star* (*Mingxing*), an entertainment weekly that unabashedly claims that "star-tracing is our job." In December 2004, Wang, together with two other private sector television producers, was for the first time invited to participate in the annual national meeting of the heads of broadcasting bureaus, the most important annual meeting of the broadcasting administration in which policy issues concerning the entire broadcasting industry are discussed and formulated. When I interviewed him on January 6, 2005, Wang spoke with great satisfaction about how his push for the further privatization of television program production, more specifically, his suggestion that television stations' in-house-produced content be limited to 30 percent of their schedule, received a favorable hearing from a deputy director of the SARFT. As he commented, this was unimaginable just a few years ago.[86]

"We have some new ideas and practices regarding media and entertainment," says a billboard mounted on top of the headquarters of Wang's Enlight Media in Beijing. Enlight Media has contributed to partially demonopolizing state broadcasting by socializing program production, a significant development in the Chinese broadcasting industry. By focusing on infotainment and targeting young audiences interested in the latest developments in popular culture, Wang has not only built his success on the Chinese television industry's entertainment turn, but also contributed to its promotion and the cultivation of a dynamic Chinese popular culture. Thus, if private television drama producers focus on entertaining an older, less well educated, and poorer audience with engaging melodramatic stories, Wang's infotainment programming specializes in entertaining China's upwardly mobile and popular culture–conscious young television audience. In both sectors, private producers serve as innovators and trendsetters in cultivating popular tastes and show state television stations and their in-house production studios the way to popularity and market success.

While proud of his business success, Wang is ambivalent about the proestablishment ideological implications of his programming. He said in a 2003 interview with me that most television dramas and entertainment programs serve as a venting mechanism for the society. In his view, there was a fundamental "dislocation in the party's propaganda theory." On the one hand, party propaganda policy still adheres to dogmatic leftist principles of enlightening and uplifting people's spirits through culture while regarding popular entertainment as trivial, vulgar, and even unhealthy. In reality, however, market-driven pop culture and soft entertainment serve a conservative role of social pacification and thus function to sustain the party's continuing political dominance. In Wang's understanding, most individuals at the upper-middle rank of the party's propaganda establishment understood the regime-sustaining role of market-driven popular culture, but dared not acknowledge such a role explicitly. However, the understanding among individuals occupying the highest propaganda positions—that is, ministry-level officials—according to Wang, was mixed. While some understood the regime-sustaining role of popular entertainment, others did not and continued to operate with a leftist vanguard mentality of culture as means of popular enlightenment, thus finding pop culture wanting, or even destructive. For Wang, this bifurcated and disjointed position in the party's propaganda theory had implications in terms of official attitudes toward his business: if his business was seen as ideologically conducive to the party's ruling, he should be recognized as such, that is, as the hero of the party's propaganda mission of sustaining social stability. Notwithstanding Wang's views of the party's reluctance to embrace him as a sign of the continuing legacy of a leftist understanding of party propaganda, by 2004, when Li Changchun declared that a market orientation is consistent with the party's ideological objective and when Wang was invited to the state's annual broadcasting industry planning meeting, there was clearly no more doubt about the state's acquiescence and, indeed, appreciation of the regime-supporting role of private media and cultural entrepreneurs. Yet Wang's own ideas and practices also embody a tension between an intellectual vanguardist notion of enlightening the public and an awareness of the conservative ideological impact of popular culture: although he adopts the word "enlight" as the English translation of the company name *guangxian* (light), he acknowledged that the company's sole business is to "entertain."

Ranked by the official *Youth of China* (*Zhongguo qingnian*) magazine as one of "the 100 young people who may influence 21st-century China" in 2001, Wang's ambition is to grow Enlight Media, which has been ranked highly by Forbes and Deloitte & Touche as one of the most promising and fastest-growing companies in the Asia-Pacific region, into China's Time Warner. Toward this end, he has rapidly diversified his company by entering into areas that are less dependent on the broadcast platform, including Internet content provision and value-added services in wireless. The company's print media platform, *Big Star*, is set to imitate Time Warner's *Entertainment Weekly*. It aims to "gather the biggest possible pleasure-seeking reading public" and eventually become "capable of competing with *Entertainment Weekly*."[87] In June 2004, Enlight Media established a subsidiary company, Enlight Film, to undertake film marketing and promotion. Although Wang operates his business in a low-key manner, he has been adept at using the market-oriented media, especially their fascination with and normative investment in the private media sector, to build a positive business environment. He is a heavy reader of the biographies of global media moguls, seeing them as his own role models, and has openly expressed his ambitions: "Five key figures influenced the development of media and entertainment industries in the West. There should be five similar individuals in China, and I hope to be one of them, making [my company] into China's Time Warner."[88]

Wang and his fellow private media producers face two major structural constraints over the further development of the private sector in broadcasting—the banning of private ownership of broadcast channels and private provision of news and current affairs. Wang is hopeful that he will be able to circumvent the first constraint. He believes that there are a number of openings within the current system. At the policy level, the state's implicit permission for the separation of ownership rights and operation rights to broadcast channels (compared with the initial step of separating the production and broadcasting functions of state broadcasters) is a further step toward the demonopolizing of state broadcasting. Along with other private content producers, he is busy setting up joint ventures with state television stations to manage specialty broadcasting channels. Secondly, the private sector can exploit uneven developments in the Chinese broadcasting industry and the uneven pattern of China's global integration. That is, while provincial-level television stations in

Beijing, Shanghai, and other more developed areas tend to "worship the foreign" and are eyeing collaborative opportunities with transnational corporations, provincial television stations in the interior as well as municipal-level stations are more willing to collaborate with domestic private producers. As usual, challenges and innovations tend to come from the margins and the parts of the state media system that have the least vested interest in the current structure. Third, just as the proliferation of local cable channels in the late 1990s and their demands for popular programming provided the opportunity for the rise of private sector content providers, Wang believes that the rise of satellite television and the state's current drive toward digital television and the development of IPTV (Internet Protocol Television) provides opportunities for private operators to secure satellite and digital channels in specialty programming and the pay television markets. Wang views American-style network television as the most efficient means of organizing the television industry in China and is hopeful of the prospects of operating a regional, even national, television network in the near future.[89]

Presently, Wang is not interested in delving into news and current affairs. He has characterized the political and social significance of his entry into the media industry as one of "saving the nation through a detour." Although Wang said in a 2003 interview that he eventually would like to produce news, whether his detoured road will lead him to his original destination seems doubtful. While Wang continues to harbor the critical mission of a journalist and espouse liberal intellectual sensibilities, business priorities are setting his company's course of development. Since news and current affairs are not a politically viable market niche for any domestic media owner, producing news does not make business sense if it would launch a confrontation with the state. Moreover, as the political and industrial environment for Wang's business operations evolves, and as the logic of capital tightens its grip on the Chinese media system, Wang may have even less freedom to entertain any serious journalistic dream.

With the entry of transnational capital and the conglomeration and accelerated capitalization of state media, Wang faces a media market that is increasingly dominated by big capital, domestic and foreign alike. To remain competitive, Wang needs to rapidly recapitalize the company with outside investment. Toward this purpose, Wang had been exploring an independent stock market listing. Meanwhile, domestic and foreign investors have expressed strong interest in investing in this highly profitable and dynamic business. On November 19, 2007, Wang gave up his quest for an independent IPO for Enlight Media by announcing a merger of the company with the QASDAQ-list ring tone provider Hurray Holdings. Under the terms of the deal, Enlight Media would inject all of its assets into Hurray, which would then change its name to Hurray Enlight

Media Group Ltd. The new company would be 42 percent owned by En-light Media, and its share could grow up to 65 percent in two years if the average share price exceeds $8.50 for 60 consecutive trading days. Wang Changtian, who assumes the position of president and CEO of the new company, becomes its single largest individual shareholder.[90]

Wang, who has and continues to make Chinese media history but, to paraphrase Marx's famous quote, did not and cannot make it as he pleases. Consequently, he has been compelled to act under the constraints of the Chinese party-state, the dictates of the market, and the logic of cap-ital. Aside from the state's political constraints, Wang sees clearly that news, especially serious news, is not the most profitable market niche, and he has learned that there is little space for political and cultural ide-alism in the media marketplace. As media scholar Ding Junjie com-mented, "Many television professionals have embraced private television institutions in pursuit of their own ideals and values. They have lofty ideals, which they think could be realized once they have moved to the private sector. Not so easy!"[91] With Wang's established business model for television production, which was the only viable one in the context of his dealings with monopolistic state broadcasters, commercialism was car-ried to a new high, to the extent that advertising time, not actual cash, was the primary currency of exchange between Wang's company and state broadcasters. This means that each program itself, not the television sta-tion as such, must be a viable and attractive advertising vehicle, and there are no such luxuries as "cross-subsidies." Now that Wang has taken En-light Media to the NASDAQ and tied its enlarged stakes in Hurray En-light Media with the increased market value of the new company's stocks, he has resolutely bid farewell to his career as an owner-operator of an in-dependent Chinese media production company. He is posited to pursue an increase in the stock value of the company as his top priority.

ACQUIRING CULTURE AND ACCUMULATING CAPITAL: THE VENTURES OF ZHEJIANG INDUSTRIALISTS

Lou Zhongfu and the Guangsha Group

On December 29, 2004, at the auditorium of the Zhejiang Broadcasting Bureau, I witnessed a grand ceremony celebrating the establishment of the Zhejiang Film and Television (Group) Ltd., a joint venture between the provincial broadcast conglomerate Zhejiang Broadcasting Group and the Guangsha Group, the province's largest private industrial conglomer-ate and the country's largest private construction company. The newly es-tablished company has a capitalization of 60 million yuan, in which the Zhejiang Broadcast Group holds a 51 percent share and Guangsha holds a 49 percent share. The input of the former includes the operational right of an entirely state-owned television channel, ZTV-5, the provincial film and television drama specialty channel, and Tianyuan Film and Television, which is the group's spin-off film and television drama production company, as well as land. Guangsha, with its Guangsha Media already operating a newspaper and a number of television drama production companies, injects real cash—29.4 million yuan. At the heart of this development is the partial privatization of the operational rights to state broadcasting—in this case, the operational rights of ZTV-5.

The event was a historical one. Like the stock listing of the *Beijing Youth Daily*, the ceremony was a political affair, a milestone in the party's cultural system reform program. In fact, not only was Zhejiang Broadcast Group one of the seven broadcast groups in the initial national trial reform program, but the two provinces of Zhejiang and Guangdong have been set up as pioneers in the development of the culture industry, or, as a slogan decorating the stage put it, building a "big cultural province" (*wenhua dasheng*). This idea of being "a big province" has particular rhetorical power in Zhejiang, one of the smallest Chinese provinces in terms of territory. Although this joint venture was described as a "strong-strong union" whereby the state sector contributed broadcast license "resources" and personnel, and the private sector provided capital and "superior" institutional mechanisms, Zhejiang Broadcast Group's 51 percent ownership and its control of the final editorial rights clearly shows who the dominant owner in this state-private partnership is. The very lineup on the stage reflected both the official nature of the event and the configuration of power between the political class and the business elite. Apart from Guangsha chairman Lou Zhongfu, the individuals sitting on the stage included officials from the SARFT, the GAPP, the Ministry of Culture, and the provincial party PD, broadcasting, and media institutions, including Liang Pingbo, the deputy provincial party secretary in charge of the cultural sector, and Chen Min'er, the head of the provincial PD.

Official rhetoric aside, to some at the Zhejiang Broadcasting Bureau, the event was like the marrying off of a daughter, and an attractive one at that. Although Zhejiang Television has an interest in further capitalizing on its television operations, this is as much a political decision as a business one. Unlike unprofitable state media outlets in other parts of the country or in other sectors, such as the financially struggling China National Radio, which received a special permit from the SARFT to contract out its music channel to a Taiwan business to improve profitability, or the exceptional case of the resource-poor Hainan provincial satellite channel, which went through ad hoc partial privatization,[92] Zhejiang Television, especially ZTV-5, is highly profitable. As one producer put it, "Our group is not short of capital. But the powers that be wanted this deal, so we did it, so as to take the lead in cultural system reform."[93] In Beijing, Wang

Changtian, who has neither the political nor financial capital to achieve his goal of operating a television channel, was jealous. He said that Guangsha got a good deal.[94]

The limited entry of Guangsha into broadcasting marked a new stage of the game in private capital involvement in the Chinese media, that is, the involvement of large private business conglomerates. As the politically orchestrated nature of the event demonstrated, the party-state has dramatized the political significance of this embrace as one more step in its reform program. Privatization, initially pursued illegally and pragmatically by rental-seeking and cash-hungry state media outlets, has been pursued as a state policy and a matter of principle. The rapid change in state policy was underscored by Chen Min'er's remark that he could have hardly imagined himself, the head of a provincial party PD, and Lou Zhongfu, a private capitalist, sitting on the same stage just three years ago.[95] Still, who is Lou and what put him on the stage?

Like Wang Changtian, Lou has a humble origin. He was born in 1954 into an impoverished goldsmith family in the central Zhejiang county of Dongyang, where the severe shortage of arable land has cultivated a long tradition in artisan trades and commerce. With only an elementary school education, he started his career as a construction worker at the collectively owned township construction company and became the company manager in 1984. Over the following decade, Lou gradually privatized and built this small rural business into the Guangsha Group, renamed Guangsha Holding Co. Ltd. in 2002, a construction and real estate–based transnational business conglomerate that operates in 28 provinces in China and more than 10 foreign countries, with more than 100 subsidiaries. The company, with revenues of 21.2 billion yuan in 2002, was the largest private business in Zhejiang Province, the fourth-largest private business in the country, and one of the top 100 businesses in China. Since 1998, Guangsha has aggressively purchased controlling shares in state enterprises in the construction business. Simultaneously ranked by *Forbes* magazine as one of China's richest men and recognized by the Chinese state as a national "model worker" and one of the 100 "Excellent Builders of Socialism with Chinese Characteristics" in 2004, Lou is the quintessential rural-entrepreneur-turned-transnational-Chinese-capitalist.

Lou's investment in media and culture derives from several interrelated motivations. As a rural entrepreneur with little education, acquiring culture, or cultural capital in both the literal and figurative senses, has been a compelling imperative. This is not just a matter of personal identity and vanity, but also one that is rooted in a sincere desire for culture and entertainment on the part of China's vast rural population. In Zhejiang Province, which boasts a well-established elite cultural tradition and well-known national literary and cultural figures, this desire on the part of the uneducated to bridge the cultural gap is particularly strong. Indeed, Lou sponsored cultural events and tried to enrich rural cultural life from the very beginning of his business career. For example, to celebrate his promotion to manager of the construction company, he sponsored three movie screenings at the county cinema.[96] As Lou's business expanded, his cultural sponsorship activities expanded in range and scope: he went from being the sole sponsor of a television drama series on Zhejiang Television in 1985, an unprecedented event at the time, to sponsoring national essay competitions and sports events. As a senior manager at the Zhejiang Broadcast Group put it, "As a peasant-originated entrepreneur, he felt his own lack of culture, and to be involved in the cultural industry is a means to raise his own cultural status."[97]

As a businessman, Lou is fully aware of the instrumental value of media and cultural sponsorships, and his cultivation of good media relations and his cultural sponsorships are precisely what have made him a household name in Zhejiang and elsewhere. This mastering of the "soft power" of media and culture, in turn, has been indispensable to Lou's business success.[98] Lou's use of journalists for favorable reporting reached the highest point when, on March 15, 1988, CCTV's *Network News* (*Xinwen lianbo*), the country's most influential television news program, broadcast a favorable news item about his company. In a sense, Lou "bought" state media for his business purposes long before he actually purchased the operational rights to a state media outlet. Lou's instrumental view of media and culture, of course, goes beyond specific business objectives. The joint venture with Zhejiang Broadcast Group is a form of political investment to the extent that it serves corporate image making and creates a favorable political context for future business expansion. As Liu Xiaoping, Guangsha's media manager, said, it is advertising in a broad sense.[99]

However, this does not mean that Lou speaks from an independent political position. Although his blacksmith father was labeled a counterrevolutionary because of his frank remarks about the misguided nature of Mao's steel-making drive in 1958, and Lou grew up as a "black child," Lou has always proactively integrated himself with the existing political system, depending on the political resources of the party-state to develop his business.[100] His various pro-establishment activities, from joining the party immediately after he obtained the management right of the township construction company, to using the party's traditional ideological education measures to cultivate the organizational culture of his company, won him all kinds of political capital. Even his cultural patronage activities are closely tied to the official ideology. For example, his 1991 national essay competition was held in the name of "celebrating the party's 70th birthday, promoting traditional culture, and enhancing concomitant development of material civilization and spiritual civilization." In short, Lou speaks "the language of the system," and this has served him and his business well.[101]

As a conglomerate involved in construction, real estate, tourism, and other industries, Guangsha also has a compelling imperative to enter the media and culture industry by establishing its own advertising outlets and promotional avenues. Even before the state officially opened up the media for private investment, Guangsha had already invested 60 million yuan in the official organ of the Zhejiang Communist Youth League in 2001 and turned the paper into *Youth Times*, an advertising-loaded commercial urban daily. In 2004, Guangsha was in talks with an urban daily in Xi'an, where the company has a big stake in the real estate market. As Liu Xiaoping put it frankly, "Guangsha invests a lot in advertising there. Since this is the case, why invest in somebody else's paper?"[102] Besides, as Lou noted himself,

> The culture industry is the last dinner. A country's economic development will eventually lead to the development of the culture industry. . . . [W]e entered the area of television drama production as early as 1993. However, our financial strength and the policy environment temporarily determined that we were not able to operate a television channel. Therefore, we steadfastly work in the main businesses of construction and real estate, waiting for the policy to loosen up [in the media].[103]

From 1993 to 2004, Guangsha invested more than 300 million yuan in its media and cultural business.[104] Lou has managed to grasp policy openings in this sector by integrating his various media and cultural businesses to establish Guangsha Media in 2004 and by successfully beating other private businesses in Zhejiang to become the joint-venture partner of the provincial broadcaster. Lou assumed the position of the deputy chair of the board of Zhejiang Film and Television Corporation and passed on the daily management of his other businesses to his sons because, as he said, "I want to do the television business myself."[105] Lou and his state sector partner plan to grow the new joint venture into a vertically integrated business in film and television entertainment, with production, distribution, broadcasting, and movie screen facilities.

Hengdian: The Hollywood of the East?

Lou's fellow Dongyang rural-entrepreneur-turned-industrial-capitalist Xu Wenrong and his Hengdian Group have even bigger ambitions. China's third-largest revenue-generating private business in 2002, Hengdian has invested much more in the film and entertainment industry than Guangsha. In fact, it had made two astonishing news headlines in 2004 before Guangsha's establishment of the Zhejiang Film and Television Corporation. On April 2, 2004, in what used to be the mountainous rural town of Dongyang City, the SARFT announced the establishment of the Zhejiang Hengdian Film and Television Industry Experiment Zone, the only one of its type in the country. Then, on October 14, 2004, Hengdian announced the establishment of Warner China Film HG Corporation ("Warner China Film"), a three-way transnational capital, state capital, and private capital joint venture between the China Film Group—China's largest state-owned film corporation—Warner Bros., and Hengdian Group. The company is the first Sino-foreign joint venture in the film and entertainment business approved under a new SARFT regulation allowing the establishment of such ventures. Warner China Film, which will "develop, invest in, produce, market, and distribute Chinese-language feature films, telefilms and animation," is described by Chairman Yang Buting as representing a "true 'dream-team'—three companies that are each leaders in their respective fields that bring vast, mutually complementary strengths and resources to the table."[106] The Time Warner news release provided the following background about its new Chinese private sector business partner:

> Hengdian Group is one of China's most powerful private enterprises, with investments in six major industries: electric and electronics, pharmaceuticals and chemicals, trade and logistics, education and consumer health, hi-tech agriculture, film and entertainment. . . . Hengdian's film and entertainment related businesses are expanding rapidly. The Hengdian World Studios feature two modern soundstages and a dozen scenic motion picture sets spanning different periods of Chinese history. . . . The Hengdian World Studios have recently received the honor of being designated by SARFT as China's first "Film and Television Experimental Zone." The designation carries with it a number of tax and other incentives designated to encourage film and television producers to avail themselves of Hengdian's locations and facilities.[107]

Like Lou, Hengdian's founder, Xu Wenrong, built his transnational industrial and business empire on the basis of township enterprises, sharing the same interest in cultural enrichment for the rural population. He built a cinema as one of his first public welfare projects after having made some money from operating rural enterprises as the village party secretary.[108] By 1995, the Hengdian Group had become China's largest rural industrial conglomerate with businesses in textiles, electronics, chemicals, and pharmaceuticals, and Xu, by then one of China's most famous rural industrialists and an NPC delegate, had developed a business interest in the cultural sector. In 1996, Xu built for free the set for the film *The Opium War*, a privately financed film by fellow NPC delegate and the well-known film director Xie Jin, to coordinate with the celebration of Hong Kong's return. The enormous media publicity the film generated for Hengdian launched Xu's new business venture in the Chinese film industry and sparked his dream to turn his mountainous hometown in central Zhejiang into the "Hollywood of the East" or "Chinawood." Since then, Hengdian Group has made a nearly 3-billion-yuan investment in its film business division, boasting a credit list that includes Zhang Yimou's *Hero* and an average of 50 films and television series each year.[109] The *Hollywood Reporter* has called this formerly unknown small mountain town "China's Hollywood,"[110] and an American director's remark that "today's Hengdian looks very much like yesterday's Hollywood" has been frequently quoted in the Chinese media.[111] As a May 19, 2006, *Los Angeles Times* report described, Hengdian World Studios, which includes 13 movie lots and covers a 25-square-kilometer area, is already the largest film base in Asia and almost twice the size of Beverly Hills. Furthermore, the local government has given the group permission to expand tenfold.[112] Like Guangsha, Hengdian's investment in film and television has not been profitable in itself; nevertheless, the group, now under the leadership of Xu Wenrong's son Xu Yong'an, is rapidly expanding the scope of its investment. They have acquired movie theater chains and are set to control 25 percent of the country's cinema market. Hengdian is also investing 800 million yuan to build a Universal Studios–type theme park, airport, golf course, as well as high-tech sound stages and more sets, including a huge set named "25,000 Li Road of Long March" for the shooting of revolutionary themes and replicas of European streets. Xu Wenrong hopes that "apart from ocean and desert, you can shoot all kinds of themes here, whether historical, war, revolutionary, or modern life."[113] The ambition, in short, is to build a high-tech global production base to rival Hollywood.[114] Although Hengdian's entertainment division generated the modest revenue of 300 million yuan in 2004, far less than the 8.2 billion yuan for its electronic business and 5.5 billion yuan for its pharmaceuticals, the entertainment division is growing much faster than the other mature areas.[115] The group, in fact, is posited to fully pursue this business while conscious of the state's broader and longer-term political, economic, and cultural development strategy and the broader and longer-term economic impacts of its new business on the region—some farmers in nearby villages, for example, have even managed to make a living by working as "movie extras."

At the local level, the Zhejiang provincial government, which has targeted film and television production as the priority area in its cultural institution reform program, took the initiative to apply through the SARFT to establish a national film and television experimental zone by building upon Hengdian's investment. In the words of deputy provincial party secretary Liang Pingbo, the province has made the development of Hengdian "the top priority of all priorities in the province's cultural system reform," promising to "mobilize the entire strength of the province to accelerate the development of the experimental zone,"[116] and calling on provincial officials at different departments "to sincerely help make the experimental zone big and strong."[117] Provincial party PD chief Chen Min'er describes the Hengdian Experimental Zone as one in which "the government acts as the supervising body, enterprises serve as the developmental agent," and together, they "carry out the double duty of institutional innovation and industrial development."[118]

One key aspect of "institutional innovation" centers on the role of the state at the central, provincial, and local levels. Apart from policy support, including a series of preferential tax policies at the national, provincial, and municipal levels, the state has incorporated the zone into its own administrative domain.[119] Although the Hengdian Group is the initial investor and operator of Hengdian Film and Television City, the state has now brought along state sector media corporations as the group's collaborators. Liang Pingbo, for example, took the heads of the three provincial media and cultural groups—the Zhejiang Broadcast Group, the *Zhejiang Daily* Group, and the Zhejiang Joint Publishing Group—to Hengdian and encouraged them to participate in the future development of the zone.[120] Furthermore, the Experimental Zone has been incorporated as a state-sponsored entity. It is now characterized as being "sponsored" (*zhuban*) by the Dongyang municipal government and collectively invested in and implemented by the Hengdian Group, the Zhejiang Broadcast Group, the *Zhejiang Daily* Group, and the Zhejiang Joint Publishing House.[121] Although the Hengdian Group manages the daily operation of the zone, the Dongyang municipal government has a management committee that serves as its nominal state administrative body.[122] In this way, the state puts a "red hat" on top of an essentially private business. Instead of being an "innovation," this is actually the continuation of the old practice of requiring an official "sponsor" for media outlets, a practice that is set to end in nonessential areas of media operations (such as book distribution) as part of the cultural system reform program. Perhaps the most telling illustration of the state's penetration into private business on the one hand and its unwillingness to give up control on the other is this: while Zhejiang provincial authorities decided to further decentralize their newly acquired film censorship power from the SARFT by setting up the provincial censorship office within the Hengdian Experimental Zone,[123] the SARFT was not willing to locate the head office of the newly established China Warner Film joint venture in Hengdian. Instead, the SARFT not only insisted on a dominant role for state capital in the joint venture—with China Film Group holding 40 percent of the share and Warner Bros. and Hengdian each holding 30 percent—but also that the head office be located in Beijing, so that the SARFT can keep a close eye on it.[124] Xu Wenrong and his eldest son, Xu Yong'an, for their part, are fully aware of their role in this state and private corporatism: "It is the SARFT and Zhejiang provincial government that have decided to forge such a national-level platform for the Chinese film and television industry. Hengdian is merely one constituting element of this platform."[125]

Still, that the central state should choose Zhejiang as a provincial cultural system reform trial site, thus enabling companies such as Guangsha and Hengdian to take a quantum leap in the media and culture industries, is not surprising. If Guangdong's selection is self-evident because of its close integration with Hong Kong and transnational media, Zhejiang boasts three crucial elements: a highly developed private sector economy, a rich cultural tradition, and strong local government support. Zhejiang, with its famous Wenzhou model of indigenous entrepreneurial capitalism, has by far the most market-oriented provincial economy in the country. In 2003 the resource-poor and geographically small province accounted for one-quarter of the total export-generated profit of China, the fourth-largest GDP of all metropolitan regions and provinces, and the highest per capita income among all provinces. The export-oriented and diversified private sector accounted for 71 percent of the provincial GDP, 60 percent of tax revenue, and 90 percent of employment. Zhejiang-based private businesses also accounted for 40 percent of the country's 500 largest private enterprises.[126]

Just as private entrepreneurs in Wenzhou have led capitalistic development in China since the beginning of the reform period, private entrepreneurs in Zhejiang have sparked the explosive growth of the culture industry in the new century. In 2002 the culture industry in Zhejiang achieved an added value of 44 million yuan and an increase of 22.6 percent over 2001, 10.3 percent higher than the overall GDP growth rate, and accounting for 5.6 percent of the total GDP. Behind the high-profile investments in the culture industry by leading private businesses is a fledgling provincial cultural economy in which the private sector plays a significant role.[127] For example, 70 percent of the 90 film and television production companies established from 2001 to 2004 were in the private sector.[128] By 2004, the province had more than 40,000 private cultural enterprises, with a total investment of 23 billion yuan and revenue of more than 30 billion yuan.[129] As the state embraces private capital in the culture industry, it has mandated Zhejiang to explore the strengths of private capital in cultural development, and Zhejiang private industrial groups such as Guangsha and Hengdian, with their three decades of accumulated capital and management expertise in other sectors of the economy, are leading the charge. Other entrepreneurs in the province have successfully built their villages into the world's biggest production bases for socks, pens, buttons, and hardware. Hengdian could conceivably emerge as a global media production base. With free use of the sets and extras costing US$2.50 for an eight-hour day, compared with US$100.00 or more in Hollywood and even Canada, Hengdian's comparative advantage is already drawing the attention of foreign producers. A Canadian producer who was shooting her film there claimed, "Labor is cheaper, all across the board. There is no union. It is a free hand for directors."[130]

As the Luos and the Xus expand their media and entertainment businesses by collaborating with state and transnational capital and by seeking capitalization through domestic and overseas stock markets,[131] they will likely become not the kind of social force with an independent voice that many liberal intellectuals have long hoped for, but, as Xu Wenrong acknowledges, a constitutive element of a state-incorporated and globally integrated media and entertainment industry.

CONCLUSION

From the initial incorporation of private newspapers in the party's postrevolutionary media system in the early 1950s and the emergence of independent citizen-run media at the onset of the reform process in 1977–1978, the nature and terms of engagement by nonstate social forces in the Chinese communication system have shifted significantly. Today, although independent citizen media are still being suppressed, and domestic private capital is still prohibited in the core news production and broadcasting functions of the communication system, nonstate business organizations have been officially recognized and encouraged to participate in a wide range of activities in the media and culture industry. The resulting system, in which state capital controls its "commanding heights" while private capital does the heavy lifting—from running the retailing shops to making the high-risk investments in television series production—has allowed the state to maintain ideological control while also making the media and cultural markets more responsive to popular tastes. During this process, the state has increasingly assumed regulatory, managerial, and gatekeeping roles, accumulating capital through rental-seeking and the strategic control of media, while outsourcing the bulk of media production and distribution work. The nature and character of domestic private media capital itself has also undergone a major transformation—that is, from the Wang Changtian–type owner-operator with a background in the media to the Guangsha- and Hengdian-type industrial conglomerates whose owners, while espousing their own cultural dreams, have a more instrumental view of media and culture and are more integrated with the existing power structure.

And yet, this is perhaps just the beginning of a more complicated process of private capital involvement in the Chinese media industry. In the summer of 2005, unconfirmed news reports about the arrest of young financial capitalist Tan Hui on bribery charges and the fate of his private multimedia empire, Stellar Mega Media, which claimed to have become the largest private media group in China in 2005, captivated the Chinese media.[132] Born in 1969, Tan cut his teeth as an employee in transnational corporations in China, became a member of China's power elite through marriage, and was an adept broker of both high political power in Beijing and the power of financial capital in Hong Kong. Instead of building his own media operations from scratch, as Wang Changtian did, or building his own business elsewhere and then "acquiring culture," as Lou and Xu did, Tan used cliental relationships with high-level state officials to acquire an astronomical volume of loans from state banks, deployed various—and sometimes dubious—investment schemes and financial instruments to purchase existing media properties, and assembled his multimedia empire overnight. In short, Tan built a media empire by manipulating high political and financial powers. Although Tan stands out in his reckless acquisitions, his blunt use of political connections, and his abuse of financial markets, he is perhaps representative of a new generation of private capitalists in the Chinese media and culture industry. Rather than viewing the media and culture industry as a crucial site of social communication and cultural expression, they see it as the new frontier for "the game of capital" (*ziben youxi*), a term the Chinese media use to describe Tan's operations.

Although the pressures of transnational integration have provided an impetus for the Chinese state to expand the scope of domestic capital participation in the media and cultural sectors, transnational capital may increasingly incorporate domestic Chinese capital in its circuits of production and distribution. The shareholding structure and the name composition of the three-way joint-venture entity—called *Zhongying Huana Hengdian Yingshi* (China Film Warner Hengdian Film and Television Ltd. Corp.) in the Chinese media and Warner China Film HG Corporation on the Time Warner website—is perhaps symbolic of the fact that Hengdian is the least powerful partner in this private and state, domestic and transnational collaboration. Instead of becoming the "Hollywood of the East," it is likely to serve as one of the production bases of Global Hollywood. Finally, although there will still be a place for the likes of Wang Changtian, Lou Zhongfu, and Xu Wenrong, as the political and financial stakes in the private media sectors are getting higher in the policy context of further liberalization and globalization and in the technological context of digital transition, individuals like Tan, with power bases both in domestic and transnational financial markets and in the ruling political class, may become increasingly important players in the private Chinese media and cultural sectors. If this is the case, the prospects for a politically independent, domestic, private media bourgeoisie will be even more unlikely. That Wang Changtian has so quickly taken his Enlight Media to the NASDAQ also confirms this analysis.

NOTES

1. Yuezhi Zhao, *Media, Market and Democracy in China: Between the Party Line and the Bottom Line* (Urbana: University of Illinois Press, 1998), 16.

2. Zhao, *Media, Market, and Democracy*, 40.

3. Confidential interview by Andy Hu, 30 May 2006.

4. Michael Schoenhals, "The Secret History of Non-State Controlled Current Information Networks in China's Cultural Revolution" (lecture at the Institute for Asian Research, University of British Columbia, 13 Sept. 2005).

5. My own research, based on primary material, including transcripts of party leaders' speeches to Red Guards provided by an overseas Chinese source whose MSN account name is "ban," supports Schoenhals' observation. In their April 18, 1967, meeting with students from the defense industry colleges, for example, central military leaders stated that the students' information networks are more "informed" (*lingtong*) than the party-state's central military headquarters, though their information was not necessarily reliable; in their August 11, 1968, meeting with Beijing student representatives, Zhou Enlai, Chen Boda, and Jiang Qing, for example, pleaded with students to follow the line of Chairman Mao and the central Cultural Revolution Leadership Group, and not to derive their own understanding of the situation on the basis of information provided by these current affairs briefs.

6. Nankai University Weidong Red Guards, "Red Guard Tabloids Are Great Things!" in *China's Cultural Revolution, 1966–1969: Not a Dinner Party*, ed. Michael Schoenhals (Armonk: M. E. Sharpe, 1996), 208.

7. Elizabeth J. Perry and Li Xun, *Proletarian Power: Shanghai in the Cultural Revolution* (Boulder, Co.: Westview Press, 1997), 211.

8. Perry and Li, *Proletarian Power*, 13–14.

9. Andrew Nathan, *Chinese Democracy* (New York: Knopf, 1985), 192.

10. Nathan, *Chinese Democracy*, 23–24.

11. Chin-Chuan Lee, "Sparking a Fire: The Press and the Ferment of Democratic Change in Taiwan," in *China's Media, Media's China*, ed. Chin-Chuan Lee (Boulder, Co.: Westview Press, 1994), 163–201.

12. David S. G. Goodman, *Beijing Street Voices: The Poetry and Politics of China's Democracy Movement* (London: M. Boyars, 1981), 1.

13. Goodman, *Beijing Street Voices*, appendix.

14. Zhao, *Media, Market and Democracy*, 34–45.

15. Hu Jiwei, "*Meiyou xinwenziyou jiu meiyou zhenzheng de wending*" (There Will Be No Genuine Stability without Press Freedom), *Shijie jingji daobao*, 8 May 1998, 8.

16. Zhao, *Media, Market and Democracy*, 42.

17. Zhao, *Media, Market and Democracy*, 35–47.

18. Zhao, *Media, Market and Democracy*, 181–194.

19. A well-known example was the *World Economic Herald*, which was banned in 1989. The paper had the World Economics Research Institute of the Shanghai Academy of Social Sciences as its official publisher but assumed semi-independent status, with actual management in the hands of its editor-in-chief, Qin Benli, a veteran liberal-minded editor. For a detailed study of the paper's technocratic

orientations, see Cheng Li and Lynn T. White III, "China's Technocratic Movement and the *World Economic Herald," Modern China* 17, no. 3 (1991): 342–388.

20. By then, the category of "counterrevolutionary propaganda" had been removed from the Chinese criminal code.

21. Because broadcasting requires more technical and infrastructural investment and because state monopoly in this sector is more total, it has been virtually impossible to establish independent broadcasting stations in urban Chinese society, where the state's surveillance power is omnipresent. The extraordinary exception, of course, was the wired radio station at Tiananmen Square during the height of the 1989 student movement.

22. Jonathan Manthorpe, "China's Rulers Uncomfortable as Public Debate Breaks Out," *Vancouver Sun*, 14 Mar. 2006, A13.

23. Daniel C. Lynch, *After the Propaganda State: Media, Politics, and "Thought Work" in Reformed China* (Stanford, Calif.: Stanford University Press, 1999), 84–93.

24. Jie Dongfang, "*Erqudao shushang*" (Second Channel Book Merchants), www.wsjk.com.cn/gb/paper24/7/class002400007/hwz55054.htm (accessed 25 Jul. 2005).

25. Zhang Yongheng, "*Zhongguo minying shuye fazhan tisu*" (The Development of China's People-Run Publishing Industry Speeded Up), www.people.com.cn/GB/paper39/10913/990434.html (accessed 25 Jul. 2005).

26. Sheng Yuan, "*Zhongguo shida baoli hangye jiemi*" (Revelations of China's Ten Most Lucrative Businesses), *Kaifang*, Jun. 2005, 71.

27. According to the Shenzhen business owner I interviewed in February 2006 in Vancouver, the private companies actually had a majority ownership in the venture, but the Central PD insisted on the state's majority ownership of 51 percent on paper.

28. Sun Zhengyi and Liu Tingting, "*2004: Zhongguo Xinwenye huiwang (shang)*" (A Retrospective View of the Chinese News Media, Part I), www.people.com.cn/GB/14677/40606/3038055.html (accessed 28 Jan. 2005).

29. Mike Meyer, "The World's Biggest Book Market," *New York Times*, 13 Mar. 2005, www.nytimes.com/2005/03/13/books/review/013MEYERL.html?ex=1150862400&en=b8d8d5f112d6f249&ei=5070 (accessed 15 Mar. 2005).

30. Liu Kang and Tian Shubin, "*Li Changchun: Weirao 'santiejin' jiaqiang he gaijin xuanchuan sixiang gongzuo*" (Li Changchun: Strengthening and Improving Propaganda Work by Focusing on "Three-Getting Close"), news.xinhuanet.com/newscenter/2003-04/15/content_833798.htm (accessed 5 Jun. 2006). See chapter 2.

31. "*Muqian woguo baokanshe zichan junshi guoyouzichan*" (All Capital in Our Country's Press Organizations Is State Capital), *Baokan guanli*, Jan. 2000, 8.

32. In rural China, unauthorized television and cable stations, sometimes set up by local governments with investment by private entrepreneurs for the combined purpose of official propaganda and profit making, sometimes set up by private entrepreneurs for the sole purpose of profit making, have spread since the 1990s. Internalizing the state broadcasters' profit-making logic, these rural entrepreneurs have come to learn that the television business is just a business like any other. Local villagers, even local officials, considering the operation of a television station as a private business and the existence of illegal television stations as quite normal, have been protective of these stations in the face of the authorities' clamp-

down. Although there is no way of knowing how widespread these stations are, a SARFT report mentioned that in 2005, it closed 5,105 authorized township-level radio and television stations, punished 173 "rule-violating" township television stations in Beijing, Liaoning, Hunan, and Henan, as well as closed 48 unauthorized township television stations in Shandong, Hunan, and Henan provinces. China News Net, "*Shenzhen 'dixia dianshitai' feifang jieshou jingwaidianshi xianxiang changjue*" (The Widespread Phenomenon of Underground Television Stations Illegally Transmitting Foreign Programming in Shenzhen), 2 Nov. 2001, news.sina.com/cn/c/2001-11-02/391284.html (accessed 13 Jul. 2004); Wang Hongwei, "*Dixia dianshitai fengchao diaocha: Zhengce zhikun cuisheng xiangzhen dianshitai*" (An Investigation into the Wave of Underground Television Stations: Policy Problems Led to the Birth of Township Television Stations), *The Bund* (*Waitan huabao*), www.so888.com/article/20040713/Sina143512.asp?id=20&sid=136&self_ID=810945 (accessed 13 Jul. 2004); Sun Wusan, "A Small Chinese Town Television Station's Struggle for Survival: How a New Institutional Arrangement Came into Being," *Westminster Papers in Communication and Culture* 3, no. 1 (2006): 54; Research Center for Reform and Development, SARFT, *2006 nian Zhongguo guangbo yingshi fanzhan baogao* (Report on the Development of China's Radio, Film, and Television) (Beijing: Shehui kexue wenxian chubanshe, 2006), 76.

33. Interview, Jul. 2004, Vancouver.

34. Lu Xingdong, "*Jiyu yu tiaozhan bingcun de Zhongguo minying chuanmeiye*" (Opportunities and Challenges Co-Exist in the Chinese People-Run Media Industry), news.xinhuanet.com/newscenter/2005-02/01/content_2534712_1.htm (accessed 25 Jul. 2005).

35. Peng Lun, "*Quxiao 'erqudao' chengwei*" (Canceling the "Second Channel" Notation), zgrdxw.peopledaily.com.cn/gb/paper384/1/class038400001/hwz226881.htm (accessed 25 Jul. 2005).

36. Wang Junping, "*Woguo minying chuanmei ye de xianzhuang ji SWOT fenxi*" (The Current State of Our Country's Private Media Industry and Related SWOT Analysis), www.people.com.cn/GB/14677/21963/39509/2987794.html (accessed 17 Jul. 2005).

37. Xie Genyu, "*Wenhua touzi tizhi gaige de liangge tupo*" (Two Breakthroughs in the Investment System in Culture), *Zhongguo xinwen pinglun*, 14 Jul. 2005, www.zjol.com.cn/gb/node2/node26108/node30205/node194994/node243713/userobject15ai3079914.html (accessed 2 Aug. 2005).

38. The State Council of PRC, "*Guowuyuan guanyu feigongyouzhi zizben jinru wenhua chanye de ruogan jueding*" (State Council Decision on the Entry of Nonpublic Capital in the Culture Industry), news.xinhuanet.com/fortune/2005-08/08/content-3325932-htm (accessed 20 Aug. 2005).

39. Wang Liming, "*Feigongyou ziben jinru wenhua chanye de touzi jiyu*" (Investment Opportunities for Nonpublic Capital in the Culture Industry), *Chuanmei*, Sept. 2005, www.sjztv.com.cn/media/MediaDetail.aspx?id=10639 (accessed 18 Jun. 2006).

40. See for example, "*Sun Jiazheng jieshou caifang, guli minying wenyi biaoyan tuanti fazhan*" (Sun Jiazheng Encourages the Development of Minying Cultural Performance Troupes), news.xinhuanet.com/politics/2006-01/12/content_4044535.htm (accessed 19 Apr. 2006).

41. Nan Xiaowei and Guo Wenjun, *"Wangba kaijin zaiji"* (Ban on Internet Cafés to be Lifted Soon), *Nanfang ribao*, 13 Sept. 2005, www.nanfangdaily.com.cn/south news/tszk/nfrb/dggc/200509130940.asp (accessed 3 Nov. 2005).

42. *"Yiwu fangkai wangba shenpi"* (Yiwu Opened up Licensing of Internet Cafés), *Jinghua shibao*, 1 Nov. 2005, www.i8china.com/news/2005/11/2176.html (accessed 22 Nov. 2005).

43. Wang, *"Woguo minying chuanmei ye de xianzhuang ji SWOT fenxi."*

44. For an excellent discussion of Internet cafés and state regulation, see Jack Linchuan Qiu and Liuming Zhou, "Through the Prism of Internet Café: Management Access in an Ecology of Games," *China Information* 19, no. 2 (2005); see also, Zhou Yongming, *Historicizing Online Politics: Telegraphy, the Internet, and Political Participation in China* (Stanford, Calif.: Stanford University Press, 2006), 139–141.

45. Carolyn Cartier, Manuel Castells, and Jack Linchuan Qiu, "The Information Have-Less: Inequality, Mobility, and Translocal Networks in Chinese Cities," *Studies in Comparative International Development* 40, no. 2 (Summer 2005): 25.

46. Yuezhi Zhao and Robert Duffy, "Short-Circuited? The Communication of Labor Struggles in China," in *Knowledge Workers in the Information Society*, ed. Catherine McKercher and Vincent Mosco (Lanham, Md.: Lexington Books, 2008).

47. E. P. Thompson, *The Making of the English Working Class*, 2nd ed. (London: Harmondsworth, 1968), 788–789.

48. Interview with an Internet scholar, Aug. 2003, Beijing.

49. Interview, Jul. 2004, Vancouver.

50. Zhou Xing, *"Guochan dianshiju shichanghua zhengce de sikao fanlun"* (A General Discussion about the Marketization of Domestic Television Dramas), *Nanfang dianshi xuekan* 4 (2004): 34.

51. Shanghai TV Festival, CV/SC-SOFRES Media, *Zhongguo dianshiju shichang baogao* (China TV Drama Market Report, 2003–2004) (Beijing: Huaxia chubanshe, 2004), 20, 24.

52. Shanghai TV Festival, CV/SC-SOFRES Media, *Zhongguo dianshiju shichang baogao*, 36, 41–43.

53. For an elaboration of this concept, see Liu Kang, *Globalization and Cultural Trends in China* (Honolulu: University of Hawai'i Press, 2004), chapter 3.

54. Zhou Xing, *"Guochan dianshiju,"* 34.

55. Research Center for Reform and Development, SARFT, 171.

56. Shanghai TV Festival, CV/SC-SOFRES Media, *Zhongguo dianshiju shichang baogao*, 216–217; see also Yik-Chan Chin, "China's Regulatory Policies on International Television Drama Flow," *Media Development* 3 (2003): 17–22.

57. Shanghai TV Festival, CV/SC-SOFRES Media, *Zhongguo dianshiju shichang baogao*, 25.

58. Cheng Ying, *"Cong woguo dianshiju shichang de fazhan licheng kan eryuan qudong de tongxiangxing yu nixiangxing"* (A Perspective on the Directions of the Dual Compulsion of the Television Market), *Nanfang dianshi xuekan* 4 (2004): 39.

59. Zhou Xing, *"Guochan dianshiju,"* 37.

60. Overinvestment and oversupply have become a problem of the industry. In 2003 television stations spent just over 2 billion yuan in television drama purchase, while more than 3 billion yuan were invested in drama production. As another indication of oversupply, more than 2,000 drama episodes remained shelved in both 2004 and 2005. Research Center for Reform and Development, SARFT, 173.

61. Liu Haibo, *"Zhengzhi yu ziben de boyi"* (A Game of Politics and Capital), *Nanfang dianshi xuekan* 4 (2004): 31.

62. Liu, *"Zhengzhi yu ziben de boyi,"* 30.

63. SARFT, *"Guanyu 'hongse jingdian' gaibian dianshiju shencha guanli de tongzhi"* (Notice on the Management of Censorship of Adoptions of "Red Classics"), 25 May 2004, www.sarft.gov.cn/manage/publishfile/103/2123.html (accessed 22 Oct. 2004).

64. Liu, *"Zhengzhi yu ziben de boyi,"* 32.

65. Cheng Ying, *"Cong woguo dianshiju,"* 39.

66. Interview, 27 Dec. 2004, Hangzhou.

67. Interview, 27 Dec. 2004, Hangzhou.

68. This point was made by Liu Kang with reference to "indigenous popular culture products" more broadly, *Globalization*, 83.

69. Yuezhi Zhao and Zhenzhi Guo, "Television in China: History, Political Economy, and Ideology," in *A Companion to Television*, ed. Janet Wasko, 521–539 (Malden, Mass.: Blackwell, 2005), 534. See also Ruoyun Bai, *Anticorruption Television Dramas: Between Propaganda and Popular Culture in Globalizing China*, Ph.D. dissertation, University of Illinois, Urbana-Champaign, 2007.

70. Geremie Barmé, *In the Red: On Contemporary Chinese Culture* (New York: Columbia University Press, 1999), 107.

71. Barmé, *In the Red*, 107.

72. Yin Hong, "Meaning, Production, Consumption: The History and Reality of Television Drama in China," in *Media in China: Consumption, Content, Crisis*, ed. Stephanie K. Donald, Michael Keane, and Yin Hong (London: Routledge/Curzon, 2002), 534.

73. Leslie Chang, "Portraying a Hero of the Revolution Has Perks in China," *Wall Street Journal*, 26 May 2000, A1.

74. Yu Hongmei, *"Jiedu women shidai de jingshen Zhenghou"* (Reading the Spiritual Symptoms of Our Times), in *Shuxie wenhua yingxiong* (Writing about Cultural Heroes), ed. Dai Jinghua (Nanjing: Jiangsu renmin chubanshe, 2000), 196.

75. Chang, "Portraying a Hero."

76. Yu, *"Jiedu,"* 205.

77. Chang, "Portraying a Hero."

78. Yu, *"Jiedu,"* 210.

79. Wang Jue, "Tuning in on Popular Tastes: Enlightened Media Sets Sights beyond Content Provision," *Commercial Weekly of China Daily*, 25 Sept. 2001, home.netandtv.com/hottag/hottag_010925.htm (accessed 26 Jul. 2005).

80. Li Xin, *"Wang Changtian men de yiyi"* (The Meaning of Wang Changtian and His Type), *Nanfang zhoumo*, 9 Dec. 2000, 21.

81. Wang Jing, *"Wang Changtian: Wo bupa chuanmei jütou qinlue"* (Wang Changtian: I Am Not Afraid of Invasion by Media Moguls) *Zhinang* 74, 5 Sept. 2001, home.netandtv.com/hottag/hottag_010905.htm (accessed 26 July 2005).

82. Huang Peijian, *"Wang Changtian: Goujian dianshi xindijia"* (Wang Changtian: Constructing a Television Syndicate), *Jingji guancha bao*, 8 Jan. 2005, www.mindmeters.com/arshow.asp?id=1570 (accessed 27 Jul. 2005).

83. Zhang Chunyan, *"Gangsi shang de 'dianshi zuofang'"* (A Television Workshop on Top of a Thin Line), *Sanlian shenghuo zhoukan*, 26 Feb. 2001, 43, home.netandtv.com/hottag/hottag_010226.htm (accessed 27 Jul. 2005).

84. Interview with a former Enlight Media employee, 22 Dec. 2003, Beijing.

85. Interview with a former Enlight Media employee, 22 Dec. 2003, Beijing.

86. Interview with Wang Changtian, 6 Jan. 2005, Beijing.

87. "*Wang Changtian jianli*" (CV of Wang Changtian), ent.sina.com.cn/v/2005-03-07/1557670952.html (accessed 18 Jul. 2005).

88. Huang Peijian, "*Wang Changtian.*"

89. Interview with Wang Changtian, 6 Jan. 2005, Beijing.

90. Wang Xing, "Merger Forms Biggest Media Content Provider," www.china daily.com.cn/cndy/2007-11/20/content_6264895.htm (accessed 2 Jan. 2008); see also Ma Quanzhi, *Dufang Wang Changtian* (An Exclusive Interview with Wang Changtian), tech.sina.com.cn/i/2007-11-19/15451860097.shtml (accessed 2 Jan. 2008).

91. Ding Junjie, "*Minying dianshi jigou, zuo wenhua haishi zuo shangye?*" (Private Television Institutions: Doing Culture or Doing Business?"), MediaChina.net, www.academic.mediachina.net/lw_view.jsp?id=601 (accessed 20 Jan. 2005).

92. The television channel initially sold 50 percent of its interest to Beida Huayi, a private Beijing company, and reoriented itself as a niche market channel on travel. Beida Huayi, in turn, merged with a subsidiary of China Poly Group Corp., a powerful state enterprise in armaments trade, real estate, and other areas to form the Beida Huayi Communications Corp. in December 2003, which assumed Beida Huayi's 50 percent stake in the satellite channel. "*Baoli shandian binggou Beida Huayi, si yi dazao yingshi chuanmei qijian*" (Poly Swift Takeover of Beida Huayi, 400 Million Yuan to Forge a Television and Film Media Flagship), tech.sina.com.cn/it/2003-12-10/0919266209.shtml (accessed 9 Jun. 2006).

93. Interview, 29 Dec. 2004, Hangzhou.

94. Interview, 6 Jan. 2005, Beijing.

95. Interview with Liu Xiaoping, 30 Dec. 2004, Hangzhou.

96. Long Zhengyang and Zhou Jianshun, *Zhongguo liliang* (Dragon Power) (Beijing: Shehuikexue chubanshe, 2005), 63.

97. Interview, 29 Dec. 2004, Hangzhou.

98. Long and Zhou, *Zhongguo liliang*, 124.

99. Interview, 30 Dec. 2004, Hangzhou.

100. Long and Zhou, *Zhongguo liliang*, 94–95.

101. Long and Zhou, *Zhongguo liliang*, 113.

102. Interview, 30 Dec. 2004, Hangzhou.

103. Zou Zhijiang, "*Lou Zhongfu: Minying ziben shishui dianshipingdao diyian*" (Lou Zhongfu: The First Case of Private Capital Testing the Water of Operating a Television Channel), *21 shiji jingji baodao*, 11 Jan. 2005, media.news.hexun.com/detail.aspx?lm=1985&id=996444 (accessed 15 Jul. 2005).

104. Zou, "*Lou Zhongfu: Minying ziben shishui dianshipingdao diyian.*"

105. Zou, "*Lou Zhongfu: Minying ziben shishui dianshipingdao diyian.*"

106. "China Film Group, Hengdian Group and Warner Bros. Pictures to Create Warner China Film HG Corporation," Time Warner News Release, 14 Oct. 2004, www.timewarner.com/corp/newsroom/pr/0,20812,724106,00.html (accessed 14 Mar. 2005).

107. "China Film Group, Hengdian Group and Warner Bros. Pictures to Create Warner China Film HG Corporation."

108. Ji Xu, *"Xu Wenrong = Hengdian,"* *Zhengquan shibao*, www.zqrb.com.cn/ReadNews.asp?NewsID=2103 (accessed 22 Jul. 2005).

109. Xiang Yihua, *"Zhejiang Hengdian yingshi chanye shiyanqu diaoyan baogao"* (A Research Report on Zhejiang Hengdian Film and Television Experimental Zone), in *Zhejiang lanpishu: 2005 nian Zhejiang fazhan baogao (wenhua juan)* (Blue Book of Zhejiang: A Report on Development in Zhejiang in 2005) (Cultural Volume), ed. Wan Bin (Hangzhou: Hangzhou chubanshe, 2005), 137.

110. Zhu Yu, *"Hengdian de 'Tiananmen' he Beijing de yiyangda"* (Hengdian's Tiananmen Is as Big as the One in Beijing), www.zj.xinhuanet.com/special/2004-03/25/content_1846221.htm (accessed 15 Jul. 2005).

111. Ji, *"Xu Wenrong = Hengdian."*

112. Don Lee, "Welcome to Chinawood," *Los Angeles Times*, 19 May 2006, hkimail.singtao.com/news_detail.asp?we_cat=7&art_id=18974&sid=8024328&con_type=1&d_str=20060519 (accessed 24 May 2006).

113. Zhang Le, *"Tanxun Hengdian yingshi chanye de lingleishengcun moshi"* (In Search of an Alternative Mode of Survival for Hengdian's Film and Television Business), Xinhua Zhejiang Channel, www.zj.xinhuanet.com/newscenter/2004-05/19/content_2156054.htm (accessed 20 Jul. 2005).

114. Zhang, *"Tanxun Hengdian."*

115. "Hollywood of East Seeks US$100m Overseas Listing," Reuters, 15 Jun. 2005.

116. Shi Yan, *"Dulan quanguo yingshi chanye shiyanqu paizhao, Hengdian jianzhi Haolaiwu"* (Holding the Exclusive License for National Film and Television Experiment Site, Hengdian Eyes Hollywood), www.zj.xinhuanet.com/special/2004-03/25/content_1846219.htm (accessed 20 Jul. 2005).

117. Shi Yan, *"Yingshichanye shiyanqu siyue guapai"* (Film and Television Experiment Site Set up in April), www.zj.xinhuanet.com/special/2004-03/31/content_1882710.htm (accessed 20 Jul. 2005).

118. Shi, *"Dulan quanguo yingshi chanye shiyanqu paizhao."*

119. Xiang, *"Zhejiang Hengdian,"* 140–141.

120. Shi, *"Dulan quanguo yingshi chanye shiyanqu paizhao."*

121. Xiang, *"Zhejiang Hengdian,"* 142.

122. Zhang Le, *"Zhejiang shengwei fushuji Liang Pingbo: Dazao Zhejiang wenhua tizhi gaige de tupokou"* (Zhejiang Deputy Party Secretary Liang Pingbo: Forging the Breakthrough Point in Zhejiang's Cultural System Reform), Xinhua Zhejiang Channel, 2 Apr. 2004, www.zj.xinhuanet.com/special/2004-04/02/content_1908157.htm (accessed 15 Jul. 2005).

123. Zhang Le and Xu Yu, *"Woguo shouge difang dianying shenchazhongxin zai Zhejiang Hengdian chengli"* (Our Country's First Local Film Censorship Center Was Established in Hengdian, Zhejiang), Xinhua Zhejiang Channel, 26 May 2005, www.zj.xinhuanet.com/special/2005-03/14/content_3871065.htm (accessed 20 Jul. 2005).

124. Zhang Le, *"Zhongying Huana Hengdian dansheng"* (The Birth of China Film Warner Hengdian), Xinhua Zhejiang Channel, 14 Mar. 2005, www.zj.xinhuanet.com/special/hengdian/news.htm (accessed 15 Jul. 2005).

125. Shi, *"Dulan quanguo yingshi chanye shiyanqu paizhao."*

126. *People's Daily* Reporting Team to Zhejiang, "*Qiantang chaoyong kai xintian*" (The Surging Waves of the Qiantang River Open up a New Sky), *People's Daily*, 31 Dec. 2004, 1.

127. Yan Yan and Zhang Le, "*Jujiao Zheshang 'wenhua touzire'*" (Focusing on the Investment Fever in Culture by Zhejiang Entrepreneurs), Xinhua Zhejiang Channel, 2 Sept. 2004, snweb.com/gb/xxdk/2004/37/a3701011.htm (accessed 20 Jul. 2005).

128. Hu Ruiting, Jiang Zhengxin, and Liu Xiaoying, "*Jinzu tuigou—Tansuo guangdian xingzheng guanli xin luzi*" (Advance Adequately and Retreat Adequately—Exploring a New Path for Broadcasting Administrative Management), in *Zhejiang lanpishu: Wenhua juan* (Blue Book of Zhejiang: Culture), ed. Wan Bin (Hangzhou: Hangzhou chubanshe, 2005), 109–110.

129. Zhang Ye and Sun Qiyan, "*Zhejiang minzi juejin wenhuachanye*" (Zhejiang Private Capital Digs Gold in the Culture Industry), Xinhua Zhejiang Channel, 29 Mar. 2004, www.zj.xinhuanet.com/special/2004-03/29/content_1870089.htm (accessed 15 Jul. 2005); Ding Wei, "*Wenhua chanye kuaisu fazhan de guanjiannian*" (A Crucial Year for the Rapid Development of the Culture Industry), in *2006 nian Zhongguo wenhua chanye fazhan baogao*, 29.

130. Lee, "Welcome to Chinawood."

131. "Hollywood of East Seeks US$100m Overseas Listing."

132. See, for example, Xie Zhu and Zhao Yanling, "*Tan Hui zhengshi beibu, keneng shexian duoxiang zuiming*" (Tan Hui Formally Arrested, Possibly Implicated in Multiple Charges), *Zhengquan shichang zhoukan*, Apr. 2005, cn.biz.yahoo.com/050429/133/9kop.html (accessed 22 Nov. 2005). However, a May 11 report based on information provided by one of Tan's companies claimed that Tan was only requested by the police to "assist investigation" and news about his arrest was inaccurate. See Liu Jun, "*Changfeng Tongxun cheng Tan Hui beibu chuanwen bushi*" (Chang Feng Communications Claims that News about Tan Hui's Arrest Is Untrue), cn.biz.yahoo.com/050511/2/9ooe.html (accessed 23 Nov. 2005).

5

Civil Rights, Legal Justice

Possibilities and Limits of Media and Internet Mobilization

If the Chinese television screen has managed to entertain the masses by offering one "hot" drama series after another, the Chinese news media and the Internet have braved the most draconian regime of party-state censorship power to create an endless flow of public controversies. From a Jiangxi school yard explosion to the "BMW incident" in Harbin, from one mining disaster after another to one legal case after another, never has the Chinese media and Internet universe generated so many widespread public controversies. These illuminating public controversies, in turn, shed light on the political economic and ideological contours of China's evolving communication system and its role in the processes of social contestation and containment. In the case studies to follow, I analyze the substantive dimensions of the Chinese public sphere and uneven terrains of discursive contestation among different social forces over the direction of China's ongoing political economic and social transformation. The two cases in this chapter center on Sun Zhigang and Wang Binyu, related media and Internet discourses, and their complicated intersections with party-state power at the local and national levels. At the center of these two cases are the issues of civil rights, economic and social rights, the rural-urban divide, the class nature of the liberal outcry for constitutional governance and China's rapidly emerging and consolidating legal system, the dynamics of confrontation and accommodation between China's urban educated strata and the Chinese state, as well as the relationship between middle-class professionalism and class rule.

The case in the next chapter centers on Lang Xianping, a Hong Kong–based economist who initiated a media- and Internet-based public policy debate on the nature and direction of the property right reform in state-owned enterprises and the process of privatization in late 2004. This case foregrounds the issues of economic democracy, property rights and ownership over means of production, and the stakes of different economic groups in China's reform process. The debates served as the background to the government's actions to halt the privatization of major state-owned enterprises through management buyouts. More importantly, they kicked off a much broader debate on neoliberalism and the direction of China's entire reform process that extended all the way to the 17th Party Congress in October 2007. Together, these two chapters reveal the specific ways in which different social forces and different kinds of power—political, economic, social, and cultural—operate within and through the media and the Internet to shape the course of China's transformation.

THE DETENTION SYSTEM AND THE DEATH OF SUN ZHIGANG

One of the most striking features of China's political economy is the urban and rural divide and the state apparatuses that enforce and maintain this divide. The household registration system, implemented in 1958 as a government response to the inflow of a starving rural population into urban centers, limits population mobility into the cities by maintaining a rigid distinction between those members of the population who have a rural household registration and those residents who have an urban registration. As Dorothy Solinger has observed, the system functions as a de facto "apartheid" system, as these two categories of population enjoy different citizenship entitlements.[1] The cradle-to-grave welfare system of state socialism under Mao, for example, was eligible only to urban residents.

Although the economic reforms have brought economic liberalization, the household registration system remains a defining feature of Chinese society. Rural residents, driven by an increasingly unsustainable agricultural sector and drawn to the economic opportunities in the cities, increasingly move into the urban areas, becoming "strangers in the city" and "second class" citizens in their own country.[2] Though the urban economy is increasingly dependent upon their labor, rural migrants must obtain temporary residence permits and are subjected to various restrictions in terms of their employment and mobility, including the need to secure a temporary work permit and a temporary residence permit.[3]

Chinese urban society, while benefiting from the labor of these rural migrants, has denied their citizenship entitlements, including basic rights such as education. This system shapes some of the fundamental features of China's modernity and the terms of its integration with the global capitalist market system. For example, the system makes possible the creation of supermodern Chinese cities with less of the slums and shantytowns typical of many third world cities. More importantly, this system put migrant workers in an extremely vulnerable position vis-à-vis domestic and transnational capital and serves as one of the key mechanisms helping to keep Chinese labor some of the cheapest in the world.[4]

In addition to effectively maintaining labor discipline, this system also serves as a powerful means of social control in China's urban centers during a period of rapid capitalistic development. At the center of this system of social control was the 1982 State Council "Measurements on the Detention and Repatriation of Vagrants and Beggars." Issued just five months before the enactment of the People's Republic's fourth Constitution on October 4, 1982, which continued the restriction of rural Chinese citizens' freedom of movement to urban areas, the regulations empowered the police to detain, shelter, and repatriate three types of "vagrants": (1) rural residents who have flowed to the city to become beggars; (2) urban residents who have become beggars on the streets; (3) other homeless street people with no livelihoods. While the overriding objective of the regulation was social control—that is, maintaining order and stability in the cities—the regulation also contained a welfare element with a provision for the state to provide food and shelter for the homeless.

A number of developments in the 1990s led to a more expansive regime of police power over the broad category of rural migrants in the cities. First, as the economic reforms deepened, the number of rural migrants expanded dramatically, further intensifying the employment pressures and social tensions in the urban centers. The original welfare dimension of the 1982 regulation was replaced with an overriding social control function, with its targets expanded from beggars and homeless individuals to the "three no people"—the segment of the migrant population who do not have an identification card, a temporary residence permit, or a work permit. Second, as the police departments became increasingly entrepreneurial in the context of reduced state subsidies and with the general development of bureaucratic capitalism, the police began to collect fines from detainees, not only to sustain the operations of these detention centers themselves, but also as a means of profit making in general. Retention and repatriation had become an industry. By 2002, there were as many as 861 retention and repatriation units in China, including 58 agricultural labor camps. Only 10 to 15 percent of those detained were the targeted individuals described in the 1982 regulation. Third, the expanded scope of retention, a shortage of police officers, and a general disinclination among the regularly trained urban police force to engage in the lowly job of rounding up beggars led to a situation in which detention centers have been typically staffed with individuals with little education, training, and discipline. Add a tendency for power abuse by the police, widespread discrimination by the urban population against migrants and other social outcasts, and in some places, an incentive system in which staff members are paid in accordance with their "performance" (i.e., the number of individuals arrested or the monetary value of fines extracted), and the result is an extremely brutal regime of social control and economic exploitation of rural migrants. This regime showed its ugliest face during politically sensitive times—for example, when cities such as Beijing and Shanghai needed to clean up their streets to greet the International Olympics Committee or other powerful international guests, or when the "two meetings" of the NPC and NPPCC take place in national, provincial, and municipal capitals. Even urban residents in the wrong place at the wrong time can be targeted.

On March 17, 2003, 27-year-old Sun Zhigang had his reckoning with this regime. Sun was born in a poor village in Huanggang City in Hubei Province, but he managed to cross the rural/urban divide by passing the university entrance exam, thus acquiring urban citizenship status. This was a rare achievement for somebody of Sun's background. In 1998, when Sun was accepted as an art design student in Wuhan Science and Technology University, he became the first person in his village since 1949 to gain urban citizenship. The whole family celebrated with banquets and the village with two movie screenings. With a carpenter father and a mother who labored on the farm, the family was so poor that Sun's younger brother had to quit school after grade eight to work as a chef, so that the family could invest in Sun Zhigang's high school education and his future. By the time Sun Zhigang attained his university degree, the family had accumulated more than 50,000 yuan in debt. Still, they were hopeful about their financial future, particularly when Sun phoned from Guangzhou to tell them about his new job, promising that he would send money home as soon as he was paid.[5]

Sun's death smashed that hope.[6] Around 10:00 p.m. on March 17, 2003, Sun, who had just moved to Guangzhou from Shenzhen to start a new job as a graphic designer in a garment factory, left the place he was renting with a friend to go to an Internet café. He had not yet obtained a temporary residence permit in Guangzhou, nor was he carrying his identification card. His timing could not have been any worse. Guangzhou's "two meetings" were about to be held, and Guangzhou's police authorities had just implemented a "strike hard" campaign in an attempt to ensure a stable environment for the meetings. As usual, the "three no people" were the targets of this campaign. Indeed, the district police department had just held a mobilization meeting that very afternoon.

Sun became one of the nearly 110 individuals who were rounded up by the police from the Huangchun police station and one of the more than 30 who ended up detained in that station. Later on that night, Sun phoned his roommate Cheng to bail him out with his identification card and cash. However, when Cheng went to the police station, he was told that Sun was not allowed to leave. No reason was given. When Cheng later spoke to Sun, Sun admitted that he had an argument with the police, although he said it was not a serious confrontation. The next morning, Sun was sent to the Guangzhou police's Tianhe District detention and repatriation center. Another friend received a phone call from Sun for help that day, but again, the police refused to release Sun. Later, Sun claimed to be sick and demanded release or medical treatment. He was sent to the detention center's medical station on the evening of March 19, two nights after his arrest, and again his friends were denied the right to see him.

Apparently, as a police investigation eventually revealed, Sun was singled out for corporal punishment because he protested and resisted his treatment and because he cried for help. Staff members deliberately decided to move Sun from one room to another and told the detainees in the other room to punish Sun: "Sun Zhigang is too noisy, we will bring him over in a while so that you can play around . . . don't hit his head and do not let out blood. No problem even if he is beaten to death. . . a person dies like an ant here."[7] And indeed, Sun was beaten to death by eight detainees on the morning of March 20, 2003. Sun's friend Cheng learned about Sun's death when he phoned the medical center later that day. The hospital's medical records show that Sun died of a heart attack.

Sun's father received the devastating news from a classmate of Sun in Wuhan. With 3,000 yuan in their pockets, Sun's father, younger brother, and other family members traveled to Guangzhou. The family didn't believe that Sun had heart disease and wanted to find out the true reasons for his death. However, without any social connections in urban China, Sun's peasant family could not make any progress. They went to the police station, the Tianhe District police office, and various government bureaus and state law enforcement institutions. They went to five Guangzhou law firms. But none of them dared to accept the case. Finally, a Guangzhou-based lawyer, who was also from the same town in Hubei and whose office had also refused to undertake the case, agreed to write a statement about the case, accepting whatever Sun's family could afford to pay.[8]

THE SUN ZHIGANG STORY AS A SCOOP FOR THE *NANFANG METROPOLITAN NEWS*

Although the ordeal of Sun's family is typical of many rural families in their dealings with the powers that be in the cities, Sun Zhigang was not a typical victim. His university education was not wasted for the family in the end. This education made him a nodal point in China's urban social networks, which played an instrumental role in connecting his family with sources of organizational and cultural power. Sun's university classmates sent money to his family members in Guangzhou for them to sustain their month-long pursuit of the truth behind his death. They also paid the 4,000-yuan autopsy fee, conducted independently by the medical college of Guangzhou's Sun Yat-sen University. More importantly, although the members of Sun's family tried to reach media outlets in vain, Sun's classmates used their networks to bring his death to the attention of China's media, legal, and intellectual communities. One account has it that a classmate who works at the high court in Beijing reached the *Nanfang Metropolitan News* (*NMN*).[9] Another story reported that Liu Jinfeng, an MA student at the Communication University of China, relayed the tragedy to Chen Feng, a newly hired *NMN* reporter in search of a news story.[10] Although the case happened in Guangzhou, clearly sources outside Guangzhou—mostly in Beijing—finally connected up with Guangzhou-based journalists.

Courage and wit were required for the *NMN* to print the story. After Chen Feng received the hot tip about Sun's death in late March 2003, his editor, Cheng Yizhong, immediately gave him permission to investigate the case. Philip P. Pan described the news production process:

> Chen, 31, teamed up with a colleague, Wang Lei, 28. They found Sun's family and persuaded them to ask a medical examiner for an autopsy. A few weeks later, the results came: Sun had been beaten to death.
>
> The two reporters briefed one of the paper's top editors. He immediately expressed interest, they recalled, and issued specific instructions. First, make sure to get every detail right. Second, get the story done fast before the authorities could order the subject off-limits.
>
> Chen and Wang moved quickly, interviewing Sun's friends, employers and relatives, and medical and legal experts. Then they tried to interview police and were told to go away at two precinct houses and city headquarters. They planned to write the story the next day.
>
> But their editor was worried. . . . He said they should have waited until the last day to contact police, because the police might call the propaganda authorities and squash the story. Then he ordered them to write it that night. The article was splashed across two pages.[11]

In addition to showing the ways in which they tactically evaded censorship and managed to get the story out, Pan's account provides a glimpse into the ways in which the journalists not only reported the "truth," but also went as far as to help to generate the "truth," including the independent medical autopsy, on behalf of members of a weak social group who did not have the cultural and financial capacities to produce such knowledge. On April 25, 2003, the *NMN* printed the scoop on Sun's death. Still, what made this paper stand out among the various media outlets that members of Sun's classmate network must have contacted, for example, the more powerful national media outlets in Beijing, the media outlets in Hubei Province (Sun's hometown), as well as the other media outlets in Guangzhou?

The *NMN*'s editorial orientation and professional culture played a crucial role in this exposure. First published in March 1995 and officially launched in 1997 as the urban subsidiary of the Guangdong provincial party organ, *Nanfang Daily*, the *NMN* is a product of the "metro paper" fever that started in the mid-1990s in the Chinese newspaper industry. As explained in chapter 2, this phenomenon began when provincial party organs, in an attempt to boost their revenue, set up daily newspapers to tap into the lucrative advertising market of China's booming metropolitans. The *NMN* was specifically set up to compete with *Guangzhou Daily*, which had successfully transformed itself from a stale party organ into a commercially successful newspaper and was raking in profits from the lucrative advertising market of the booming Guangzhou City. While *Guangzhou Daily* appealed to the more established Guangzhou urban middle-class market, the *NMN*, being the newcomer, had to blaze a new trail and cultivate a new market. The paper went down-market by establishing a readership through street sales and, more specifically, by catering to the "new Guangzhou people," that is, the outsiders, or the migrant population. This group not only includes rural migrants, but also the young, educated, and white-collar population that has been drawn to Guangzhou and the nearby Pearl River delta from the rest of the country because of its employment and business opportunities.

Cheng Yizhong, born in 1965, and the youngest of the three-person committee organized by the parent newspaper to set up the new paper in 1994, was himself such a migrant. The son of peasants from Anhui Province, Cheng landed a job with *Nanfang Daily* after graduating with a degree in literature from Guangzhou's Zhongshan University in 1989. He quickly established himself as a top editor. In March 1995, 30-year-old Cheng became the deputy editor of the *NMN*. Cheng not only easily identified with the life experiences of somebody like Sun Zhigang, but also intentionally targeted the paper to the social stratum that Sun Zhigang was a part of. Cheng's competitors confirmed the readership orientation of the paper, although in a derogatory way. A top executive of *Guangzhou Daily*, for example, specifically said in an interview I conducted in 1998 that while his paper had the more respectable middle-class readership, the *NMN* readership had a lower social status; it is a paper for the "laborers" (*dagong zi*).[12]

Set in the tabloid format, the *NMN* imitated the sensationalist style of Hong Kong's commercial *Apple Daily*. It quickly attracted attention with some of the most dramatic and sensationalist stories of the time. Philip Pan writes how readers who picked up the *NMN* on September 1, 1997, found a different kind of Communist Party newspaper. Instead of the latest pronouncements of the party, a quarter of the paper's 16 pages were devoted to the death of Princess Diana. In this way, "the tabloid stunned its rivals: almost every newspaper in China had covered Diana's death with only a few hundred words."[13]

If the Diana story established the paper's sensationalist reputation, another "soft" or "nonpolitical" topic, the 1998 World Cup finals, helped the paper to not only build a loyal readership locally and nationally, but also to cut its teeth in critical commentary. The paper mobilized all its resources to provide some of the most elaborate and colorful coverage of the event—eight pages a day for 43 consecutive days. More importantly, it employed a talented group of writers who provided some of the most critical analyses of the political economy and culture of China's soccer establishment, especially the China Soccer Association, the state authority in charge of Chinese soccer development (the part of the Chinese political establishment that is least powerful, therefore, the "weakest link" in the Chinese power structure). As Yang Xiaoyan, a seasoned observer of the Guangzhou newspaper scene puts it, although soccer was the specific topic, the paper's analysis of the political economy of China's soccer establishment, especially the intertwining logic of state directives and commercial imperatives and the resulting contradictions and tensions, as well as the bureaucratic political culture of the soccer establishment, showed it to be symptomatic of broader power relations in the Chinese society.[14]

Gradually, the paper extended its sensationalism and critical commentary into more critical realms of Chinese social life, cultivating a professional culture and a liberal editorial orientation that has pushed the boundaries of what is politically permissible. In the area of news, the paper, which started with less than 100 reporters and began by rewriting sensationalist stories from the Internet, has developed an extensive reporting team with certain professional standards. It quickly distinguished itself with more critical reporting on social problems such as crime and corruption. Moreover, as Pan wrote, while other newspapers avoided angering local officials, by muckraking only in other provinces, the paper focused on hard-hitting reporting in its own city and region.[15] This is an extraordinary stand in China's journalistic environment. As I have written elsewhere, a number of factors in the broad political economy of the Chinese media have led to the growth of investigative journalism since the 1990s. These include commercialization and growing market competition among news outlets catering to the urban audience, the emergence of a

new generation of enterprising and well-educated journalists, and journalists' growing sense of the liberal watchdog model, coupled with the
party-state's anticorruption imperative and political agenda of maintaining legitimacy and defusing and containing social tensions. However,
much of this type of journalism can be categorized as "watchdogs on
party leashes," because they avoid the most sensitive political and social
issues, and their targets are limited to low-ranking officials.[16] Of the two
best known watchdog media outlets, CCTV's *Focus Interviews* typically
addresses topics and issues that are already in the official reform agenda
and limits its targets to power abuse by village- and township-level officials, despite the fact that it is a central-level media organization. *Nanfang
Weekend*, a sister paper of the *NMN*, while well known for producing
some of the most critical watchdog stories, normally muckrakes outside
Guangdong Province. By muckraking in its own region, the *NMN* established itself as the critical media outlet of the economically dynamic Pearl
River delta. In particular, its cultivation of the migrant readership made it
the most popular paper in the migrant cities of the Pearl River delta. For
example, it was so popular in Shenzhen that press authorities tried to ban
its distribution in the city.[17] In the area of commentary, leading liberal intellectuals were invited to write editorials on topical issues. Consequently,
the paper established itself as a serious intellectual forum for elite liberal
intellectuals, as well as a popular paper among China's new lower-mid-
dle working-class population. The paper's editorial and commentary sections are comparable with those of the *New York Times*, while its news
pages put it on par with *USA Today*. The result has been a paper that is
both popular and respected, an agenda-setter and opinion leader in the
Chinese commercial media sector.

The paper was an instant commercial success. Circulation climbed from
80,000 at the end of 1997 to 380,000 a year later,[18] and to over a million by
the early 2000s. It created an economic miracle in the Chinese newspaper
industry by already earning a profit in the third year of its operation.
Moreover, as the reputation of the paper grew, its profit margins increased
spectacularly, from 3.76 million yuan in 1999 to 21.41 million in 2000, 24.85
million in 2001, 64.22 million in 2002, and 116.00 million in 2003.[19] In 2001,
Cheng Yizhong was promoted to the position of the paper's editor-in-
chief. Unlike the other two well-known, commercially successful Chinese
urban papers, the *Guangzhou Daily* and the *Beijing Youth Daily*, both of
which prioritized commercial expansion and the accumulation imperative, the *NMN* remained the editor's paper. Politically, the paper pushes
the limits of censorship, best exemplified in its reporting of the outbreak
of SARS between February and March 2003. At the same time, it has focused on its core journalistic mission and invests in professional excellence. Not surprisingly, the paper's newly established in-depth reporting

department was precisely what afforded the newly hired investigative reporter Chen Feng the opportunity to report the Sun Zhigang case.

In the larger context, the unique organizational culture of the *Nanfang Daily* Group is a significant factor in the making of the *NMN*. Although all papers are under party control in China, and the wave of conglomeration has swept across the entire newspaper industry, not all party organs are the same, nor does every conglomerate adopt the same strategy. Contrary to the *GD* group, which expands by venturing into other business sectors and by buying smaller publications, the *Nanfang Daily* Group expands by staying within the core newspaper business, pursuing excellence in journalism, and by launching and nurturing new, innovative, politically courageous, and intellectually relevant newspapers of regional and national influence—from *Nanfang Weekend* in the 1980s to the *NMN* in the 1990s and, since the 2000s, *21st-Century Business Herald* and the now defunct *21st-Century Global Herald* (*Ershi shiji huanqiu baodao*). Thus, the broad political economic analysis I have presented so far must be supplemented by a more specific analysis, because the organizational culture of individual media organizations, and the social background and value orientations of media gatekeepers such as Cheng Yizhong, also matter. My fieldwork in Guangzhou confirmed this difference in managerial strategies and professional culture at different newspapers. A former journalist who worked at the *NMN* recalled that newly hired reporters were imbued in a professional culture of building the best reporting staff of the country and becoming the best reporters.[20] In contrast, there is a famous joke about Li Yuanjiang and his treatment of journalism as a mere tool for profit making at the *GD*: when journalism school interns arrived at the paper, Li Yuanjiang would first arrange for them to see the newspaper's printing factory, letting them know that a newspaper is simply a money-printing machine, and on the second day he would arrange for them to visit the janitors working for the newspaper, so that young journalists wouldn't entertain any illusions about professional ethos.

In short, this is the broad organizational and professional context within which the *NMN* became the paper that exposed the Sun Zhigang story. If the failure of Sun's family members to reach the media on their own underscores the limits of urban-based media professionalism, the very publication of the story shows professional journalism, citizen consciousness, as well as the social reform ethos of Chinese journalists at its best. Of course, as a subsidiary of the *Nanfang Daily* Group, which is the party organ of the Guangdong provincial party committee, the *NMN* does have the political advantage of not having to administratively subordinate itself to the Guangzhou party-state authorities, where the case occurred. Still, it is one thing to expose other branches of the local state; it is another to expose the most powerful branches of the local state, the law enforcement agencies.

ELITE INTELLECTUAL AND POPULAR MOBILIZATION
THROUGH MEDIA AND THE INTERNET

Entitled "The Death of Detainee Sun Zhigang," the April 25, 2003, *NMN* exclusive was splashed across two pages. Illustrative of the fact that the newspaper had developed a mature professionalism that transcended its initial sensationalism, the story was structured in a matter-of-fact manner. A narrative about what happened to Sun based on various interviews, evidence of the independent autopsy report, as well as background material about the detention system made up the bulk of the story. Significantly, the headline framed Sun Zhigang vis-à-vis the detention system as a "detainee" without foregrounding his university graduate status. Nor did the story dramatize the emotional devastation and the ordeals of the family in their monthlong search for the truth behind Sun's death. The story reported the desperation and, indeed, the resignation of the family in its last paragraph by saying that "members of Sun's family are now somewhat regretful for supporting Sun Zhigang's university education. If he was not educated, he would not have insisted on principles, and perhaps he would not have been killed."[21]

Nevertheless, the *NMN* made its advocacy and social reform agenda clear by publishing the story and framing it against the detention system. Furthermore, one of its editors took the initiative of mobilizing social reform around the story by posting a message on Century China (*Shiji Zhongguo*), the most popular Internet forum for liberal intellectuals: "I am coming here, the leading website for Chinese intellectuals, to invite you to write. This is the time that intellectuals must stand up to act as citizens for social justice. We need to not only demand a just solution to this individual case but also reflect on the big picture behind this tragedy." The editor left his e-mail address and promised to publish some of the best responses in his paper.[22]

The story, which immediately spread to the Internet that same day and was widely reported by media outlets in the country the following day, caused a national sensation. Hundreds of people called and sent faxes to the newspaper to express outrage or to tell their own stories of police abuse, and tens of thousands posted messages on the Internet. Sun was not the first victim of China's detention and repatriation system; nor was this the first time that the news media reported deaths resulting from the enforcement of the retention system. As an Internet posting put it, there had been many similar news reports, including a January 26, 2003, *GD* story about the deaths of two female migrant workers in the hands of detention police. Although the case caught the media's attention and stirred up a big sensation, with promises by authorities to investigate, there was no follow-up at all.[23]

But the story was different this time. Although Sun had a rural background, his university education had earned him membership in China's educated social strata. He was not supposed to be detained, let alone beaten to death. If he was mistakenly rounded up, he should have been released immediately once he explained his status. Not surprisingly, on the Internet, including authoritative websites such as Xinhua Net, the *NMN* story was circulated not under its original title "The Death of Detainee Sun Zhigang," but under the headline "University Graduate Detained Because of Lack of Temporary Residence Permit and Beaten to Death." This is a significant discursive transformation and rearticulation. The technical term "detainee" has been replaced by the social category "university graduate." Moreover, "Sun Zhigang" as a specific individual has disappeared in the new headline. Instead, one of the collective categories to which he belonged, "university graduate"—which carries all the connotations of knowledge and elite status—has become the subject. Yet Sun's more current status in the labor force, that is, as a graphic designer in a garment factory—the collective category of "company employee" or "white collar worker"—was not invoked. In other stories, Sun Zhigang was no longer a "university graduate" (*daxue biyesheng*) but simply a "university student" (*daxue sheng*). Although the label was incorrect, it adds the connotations of innocence and youth. From his "university graduate" and "university student" status, Sun Zhigang, in subsequent news media and Internet reports and commentaries, became a symbol for the more generalized category of "citizen" (*gongmin*) in an emerging liberal citizen rights discourse. This eventually became the dominant framework of media and Internet discourse around him.

In short, as the Sun Zhigang story gained wide media and Internet attention, it became framed first and foremost as a citizenship rights case, specifically, civil rights in terms of personal freedom and security against arbitrary state and administrative power, a cause that urban citizens can identify with. That Sun, somebody who had already gained urban citizenship, was detained and beaten to death, horrified the urban citizenry, as his experience went beyond the "bottom-line" limits of the detention system.[24] Rural migrants, the social category to which Sun was mistakenly assigned, their "second-class" status, and their social justice—that is, Sun as a symbol for weak social groups—had assumed secondary importance. An Internet keyword search on December, 15, 2005, lent support to this observation. Of the 251,000 items that contained "Sun Zhigang" in a Google search, the term "citizen" appeared 71,000 times, the term "university student" appeared 64,700 times, and the term "peasant worker" ("*mingong*," which would be inclusive of the term "*nongmin gong*" in the search) appeared 23,000 times. Consistent with this pattern, the term "citizenship rights" (*gongmin quanli*), which is associated with the more general citizenship rights framework, appeared 49,500 times, while the term "social justice" (*shenhui gongzheng*), which articulates more closely with a social justice for rural migrants framework, appeared 35,000 times.[25]

Sun's university graduate social status and the liberal civil rights frame made him easily identifiable not only with China's intellectual community, but also with the much larger community of China's Internet users, which played an instrumental role in the event.[26] Although authorities in Guangzhou quickly suppressed the *NMN*'s further reporting of the case, the story took on a life of its own throughout China. Both Sun's direct and indirect classmate networks and China's Internet community at large were mobilized. Here some background on the socioeconomic makeup of China's active online community is necessary. Although China's online community has expanded exponentially since 1997, reaching 68 million people around the time of the Sun Zhigang controversy in mid-2003, and 110 million by early 2006,[27] Chinese Internet users are disproportionately young, male, urban, and college educated—exactly the same profile as that of Sun Zhigang. Workers and farmers, the two largest social groups, amounted to only minuscule percentages of the online population.[28] The groups that make up the numeric majority of China's online population, students (30.1 percent), service and office workers (28.1 percent), and technicians (15.9 percent), constitute the lower segment of China's "middle class" or "middle social strata" in structural terms (if not in numerical terms) and act as a buffer between the ruling elites and their business and intellectual allies on the one hand and the workers and farmers on the other. As Dong Han has observed, this group plays an important, though necessarily divisive and fragmentary, mediating role in class conflicts in Chinese society. On the one hand, they are the beneficiaries of China's urban/rural divide and the economic reforms—they share part of the surplus extracted from the rural population while evading the massive layoffs that have been experienced by urban industrial workers in the state-owned enterprises. Contempt for manual labor and the superiority secured by the urban-rural divide always result in these groups' conscious social distinction from factory workers and farmers. On the other hand, these social groups were troubled by the negative economic consequences of market reforms in housing, health care, and education, as well as other pitfalls of the party-state's authoritarian politics, including corruption, malfunctioning public services, increased crime rates, arbitrary government administrative power and police brutality, and worsening environmental problems. Their socioeconomic status, plus their family and social links with factory workers and the rural population, make it possible for them to side with the people at the bottom of Chinese society.[29] The most outspoken among these groups in cyberspace are the so-called angry youth (*fenqing*) and marginal middle-aged intellectuals or grassroots social analysts (the "angry middle-aged," or *fenzhong*) who

rp identify with migrant workers

have never had access to the mainstream media. Thus, although cyberspace does not constitute a battlefield between China's ruling elites and the disenfranchised per se, as the latter are largely without Internet access, class conflicts between the ruling elites and the disenfranchised workers and farmers, as well as the fact that the majority of Internet users belong to the bottom segment of urban-based "middle social strata," are the necessary places to start to understand Internet discourses in China.[30] Moreover, by 2003, with the turning of the "old leftists" to the Internet through the establishment of the Mao Zedong Flag website and the resulting coalescence of various leftist discourses, Chinese Internet discourses had become more politicized and inflected with a heightened sense of class conflict.

Sun's tragedy struck a responsive chord among the economically less privileged but socially progressive segment of the urban "middle social strata," especially the Internet users of Sun's age and educational background.[31] Sun's classmates, with their social capital and economic resources, were the ones who persistently pushed forward the "Sun Zhigang event," from carrying the news to the family, to donating funds, seeking legal assistance, appealing to the media, and eventually writing on the Internet on his behalf. The point, then, is that the media and Internet alone, in the absence of necessary interpersonal networks and social agents willing to identify with a particular cause, will not necessarily lead to any effective public mobilization. In addition to the crucial role of this social network in gaining the media's initial attention on the case, the following account, provided by a participant in this mobilization, offers further evidence of the structure of this social network and its mobilizing power:

> I do not personally know Sun Zhigang. He was merely a classmate of one of my university classmates. When I passed on the story of Sun's death to one of my classmates, he cried. He also works in the press. So he asked me to help him to produce a follow-up report. . . . I had just returned from Hangzhou and was under quarantine (from SARS) in Wuhan. So I entrusted the task to Gao Hong, a female friend of mine who studies comparative literature. She agreed without hesitation and set out to make appointments with her professor friend, journalist friend, and lawyer friend, as well as finding Sun's family members who were still in Guangzhou. At 2:50 a.m. last night, she sent me the article . . . however, when I sent this article to my classmate, he told me that he could not publish it in his paper. The reasons were unclear.[32]

This article, written on April 28, 2003, was posted on the Internet the following day and consisted of interviews with reporter Chen Feng, literature professor and feminist activist Ai Xiaoming, civil rights lawyer Zhong Yujie, as well as Sun's brother and uncle. It became a key piece in the follow-up to the *NMN*'s initial story. In the article, the three professionals—a journalist, a professor, and a lawyer—spoke for as well as with members of Sun's family and assumed the role of social advocates, coordinating the mobilization activities. Reporter Chen Feng clarified that the objective of Sun's family was not to seek financial assistance, but to seek truth and justice. Lawyer Zhong spoke on behalf of Sun's family, asking those with social status and media and Internet access "to calmly use your own social status" to help the Sun family in the pursuit of truth. Chen Feng cautioned against extreme responses proposed by some Internet users and suggested strategies such as financial donations and phoning government offices to call attention to the case.

A major *NMN* follow-up story that was censored was published in *China Youth News* on April 26, 2003. It also found its way onto the Internet. Under the title "The *NMN*'s Unpublished Follow-up Report about the Unnatural Death of Sun Zhigang," the piece was forwarded with the following note on the censorship: "When on-duty editors were rushing to work on the follow-up story on the afternoon of April 25, a phone call from the provincial propaganda department [of Guangdong Province] demanded a stop to all reporting on Sun Zhigang. The following are parts of the draft reports I copied from them at noon."[33]

The immediacy, not to mention the revealing nature, of the material, including the monthlong ordeal of the Sun family, had a dramatic impact and led more Internet users to write from different angles, creating a powerful multidimensional public discourse about broader issues of police brutality against ordinary citizens, the injustice of the detention regime, and social inequality in general. Some reported similar stories of police brutality and encounters with the detention system. Others, especially more prominent intellectuals, posted powerful pieces on the Internet, appealing to the authorities to investigate the case and critiquing police brutality and unlimited police and administrative power, the injustice of the detention system, as well as the broader household registration system and urban rural inequality. Widespread and influential pieces included Ai Xiaoming's "Live in Fear"[34] and farmer rights activist Li Changping's "Sun Zhigang Died for Me."[35] Speaking to official discourses, Professor Ai wrote,

> Guangzhou is a beautiful city. Every day, real estate advertising celebrates the beauty of new life. But if an outsider worker has no right to enjoy the freedom of walking on the streets at night, what is the meaning of this beauty? Guangdong's economic development depends on attracting more foreign investment, but if there is no responsibility and accountability for this kind of murder under broad daylight, where is our society's sense of justice? How can we claim that we live in a society in which the human rights of citizens are protected? . . . How can I know that the next victim won't be my own son, my students, or myself? As a woman, a mother, and a teacher, I call upon the chair of Guangdong NPC . . . to protect the rights of weak social

groups, secure the safety of migrant laborers, and severely punish Sun Zhigang's murderers.[36]

Li Changping used the opportunity to voice his more systematic critique of glaring social injustice and the rapidly expanding and increasingly blunt operation of political economic power by a small minority in Chinese society against ordinary Chinese citizens in general—"us" as an all-inclusive citizenry as opposed to the small ruling elite:

> The death of Sun Zhigang made me think about a lot of things. We have enacted more than 2,000 laws, and yet more and more people are coming to Beijing to petition. The population of the "petition village" near Beijing's South Railway Station has reached more than 10,000. This is unprecedented. Plainclothes police from each province are regularly stationed in Beijing; more and more petitioners are detained, sentenced, some have even evaporated. . . . Before the detention and repatriation system was a welfare system, its targets were rural migrants with no livelihoods. Now, what kind of a system has this become when its targets include university graduates? . . . Before it was the rural/urban duality; now, if you are a resident of Wuhan and you go to Beijing, Shanghai, and Guangzhou, you can be detained as well. . . . [O]ur society is fragmented into countless political economic interest cliques, and after a small minority become the holders of vested political and economic interests, they utilize laws, regulations, institutions, power, and state apparatuses to sustain and expand their vested interests. As the hundreds and thousands of rural migrant laborers, the hundreds and thousands of laid-off workers, and the hundreds and thousands of university graduates seek their opportunities for survival and development, how many more will become Sun Zhigang! . . . Sun Zhigang died for us. If we ignore his death today, tomorrow will be our date of death.[37]

Although Guangzhou and Guangdong authorities may have wished to ignore these messages, national media exposure and Internet mobilization made it increasingly difficult for them to cover up the case. To be sure, just as there is a hierarchy in discursive authority in the Chinese media, there is a hierarchy in discursive power in China's cyberspace. On May 4, 2003, nearly 10 days after the *NMN*'s initial exposure, People's Net, the *People's Daily* website, posted an authoritatively worded article under the title "The Sun Zhigang Case: Who Continues to Pretend to be Deaf and Mute?" Although the article was authored by "net friend Jing Xiuwen," it was written in the style of a *People's Daily* editorial, with a penetrating analysis of a bureaucratic culture in which officials put their own personal interests above justice, fairness, and the interests of the people.[38] The authorities in Guangzhou took this article seriously. Under the headline "Hu Jintao and Wen Jiabao Surfed the Net: Paying Attention to the People's Net Reporting of the Sun Zhigang Case," the *Nanfang Weekend* reported that this article finally "increased the determination of the police to investigate the case."[39]

On May 13, 2003, the Xinhua News Agency reported the arrests of 13 suspects in connection with Sun's death. The report also indicated that the case had caught the attention of central and Guangdong provincial authorities. The secretary of the central Political and Legal Commission and the Ministry of Public Security issued several instructions for a thorough investigation of the case, and the ministry sent a work team to supervise the investigation. The standing committee of the provincial party committee of Guangdong Province held special sessions to discuss the case and ordered an in-depth investigation.[40] Special investigative teams constituted by the Ministry of Public Security as well as provincial and municipal authorities undertook the investigation.

As journalists at the *NMN* had hoped, the debate went beyond the Sun Zhigang case itself to a broad intellectual mobilization for civil rights and for the state to abolish the detention system per se, including an examination of its constitutionality. On April 29, 2003, more than a hundred leading intellectuals issued an open letter to the NPC calling for the repeal of the detention and temporary residence permits system. This led to more petitions by Chinese intellectuals from different disciplines and with different political and ideological orientations. Especially influential was a petition by three newly minted legal scholars calling for a constitutional review of the 1982 regulation. Although the authors of these appeals signed themselves as "Chinese citizens," as with Sun, their social status—having doctorate degrees and being affiliated with elite universities—garnered them media and Internet attention and discursive authority.

Because of the dominant framing of the issue as one concerning the rule of law, arbitrary administrative power, police brutality, and the basic civil rights of individual citizens, liberal and "new left" intellectuals, notwithstanding their ideological divisions, shared common concerns. A posting at the Century China forum, entitled "Why Intellectuals Must Lift Their Eyes from Books," celebrated this unprecedented unity on the part of China's intellectuals, their sense of social responsibility, and their shared "bottom-line positions":

> These public intellectuals, regardless of North or South, of left or right, of science or arts, of high or low ranks, have gradually lifted their eyes from their books. They have called discussion meetings, held seminars, published articles in the media, given media interviews, exchanged views with Internet users in chat rooms, issued joint petitions. . . . [T]his is the power of public intellectuals; this power can wake up public consciousness, influence government policies, and promote social progress.[41]

At the *NMN*, Cheng Yizhong kept the paper at the forefront of the campaign, asking his reporters to follow up with investigations in the face of censorship orders and sending articles to the Internet and *China Youth*

News in Beijing to bypass local censorship, and later on, after Guangzhou authorities could no longer censor the story, the *NMN* published a series of influential and widely circulated special reports and editorials advocating the abolishment of the detention system, including reporter Meng Bo's "Six Questions about the Retention and Repatriation System."[42]

The impact of the mobilization was immediate. On June 4, 2003, 23 officials in various Guangzhou municipal police, public health, and civil affairs departments received party and administrative disciplinary actions—eight police chiefs and police officers at the Tianhe District and its Huangchun branch were fired. On June 9, 2003, the Guangzhou Intermediate Court issued criminal sentences to the 18 individuals directly responsible for Sun's death. On June 20, 2003, Premier Wen Jiabao signed State Council Order Number 381, abolishing the 1982 regulation and replacing it with "Measurements Regarding the Assistance and Management of Vagrants and Beggars without Subsistence in the Cities."[43] The new regulation not only prohibited local state agencies from detaining people against their will or imposing charges or fines on them, but also included sweeping welfare program reform aimed at "assisting vagrants and beggars in cities, ensuring their basic livelihoods, and perfecting the social welfare system."[44] It charged governments at the county level and above with the responsibilities of establishing assistance centers that provide food, shelter, and emergency medical care for vagrants and beggars, contacting their family members and working units, as well as covering the transportation costs for these individuals to return to their place of origin. Moreover, it stated that these centers "shall not refuse to provide timely assistance to those who are eligible" and that "in the case of an assistance center failing to fulfill its duties, eligible individuals can report to local civil affairs departments, which, upon investigation, shall not only order the assistance center to provide immediate assistance, but must also impose disciplinary punishments against responsible individuals."[45] In short, the new regulation not only abolished the social control function of the 1982 regulation, but also empowered vagrants and beggars to claim their rights to subsistence from the state.

BEYOND SUN ZHIGANG: INTELLECTUAL AND BUREAUCRATIC POLITICAL BACKLASHES

Neoliberal Intellectual Backlashes and the Limits of Citizen Rights Discourse

Although the media, China's intellectual community, and the Internet demonstrated unprecedented mobilizing power in advocating civil rights and social reform through the Sun Zhigang case, this mobilization has clear internal limits.

First, there is the issue of the apparent elitism of the media and Internet discourses themselves. As noted earlier, Sun's "university graduate" or simply "university student" status became the crucial element in the newsworthiness of the story. If Sun had not been a member of the elite social strata, the story would probably not have unfolded the way it did. As Kuang Xinnian put it, "That Sun Zhigang was beaten to death was an accidental story. This is not because detention, beating, and death do not happen on a frequent basis, but because it is extremely rare that a university graduate is beaten to death, because the detention system aims not at the elite strata, but at the peasant strata."[46]

Second, as with similar cases of media-induced and central authority–mandated deliveries of legal justice, the political imperative of appealing to public outrage led to swift, severe, but not necessarily legally sound court decisions. In the end, as in many other similar cases, what the case reaffirmed was not the rule of law as such, but the effectiveness of high-level political intervention in the law and order process. As Sun Liping has observed, there is a profound dilemma in the current interaction of media, political power, and legal justice. The intervention of political power may lead to unfair legal decisions, and yet, in the context of widespread power abuse, political intervention remains the only means to ensure the delivery of justice in some cases.[47]

Third, although media- and Internet-based elite and popular mobilization led the State Council to abolish its earlier regulation, the more substantive appeal of liberal legal scholars about the constitutionality of the regulation was bypassed by party-state authorities. In particular, liberal scholars who had wished to use the case to promote constitutional governance were not able to make any substantive progress in this regard. In fact, Xu Zhiyong, one of the three newly minted legal scholars who issued an open letter calling for a constitutional review of the 1982 detention regulation, noted that while the abolishing of the regulation itself was one objective, another "more important objective" was the procedural issue of the case—that is, to establish the authority of the Chinese Constitution and the power of the NPC in constitutional review. Thus, for Xu, the result was far from what he and his colleagues had hoped for.[48] That Xu ranked the civil rights objective as being "more important" and that he and many of his fellow crusaders couldn't care less about the actual social gains of the campaign, namely, the state's granting of welfare entitlement rights to the vagabonds, is indicative of the social bias of an emerging liberal citizenship rights discourse that prioritizes civil and political rights over economic and social rights.

- Gov over powered
- no legal process
- media failed to adress bigger issue
↳ just got end result

In fact, although there was a broad consensus about the civil rights of rural migrants and the undesirability of the detention and repatriation regime, other than calling for the repeal of the 1982 regulation within a discourse of civil rights and constitutional governance, the dominant framework of the media and Internet discourses did not offer any critical reflection on China's developmental path, which created the problem in the first place, nor did it address migrant workers' economic and social rights, let alone the class interest of migrant workers and their conflicted class relationships within Chinese urban society. The discourse on the civil rights of Sun Zhigang and rural migrants, although powerful in posing a challenge to an autocratic state and its arbitrary use of police force against individuals, conceals profound class inequalities between rural and urban society and the very fact that the detention system was put in place not by an abstract evil state bent on curtailing the civil rights of every individual, but to protect the socioeconomic interests of the urban population against rural migrants, and as part of China's developmental strategy that has condemned rural residents to "second-class citizen" status. To add more irony to the liberal appeal to constitutional authority, as one commentator pointed out, although the first Constitution of the People's Republic of China, enacted in 1954, guarantees citizens' freedom of movement, that clause was removed in subsequent constitutions; thus, "the detention and repatriation system has a constitutional basis."[49] What is at stake, as this commentator noted, is justice and equality for the rural population. In short, it is perhaps fair to say that market-oriented urban media, urban intellectuals, and Internet users crusaded on behalf of Sun Zhigang primarily from the perspective of universal citizenship rights, not from the perspective of rural migrants as a social class and their potentially conflicting interests with Chinese urban society within the context of China's modernization strategies. Members of urban society identify with Sun Zhigang because their own individual rights are under threat by state and administrative power as well. In this sense, their crusade on behalf of Sun Zhigang was a crusade for the civil rights of all citizens. Within this context statements by urban intellectuals such as "Sun Zhigang died for me" make sense.

Perhaps significant is that the central authorities, rather than the media and Internet crusaders, ended up going beyond the civil rights discourse to address the social rights of the urban homeless in the aftermath of the Sun Zhigang case. The new party leadership, in an attempt to display its newly affirmed "people-oriented" mixture of reformist populism and paternalist governance in the midst of managing a SARS crisis, not only abolished the disciplinary detention regime, but also replaced it with a welfarist regime of social entitlements for the urban homeless.

Not surprisingly, the government's "generous" welfarist regime led to a conservative intellectual backlash in Chinese cyberspace. Xu Xiangyang, a neoliberal economist, charged humanistic intellectuals with irresponsibility and the government with capitulating to the destructive force of "vagrant populism."[50] To abolish the social control function of the state's coercive regime against rural migrants and to replace it with the new welfare system is, in Xu's view, to invite the destruction of China's fragile urban civilization by a flood of rural migrants, which in Xu's view embody the forces of barbarism, evil, and chaos. In an Internet posting on August 3, 2003, Xu warned against the increasing pressure of rural migration on the city following China's WTO accession and invoked the specter of urban China engulfed by the destructive force of rural migrants with the ending of the detention system.[51] Xu not only defended the rationality of the detention system in securing China's "fragile urban civilization," but also derided the new regulation for its impracticality and its enormous "economic cost." In particular, Xu faulted its populist thrust:

> Populists made [provision for the poor] the complete responsibility of the rich and the right of the poor. This notion found its fullest expression in the new regulation: I am poor, therefore I have the right to food, shelter, medical care, and transportation, and the provision of these becomes the responsibility of the government. If I cannot afford these, I have the right to appeal. . . . [A]t its most powerful, populism ostensibly promotes class struggle, turning the state into a violent instrument that functions to deprive property owners.[52]

Claiming that populism as a form of mob rule had assumed a dangerously dominant discursive position in China, Xu censured the Chinese government for following the moralistic impulse of China's humanistic intellectual community and conjured the specter of totalitarianism in the resulting state and society interaction:

> If the mainstream discourse of the entire society is controlled by this trend, the resulting state and society interaction will inevitably lead to the softening of government, the derailing of social norms, rather than the spread of a free order. . . . [W]hen the repatriation system was replaced by the assistance system, many sounded victorious applause, but instead of viewing it as a victory of the human rights value of liberalism, it is a victory of the humanistic value of populism.[53]

Xu's article underscores China's neoliberal intellectual circle's unwillingness to make class compromises and their long-standing fear of populism, which was seen as the ideological underpinning of Maoism and all the evils that Maoism stood for. By moving beyond the liberal civil rights discourse and attacking the government's welfarist policy, Xu posed challenging questions about China's developmental path and the appropriate role of the state in China's increasingly class-divided society: a minimalist, neoliberal state that performs the function of social control and secures negative freedoms or a welfarist, socialist state that not only guarantees civil rights for all, but also social rights for the poor. However, instead of engaging in a more comprehensive debate with Xu on China's developmental path, the relative merits of civil rights and social rights, as well as the appropriate role of the Chinese state, Internet users heaped verbal abuse on Xu. Consequently, Internet discourse on the topic degenerated into symbolic violence against an unpopular position.[54]

Bureaucratic Political Backlashes and the Contestation of Bureaucratic and Professional Cultures

Apart from their internal limits, media and Internet discourses continue to be constrained by the complicated web of vertical and horizontal bureaucratic political power at the central and local levels. As discussed above, the State Council responded to the media and Internet-based mobilization by abolishing the 1982 regulation through the administrative, rather than the constitutional, route and issuing a new regulation whose welfarist provisions infuriated Hayak-inspired neoliberals such as Xu Xiangyang. *Tactic allows for more criticism*

Xu was not alone. The State Council's change of rules led to an immediate backlash within the Chinese state's law and order apparatuses. As "My name is Sun Zhigang" became the defiant answer to police queries about an individual's name on the streets, police were almost on strike in Guangzhou, Shenzhen, and other south Chinese cities, complaining that without the power to detain suspects they could not stop burglaries and other minor crimes. Contrary to the original fanfare about the State Council's new regulation, there was little media reporting on the challenges of implementing this regulation, including the substance of a September 26, 2003, State Council meeting that discussed this issue and in which Premier Wen Jiabao may have made concessions to the state's law enforcement agencies in terms of the implementation of the new regulation.[55]

Most significantly, local authorities in Guangzhou and Guangdong launched a major counterattack against the media. To be sure, central government and popular pressure forced local law and order authorities to hand legal and administrative punishments to those who were directly and indirectly responsible for Sun's death. But local authorities were furious about the negative national media publicity, and the *NMN* quickly became the target of bureaucratic political retaliation. In a development that was highly counterintuitive to those who tend to reify the rule of law as a means to constrain arbitrary state power, authorities in Guangzhou turned to the instruments of law to retaliate against journalists and to crush an emerging culture of independent journalism.

Between July 2003 and September 2004, Guangzhou law and order authorities, with the implicit support of the Guangzhou municipal and provincial leaderships, carried out a major investigation into the finances of the *NMN*. Three top executives of the paper were arrested and charged—general manager Yu Huafeng, *Nanfang Daily* editorial board member Li Minying (who functions as the *NMN*'s director), and *NMN* editor-in-chief Cheng Yizhong—for economic crimes based on the paper's bonus payment practices. On March 19, 2004, Yu Huafeng was sentenced to 12 years in prison for embezzling public funds by transferring bonus funds from the newspaper's advertising department to be distributed among editorial personnel, for receiving 100,000 yuan as his own share of the bonus, and for bribing Li Minying by paying him a bonus. Li Minying was sentenced to an 11-year jail term for accepting the payment. On the same day, Cheng Yizhong was arrested for the embezzlement of public funds and for "privately dividing up state assets." His home and office were searched by Guangzhou police, who also stormed the *Nanfang Daily* Group headquarters. As many as 20 other editors and business managers at the *NMN* were interrogated by the prosecutors.[56]

These actions stunned Chinese journalists, intellectuals, and the Internet community. The relatively small amount of money involved and the ambiguous nature of the charges—especially the blurred line between legitimate bonuses and the illegitimate embezzlement of state funds that is systematic in any Chinese news organization under the "cause-oriented undertaking run as a business" model—made the retaliatory nature of the investigations all too obvious. Like the Sun Zhigang case, extensive media, Internet, and intra-elite petitions were generated on behalf of the *NMN* and its top management. Beijing-based journalists, journalism scholars, and literacy figures issued open letters, set up special websites to report on the latest developments of the case, and petitioned the authorities for the release of those arrested.[57] Legal scholars in Beijing and Shanghai argued that the *NMN* editorial board's bonus allocation was a legitimate practice under the market economy. Within the local power elite, former Guangdong provincial leaders Ren Zhongyi and Wu Nansheng either wrote or spoke in person to Zhang Dejiang, the Guangdong provincial party secretary, to review the case. Local intellectual and media elites, including leading professors at Guangzhou's Sun Yat-sen University, senior managers and senior journalists at *Nanfang Daily*, as well as staff members at the *NMN*, also wrote to Guangdong provincial authorities, demanding the release of the arrested journalists.[58] Domestic and international media coverage of the case, as well as wide publicity of the petition activities, also helped to put pressure on the Guangzhou and Guangdong authorities. The intervention of President Hu Jintao and Premier Wen Jiabao, as well as "the 'sincere advice' of foreign governments" was also reported.[59] On June 15, 2004, the Guangzhou Intermediate Court reduced the prison sentence of Yu Huafeng from 12 years to 8 years and that of Li Minying from 11 years to 6 years on appeal. Although Cheng Yizhong was later released without any charge, he was barred from going to Senegal in April 2005 to receive a UN press freedom award. On July 20, 2005, the Guangdong Higher People's Court rejected Yu Huafeng's appeal of his eight-year jail sentence, and almost a month later, more than 2,300 journalists filed a petition calling for the release of Yu and Li.[60] Clearly, Guangdong provincial authorities, and perhaps even central authorities, were not prepared to yield to domestic journalistic pressure or appreciate international recognition of those who struggle for journalistic autonomy.

The *NMN* case underscores the fragile political economic base of China's nascent culture of independent professional journalism. The case represents a major contestation between the entrenched local bureaucratic culture and the professional culture of the *NMN*. Embedded in the practices of the *NMN*, and refined and articulated by Cheng Yizhong in his role as the editor-in-chief of the newly established *Beijing News* in 2003, this nascent professional culture promotes the "public interest" and what China's new generation of media professionals assume to be the universal value orientations of media institutions. The *Beijing News* adopts the slogan of "Responsible for Reporting Everything" as its motto and endeavors to "guard the interests of the country and the people, appeal to rationality, check against administrative power, pursue truth and virtue, defend public justice, and expose the ugly and the evil."[61] It further argues that "these are universalistic and ultimate values of media in every country and regardless of social systems," and in an attempt to speak to the official discourse, Cheng claims that "these are also the values consistently advocated by the governing party of our country, that is, to employ power for the people, to be concerned about the people, and to pursue the interest of the people."[62] Such a value orientation has put Cheng and the kind of journalism he practices in direct conflict with actually existing bureaucratic culture, which centers on the use of public office for the self-interest of officials and bureaucratic self-preservation. From the perspective of this bureaucratic culture, especially the career ambitions of officials, the *NMN*'s exposure of the Sun Zhigang case was a major setback.

There were strong bureaucratic motivations for political retaliation in particular and for curbing the further growth of this new brand of assertive journalism in general. At the rank-and-file level, a Guangzhou police officer who received a three-year prison sentence for his involvement in the Sun Zhigang case reportedly threatened Zhu Huisheng, public security bureau chief of Guangzhou City, at the time of his sentence: "I will bring death to you if you do not bring death to the *NMN*!"[63] At the Guangzhou municipal level, Zhang Guifang, deputy party secretary in charge of Guangzhou's law and order apparatuses and responsible for establishing Guangzhou's draconian migrant detention regime, took the same attitude toward the media. In a June 2003 meeting aimed at drawing a lesson from the Sun Zhigang case, Zhang stated a plain truth about China's bureaucratic culture and benefits of an obedient media: there were similar cases of detention deaths all over the country; if not for the reporting of the *NMN*, there would not have been a problem. At this meeting an agenda was set to punish the *NMN*, and Zhang assumed the leadership role of a special investigation team.[64] At the provincial level, Zhang Dejiang, former party secretary of Zhejiang Province who was appointed a political bureau member and Guangdong provincial party secretary in November 2002, had made the taming of Guangdong's outspoken media one of his major political objectives. In 2003, Zhang Dejiang suspended the publication of *Nanfang Daily*'s newly established paper, *21st-Century Global Herald,* for its interview with liberal party elder Li Rui and changed the upper management of the *Nanfang Daily* Group. As part of this change, he replaced the editor-in-chief of *Nanfang Weekend* with his own protégé Zhang Dongming, the news bureau chief of the Guangzhou PD. This was considered a blunt assault on the growing journalistic culture and led to the departure of a number of independent-minded reporters from the paper. Still, Zhang Dejiang was unhappy with the *NMN* and other media outlets' reporting of the outbreak of the SARS epidemic. In November 2003, when the *NMN* broke censorship rules by reporting the reemergence of SARS, the responsible reporter and editor at the *NMN* were punished, and Zhang reportedly shouted, "I did not expect that Guangdong's media would be so difficult to control!"[65] Even after Hu Jintao and Wen Jiabao had instructed that local officials should not suppress information regarding SARS, Guangdong authorities still imposed all kinds of restrictions on news media, including prohibiting the transmission of Xinhua and CCTV news, leading one commentator to say that "only in Guangdong can somebody dare to suppress stories by Xinhua and CCTV."[66] In short, Zhang's instrumental view of the media—that it must be the mouthpiece of the party and anything beyond this is considered rebellious—and his private instrumentalism—seeing himself as the embodiment of the party—have led to a serious clash with the idea of journalistic autonomy. When Guangzhou municipal authorities decided to investigate the *NMN*'s finances, Zhang agreed and instructed as a matter of principle that "the *NMN* should not only supervise others, but should also accept supervision [by others]."[67] Reflective of the broad local political consensus against the *NMN* at both the Guangzhou municipal and Guangdong provincial levels, Huang Huahua, Guangdong provincial governor, instructed that the investigation should be "carried to the end."[68]

Apart from the ideological limits of a liberalism-inspired professionalism and its inconsistency, issues I will discuss in the next section and in the conclusion, the case also demonstrated that China's fledgling culture of professional journalism rests on fragile economic grounds. That the Guangzhou law and order authorities were able to prosecute media managers for economic crimes based on the paper's bonus payment system is the result of the unique political economy of China's state media organizations. On the one hand, media organizations such as the *NMN* are state-owned institutions and journalists are considered state employees—and thus are subject to state prosecution for the economic crimes of accepting bribes and embezzling public funds. On the other hand, these media organizations are functioning as market entities and engaging in profit-making activities. Typically operating under a responsibility system, subsidiary media outlets such as the *NMN*, after handing in a set amount of revenue to the parent organization, are given the financial autonomy to dispose of surplus revenue through reinvestments, bonus distribution among management and staff, housing, and other welfare provisions. The bonus system at the *NMN* is widely practiced in China's state-owned and financially decentralized media industry. In fact, the amount involved in the *NMN* case revealed that the scope was more restricted than at many other media organizations. As a petition by five Beijing-based media scholars and journalists put it, if the case against the *NMN* could be established, then almost all of China's state enterprise managers are guilty of the same crimes.[69] As is widely agreed upon among observers of China's media, the *NMN* is among the least guilty of financial mismanagement—in fact, most observers were astonished at the fact that the thorough investigation of the paper's books only led to the discovery of a problem with the paper's bonus system. Given that more serious problems of corruption and the embezzlement of public funds are not uncommon in Chinese media organizations, the chilling effects of the *NMN* case on other media organizations cannot be underestimated. Although intellectual and intra-elite mobilization resulted in reduced sentences for Yu Huafeng and Li Minying, as well as the release of Cheng Yizhong, Guangzhou law and order authorities set a powerful precedent.

THE WANG BINYU CASE: LEGAL JUSTICE, CLASS RULE, AND MEDIA PROFESSIONALISM AS CLASS CONTAINMENT

In the fall of 2005, more than two years after the Sun Zhigang case, the life of Wang Binyu, another 27-year-old young man, became the focal point of a media and Internet controversy of a very different order. Unlike Sun, Wang did not make it to the other side of the urban/rural divide. Sun was an innocent victim of the police. In contrast, Wang killed four other individuals. Born in an impoverished rural village in Gansu Province in the northwest, Wang lost his mother at the age of six and had to quit school before finishing grade four. He became a migrant worker at the age of 17 and by 2005 had worked as a manual laborer in various locations for 10 years, enduring all forms of humiliation and exploitation. On May 11, 2005, in a small city in Ningxia, Wang Binyu made his last attempt to collect his 5,000-yuan unpaid wage from his boss in the private construction sector, as his father had broken his leg and was in urgent need of the money for treatment. Before this, Wang had sought a legal order to collect the unpaid wage, but the authorities told him that the process would take at least three to six months and referred him to the labor arbitration system through the government's labor department. Wang obtained an administrative order in his favor, but the labor department failed to enforce its decision. By May 11, Wang not only had not received his salary, but also had been locked out of his dorm by the boss. When Wang went to his boss's residence to ask for the salary, people inside refused to open the door. When Wang insisted, he was cursed, kicked, and slapped in the face by his foreman, his boss's wife, as well as others in the vicinity. Long-repressed frustration exploded. Wang took out a fruit knife and went on a rampage. He killed the four people present and injured another, then immediately turned himself in to the police. Wang was sentenced to death in the first trial in June 2005.

On September 4, 2005, three journalists from Xinhua News Agency, after having conducted more than 10 hours of interviews with Wang, publicized Wang's case. The Xinhua story detailed the wretched life of Wang and his family, showed sympathy for Wang and his fellow migrant workers, and called for the whole society to pay more attention to the rights of migrant workers. The story not only gave Wang, a soon-to-be-executed migrant-worker-turned-murderer, his final voice in the country's most authoritative news outlet, but also framed Wang as somebody who was eager to use his own tragic case to appeal for economic and social justice for his fellow migrant workers.[70] This story, while extraordinary in using Wang to dramatize the problem of unpaid wages to migrant workers, fits in with the tenor of official propaganda under the Hu Jintao leadership. As discussed in chapter 1, as part of their attempt to readdress the massive social deficit of the economic reforms and reestablish the party's hegemony, the new leadership has tried to cultivate a pro-people image and expressed its determination to improve the lot of China's underclass, from addressing rural poverty to helping migrant workers to collect their unpaid wages. To highlight the story's social justice and social stability frames and the official news agency's crusade for the importance of "paying workers according to the law"—that is, workers' economic rights as guaranteed and enforced by legally binding labor contracts—the Xinhua News Agency issued a commentary on the same day, entitled "Never Ignore the Basic Wishes of Migrant Workers." Speaking mainly to party officials in the typically paternalistic tone of party journalism, the article stated that the case of Wang "highlighted the shortcomings of our work in protecting the legal rights of migrant workers, making us realize how important it is to fulfill migrant workers' basic wish of getting salaries on time and in full amount." The article noted increased instances of desperate and violent attempts by migrant workers to get their unpaid wage and their negative consequences on social stability. It also noted the formidable legal barriers for workers and deplored ineffective law enforcement in this area, urging law enforcement agencies to improve their work.[71]

However, perhaps beyond the expectations of the Xinhua journalists, the story immediately touched a sensitive nerve in society and set off a heated media and Internet debate. Media and Internet debate crystallized on Wang's pending execution and the deprivation of social justice for Wang and his fellow migrant workers. Internet opinion overwhelmingly sympathized with Wang, arguing that Wang's action was an understandable reaction to the social injustice he faced. A large-scale campaign to rescue Wang from the death penalty soon developed. Drawing on a broad notion of justice, "arguments against the death penalty refused to treat the case as an isolated criminal act but to place it within a large social context."[72] Internet crusades on behalf of Wang thus threatened to shake a criminal justice regime based on individual rights. Yes, Wang needs to be brought to justice, but what about the class-based social justice of the 100 million migrant workers that Wang symbolizes?

The politicized framing of Wang's criminal act exposed the bifurcated and class-based nature of an emergent rule of law system. On the one hand, this system fails miserably to enforce labor contracts on behalf of workers—by the middle of November 2004, incomplete government statistics reported that migrant workers were owed 100 billion yuan in unpaid salary (the costs of collecting this 100 billion yuan are estimated to be 300 billion yuan).[73] On the other hand, it has been swift and ruthless in enforcing criminal justice. Subsequent media and Internet debate ignored Xinhua News Agency's focus on strengthening the enforcement of migrant workers' legally entitled economic rights. Legal opinion on the death penalty, meanwhile, was divided. One side focused on criminal justice and insisted on upholding the authority of the rule of law. The other side, however, maintained that the injustice of the judicial system itself, that is, its inability to deliver economic justice in the first place, led to Wang's resorting to violence; thus, to "save Wang Binyu is to save the legal system itself."[74] The editorial opinions of China's most popular media outlets were also divided. More specifically, initial sympathy toward Wang and the broad concept of social and legal justice was quickly overwhelmed by a more calculated reasoning on behalf of the "rule of law," "judicial independence," "professionalism," and even overt expression of class contempt toward migrant workers. The divided opinions of the *Beijing News* and the *NMN* are particularly noteworthy.

The *Beijing News* took the lead in voicing opinion against Wang's death penalty sentence with two commentaries on September 7 and September 9, respectively.[75] Both articles accepted a popularly perceived notion of social justice, insisted on placing the case in the broader social context, while opposing limiting the notion of justice to an "abstracted" act of murder.[76] The September 9 article even cited a legal precedent in 1979 in which an individual who killed three people under similar circumstances was spared the death penalty. In contrast, the *NMN* quickly revealed its role as an agent of social control and class containment in this case. On September 12, the *NMN*, which had played such an important role in the Sun Zhigang case, published an unsigned editorial, arguing that media coverage of the case had violated the principle of "journalistic professionalism."[77] Entitled "Pathos Cannot Cover up True Facts, Sympathy Should Return to Professional Principles," the editorial traced the process by which the Wang Binyu case came into public attention, charging the media with a "disturbing tendency at the level of facts gathering"—that is, for failing to focus on Wang's murderous actions per se and foregrounding the context and background of Wang's actions instead. Specifically, the editorial noted that there had been three news reports on Wang before he got national attention in early September and that the earlier the report, the more it focused on the case itself. But as follow-up reports were produced, more background stories were covered, which, according to the editorial, was against the principles of "journalistic professionalism." Implicitly, then, the *NMN*, revealing its attempt at containing a potential class conflict, blamed the September 4 Xinhua News Agency story for being unprofessional and for sowing the seeds of the subsequent public opinion outrage. As discussed previously, in its handling of the Sun Zhigang case, the *NMN* had not only gone as far as "creating" facts (including helping with obtaining the autopsy results) and providing ample background stories about Sun and the broad context of the detention system, but also had directly called for reflection "on the big picture behind this tragedy [of Sun Zhigang]" and mobilized Internet opinion on behalf of Sun and the citizenship rights cause. In contrast, the "relevant facts" of the Wang case for the *NMN* were what took place at the locale of the killing. These were the presumably objective and neutral facts that the media should focus on exclusively. To dig up background stories and place Wang's criminal act in a broader social context was "unprofessional." Different notions of what counts as being professional and as "objective news" and "relevant facts" are clearly at play.[78] Thus, while the NMN was practicing advocacy journalism in the Sun Zhigang case and in its crusade for civil rights, it was now calling for a more restricted and pro-establishment regime of "objective reporting" in the Wang Binyu case. In other words, facing a popular mobilization that threatened to stir up class conflict and reveal the class nature of the emerging law and order regime, the NMN called for the media to "return to the professional principles" of detached, factual reporting, and to provide a "cool-minded and rational guiding voice" to public opinion.

Challenging any simple "state" versus "market" dichotomy, this time the NMN, one of the leading market-oriented media outlets that has often found itself pushing the limits of the party-state's censorship, rather than the Xinhua News Agency and party propaganda authorities, was the organization that called for "correct guidance" to public opinion. That Sun was murdered by the police and Wang murdered four people certainly made a difference in their respective media treatments. My purpose in juxtaposing these two cases has been to highlight the discursive boundaries they each demarcated and to demonstrate how they foregrounded the complex articulations between statist agendas and societal interests. In particular, I want to underscore the point that professionalism, which for most Chinese media theorists and practitioners symbolizes the not-yet-realized dream of journalistic autonomy from the party-state, reveals its nature as a means of class containment. In the context of increased class antagonism, to embrace the presumably universal values of journalistic professionalism and judicial independence is to negate class divisions and conflicts, and this could only mean collaboration with the status quo.[79]

While divided opinions between the two closely related, leading mass appeal urban papers, Beijing News and the NMN, reflect the fluidity and the highly contested nature of the Chinese discursive field, the NMN was not alone in its mobilization of a particular notion of journalistic professionalism for the purpose of class containment. An editorial in China News Weekly (Zhongguo xinwen zhoukan), a privately funded, trendy news weekly published under the sponsorship of China News Agency, was quick to echo the NMN's editorial line, for example, by calling for "a vigilance against public opinion bias." As with the NMN, the editorial identifies this bias as including a tendency to downplay the details of Wang's murderous acts, to focus instead on the "abstract" aspects of his life story, his plights, and his frustrations, as well as the broad framing of Wang as a symbol of the migrant working class and his violence as a desperate, class-based act of resistance.[80]

Other widely circulated newspaper articles similarly display a strong class containment dimension, while clearly constructing migrant workers as the internal "other." Signed by Xiao Yugen and entitled "It Is a Dangerous Signal That Public Opinion Sympathizes with Murderer Wang Binyu," a story in the *China Youth News* was blunt in its hegemonic mission to displace class politics and defuse class conflict.[81] The commentary not only recognized public sympathy for Wang as a challenge against the rule of law, a dangerous phenomenon that needed to be dealt with carefully, but also glossed over the class dimension. In particular, the article constructed a dichotomy between Wang as an "extremely minuscule minority," whose distorted psychology was unworthy of too much of the attention, with "the absolutely vast majority of the common people." Because this vast majority of "common people" are the ones "we" interact with on an everyday basis and the ones who constitute the main body of the "harmonious society," theirs are the feelings that deserve our total attention. Another commentary by the same author, initially published in *Modern Express* (*Xiandai kuaibao*), cast the "us" versus "them" frame in a different manner. It essentially called for increased attention to improve the lot of the migrant workers on the part of "us" so that "they," the dangerous and "low quality" others, can be contained by the urban society.[82] Invoking the prevailing "quality" (*suzhi*) discourse among the urban and educated elite,[83] a discourse that would be viewed as racist if it were invoked in a multiracial society by one racial group toward another, the article, entitled "Migrant Worker Killed Four People in a Row Because of Very Low Quality," started by acknowledging the urban and rural divide and the kind of exploitative experience migrant workers face. It then concluded that these people, "given their education and experience, are not likely to challenge the system." Still, according to the article, when cornered these people, because of their "low qualities," which include not only their low educational levels and weak legal awareness, but also their inability to control their own temper, could become a dangerous social force. That the very title of the article—in which Wang Binyu, who was constructed as belonging to a "miniscule minority" in the other article, had now come to stand for his entire social class of migrant workers (*mingong*)—could have appeared at all in the Chinese popular press and gained wide circulation on the Chinese Internet is itself testimony to the profound class bias of the Chinese symbolic universe. Indeed, the title was very likely written by the editors precisely for its presumed potential to resonate with readers. Thus, if Sun Zhigang is one of "us" and he died for "me," mainstream media and Internet discussions invariably presume the "otherness" of Wang, who deserved a harsher justice either because of what he had done to "us,"[84] or because he and his kind are here to stay in the cities and if cornered, could endanger "us."

Online leftist voices, which had gained momentum by 2005, immediately turned Wang into a symbol of critique against the party's betrayal of the working class and a rallying point for attacking the "bourgeois" nature of the legal system, thus raising fundamental questions about the morality of law and the democratic nature of the liberal discourse on the "rule of law." On September 12, 2005, a coalition of leftist websites initiated an online petition in an attempt to save Wang from the death penalty.[85] The Utopia website, moreover, took the unprecedented action of organizing an offline seminar on Wang.[86] The leftists' class-based analysis of the case, their framing of it as a confrontation between the exploiters and the exploited, and their interpretation of the state's treatment of Wang as a litmus test of its true class color not only broadened the scope of the debate, but also raised its stakes. The following poem by Liu Lu, initially posted on the web on September 16, captured the sense of outrage and resignation on the part of the politically conscious left in its politicization of the Wang Binyu case. The poem's sense of class solidarity and its attack on the state's betrayal of the working class, meanwhile, contrasts sharply with the "us" versus "them" frame in the popular media, not to mention the *NMN*'s cool-minded "journalistic professionalism":

Wang Binyu, You Are the Death of the State[87]

With two kitchen knives, a marshal some had won[88]
You were pushed to the execution ground for holding only one
What logic of this world—So cruel, so absurd!
Wang Binyu, blame yourself if you must
Why bring yourself to life if this is what you deserve?

This world of the good times
Is neither yours nor mine
The neon lights so red, the fine wine so green
Are neither yours nor mine
Although it is your blood and my tears
That make them flare and shine
And although those skyscrapers stabbing straight into the clouds
Are propped up by the skeletons of our brothers

Never have we been acknowledged by this State
Which denies even the smallest pay for our sweat and might
Why are their laws so unkind
In depriving the living rights of every you and I

As you are about to die
Your name and stories spread online

A group of souls equally lowly
Begs for you day and night
In begging for you they beg for their own rights
But begging never slows the pace of the law-representing gun
For dealing with those like you and I
The level of hesitation this State shows is absolutely none

Some say to execute you is to execute the Communist Party, mighty and great
I say your death makes the death of this State
Wang Binyu, my brother
When even you, the most tolerable common folk, would rather die than to suffer
This State is smothering herself by smothering the lower

Wang Binyu, my brother
For you the moon this mid-autumn will be battered
Even thousands of years from now our offspring will still remember
Year 2005's death of the State

On September 17, 2005, an open letter to the country's highest law-making and judicial authorities by "citizen Huang Jiaxin," entitled "Can't Shoot Migrant Worker Wang Binyu on the Execution Ground of the Communist Party," dropped yet another rhetorical bomb in Chinese cyberspace. The letter, originally posted at the Protagonist website, argued that a legal system that had never protected Wang's legally entitled economic rights had no legitimate ground to exercise "dictatorship" over him. It further argued that if the party executed Wang, the party would undermine its own proclaimed class base and violate the spirits of the tens of millions of revolutionaries who shared Wang's background and who fought for the revolution and, consequently, undermine its own legitimacy for ruling.[89]

On September 21, four days after Huang's explosive open letter, the central party-state, which had acted as the "good guys" in the Sun Zhigang case, apparently decided that it was time to give Huang an answer and to give closure to the case. It ordered the media and online forums to shut up.[90] The Utopia website was ordered to shut down for organizing the offline seminar.[91] The second trial of Wang opened on September 29, 2005, with the authorities violating the law by denying Wang the opportunity to meet up with a lawyer that his father had chosen, let alone to allow the lawyer to represent him. To add further insult to Wang, his family, and his sympathizers, while the legal system demonstrated its swift efficiency by upholding Wang's death penalty and executing him immediately on October 19, 2005, Wang's salary remained unpaid even after his execution.[92] Most astonishingly, apart from a strictly enforced ban on unauthorized news reports of Wang's second trial and the execution, so that no more new material on Wang was generated, the state's censorship regime did more symbolic violence by selectively deleting material that had already been published by mainstream newspapers and circulated on mainstream websites. In particular, articles that challenged the death penalty, including the two *Beijing News* articles that had been carried by the Xinhua Net, were deleted.[93]

CONCLUSION

The Sun Zhigang and Wang Binyu cases were by no means isolated. There have been many other similar cases of media and Internet mobilization involving various social groups and individuals, from farmers to urban residents, tenants, carriers of transmissible diseases, and private entrepreneurs. Similarly, although the *NMN* stood out in mobilizing a double-edged regime of "professional journalism" in an attempt to crusade for liberal civil rights against arbitrary state power on the one hand and contain class conflict on the other, it exemplifies the media's increased activism in the Chinese public sphere. For example, 2003 alone witnessed the establishment or the expansion of "current affairs commentary" pages in more than 100 media outlets.[94]

Inspired by the media and Internet crusades on the Sun Zhigang case, *China News Weekly* proclaimed 2003 "the year of citizenship rights" in its end-of-year special issue. It attributed this to a growing rights consciousness among various social groups who no longer take the beneficial nature of "the reform" for granted, a social reform impulse among journalists, lawyers, writers, and university-based public intellectuals, an active Internet community, as well as the pro-people pronouncements of the new party leadership. Writing at the end of 2003, Wang Yi, a liberal civil rights activist (and a newly converted Christian who gained an audience with U.S. president Bush in May 2006), similarly noted that citizen rights actions helped to restore the public to the center of politics, turning the political arena into a space that is indispensable to the interest of every individual. Wang Yi hoped that the dispersed and individualized nature of citizen rights actions and the participation and intellectual stewardship of rational-minded public intellectuals with mild social reform objectives would gradually dissipate the danger of drastic social upheavals and "to the greatest extent minimize the risk of radical populism."[95] That is, by crusading for citizens' rights, market-oriented liberal media outlets and their middle-class allies hope to defuse social conflicts, transform the postrevolutionary party-state into a liberal constitutional polity, and contain the threat of yet another radical social revolution.

However, these social reformist–oriented, rights-based, and media- and Internet-supported actions, because of their challenge to vested bureaucratic interests, have inevitably met bureaucratic resistance. The *NMN*'s conflict with local bureaucratic power over the Sun Zhigang case not only underscored the formidable challenges the media face, but also the media's own fragile political economic bases. Moreover, as liberal indifference to, and neoliberal backlash against, the state's granting of social rights to the vagrants in the aftermath of the Sun Zhigang case, together with the Wang Binyu case, have made crystal clear, there are differences both in rhetoric and substance between the struggle for civil rights and the struggle for economic and social justice. On the one hand, liberal intellectuals and the market-oriented urban media prioritize civil rights and fight for the freedom from an obtrusive state. The economic and social rights of the low social classes, meanwhile, have not been their primary concerns. On the other hand, leftist discourses apply the language of class exploitation to contemporary Chinese society and reappropriate the symbols of the communist revolution to argue for the economic and social interests of China's low social classes. Arbitrating these two competing discourses is the Chinese state, which rejects liberal constitutionalism on the one hand and suppresses the discourse of class exploitation on the other,[96] while trying to appease the low social classes with paternalistic and "pro-people" redistributive politics and the selective instrumental mobilization of a "rights" discourse.[97] Again, I wish to emphasize that while the media and liberal intellectuals crusaded for civil rights through the Sun Zhigang case, the state went beyond this appeal to grant the vagrants their social welfare rights. Similarly, the Xinhua News Agency, not the urban market-oriented media, was the organization that initially used the Wang Binyu story to argue for the importance of fulfilling migrant workers' most basic economic rights of having their wages paid. Sun Zhigang, confident that he would be paid with his white-collar job, probably would have been happy if the state had simply left him alone. Wang Binyu, however, desperately needed his capitalist employer to abide by labor laws. Meanwhile, deprived of the basic labor right to self-organization and collective bargaining, he had to rely on the state to enforce his economic rights. The Sun Zhigang case demonstrates the mobilizing power of a widely shared media- and Internet-led social consensus on civil rights vis-à-vis the arbitrary power of the state and a punitive bureaucratic culture of self-preservation and mutual protection. The Wang Binyu case, on the other hand, brought to the fore the issue of antagonistic class conflicts and revealed the class nature of the emerging discourse on the "rule of law" and journalistic and judicial neutrality. With a divided and conflictual public sphere, the state's swift execution of Wang, and the silencing of public debate on the case, the individual-based criminal justice system was up-held. The economic rights of the migrant working class and the need to secure these rights through the legal system, a topic that the Xinhua News Agency had initially hoped to foreground, however, fell off the agenda of media and Internet discussions on criminal justice, the technicalities of the case, as well as the mobilization to save Wang Binyu from the death sentence. No media commentators rushed to proclaim 2005 "the year of economic rights for workers and farmers."

Whether a liberal notion of negative freedoms—the overriding agenda of market-oriented urban media and the liberal intellectual community—can effectively satisfy the most urgent needs of China's vast laboring classes and thus contain class conflicts remains an open question. For its part, China's online leftist community has been vocal in condemning class exploitation, serving as a permanent thorn in the side of the party by constantly reminding it of its revolutionary legacy and charging it with betraying the working class. However, there is clearly no broad, urban-based social reformist movement that could lend a concrete hand to workers' struggle for their economic and social rights. Still, as I examine media and Internet debates on the more fundamental and divisive issue of property rights in the next chapter, discursive domination and contestation remain fundamental to social struggles, although some online activists are fully aware of the limitations of online activism as well.

NOTES

1. Dorothy Solinger, *Contesting Citizenship in Urban China: Peasant Migrants, the State, and the Logic of the Market* (Berkeley: University of California Press, 1999).

2. Li Zhang, *Strangers in the City: Reconfigurations of Space, Power and Social Networks within China's Floating Population* (Stanford, Calif.: Stanford University Press, 2001).

3. Solinger, *Contesting Citizenship*, 83, cited in Anita Chan and Hong-Zen Wang, "The Impact of the State on Workers' Conditions—Comparing Taiwanese Factories in China and Vietnam," *Pacific Affairs* 77, no. 4 (Winter 2004–2005): 637.

4. Chan and Wang, "The Impact of the State on Workers' Conditions," 629–646.

5. "*Bei fengsha de Sun Zhigang shijian houxu baodao*" (The Censored Report on the Sun Zhigang Case), www.peacehall.com/news/gb/yuanqing/2003/04/200304270429.shtml (accessed 17 May 2005).

6. For an official account of the events that led to Sun's death, see Liu Jianhua and Lu Pingxin, "'*Shourong' bian 'Jiuzhu'*" (From "Detention" to "Assistance"), in *Zhongguo renquan zai xingdong* (China Human Rights in Action), ed. Dong Yunhu, Wang Jinjun, and Chang Jian (Chengdu: Sichuan renmin chubanshe, 2005), 207–213.

7. Cited in Mao Sheng, "*Cong xinwen shijian dao gonggong shijian*" (From a News Event to a Public Event) (master's thesis, Communication University of China, 2004), 5–6.

8. "*Bei fengsha de Sun Zhigang shijian houxu baodao.*"

9. Dai Hongbing, "*Sun Zhigang jiaren jiangshu Guangzhou benzou yi mumu, zhuiwen siyin chuchu pengbi*" (Sun's Family Reported the Difficulties in Finding the True Cause of His Death in Guangzhou), *Yangzi wanbao*, 14 Jun. 2003, news.sina .com.cn/c/2003-06-14/1318219106s.shtml (accessed 17 May 2005).

10. Mao, "*Cong xinwen shijian dao gonggong shijian*," 6.

11. Philip P. Pan, "In China, an Editor Triumphs, and Fails," *Washington Post*, 1 Aug. 2004, A01, www.washingtonpost.com/wp-dyn.articles/A30835-2004Jul31 .html (accessed 24 Mar. 2006).

12. Interview with a *Guangzhou Daily* deputy editor-in-chief, Aug. 1998, Guangzhou.

13. Pan, "In China, an Editor Triumphs, and Fails."

14. Interview, Jul. 2004, Vancouver.

15. Pan, "In China, an Editor Triumphs, and Fails."

16. Yuezhi Zhao, "Watchdogs on Party Leashes? Contexts and Limitations of Investigative Reporting in Post-Deng China," *Journalism Studies* 1, no. 4 (Nov. 2000): 577–597.

17. Joseph M. Chan, "Administrative Boundaries and Media Marketization: A Comparative Analysis of the Newspaper, TV and Internet Markets in China," in *Chinese Media, Global Contexts*, ed. Chin-Chuan Lee, 159–176 (New York: Routledge, 2003), 163.

18. Pan, "In China, an Editor Triumphs, and Fails."

19. "*Nanfang Dushi An*" (The *NMN* Case), www.peacehall.com/news/gb/ china/2004/05200405071547.shtml (accessed 17 Oct. 2004).

20. Interview with Liang Yan, 15 Apr. 2005, Vancouver.

21. Chen Feng and Wang Lei, "*Beishourongzhe Sunzhigang zhisi*" (The Death of Detainee Sun Zhigang), *Nanfang dushi bao*, 25 Apr. 2003, news.sina.com.cn/s/2003-04-25/11111016223.html (accessed 17 May 2005).

22. Barrett McCormick, "Censorship, Sensation and Accountability in Chinese Media" (paper presented at the "Conference on Grassroots Political Reform in Contemporary China," Fairbank Center for East Asian Research, Harvard University, 29–31 Oct. 2004), 39.

23. Mo Ke, "*Sun Zhigang zhisi de houxu baodao huibuhui buliaoliaozhi*" (Will the Follow-up Reporting of Sun Zhigang's Death Go Anywhere?), www.people .com.cn/GB/guandian/30/20030430/982989.html (accessed 17 May 2005).

24. Bao Limin, "*Sun Zhigang men de shengli: Ruguo zhikao meiti de liliang gouma?*" (The Victory of Sun Zhigang and His Fellows: Is the Power of Media Alone Enough?), news.xinhuanet.com/newmedia/2004-10/28/content_2147616.htm (accessed 12 Dec. 2005).

25. The search was conducted on 12 Dec. 2005.

26. Luo Gang, "*Wangluo gonggong kongjian: Keneng de he bu keneng de*" (The Possibilities and Limits of China's Internet Public Space) (paper presented at the

"Media Technology, Creative Industries, and Cultural Significance" conference, Taipei, 24–25 Sept. 2004), 8.

27. For survey data on various years, see www.cnnic.net.cn/index/0E/ 00/11/index.htm.

28. In fact, the China Internet Network Information Center biannual survey does not even use workers and farmers as distinctive and stable social categories. At the time of the Sun Zhigang controversy, for example, a category that includes "workers in agriculture, forestry, animal husbandry and fishery" made up 0.9 percent of the online population, while the category of "production and transportation facilities operators," which presumably includes industrial workers, chauffeurs, and taxi, truck, and bus drivers, made up 5.8 percent of the online population. The CNNIC's 16th Survey, reporting the results of questionnaires gathered before and on June 30, 2005, put the respective numbers at 1.2 percent and 5.8 percent. For these survey reports, see www.cnnic.net.cn/index/0E/ 00/11/index.htm.

29. Dong Han, "Class Division and Conflicts in Media and Internet Discourse in the Case of Wang Binyu" (unpublished manuscript, May 2006), 6–8.

30. Han, "Class Division and Conflicts," 7.

31. Luo Gang, "*Wangluo gonggong kongjian,*" 8. The gender dimension is also important. In China's media and Internet universe, Sun commands a higher symbolic value than, say, female rural migrants without a university education, or even a female university graduate.

32. Gao Hong and Tang Hongmei, "*Sangzhong weishei erming: Zuoye de zhuanfang—Guanyu Sun Zhigang*" (Death Bell for Whom: Last Night's Interview about Sun Zhigang), originally cited in Luo Gang, "*Wangluo gonggong kongjian,*" 9, www.bsszts.com/asp.bbs/showtopic.asp?TOPIC_ID=1343&Forum_ID=64 (accessed 17 May 2005).

33. "*Bei fengsha de Sun Zhigang shijian houxu baodao.*"

34. Ai Xiaoming, "*Shenghuo zai kongju zhong*" (Live in Fear), www.genders.zsu.edu.cn/board/focus/display.asp?id=8 (accessed 17 May 2005).

35. Li Changping, "*Sun Zhigang tiwo ersi*" (Sun Zhigang Died for Me), www .mlcool.com/html/ns001718.htm (accessed 17 May 2005).

36. Ai, "*Shenghuo zai kongju zhong.*"

37. Li, "*Sun Zhigang tiwo ersi.*"

38. Jing Xiuwen, "*Sun Zhigang an: Shisheizai zhuanglong zuoya?*" (The Sun Zhigang Case: Who Is Pretending to be Deaf and Mute?), www.people.com.cn/GB/ guardian/30/20030504/984197.html (accessed 18 May 2005).

39. Lin Chufang and Zhao Ling, "*Hu Jintao Wen Jiabao shangwang: Guanzhu Reminwang baodao Sun Zhigang an*" (Hu Jintao and Wen Jiabao Surfed the Net: Paying Attention to the People Net's Reporting of the Sun Zhigang Case), *Nanfang zhoumo,* 6 Jun. 2003, news.0898.net/2003/06/06/69724.html (accesed 12 Dec. 2005).

40. McCormick, "Censorship," 18.

41. "*Zhishi fenzi wei he bixu cong shubenshang taiqitou*" (Why Intellectuals Must Lift up Their Eyes from Books), www.cc.org.cn/old/pingtai/0306113015.htm (accessed 18 May 2005).

42. Meng Bo, *"Liuwen shourong zhidu"* (Six Questions about the Detention and Repatriation System), *Nanfang dushi bao*, www.peacehall.com/news/gb/yuangqing/2003/05/200305312313.shtml (accessed 17 Oct. 2003).

43. State Council of the PRC, *"Chengshi shenghuo wuzhuo de liulang qitao renyuan jiuzhu guanli banfa"* (Measurements Regarding the Assistance and Management of Vagrants and Beggars without Subsistence in the Cities), news.xinhuanet.com/zhengfu/2003-06/22/content_931160.htm (accessed 13 Dec. 2005).

44. State Council of the PRC, *"Chengshi shenghuo."*

45. State Council of the PRC, *"Chengshi shenghuo."*

46. Cited in Mao, *"Cong xinwen shijian dao gonggong shijian,"* 19–20.

47. Sun Liping, *Shiheng: Duanlieshehui de yunzuo luoji* (Imbalance: The Logic of a Fractured Society) (Beijing: Shehui kexue wenxian chubanshe, 2004), 176.

48. Xu Zhiyong, *"Weihu xianfa quanwei, jiuji gongmin quanli"* (Upholding Constitutional Authority, Supporting Civil Rights), *Zhongguo xinwen zhoukan* 47, 22 Dec. 2003, 29.

49. Bo Shouxing, *"Sun Zhigang shijian yu shehui gongzheng"* (The Sun Zhigang Case and Social Justice), www.people.com.cn/GB/paper1631/9518/880081.html (accessed 12 Mar. 2006).

50. Xu Xiangyang, *"Dui feizhi shourong qiansong zhidu de huanwei sikao—Jianping zhishifenzi de rendaozhuyi qingyi"* (A Different Perspective on the Abolishing of the Detention and Repatriation System), 21exit.com/51/Article_Show.asp?ArticleID=1128 (accessed 18 Jun. 2006).

51. Xu, *"Dui feizhi shourong."*

52. Xu, *"Dui feizhi shourong."*

53. Xu, *"Dui feizhi shourong."*

54. Luo, *"Wangluo gonggong kongjian."*

55. Wu Guoguang, "The Birth of Sophisticated Propaganda: The Party-State and the Chinese Media in Post-Reform Politics" (paper manuscript made available to the author), 13.

56. *"Nanfang dushi bao an jishi"* (A Chronology of the *NMN* Case), www.peacehall.com/news/gb.china/2004/07/200407091335.shtml (accessed 16 Oct. 2004).

57. *"Guanzhu Nanfang dushi bao an"* (Pay Attention to the NMN Case), www.peacehall.com/news/gb/chain/2004/04/200404212228.shtml (accessed 17 Oct. 2004).

58. *"Nanfang dushi bao an jishi."*

59. Leu Siew Ying, "Outrage Promoted Editor's Release: Intellectuals' Online Debate Spurred Mainland Leaders to Listen to Reason," *South China Morning Post*, 31 Aug. 2004.

60. Lew Siew Ying, "China: Journalist Jailed for Eight Years Lost Appeal," *South China Morning Post*, 30 Jul. 2005, www.asiamedia.ucla.edu/article.asp?parentid=27429 (accessed 9 Aug. 2005).

61. *"Nanfang duoshi an: Yu Huafeng, Cheng Yizhong xiansheng jianjie"* (The *NMN* Case: A Brief Introduction to Yu Huafeng and Cheng Yizhong), www.peacehall.com/news/gb/china/2004/05/200405071547.shtml (accessed 17 Oct. 2004).

62. *"Nanfang duoshi an: Yu Huafeng, Cheng Yizhong xiansheng jianjie."*

63. Zhan Jiang, "*Zhang Dejiang xiansheng: Ni shifou kaolü huiying?*" (Mr. Zhang Dejiang: Would You Please Respond?), Zhan Jiang's open letter was initially posted on the Internet, personal correspondence, 5 Jan. 2005.

64. "*Nanfang duishi bao an jishi.*"

65. Xu Wenzhong, "*Nanfang dushi bao zhengsu guocheng jiemi*" (Revealing the Process of Punishing the *NMN*), *Zhonghua tansuo* (Supplement to *Ming Pao*, Vancouver), 3 May 2004, 2.

66. Xia Wenshi, "*Feidian huoshou Zhang Dejiang*" (Zhang Dejiang, the Chief Problem Source of the SARS), *Kaifang*, May 2003, 12.

67. Wang Jianmin, "*Cong zhengyi zhiyan dao fuchu daijia*" (From Speaking Out for Justice to Paying a Price), *Zhonghua tansuo*, 3 May 2004, 14.

68. Wang, "*Cong zhangyi zhiyan dao fuchu daijia.*"

69. Zhan Jiang, Wang Keqing, Zhao Mu, Chen Feng, Liu Chang, Zhong Ze, Chen Jieren, and Hu Xiaotong, "*Guanyu Nanfang dushi bao wenti de huyushu*" (A Petition Letter Concerning the *NMN* Issue), www.peacehall.com/news/gb/china/200404/200404152346.shtml (accessed 17 Oct. 2004).

70. Meng Zhaoli, Liu Jiaqian, and Liu Xiaoli, "*Xinhua shidian: Siqiu Wang Binyu de daobai*" (Xinhua Viewpoint: The Words of Death Row Prisoner Wang Binyu), news.xinhuanet.com/newscenter/2005-09/04/content_3440619_1.htm (accessed 12 Jun. 2006).

71. Zhang Jiangao, "*Xinhua kuaiping: Qianwan bie moshi nongmingong de jiben yuanwang*" (Xinhua Express Commentary: Never Overlook the Basic Wishes of Migrant Workers), news.163.com/05/0904/10/1SQ5BU460001120U.html (accessed 12 Jun. 2006).

72. Han, "Class Division and Conflicts," 12.

73. Cui Li, "*Nongmingong weiquan chengben diaocha: Zhuitai yiqianyi qianxin xu sanqianyi chengben*" (A Survey of the Costs of Migrant Workers' Pursuit of Their Rights: It Costs 300 Billion Yuan to Get the 100 Billion Yuan Unpaid Salary), news.xinhuanet.com/legal/2005-06/09/content_3061559.htm (accessed 13 Jun. 2006).

74 Guo Ruo, "*Gao Zhisheng lüshi huyu zhengjiu Wang Binyu zhengjiu sifa*" (Lawyer Gao Zhisheng Appealed to Save Wang Binyu and Save the Legal System), www.epochtimes.com/gb/5/10/1/n1071887.htm (accessed 12 Jun. 2006).

75. Gao Yifei, "*You biyao pan Wang Binyu sixing ma?*" (Is It Necessary to Sentence Wang Binyu to Death?), *Xinjing bao*, 7 Sept. 2005, www.scol.com.cn/comment/mtsj/20050907/20059792745.htm (accessed 18 Jun. 2006); Chen Bulei, "*You Wang Binyu xiangqi le Jiang Aizhen*" (From Wang Binyu Case to Jiang Anzhen), *Xinjing bao*, 9 Sept. 2005, www.scol.com.cn/comment/mtsj/20050909/20059992136.htm (accessed 18 Jun. 2006).

76. Han, "Class Division and Conflicts," 12.

77. "*Nanfang dushi bao pinglun: Beiqing buneng zhebi zhenxiang, guanhuai huigui zhuanye zhunze*" (The *NMN* Editorial: Pathos Cannot Cover Up True Facts, Compassion Must Gear toward Professional Principles), www.genderwatchina.org/pages/shownews.asp?id=884 (accessed 15 Dec. 2005).

78. For a discussion of the multifaceted regime of journalistic objectivity, see Robert A. Hackett and Yuezhi Zhao, *Sustaining Democracy? Journalism and the Politics of Objectivity* (Toronto: Garamond Press, 1998).

79. Han, "Class Division and Conflicts," 15.

80. *Zhongguo xinwen zhoukan*, *"Difang Wang Binyu an de yulun piancha"* (Be Vigilant against Public Opinion Bias on the Wang Binyu Case), www.ncn.org/asp/zwgInfo/da-KAY.asp?ID=65918&ad=9/27/2005 (accessed 15 Dec. 2005).

81. Xiao Yuhen, *"Yulun tongqing sharenfan Wang Binyu shi weixian xinhao"* (It Is a Dangerous Signal That Public Opinion Sympathizes with Murderer Wang Binyu), *Zhongguo qingnian bao*, 9 Sept. 2005, www.peacehall.com/news/gb/pubvp/2005/09/200509181411.shtml (accessed 13 Jun. 2006).

82. Xiao Yuhen, *"Mingong liansha siren yuanyu suzhi taidi"* (Migrant Worker Killed Four People in a Row Because of Very Low Quality) *Xiandai kuaibao*, 6 Sept. 2005, star.news.sohu.com/20050906/n240343966.shtml (accessed 18 Jun. 2006).

83. For an excellent analysis of this discourse, see Ann Anagnost, "The Corporeal Politics of Quality (Suzhi)," *Public Culture* 16, no. 2 (Spring 2004): 189–208.

84. Han, "Class Division and Conflicts," 23.

85. For the original petition, see www.zgysj.com/2005/200510c.htm#%B5%B6%CF%C2%C1%F4%C8%CB (accessed 13 Jun. 2006).

86. I am grateful to Andy Hu for providing this information.

87. Liu Lu, *"Wang Binyu, ni jiushi Guoshang"* (Wang Binyu, You Are the Death of the State), www.peacehall.com/news/gb/china/2005/09/200509160016.shtml (accessed 15 Dec. 2005). I am grateful to Andy Hu for translating it into English.

88. In reference to the revolutionary legend of He Long, who became a communist hero and a founding father—one of the ten marshals—of the People's Republic of China. He launched his revolutionary career by killing two corrupt tariff officials with two kitchen knives. The lore of "two kitchen knives stirred up a revolution" is known to every schoolchild as part of the party's revolutionary history.

89. Huang Jiaxin, *"Buneng zai Gongchandang de xingchang shang qiangsha nongmingong Wang Binyu"* (Can't Shoot Migrant Worker Wang Binyu on the Execution Ground of the Communist Party), www.snzg.net/shownews.asp?newsid=7841 (accessed 13 Jun. 2006).

90. Han, "Class Division and Conflicts," 20–21.

91. The website reopened in October 2005, at www.wyzxsx.com, on the condition that it focus purely on academic discussion. Andy Hu, "Swimming against the Tide: Tracing and Locating Chinese Leftism Online" (master's thesis, School of Communication, Simon Fraser University, 2006), 147.

92. Han, "Class Division and Conflicts," 16.

93. This was initially revealed by Dong Han in his Internet searches in March and April 2006. My own research in June 2006 confirmed this pattern.

94. Wang Yi, *"2003 gongmin quanli nian"* (2003: A Year of Citizen's Rights), *Zhongguo xinwen zhoukan* 47, 22 Dec. 2003, 21.

95. Wang, *"2003 gongmin quanli nian."*

96. As Eric Florence argues, the discourse of class exploitation invokes a capitalist society, which is antithetical to a party that grounds its moral foundation on a rejection of capitalist social relations. Eric Florence, "Migrant Workers in the Pearl River Delta: Discourse and Narratives about Work as a Site of Struggle," *Critical Asian Studies* 39, no. 1 (2007): 145-146.

97. For an analysis of the nature and limits of this discourse, see Elizabeth J. Perry, "Studying Chinese Politics: Farewell to Revolution?" *China Journal* 57 (Jan. 2007): 19-21.

6

Challenging Neoliberalism?
The "Lang Xianping Storm," Property Rights, and Economic Justice

Between the Sun Zhigang case in 2003 and the Wang Binyu case in 2005, another major media and Internet debate, the "Lang Xianping storm," was raging in the Chinese symbolic universe. As discussed in chapter 1, accelerated market reforms in the post-1992 period were implemented with the suppression of public debates about their political and social implications. In reality, Deng's "no debate" policy was aimed at suppressing leftist opposition against further capitalistic developments. It created the ideological space for the ascendance and entrenchment of neoliberal influence in economic and social development. Operating with the implicit assumption that the only legitimate form of capital is private capital and pressing for "state retreats and people advances" (*guotui minjin*), neoliberal economists claimed that the problem with state-owned enterprises (SOEs) is the "absence of the owner." Transferring state property into the hands of private capitalists thus became a key reform objective of neoliberal economists and government officials. This discourse gained legitimacy and obtained prominence at the 15th and 16th party congresses in 1997 and 2002. The year 2003 was to become the year of management buyouts (MBOs)—a privatization scheme whereby former state enterprise managers privatize the enterprises they manage.[1]

In practical terms, post-1992 economic reforms have implemented the accelerated restructuring, including privatization, of SOEs without the necessary legal framework and without the mediating mechanism of a competitive market. This has been carried out under euphemisms such as "property right reform" (*chanquan gaige*) and "system transformation of SOEs" (*guoqi gaizhi*)—partly because restructuring encompasses a whole range of forms of ownership transformation and partly because of its clear political connotation, the straightforward term "privatization" has been avoided in official discourses. In many cases, SOEs were sold to domestic, private capitalists or foreign firms at prices agreed upon by local officials and the purchasing companies.[2] With the MBO scheme, SOEs have been sold to their managers in "black-box deals" in which government officials and SOE managers agreed upon a price without public tendering. To be sure, restructuring may have resulted in efficiency in a narrow sense,[3] and not all cases of privatization necessarily involve asset stripping, official corruption, and massive layoffs. Nevertheless, this has been a fundamentally unfair process, leading to the enrichment of former SOE managers, private and foreign capitalists, and government officials, while tens of millions of former SOE workers have either been laid off or lost pensions or other forms of welfare entitlements. Moreover, although this economic injustice has been widely perceived and experienced at the popular level, there was little media discussion. The result was a huge gap between the media agenda and popular concerns.

Lang Xianping, like the proverbial boy who points out that the emperor has no clothes, called attention to the injustice of this process in the popular media and on the Internet. Moreover, the attention opened the door for a wide debate on the directions of the Chinese reform process in 2005 and 2006. A detailed examination of the case and its aftermath demonstrates the extent of neoliberal hegemony on economic issues in China, the market-oriented media's symbiotic relationships with neoliberal economists and entrepreneurs, and the possibilities and limits of challenging neoliberal ideological domination through the media and the Internet. This examination also highlights the stratified nature of media and Internet discourses, divisions within and between elite and popular discourses on the issue of economic justice, as well as fundamental struggles over the future direction of China's social transformation.

LANG XIANPING, MEDIA MOBILIZATION, AND CRACKS IN NEOLIBERAL HEGEMONY

Just as there had been other media reports about problems with the detention system before the Sun Zhigang case, domestic economists of different ideological orientations had voiced concerns about the problematic process of SOE privatization since the early 1990s. Liberal scholar Qin Hui, who favors privatization but argues for a more equitable process, for example, published articles in 1992 and 1993 to raise concerns about the unfair nature of privatization through MBOs when the first case was implemented in China.[4] However, Qin's articles, published in small-circulation intellectual journals such as *Twenty-first Century* and *Orient*, were largely inaccessible to the policy-making elite and the larger public. "Old left" journals such as *Pursuit of Truth* and *Mid-Stream* also published articles condemning the privatization of the SOEs and the loss of state assets throughout the 1990s. These publications not only had limited distribution, but also had little legitimacy among the popular media elite. Popular writer He Qinglian was another marginalized critical voice. She drew attention to the "distorted" market logic in Chinese economic practices and raised the moral and social justice dimension of the economy in the early 1990s, at a time when neoliberalism was just taking hold in Chinese economic discourse. As a woman and a journalist with only a master's degree in economics, she was viciously attacked by academic economists for bringing moral issues into economics and, even worse, for not knowing what she was talking about. Although her book *Modernization's Pitfalls* (*Xiandaihua de xianjing*), in which she depicted the massive loss of state assets through the "rental-seeking" phenomenon, was very popular in the late 1990s, it had little impact in holding back the ascendancy of neoliberal economics, let alone in challenging the neoliberal economic and social policies of the Jiang Zemin era.

By the summer of 2003, as the Hu Jintao leadership began to readjust the party's developmental policies and ideological orientations, "the Central Party Committee had became very interested in research into the topic of neoliberalism"[5] and instructed the Chinese Academy of Social Sciences (CASS) to establish a project group on this topic. On June 10, 2004, at the launch of this group's report, a book entitled *An Assessment of Neoliberalism* (*Xin ziyou zhuyi pingxi*), established social scientists and party theoreticians organized a seminar criticizing neoliberalism. *Guangming Daily*, the central party organ in the theoretical and ideological field, published a news story on the seminar under the headline "Beware of the Influence of Neoliberalism in Our Country." Characterizing neoliberalism as "the theoretical expression of international monopoly capitalist class on globalization," the news report acknowledged the spread of neoliberalism in China and concluded,

> The scholars emphasized, our country's reform and openness is the improvement of the socialist system and the development of socialism with Chinese characteristics, and it is by no means taking the capitalist road as prescribed by neoliberal theory. Practices have proved that neoliberal theory has experienced serious setbacks in some Latin American countries and in Russia. Consequently, it has encountered resistance in many developed countries and across vast numbers of developing countries. Workers in our country's philosophy and social sciences fields should actively mobilize themselves to counteract the challenge that neoliberalism has posed for Marxism, so as to consolidate the guiding role of Marxism in the ideological and social sciences domains.[6]

However, as a traditional party organ, *Guangming Daily* not only does not have any popular subscription base, but it also speaks from a perspective that does not appeal to the gatekeepers of the market-driven popular media sector. In fact, many among China's intellectual community—especially new intellectual elites in the social sciences and humanities—regarded the paper as an ideological bastion of the "old left." Nor do party theoreticians connect their theoretical agenda of critiquing neoliberalism as a foreign ideology with any critical examination of concrete domestic policies and developments.

Whether calculated or not, it took Lang, a self-described "bourgeois" metropolitan economist with a background in journalism and the necessary skills to package a story for the popular media, to provoke a public policy debate on SOE privatization, thus localizing the critique against neoliberalism in China. Before he became a professor of finance at the Chinese University of Hong Kong in 2001, Lang, with a Ph.D. from the University of Pennsylvania's famous Wharton School, already had teaching appointments in a number of elite U.S. universities and was an adviser to the World Bank on corporate governance. Lang's status as a world-class economist impressed the Chinese media and endowed him with the necessary discursive authority to be taken seriously.[7]

From June to August 2004, Lang publicly challenged a number of well-known private Chinese companies and their owners for their problematic privatization of state assets. Lang's first two targets, Haier CEO Zhang Ruimin and TCL chairman Li Dongsheng, both star private entrepreneurs, tried to deflect his criticism by putting forward low-key public responses. On August 9, 2004, Lang launched his challenge against Greencool, a massive industrial conglomerate that had emerged with dazzling speed through the takeover of SOEs. In a public lecture at Fudan University in Shanghai, Lang employed the case study method and used popular martial arts metaphors to demonstrate the strategies through which Greencool board chairman Gu Chujun privatized state enterprises, raising questions about the legality and accountability of the process. Lang's broad appeal and provocative intention were revealed by both the title and the concluding remark of the report that was the basis of his lecture. The title read "Greencool: Feasting at the Banquet of 'State Retreats and People Advance.'" The conclusion stated, "Is Gu Chujun the model of 'private entrepreneur' that we can expect from over ten years of economic reform? If Gu is the model for China's private entrepreneurs, I will have to cry for China's future."[8] On August 10, Shanghai's *Oriental Express* (*Dongfang zaobao*) and Hong Kong's *Business Journal* (*Shangbo*) published excerpts of Lang's report. Other media outlets quickly took note. On August 14, the NMN gave Lang's analysis prominent play by publishing three lengthy articles, including an interview with Lang, under the provocative title "Private Capital's Ability to Make State Enterprise Profitable in Doubt." Gu threatened to sue Lang for slander. Lang grasped the opportunity to escalate media attention and took the case to the court of public opinion. He traveled to Beijing to reveal Gu's lawyer's letter to the media on August 16 and went on Sohu's chat room to mobilize Internet users on the following day. The Beijing media, including *China Youth News*, reported the Lang-Gu case widely. The Internet also exploded with news and comments.

However, mainstream economists, who had been powerful advocates of privatization, were silent. The market-oriented urban newspapers, with their heightened social reformist ethos, crusading spirit, as well as their commercial imperative to generate excitement, found this silence disappointing and made this itself the news. On August 18, 2004, *Beijing Youth Daily* warned that a new wave of state asset losses was in the making and called for "the adequate attention of the entire society" so that this increasingly serious phenomenon could be curbed. The paper warned, "After more than 20 years of reform and after the entire society has paid high enough prices and tuition fees for the social transformation, if we continue to tolerate this round of large-scale, theoretically informed, and well-planned plundering of state assets, we will not be able to explain ourselves in history."[9]

On August 18, Pei Ying, an intern reporter from *Beijing Morning Post* (*Beijing chenbao*), a market-oriented subsidiary of the *Beijing Daily* Group, published a story under the headline "Lang Xianping: My Only Regret Is to Fight Alone." The article, an exclusive interview with Lang, focused on Lang's confrontation with Gu and was punctuated with provocative subheadings such as "Outrage!" "Warning!" and "Regret!"[10] On August 20, the paper published a commentary by Wang Han, who pointedly provoked mainstream economists. Wang deplored the fact that Lang did not have a single supporter among domestic mainstream economists, challenging their "collective loss of speech" and calling forth "their sense of social responsibility" and "academic conscience."[11]

Although Wang Han was also an intern—somebody with the lowest level of discursive authority within the newspaper, the piece charged itself with an enormous responsibility, that is, to provoke a debate of fundamental public importance among China's economists—arguably the most powerful discursive community in China's reform process.[12] These articles, together with similar pieces in other papers, put China's mainstream economists on the defensive and compelled them to respond. Within this context, "mainstream economists" are not party-state economists per se, but those "of the neoliberal school who have dominated China's 20 years of property right reform—the designers, participants, and beneficiaries of market reforms who make up part of the dominant power group [*qiangshi jituan*]."[13]

Lang and his journalist supporters continued to push forward the debate. For example, on August 23, at a "meeting the readers" tea party held by a group of mainstream economists at the Beijing Library, a young female reporter stunned them with a question about why they have a "collective loss of speech" over the Lang versus Gu controversy that had gained so much attention in the media and on the Internet.[14] Forced to respond, Zhao Xiao, a Peking University economics professor, warned against arousing popular resentment of SOE reform. Then, on August 28, two business newspapers interviewed Peking University's prominent neoliberal economist Zhang Weiying, who attacked Lang for having the selfish motive of seeking fame. Zhang's personal attack, his dismissal of the relevance of popular opinion in economic matters, as well as his moralistic plea that private entrepreneurs should be well treated by society further galvanized Lang's supporters.[15]

On that same day in August, the two competing discourses clashed with each other in north and south China. In Beijing, a supporter of Lang Xianping organized a seminar entitled "State Asset Loss and the Development of State-Owned Economy." The Beijing meeting was intended to be inclusive, as both "mainstream" and "new left" economists were invited. However, with the exception of state economist Zhang Weikui, a deputy director of the powerful Enterprise Research Institute of the State Council Development Research Center, no mainstream economists showed up. Instead, they were in Shenzhen participating in the annual "China's Entrepreneurs Summit Forum." At the Beijing conference, Lang and left-leaning economists moved beyond Lang's case studies to criticize the overall neoliberal economic orthodoxy that has dominated intellectual and policy discourses on SOE reform in China. Lang exposed the ideological nature of neoliberalism and the fallacy of neoliberal economists' single-minded pursuit of privatization. Using the commonsense metaphor that just because a housekeeper does a good job does not mean that he or she should assume ownership of the house, Lang underscored the injustice of managers privatizing SOEs. At the same time, he contrasted the practice of MBOs abroad with Chinese practices and revealed the ridiculous nature of Chinese practices: SOE managers borrowed money from state banks to purchase state assets at a price they set for themselves. He also pointed out that property rights reform had been guided by two fallacies: that privatization is the only solution and that there is an absence of owners in SOEs. Lang took the party's schoolbook theory seriously by stating that SOEs belong to the Chinese people, and he reminded everybody that the privatization of SOEs has not gained the approval of the Chinese people.

Lang is no radical Marxist economist. Yet reflective of just how right-leaning the "goalposts" of the ideological debates in the mainstream economic and even media fields are, he was labeled a "leftist." Describing himself as a "bourgeois economist" and commenting that "if even I am considered too left-leaning, then anyone more right-leaning [than I am] is definitely wrong,"[16] Lang is an institutional economist and a Keynesian liberal in the Western context. Conscious of the need for class compromise, he reminded his Chinese colleagues of a basic Marxian doctrine: the exploitation of surplus value by private capitalists led to a hundred years of socialist revolution. He warned that the unaccountable transfer of public assets into the hands of private capitalists, plus the excessive exploitation of the surplus value, may lead to another social upheaval. Lang barely made any references to the interests of Chinese workers in his remarks, and he repeatedly stated that his primary concern was to protect the interests of medium-sized and small investors. Still, Lang's challenge against neoliberal orthodoxy, including his insistence that the objective of SOE reform should be the maximization of public welfare, not some abstract and ill-defined notion of efficiency, his argument for the necessity of a strong state to promote equity in the economy, as well as his questioning of the blind trust in private ownership, made him a "radical" or "leftist" economist in China.[17]

THE OPENING UP OF DISCURSIVE SPACE FOR "NEW LEFT" DOMESTIC ECONOMISTS

The August 28 Beijing seminar played an instrumental role in challenging neoliberal hegemony in the economic field. By launching an attack on neoliberalism, Lang, an outsider, opened up a discursive space for left-leaning domestic economists, who have long been marginalized and excluded from mainstream academic, media, and public policy forums. They jumped at the opportunity and became the most vocal voices in the debate. Zuo Dapei, a leading "new left" economist at the Chinese Academy of Social Sciences, proclaimed as he entered the Beijing seminar room: "Who said that economists suffered from a loss of speech? I, for one, never have! I spoke out about the loss of state assets six years ago!"[18] Other marginalized economists became emotional as well. One account wrote,

> Perhaps because they have not had a chance to speak into the microphone for a long time, they eagerly wanted to speak . . . to speak out about the unfair treatment of their scholarship. One participating scholar said, "I must challenge the monopoly of those people [i.e., mainstream neoliberal economists]." Another economist protested, "In the past, we didn't have the equal opportunity to participate in discussions. We cannot even get our papers published."[19]

Attaining their dominant ideological position by ignoring, marginalizing, and suppressing oppositional voices in public discourses, neoliberal
economists have operated as the organic intellectuals of China's rising
propertied class during the reform process—serving as their board members, lobbyists, publicists, and strategists, while enriching themselves
with consultant and speech fees and stock shares. The experience of Zuo,
perhaps the best known "new left" economist, is illustrative of the supremacy of neoliberal discursive power. Zuo is no Maoist ideologue of the
old generation. Rather, he belongs to the new generation of reform-era
economists trained in market economics. In fact, he is an expert in
post–World War II German neoliberal economic thought and he boasts
two postdoctoral posts in Germany and research papers written in German. In February 1994, *Economics News* (*Jingji xiaoxi bao*), a specialized
trade paper for economists, published an article by Zuo criticizing the
dominant economic orthodoxy of the time. This orthodoxy insisted that
the Chinese economy was not overheated and opposed the government's
macroeconomic adjustment policy. The article, not surprisingly, received
no response from mainstream economists. Furthermore, when the editor-
in-chief of the paper phoned up another leading mainstream economist to
solicit a contribution later on, that economist expressed outrage at the paper for publishing Zuo's article at all. The economist further indicated
that four other fellow economists had asked him to boycott the paper as a
publishing outlet in retaliation against the publication of Zuo's article.[20]
Similarly, although Zuo's 2002 book *Confused Economics* (*Hunluan de
jingjixue*), which presented a systematic critique of what Zuo called "economic liberalism with Chinese characteristics," sold well in the market,
and mainstream economists were talking about it privately, only one
economist cared to review it in a public forum. For Zuo, this was a form
of censorship by omission. However, Zuo provided no evidence that the
government had ordered that his book receive this "cool treatment."

Zuo's experience is important. It challenges any one-dimensional
analysis that attributes discursive disciplinary power either to the iron fist
of the state or to the structural bias of the market, or a combination of
both. To be sure, the power of neoliberal economists as a collective discursive community is no match for that of the state or the market, and
they do not act independently of these two vectors of power. Nevertheless, in the context of China's economic reforms, when economics has become the most powerful academic discipline and when economists occupy key positions in different branches of the state, in government
research institutions and think tanks, in universities, in the media as the
most-quoted expert sources, not to mention as advisers to businesses, this
power is formidable. In the Chinese media, the names of some economists
are closely linked to specific economic policies, and they signify both discursive and institutional power. For example, Wu Jinglian, the most vocal

advocate of marketization, has long been known as "Market Wu," and he heads a powerful research institute under the State Council. Li Yining, who advocated the restructuring of SOEs into shareholding companies, is known as "Shareholding Li," and he is a deputy chairman of the Finance and Economic Committee of the NPC.

Given this highly unequal discursive, political, and organizational power between contending economic perspectives, it is not surprising that Zuo and his fellow left-leaning economists seized the opening in the media and quickly turned their academic positions into political appeals. On August 28, 2004, the same day the Beijing seminar took place, Zuo and two other left-leaning economists issued an open letter to the highest levels of party and state leadership. They pointed out that the problem of state assets plundering is more serious than what Lang had revealed. They not only demanded that the top leadership stop MBO practices, investigate and audit existing MBO practices, and openly report the results of the audits in the *People's Daily*, but also called for a thorough rethinking of the entire direction of SOE reform. They wrote,

> With the all-out privatization of SOEs, workers have been laid off en masse, while a few became billionaires. As workers lost their status as the masters of the state, the nature of the state will be transformed. . . . [T]he Communist Party will become the party of the rich, the party of private property, with the social basis of the governing party being seriously undermined.[21]

In another statement issued to the media at the same time—posted in its entirety by Sina on September 1 and reported by the *Beijing Morning Post* on September 2—Zuo not only delineated the political implications of privatization, but also called for a struggle against the perpetuators of unaccountable privatization and a Russian-style oligarchy:

> I sound an alarm for the entire Chinese nation: the people's property and their future are in danger! . . . We not only face real capitalism, but also face the worst form of crony capitalism. . . . We need a genuine settling of the scores with those who expropriate the people in the name of "system transformation," with those corrupt officials who promote crony capitalism, and with those individuals who consciously support the expropriation of the people. [We] should no longer tolerate their crimes. [We] must re-expropriate the expropriators and reclaim the power of the people!

THE MARKET-ORIENTED DAILIES, THE VALUE OF PUBLIC DEBATE, AND THE "PUBLIC INTEREST"

By late August 2004, the debate had become a media event, and Lang a public symbol. With the participation of tens of thousands of Internet users, economists, legal scholars, and public intellectuals in other fields, the debate's scope of public involvement was second only to the Sun Zhigang case in 2003. The terms of the debate were quickly and progressively enlarged and deepened: from Lang Xianping versus Gu Chujun to the property rights reform of the SOEs, to the entire topic of SOE reform, to a debate between contending economic paradigms over such fundamental issues as the respective roles of the private and state sectors and the role of the state, and ultimately, to a debate about the trajectory, consequences, social orientations, and future directions of China's entire reform process. The "no debate" curse imposed by Deng and sustained by the Jiang Zemin leadership seemed to have been finally dispelled. This had been unprecedented in Chinese public life since 1992.

Thus, one of the world's most tightly controlled media systems produced perhaps one of the most heated debates on neoliberal economic policies and practices and their consequences. To be sure, just as the Sun Zhigang and Wang Binyu cases involved the ingredients of sensational journalism, this debate involved a celebrity scholar, a lawsuit, conflicting personalities, personal attacks, and other "newsworthy" elements. The media-savvy Lang Xiaping was extremely adept in delivering timely and media-friendly content. Most importantly, however, Lang struck a responsive cord in the Chinese public consciousness. The media, for their part, displayed an extraordinary sense of social responsibility and public spirit. This is particularly significant in the context of sustained political censorship, the general commercial logic that encourages the media to pursue the trivial and to avoid controversial issues, and journalistic corruption that passes off publicity pieces for businesses and entrepreneurs as news. The event demonstrated the agency of many Chinese journalists and their commitment to an expanded public sphere during China's epochal transformation.

At the same time, because the Chinese media system has a highly fragmented structure, different types of media outlets played different roles, and they displayed different value orientations, demonstrating different degrees of involvement in the debate. The market-oriented sector, consisting of metropolitan urban dailies and the business papers, was the main forum. These newspapers, together with the embattled *China Youth News*, were at the forefront in carrying Lang's initial critiques of the three companies, his views, as well as in soliciting the perspectives of other economists.

There was, however, a clear difference in perspective between the popular urban dailies and the business press. The urban dailies more clearly identified themselves with Lang's perspective in their reporting and were more proactive in promoting the debate in their commentaries. As discussed in chapter 2, the urban dailies make up the most resource-rich segment of the Chinese press because of their state-granted privilege to tap into the most lucrative metropolitan advertising markets. They also have relatively more political capital because, as the subsidiaries of central and provincial-level party organs, they have higher political status in accessing official sources and can claim provincial and above-level political authorities as their power base. Their political and economic positions, in turn, have allowed them to recruit some of the best journalistic talents. Consequently, these newspapers have become the agenda-setters of China's popular media and, as they themselves are eager to claim, China's "new mainstream media" (in contrast to the "old mainstream media" of central and provincial party organs—their parent papers). Moreover, through both their capacity and their state-secured monopoly to produce original news, they are the agenda-setters of China's commercial websites, which are banned from having reporters of their own.

The *NMN* and the *Beijing Morning Post* in particular played instrumental roles in this debate. They produced some of the earliest and most widely circulated articles. Of particular significance was the current affairs commentary in these papers—a genre that can be traced back to the *NMN*'s soccer commentaries. In these commentaries the papers issued the calls that put mainstream economists on the defensive, arguing for the importance of public debate on the topic. The *NMN*, consistent with its role in the Sun Zhigang case, not only printed three lengthy articles detailing Lang's arguments as early as August 14, but also published a commentary on August 31 calling for the expansion of the debate on the direction of reform in other areas of critical public importance, including education and health care. Reflecting a broader and more radical analytical framework, the commentary discussed the "Lang Xianping Storm" in terms of "empowering the public with the right to participate in discussions and the right to know," believing that "the participation of the masses and their thinking" are crucial in the search for reform strategies and the formation of social consensus over core guiding principles for China's reform process.[22] In contrast to the elitism of neoliberal economists who accused Lang of playing into "irrational popular sentiments," and in contrast to Lang himself, who advocated a paternalistic notion of elite democracy and saw this democracy as the result of an appropriate level of economic development under authoritarianism, the *NMN* commentary stated that the debate must not be limited to experts. It argued that the Chinese public had the necessary intellectual abilities to carry out a constructive public debate and that the public was capable of finding solutions to issues of fundamental importance. What the paper called forth, then, is a broader notion of democracy in which public deliberation plays an important role in shaping the policies and value orientations of China's ongoing transformation. In an implicit response to Zhang Weiying's charge that Lang was motivated by his quest for fame, a commentary in the *Beijing News* welcomed the emergence of an "academic star" who dared to criticize business in the name of public interest. The paper noted the dominance of mainstream economists in the media and considered this to be a problem:

> This kind of "academic star" is all too rare. Aren't some mainstream economists holding discursive power in the mass media? They often show up in the print pages and television screens. They travel back and forth from and to major business enterprises and busy themselves with being their "consultants." They frequently speak at forums all over the country. . . . Why is it an issue with an extra "academic star" like Lang? . . . How could he hurt entrepreneurs? We should know that it is the dominance of a single voice that has hurt the SOE reform.[23]

Still, it left the more established *China Youth News* to publish the most poignant critique of a dominant knowledge-money-power regime in the Chinese social structure. This article argued that Lang's criticisms challenged not only a few individuals, but an entire group and the unspoken rules behind this group. This group pursued the interest of capital and little in terms of public interest. It cited examples of the interlocking relationships between elite economists and capital and moved on to describe the formation of a "super-stable" power, money, and knowledge regime:

> One famous economist serves as an adviser or an independent board member in nine publicly listed companies. Another economist serves as an adviser to 15 companies, enjoying an annual income ranging from 30,000 to 200,000 yuan from each company. These individuals hold important positions in government think tanks at various levels. Their words have an impact on high-level decisions one way or another. Under the leadership of some of the so-called mainstream economists, more and more people embrace capital, accept money from them, reason for them, conduct research for them, and speak for them. Under such an intertwining relationship, the research and analysis of some economists takes on the color of capital. . . . When speaking for capital becomes a hegemonic discourse, there is an atrophy of academic freedom and freedom of expression in the economic field, as the implicit rules of this discursive hegemony encourage conformity and discourage dissent . . . the collusion among capital, power, and economists may lead to a "super-stable" structure of a vested interest group, an alliance that divides up the benefits of reform to the exclusion of the ordinary people without power, money, and discursive power.[24]

The article noted that the existence of this structure of vested interest holders has become an obstacle for reform and that intellectuals with a social conscience must maintain an ethical bottom line and argue for the "public interest" in their research. The article had such a wide resonance among the urban dailies that *Yanzhao Metropolitan News* (*Yanzhao dushi bao*) paraphrased its main arguments and presented them as its own. This abridged version, in turn, gained circulation on the Internet.[25]

The urban dailies, in their reporting of news, in their framing of headlines, as well as in their choice of interview subjects, clearly showed sympathy for and identification with Lang and left-leaning economists. In contrast to the "special interests" of entrepreneurs and economists with vested interests in private businesses, these papers speak on behalf of the "public interest." The *Beijing Morning Post* and *China Youth News* each stood out for their unprecedented inclusion and reporting of Zuo Dapei and his ideas. To be sure, both papers went only so far as to publish Zuo's warning against a Chinese-style Russian oligarchy. They did not publish Zuo's more radical warning against the danger of fascist-style crony capitalism or his call for settling scores with private entrepreneurs, neoliberal economists, and corrupt officials responsible for spontaneous or illegal privatization. This demonstrates the limits of the Chinese press discourse on the "public interest" and its operation within the hegemonic framework of maintaining social stability. Other market-oriented media outlets were more explicit in their role of policing the discursive boundaries. *China News Weekly* (*Zhongguo xinwen zhoukan*), which would issue the most stern editorial voice against a class-based public opinion mobilization during the Wang Binyu debate in September 2005, for example, stated that the call for settling scores with past proponents of spontaneous privatization was "a dangerous political appeal." "If certain injustice in the reform process has aroused a psychology of discontent and resentment among certain social groups, a responsible way is to explore the adaptation of certain measures to alleviate this psychology. However, it is to nobody's interest to inflame it, turning it into social conflict."[26]

A STUDY IN CONTRAST: THE BUSINESS PRESS AND OTHER SPECIAL INTEREST PAPERS

In contrast, and perhaps predictably, business papers consistently supported neoliberal economists and private entrepreneurs. The most active business papers included the longer-established *Chinese Industrial and Commercial Times* (*Zhongguo gongshang shibao*) and newly established ones such as Guangzhou's *21st-Century Business Herald*, Beijing's *Economic Observer*, and various papers specializing in the stock markets. Of course, the business press is by no means monolithic. Lang's reputation as a defender of the interests of medium and small investors received wide endorsement in various stock market papers, which count on these investors as their core readers.

Although a number of business papers provided some of the most comprehensive and up-to-date reports of Lang's ideas, as crucial sites whereby the bloc of business, political, and academic power is constituted, major business papers served as the prominent forums for private capitalists and neoliberal economists throughout the debate. For example, one of the earliest rebuttals of Lang by Zhang Wenkui was published by the *21st-Century Business Herald* under a Cultural Revolution–style declarative headline, "The Direction of SOE Property Right Reform Is Not Allowed to Be Changed."[27]Other business papers also rushed to publish interviews with Zhang.[28] Similarly, Zhang Weiying's lengthy and controversial rebuttal of Lang was published by the *Economic Observer* in the form of an interview on August 28. The paper failed to get an interview from Zhou Qiren, another well-known Peking University neoliberal economist, because Zhou initially did not intend to take Lang seriously and had resorted to the marginalization-through-neglect strategy. As Lang and the voices of his supporters gained media attention, Zhou and the paper quickly reconnected with each other, and the paper published a major interview with Zhou on September 13.[29]

One paper in the business sector that was particularly outspoken on behalf of China's ascending capitalist class was *Chinese Industrial and Commercial Times*, the official organ of the All China Industrial and Commerce Association. Like its more recently established peers, the paper followed the debate closely. Its framing of the news events, however, showed a significant difference from the urban commercial dailies. A comparison of its reporting of the August 28 Beijing seminar on "State Asset Loss and the Development of State Sector Economy" with that of the *Beijing Morning Post* is perhaps most illustrative. The *Beijing Morning Post*'s short report was headlined "Five Scholars Support Lang Xianping in Beijing," and in the text, the report highlighted the perspective of "new left" economists such as Zuo Dapei. In contrast, the August 30 *Chinese Industrial and Commercial Times* story about the seminar was headlined "'Heroes' of All Brands Collectively Absent, Lang Xianping the Single Player at Seminar." This headline thus completely ignored the fact that economists to the left of Lang were not only present, but also very vocal at the seminar. Consistent with the framing of the headline, the report started with the sentence, "The Lang Xianping of August 28, somewhat lonely, somewhat helpless," and moved on to report the content of Lang's keynote speech.[30] There was no mention of other participants, their ideas, and the dynamics of the conference. The paper's ideological stand, including its intolerance of debates on public policy, was also expressed in a strongly worded editorial on September 7, entitled, "Private Enterprises Are Not Responsible for Loss of State Assets." The article reiterated the neoliberal perspective about the efficiency and magic power of privatization. Instead of acknowledging the relevance of the values of equity and social justice, it only concerned itself with economic growth: "If we have to speak with facts, why don't we do a calculation of how much state tax revenues have increased, how much societal wealth has increased?" More importantly, the concluding paragraph of the article invoked both the authority of the Chinese Constitution, which has incorporated a clause promoting the private economy, and the pro–private sector words of Premier Wen Jiabao to dismiss not only the relevance of Lang's challenge, but also the relevance of scholarly debates all together: "In China, development is an irrefutable argument. Any 'empty talk,' 'free talk,' not-fact-based, unrealistic so-called scholarly debate will in no way fundamentally undermine this course of development."[31] What this paper advocated, then, is a restoration of the "no debate" regime in the Chinese public sphere.

Within this context, journalists in China are increasingly conscious of the role of the press business in securing discursive dominance in the Chinese public sphere. Commenting on the unprecedented recruitment campaign launched by the *First Finance Daily* (*Diyi caijing ribao*), a business paper established in Shanghai in November 2004 as a cross-media and cross-regional joint venture by Shanghai's SMG, the *Beijing Youth Daily* Group, and the *Guangzhou Daily* Group, a commentator at Shanghai's *Liberation Daily* wrote of this new paper's ambitions: "Objective: discursive power. . . . [I]n the United States, the business press is a powerful force, government listens to it for its policy choices, all the CEOs heed what Wall Street papers say."[32] The article then moved on to say how China's business press, which has not yet achieved this level of discursive power, had more work to do. That a writer for the *Liberation Daily*, Shanghai's party organ, should comment on the ascending discursive power of China's business press with such favor is a significant statement in itself.

As discussed in chapter 2, the same process that has witnessed the rapid rise of the urban commercial dailies and the massive expansion of the business press has also witnessed the relative decline in the discursive influence and financial resources of papers targeting workers, farmers, and women. The *Workers' Daily*, the only national paper that supposedly has a mandate to speak to, if not for, the working class in China, was silent in the debate. A content search from late August to the end of October 2004 showed no coverage of the debate at all. This is astonishing, given the fact that SOE reform is so closely tied to the interests of workers. At a time when economists like Zhang Weiying have called upon society to "treat well those who have made a contribution to society" (portraying SOE managers as the exclusive group that has made such a contribution), the *Workers' Daily* chose not to make the point that perhaps tens of millions of workers, and indeed generations of workers, have also contributed to the building-up of the SOEs in the more than 50 years of the

People's Republic.[33] Similarly, given that women workers have suffered disproportionately during the SOE privatization process, as the layoff policy is one of "ladies first," and the reemployment rate for women is 19 percent lower that that for men,[34] the complete silence of *China Women's News* on the debate is also significant. What is important to emphasize, once again, is that the current irrelevance of the *Workers' Daily* and the *China Women's News* was by no means a "natural outcome." One of the articles in the November 18, 1998, inaugural issue of *China Women's News'* short-lived *Weekly Review* supplement, for example, was precisely about the mainstream media's revisionist discourse of portraying SOE workers as parasites "fed" by the state and the SOEs. Under the title "Who on Earth Feeds Whom?" the article stated, "If workers are regarded as being 'fed,' and let go when they can no longer be 'fed,' while their rights as the creators of the accumulated value of state assets are completely disregarded during the property right reform process, this is unjust."[35] The article brought back the "labor theory of value" and concluded, "in a country where the question of 'who feeds whom' was supposed to be answered ever since Marxism was first introduced, it is astonishing that this complete ideological inversion not only happened at all, but also manifested in the self-proclaimed 'main melody' media."[36] Although no one knows how the *Workers' Daily's* short-lived urban supplement, the *New Journal*, might have contributed to the debate, this article may give some clue as to how the *Weekly Review*, if it were allowed to continue, might have contributed to the current debate.

THE INTERNET AND THE VOICE OF THE "POPULAR"

The Internet was the most vibrant forum in the debate. It served as a distribution outlet for the earliest newspaper stories about Lang's lecture, and later, major portals circulated Lang's talks, press articles, and served as exclusive outlets for the views of many participant economists. On August 30, Sohu, which had Lang Xianping as its chief financial commentator at the time, established a special site entitled "The Great Debate on SOE Property Right Reform."[37] Apart from the three major commercial portals, Sina, Sohu, and Netease, major Internet forums such as www.blogchina.com, the Century China Forum at www.cc.org.cn, and the *People's Daily's* "Strengthening the Nation" web forum at www.qglt .com served as key sites for the debate.

The Internet both broadened and deepened the debate. The major websites of official media outlets carried articles by "grassroots economists," that is, grassroots writers or economists who do not necessarily have economics-related academic positions (on par with the nationalistic-oriented "grassroots foreign policy experts" who served as critics of China's foreign policies on the Internet), and non-economists who framed the issue beyond economics. Like the Sun Zhigang case, the views of leading public intellectuals received wide attention. The Nanfang Net, for example, carried an article under the banner "Wang Xiaoming Supports Lang Xianping: Economics Is Not What Is Being Argued About!" In the article, Wang, a Shanghai-based literature professor, noted that although he had remained on the sidelines of the debate because he is not an economist, he had realized that the economists were actually not making points about economics, but politics: that economist Zhang Weiying's privileging of the maximization of wealth over equity was not an economic argument, but a political one; that Zhang's disregard for workers' contributions to society was not merely an economic issue; and that domestic economists' attack of Lang's motive was not very scholarly. What Wang pointed out, then, is the political dimension of neoliberalism. Wang argued that the SOEs are the cumulative assets of state socialism under the then low-wage and low-consumption economic regime and that the entire population contributed to their accumulation. Furthermore, Wang made an ideological distinction between the semantics of "state ownership" (*guoyou*) and "all people's ownership" (*quanmin suoyou*) (the former somehow replaced the latter in official discourses during the reform period) and drew attention to the cultural and ideological background of the current disposal of this asset:

> What kind of environment and factors support the steady and open plundering of assets owned by the whole people (including each of us) at such a broad scale? From the perspective of culture, what role has been played by the thoughts and ideas that have been popular over the recent decade, including modernization, connecting with the world track, market economy, private ownership, the holy logic of investment-output, incentives, MBO, state assets as local government assets, etc.? Although these ideas perhaps each have their respective values on their own, in the specific context of China, why have they helped to promote this massive tide of plundering?[38]

Wang's article itself became a source of debate. On the one hand, a certain Li Damiao in the "Real Name Forum" issued a hostile right-wing diatribe against Wang for being nostalgic about the Cultural Revolution and the "happy banquet of communism" and for opposing reform. As I discussed in chapter 1, this rhetorical strategy of accusing somebody of being nostalgic for the horrendous Cultural Revolution has been the most effective and most feared ideological weapon in the hands of right-wing ideologues and neoliberal reformers in China. On the other hand, Wang's point was picked up by an article initially published in a business journal and then widely circulated on many major websites, including the People's

Net. This article acknowledged that the Maoist path of capital accumulation is "against the natural law," while claiming that there has been extremely little opposition to the market economy and SOE reform. Nevertheless, it argued that mainstream economists' single-minded pursuit of "economic rationality" is problematic. Reflecting an urban middle-class fear of growing resentment from below *and* the need for social reform as a means of class containment—the same instrumentalist rationale behind Lang's call for social justice as a value in SOE reform—the author wrote,

> Strangely, at a time when the higher-level leadership has already had considerable awareness of the need to be concerned with weak social groups that are being sacrificed and hurt and the need to make necessary concessions, a whole group of mainstream economists continues to emphasize "economic rationality," indulging themselves in the myth of growth. I must once again emphasize my deepest apprehension about the psychology of resentment in society . . . which will only amplify through communication and accumulation. . . . I feel extremely anxious with the things I hear and see after I step out of the fancy office tower where I work. I plead sincerely to every Chinese economist with a sense of social responsibility, to leave behind books and statistics, and entrepreneur's salons filled with the powerful, to leave those eloquent high-level forums merely for a while, and to spend a month to go down [to the grassroots] to take a walk, have a look, and then continue this debate.[39]

Trying to remain true to its name, the *People's Daily* website posted articles that spoke on behalf of the "people." While the media blamed mainstream economists for a loss of speech, one article argued that the real group that had lost its voice was "certain local government officials" who colluded with entrepreneurs and betrayed the will of the public in SOE reform. However, instead of calling for political democracy so that the public would have control over officials, the article left the task to the party-state's disciplinary inspection and supervision departments and called for the adherence to the "market economic logic" of "efficiency to be arranged by the market, and equity to be managed by the government" and the construction of a "social security and public welfare system."[40] Another article on the website deplored the public's lack of voice—China's silent majority. However, the article repeated the same solution: "We do not wish to stop SOE reform, but we hope SOE reform can truly take the path of legalization and marketization." Reflecting the hegemony of market economics, it called for a "fair, just, and transparent" market competition mechanism.[41]

Mainstream commercial websites, while carrying more articles by neoliberal economists, also gave some space to "new left" economists, including full-length articles by Zuo Dapei. The entire text of the open letter by Zuo and his fellow left-leaning economists, for example, found its place on commercial websites. Sina and Sohu each carried one exclusive article from Zuo to demonstrate their inclusiveness. Another of Zuo's articles found its place on the web version of the *Guangming Daily.*[42] In the article, Zuo pointed out that although the media and public opinion supported Lang's opposition to unaccountable privatization by SOE managers, Lang's argument for "big government" received an overwhelming rejection. Zuo said that those opposing Lang's call for "big government" were made up of two types, neoliberal economists, who would like to see "entrepreneurs who have acquired or even stolen capital control the entire society," and the majority, who seemed to have conflated the unlimited *power* of government officials with state *capacity.* He argued that the problem with China is that officials are too powerful while the state's capacity to regulate the economic sectors that are basic to the public welfare is lacking and ineffective, and its capacity to provide social welfare is limited in comparison with the state in Western Europe and the United States. In this way, Zuo's article tried to move beyond the simple condemnation of unfair privatization to the topic of reforming the Chinese state.

The heated debated among Internet users—one count by Sohu claimed as many as 30,000 Internet commentaries on the topic[43]—and their overwhelming support for Lang became an important form of symbolic power in itself. A Sina survey of more than 40,000 Internet users showed a support rate of more than 90 percent in favor of Lang.[44] In contrast, Zhang Weiying, the most outspoken neoliberal economist, only received a support rate of 5 percent.[45] These figures were then widely cited by the print media, and these numbers, perhaps more than the arguments of Lang and his "new left" economist supporters, helped to put neoliberal economists on the defensive. Their attempt to discredit this Internet-based popular opinion as emotional and irrational only further provoked Internet users.

Thus, China's Internet, because of its relatively open environment, has become the surrogate "public" in Chinese public communication. This public is a peculiar one. In addition to the "old lefts" who were compelled to use the Internet, as discussed in chapter 1, this active Internet public includes leading humanistic intellectuals who have access to mainstream print media but aim to enlarge the Chinese public sphere, young university faculty members, social critics, grassroots leftist commentators who do not have ready access to mainstream print media, white-collar workers, and the general category of "angry youths" (*fenqing*), made up of mostly university students. In terms of social background, this group of educated urban youth is perhaps highly comparable to the "new left" youth in the West in the 1960s. As revealed in chapter 5, Sun Zhigang and individuals mobilized on his behalf provided glimpses of the social composition of this network. As Internet users and thus citizens of the "newly industrializing China,"[46] they mediate between the ruling classes and the underclasses, and their organic ties to the other two Chinas—the state socialist China and rural China—are still too close to be severed. Although their consumerist orientations and nationalistic passions have been widely documented in the Western media and academic literature,[47] as the previous chapter demonstrated, this same group of socially conscious and politically engaged youth, like their counterparts in the antiglobalization social justice movement in the rest of the world, have been outspoken social critics of China's reform program. If the neoliberal economists who dominate academic and media discourses tend to speak on behalf of China's raising capitalist class, Internet users displayed more concern for social justice and claimed to speak on behalf of ordinary workers and farmers. These socially engaged individuals with symbolic resources made up the core of China's active "public" in this discussion. They participated in the debate either out of genuine commitment to social justice or out of the felt need for class compromise—that is, the fear that the resentment of the losers of the reform process outside the fancy classrooms and office towers may one day threaten those inside. Additionally, with the increasing difficulty of finding decent employment after a university education, many urban youths may have also come to realize their own precarious social economic status, thus sharing similar concerns with China's underclasses.

The formation of this Internet public and the parameters of their participation, of course, are heavily mediated. Like print media outlets, major websites themselves played important filtering and editorial roles. When posting a forum by three leftist economists, Sina, for example, put up a disclaimer, saying that it carried the article to spread information, but did not necessarily endorse its views.[48] However, the website did not feel the need to do so when it held forums featuring neoliberal economists. Moreover, Sina left out significant parts of the forum, which found their way into other, less mainstream websites such as Agriculture China (*Sannong luntan*).

The editorial role of Sohu is perhaps most illustrative. For example, in a webpage that recounted the milestones of the debate, there was, conspicuously, no mention of the open letter by Zuo Dapei and his fellow "new left" economists. Nor did the website list any articles written by non-economists, including almost all the newspaper commentaries that expanded the scope of the debate and challenged the dominant knowledge-power regime. In an editorial that framed the entire debate, Wang Zihui, editor-in-chief of Sohu Finance, blamed unwanted "noises" for undermining the "efficiency" of the debate and called for rationality in the media, while trying to articulate what he conceived to be the "collective unconsciousness" emerging from the debate. The editorial claimed that the negative consequences of reform were "inevitable" and that an "unconscious consensus" was emerging among economists. This "consensus," however, is nothing short of Sohu's articulation of a hegemonic perspective about the inevitability of privatization. Wang called upon the media: "At a time when this 'unconscious consensus' is crystallizing, the media, while providing a discursive platform for the academic community, must respect and nurture this objectively existent 'unconscious' consensus, locking it up as the goal of our discussion to improve the efficiency of our discussion."[49]

Thus, contrary to commentaries in urban dailies that called for broadening the debate, Sohu as a website aimed to limit the scope of the debate, advising the media to act more self-consciously to forge a consensus in favor of further privatization. The Internet's role in providing broader perspectives, therefore, contrasts sharply with the hegemonic editorial orientation of Sohu, which was narrower than some of the urban daily newspapers. From Sina's "double standards" in its editorial practice to Sohu's attempt to limit the scope of the debate and its call for the media to focus on an "objectively" existent consensus in 2004, it is only one step away from the *NMN*'s call for the media to focus on the "objective" facts of Wang Binyu's killings in 2005. As the terms of public debates extended from state enterprise reform, which is considered an "urban issue" affecting members of Chinese urban society including state enterprise workers, to encompass the urban/rural divide and the economic rights of migrant workers as the urban society's collective "other," one witnesses the intensified terms of social conflict and thus narrower definitions of journalistic neutrality.

The voices of Chinese workers—specifically urban-based state enterprise workers, the group that had much at stake in this debate—were absent in mainstream commercial websites. It took the *People's Daily*'s "Strengthen the Nation Forum" to call attention to the missing voice of workers in the debate. The following discussion, generated by a remark of a "Mr. Yundanshuinuan" (a self-identified fifty-something laid-off worker), posted on September 23, 2004, demonstrates how this official web forum tried to maintain its discursive hegemony:

[subject post, or *zhutie*]:
　　Mr. Yundanshuinuan: Odd discussion on the loss of state assets: the sole missing voice is that of the workers.
　　[follow-up posts, or *gentie*]:
- State enterprise workers have no right to speak, their only right is to be laid off.
- Where are the political leaders of the people? Come out and speak a word of justice for the proletariat and do one good thing.

- I appeal, with my blood, to the Central Committee to immediately stop and reexamine a process of state enterprise reform that is dominated by power and money!
- Who is listening even if workers are speaking out?
- Where can workers speak out?
- The reform should enrich workers and farmers. Why not?
- How many super rich individuals have been created through the plundering of state assets?!
- How much say have the masses of workers had in the more than 10 years of SOE reform? Oh, government, who do you represent?
- This article points out a key problem in SOE reform, and it shames power holders and scholars. Really admirable.
- Hope the chair of the All Federation of Trade Unions and the chair of trade unions at various levels join the discussion.
- There is no lack of workers' voices. Many netizens are workers. What is lacking at the present is the voice of political leaders.
- This is easy to understand. The industrial working class is no longer the leading class today. Their words have no weight. It is not that they are not speaking; it is that nobody listens to them.
- In the eyes of the elite, workers and farmers are superfluous.
- The duty of the leftists on "Strengthening the Nation Forum" is to speak for workers.
- Encourage the masses to participate in the Lang Xianping and SOE reform debate. This is the only way to steer the discussion in the correct direction.
- The participation of the masses in the debate of ideas is the only way to obtain truth. This is the core issue in the current debate.
- In fact, it is not just in the area of enterprise reform, many government policies are the results of experts. They have become the speakers for policy.
- The absence of the voice of farmers is even more apparent. Since the SOEs are "state assets," why not allow farmers' participation?
- Isn't the state representing the working class? Doesn't the State Assets Management Bureau exercise its power on behalf of workers? Perhaps the state no longer represents the workers?
- If one wants to listen more to the voices of workers, I suggest economists base themselves in the enterprises for two or three months, visiting at least several enterprises and participating in labor.
- At this point, many workers only know that they are not willing to be bought out of their jobs, but they are unable to speak more about what's wrong.
- Correct. Many Chinese economists have no idea about the plight of Chinese workers.
- If workers were more educated and could get on the web, they wouldn't wait until today.
- Good point. Precisely because workers cannot afford to buy computers and you are highly educated, it will be up to you to help them more.

- Wrong, what is lacking is the voice of the whole people as the property owners. Everyone is a shareholder of SOEs and each has a stake.
- This strange phenomenon clashes with our Constitution and the nature of our state! This is so inconsistent with the working-class political party of ours!!
- Because workers are busy with work, they are shouldering the costs of reform quietly, believing in the party and the government. They are the ones who truly sacrifice, and they are the backbone of our nation.
- What is odd is that in an issue that is of fundamental concern to the majority, the voice of this majority is missing.
- Workers are laid off, how can they have a voice?!
- Workers should not only have voices on the issues of SOE system transformation, but also have the deciding power.
- I used to be a state enterprise worker. Support Lang Xianping. The phenomenon of the loss of state assets should no longer be continued. Zhang Weiying and his type have misled the country and hurt the people.[50]

By permitting this discussion, the *People's Daily*'s chat room provided a highly confined and well-monitored venting place for workers and their sympathizers. At the same time, it managed to render the voices of frontline workers and their concrete struggles nonexistent.

MARGINAL LEFTIST WEBSITES, BLOGGERS, AND THE VOICES OF WORKERS

Marginal leftist websites, some hosted overseas due to domestic repression, others constantly struggling for a precarious domestic existence under the party's censorship regime, were left to carry the more urgent voices of frontline workers and to report on their struggles. These websites provided vivid descriptions of the actual process of spontaneous privatization by government officials, state enterprise managers, and private entrepreneurs, and on workers' ongoing struggles against being expropriated. In fact, workers were protesting against this very process just as the "Lang Xianping Storm" was in the making. In Xianyang City, Shaanxi Province, more than 6,000 workers, mostly women, were on strike at the Tianwang Textile Factory, a former SOE, in September and October 2004 to protest against a privatization deal that, according to the workers, constituted a loss of state assets and, more importantly for them, forced them to sign unfair labor contracts and undermined their wages and benefit entitlements.[51] In Chongqing, workers at 3403 Factory, a former military factory, waged a strike on August 18, 2004, the same day the *Beijing Morning Post* published "Lang Xianping: My Only Regret Is to Fight Alone." The factory, which workers claimed was worth nearly 200 million yuan, was sold behind the backs of its 3,000 workers in June 2004 to a private entrepreneur for a mere 22 million yuan, with only 2 million yuan paid before the August 2004 takeover.[52]

This story, in the form of a blog filed under the name "Workers of Chongqing 3403 Factory" and circulated in a number of leftist websites, including the October issue of *China and the World* webzine, provided a far more compelling and vivid example of the "plundering of state assets" than Lang's studies. If Lang's only source was publicly available financial information of the concerned companies, this blog spoke with the firsthand knowledge of workers who witnessed the process and were actually engaged in the struggle to protect their own means of production. In contrast to neoliberal platitudes about SOE inefficiency, the workers argued that misguided government policies and "ill-intended management" were the primary reasons for the demise of SOEs. In this case, the purchasing company, called Naide, was itself a former SOE. It became the private company of factory director Lin Chaoyang in 1998 under the Chongqing government's SOE privatization program. After acquiring control of Naide, Lin used it as a base to enrich a private enterprise set up in his brother's name, and he then targeted 3403 Factory just 30 kilometers away. He colluded with 3403 Factory manager Zhang Chengyi to form a joint-venture business—a common strategy to hollow out an existing SOE. Furthermore, as another "hollowing out" strategy, Zhang allowed Lin free use of the 3403 Factory floor to produce for another private company under Lin's name. By June 2004, 3403 Factory was on the verge of bankruptcy, and Lin, whom workers believe had bribed Zhang and Chongqing officials, became its designated "backdoor" purchaser. The price of 22 million yuan was set by government officials, and there was no public bidding process. Zhang Chengyi became the deputy manager of Naide and received a handsome "salary" without actually having to work. Moreover, news about the factory's sale was concealed from workers. When workers finally learned about it, they mobilized to protect the factory and offered to collectively buy it with a 10,000-yuan investment each—with 3,000 of them, this would mean an offer of 30 million yuan, much higher than the 22-million-yuan selling price. This led to prolonged struggles between workers on the one side and Lin, Zhang, and government officials on the other. By August 25, 2004, the sign-off date of the first blog, more than 300 police officers had stormed the factory.

After explaining how both civilian and military authorities involved in the supervision of the factory had been "bought off" by the factory's management, and that there was no hope either for a local governmental solution or for a legal settlement, one worker activist/blogger issued the following appeal:

I swear with my conscience as a Chinese citizen about the truthfulness of my report. Chongqing City is under the control of dark forces, and it is impossible to solve this problem locally. We, several thousands of workers, have sent joint letters to the secretary of the Central Inspection and Discipline Commission Wu Guanzheng, [CCTV's] *Focus Interviews*, etc. But we do not know whether our mail has reached them, as it is possible that it might have been blocked by dark hands . . . how we hope the Central [Committee of the CCP] can intervene . . . but the sky is high and emperor is far, how can the Central know of a strike carried out by workers for justice thousands of kilometers away? . . . Our only hope is to issue an urgent appeal for the support of the country's justice-minded individuals, please send news about the strike to the Central or influential media outlets.[53]

This blog, filed by "Recent Developments in Protecting the Factory," reminds one of the plights of Sun Zhigang's family members in trying to get media attention. The blog said that "144469160," who had filed an earlier report, was a participant in the strike and because he "is currently in trouble, I carry on his task to report." This blogger explained that they were already under police surveillance, had lost partial freedom, and consequently, were unable to file timely reports and that they were afraid to use their true names.[54] The blogger signed off by describing an imminent police crackdown against the workers.[55] Subsequently, a posting in the *China and the World* webzine, entitled "The Privatization of State-Owned Enterprises Will Eventually Lead to Revolution—To the Fourth Plenum of the Communist Party 16th Congress" and signed by "workers of 3403 Factory in Chongqing," reported that at about 3 a.m. on August 30, 2004, the Chongqing government mobilized more than 1,200 police to suppress the strike. Workers' organizers were arrested, resulting in several serious injuries.[56]

In addition to reporting on the actual struggles at 3403 Factory, workers or their organic intellectuals directly participated in the ongoing Lang Xianping debate. On August 28, 2004, the very day Lang and left-leaning economists were meeting in Beijing and "mainstream economists" were meeting in Shenzhen, *China and the World* published an article that took issue with Zhang Wenkui's just-published article in *21st-Century Business Herald*. In his article, Zhang made a sweeping claim that property rights reform ought not to be stopped because it is "based on more than 20 years of exploration and praxis by the whole nation from the top to the bottom and from all concerned interests" and that the "government's policy on SOE reform, especially property right reform, is systematic, consistent, and responsible and is based on numerous studies and investigations and repeated discussions." The workers' article, signed by "Ordinary Workers at Chongqing 3403 Factory and Chongqing Naide Industrial Corp.," challenged Zhang's claim about the popular base of the policy. It cited the deep resentment and massive resistance of millions of workers, some having been so desperate that they resorted to suicidal attacks in which they and factory owners died together. Furthermore, the letter exposed the superficial and manipulated nature of these studies and investigations, which in turn have led to problematic policy statements by party-state leaders that run against the interests of workers. What this article provided was a workers' perspective on the political economy of official knowledge production and how this knowledge is used by power-holders and translated into policy. Typically, the workers pointed out, these so-called studies and investigations were carried out in a factory preselected by local officials, under the arrangement of local officials and factory managers, and excluding workers' input. Under such circumstances, factory leaders repeated neoliberal platitudes about problems with SOEs, such as overemployment (but not counting the cronies of the factory's management), workers' predisposition to eat from the big iron rice bowl and their lack of motivation (but excluding the management's relatives and cronies who are not only unproductive laborers but also live their lavish lifestyles at factory expenses), and high production costs (but not counting their own personal expenses and their practice of selling low and purchasing high from private factories run by their family members). The article provided examples of such manipulated research and study tours by top state officials, including the fact that when Vice Premier Wu Bangguo conducted a study tour of reemployment in Chongqing, Naide was the chosen site, and during the visit, the factory bribed a worker with special benefits and only allowed this worker to report to Wu. The article concluded, "No wonder Zhu Rongji [the former premier] and Wu Bangguo speak in unison in a Xinhua report to say that 'the fundamental reason for the loss and bankruptcy of SOEs is overemployment.'" The article charged official researchers such as Zhang for making false claims and "sucking up the sweat and blood of the people on the one hand and illegally receiving bribes from those who got rich instantly from the reforms on the other." It argued that the misleading research of people like Zhang and the support of government officials are precisely what encourages private entrepreneurs to plunder state assets with such madness on such a massive scale.[57] In the context of the famous CCTV *Focus Interviews'* exposure of how Zhu Rongji was cheated by local officials in Anhui Province in one of his inspection tours regarding the country's liberalized grain market, the workers' challenge against the dominant knowledge and power regime is particularly poignant.

Through these blogs, 3403 Factory workers developed their own analysis of the reasons for the demise of SOEs, offering their critiques of the money-power-knowledge regime of the ruling classes and the undemocratic nature of both state policy making and the SOE privatization process.

Furthermore, they fought for their collective ownership of the company as an alternative to corporate privatization. They also issued urgent calls to the Internet community to communicate their struggles. Unlike Sun's civil rights case in 2003 or even Wang Binyu's death penalty case in 2005, however, there was no mainstream media response and little Internet mobilization on behalf of workers even in the midst of the "Lang Xianping Storm"—even though written material about the 3403 Factory case was distributed to journalists and economists at the August 28, 2004, Beijing seminar on "State Asset Loss and the Development of State-Owned Economy."[58] The contrast between the Sun and Wang cases on the one hand and the 3403 Factory case on the other, and the degree of media and Internet openness in these three areas—one an individual-based civil rights appeal, one a class-based appeal on workers' minimum economic right to be paid, the other a class-based appeal concerning the fundamental right of the different economic classes in controlling the means of production—is thus obvious. That is, while the media, urban intellectuals, and the Internet community were willing to mobilize themselves fully around Sun Zhigang and partially round Wang Binyu, this active "Chinese public" with symbolic power was *not in a position* to fight for the class interests of Chinese workers as potential owners of the means of production. In fact, the news media, given their own institutional setup and operational mechanisms, are often guilty of the same superficial, manipulated, and one-sided research and analysis that have contributed to a policy-formation process detrimental to the interests of workers. They are the main channels of propaganda for government officials and factory managers, and they play a major role in amplifying neoliberal reform ideas.

Moreover, contrary to the Sun Zhigang case and signifying the state's complicity in pursuing capitalistic transformation of the Chinese economy, even the mere discussion of the topic on marginal websites was censored, not to mention the difficulty of getting the topic onto web forums sponsored by major media outlets such as Xinhua's "Development Forum" and the *People's Daily's* "Strengthen the Nation Forum." The following discussion, generated between August 28 and August 31, 2004, at the "Protagonist Forum," reveals the communication conditions and politics of a politically conscious, yet marginalized web community. The discussion about the relationship between domestic working-class struggles against privatization and nationalistic struggles against foreign capital is reflective of long-standing and recurring intellectual debates on the left.

[subject post]:
Chongqing 3403 Factory: 200 million yuan worth of state assets was sold at 22 million yuan; workers demanded democratic management and production for self-salvation, bloody conflict occurred.

[follow-up posts]:

- Can the good leading comrades within the party who are said to exist in large numbers, especially those respected senior leaders, contact the workers in the factory?
- Can it be that the webmaster constantly deletes these postings, which do not violate the Constitution, in order to coordinate with the boss of Naide?
- Perhaps the Naide boss does not want to hear the news that Beijing's left-wing scholars requested that reporters from left-wing media abroad come to Chongqing to find out the situation?
- Why can't old and new leftists mobilize 10 percent of the energy they mobilized for the petition to commemorate Mao's anniversary, to support the real struggles of Chongqing workers?
- This issue revealed that after more than several decades of revolution, some people still have answers to questions such as who creates wealth and who sustains whose life upside down. How can such individuals call themselves communists and become leaders?
- Unable to post this article at Xinhua's "Development Forum."
- This article was posted at "Century Solon Forum." It attracted more than 100 hits within 10 minutes, and the webmaster quickly deleted it.
- I tried several times to put postings about concrete examples of workers' struggles on the "Strengthen the Nation Forum" and "Development Forum," but they were all quickly deleted. Worker's right to public opinion has been completely deprived under the pretense of stability!
- Oh, how painful it is that we see our worker brothers suffering in front of our eyes, but there is nothing that we can do!!!
- Several leftists at "Protagonist" gave me a good impression.
- I have even more admiration for those who have real actions.
- What are you up to? Selling us out to the government to get ahead with your own position?
- So you know the danger of undertaking real struggles.
- I propose . . . a petition to support 3403 Factory.
- I support a petition, but it is a must to step down from this forum! Otherwise, it is of no consequence.
- Agree. Groundwork must be carried out beyond this forum.
- There will soon be a petition organized in support of the railway industry [against foreign capital, especially Japanese capital involvement in the building of the high-speed railway between Beijing and Shanghai]. We cannot spread ourselves too thin.
- Without the power of the working class, it won't be possible to protect any industry. You know it all too well that many industries have been dominated by foreign capital.
- The railway industry has strategic importance and it cannot be left in the hands of foreigners.
- This is not a comparison between the entire railway industry and one factory. The "High-speed Railway" case and "3403 Factory" case should not be seen in isolation. They are connected. It is a question about the choice of the lines of struggle.

- They both involve petition and mass mobilization. What's the difference in policy line? You are too single-minded.
- No, I am not. It is a question about recognizing the principal contradiction in the domestic situation and the relationship between proletariat revolution and patriotism.
- Since they are both about petitions, can't they be carried on simultaneously?
- No. The Patriots' Alliance is organizing the petition about the "High-speed Railway."
- May this material be gathered together and be integrated with our support for Lang Xianping, so as to stop SOE property rights reform?
- I appeal to the entire working class in Chongqing with industrial workers as its core force, unite and oppose privatization.
- Isn't Zhu Yunchuan from Chongqing's *Modern Workers' Journal* [*Xiandai gongren bao*]? Can't he be of some help, providing an update report on the situation at 3403 Factory?
- The original Chongqing *Modern Workers' Journal* has been privatized. It no longer knows the specific situation at 3403 Factory, and there is no way that it can report its current situation to us.
- There are many similar situations in Chongqing, and we have become desensitized. Local media are unable to report and feel disloyal to the party if they report to foreign sources, how frustrating!
- Support 3403 Factory workers in their unified and resolute struggle against the capitalist roaders within the party, protecting their own basic rights.
- This is not a problem about the governing ability of the governing party, is a problem about the political consciousness of the governing party.
- Support workers' struggle for subsistence, oppose the selling out of fundamental interests concerning the life and death of workers!
- Bloody conflicts signify the acute degree of class struggle in certain areas, but the key problem lies in the indifference and letting-loose attitude of the local municipal party committee and the powers that be above![59]

THE PEOPLE'S DAILY, CCTV, AND SOHU: VOICE OF STATE AND VOICE OF CAPITAL

The provincial party organs were almost irrelevant in the debate. Of the 72 major articles on the debate collected by the Beelink website, only 2 articles—both by Shanghai's *Liberation Daily*—were from this sector. However, the position of two central party-state media outlets, the *People's Daily* and CCTV, is significant. Though the *People's Daily's* website actively participated in the debate, the *People's Daily* proper did not even acknowledge the existence of the debate. However, the paper played an instrumental role by publishing an authoritative September 29, 2004, article by the Research Office of the State Council Asset Management Bureau.

The article made no reference to the debate, but the fact was confirmed that the direction for the article came from the central party leadership as a formal response to the raging debate.[60] The lengthy article affirmed the direction of property rights reform in the SOE sector but called for a halt to the practice of MBOs in large SOEs and a tightening up of the state's oversight of privatization in medium and small SOEs.[61] In the typical official style of "dialectics," the article defined SOE reform as the "strategic readjustment of the distribution and structure of the state sector" and rejected it as wholesale privatization. It stated that to understand this as "only speaking of 'advance' without 'retreat' is one sided," just as it is incorrect to interpret it as "state retreats and people advance" and "state-owned economy to retreat from all competitive sectors." The article acknowledged all kinds of problems in the interpretation of the central government's policies and the de facto practice of eliminating state capital in all competitive economic sectors at the local level, even to the point of using the party's traditional method of mass mobilization to achieve privatization targets and undermining the interests of governments, creditors, and workers. However, by remaining silent throughout the debate, the *People's Daily* helped to contain the debate within the less official "new mainstream" discourse, while maintaining its own authority as the official "mainstream" paper that follows the "no debate" policy.

In contrast, CCTV's role in the debate was a subject of controversy, and this has significant implications for understanding communication politics in China. Although CCTV programs such as *Focus Interviews* claim to address issues of public concern and promote social justice, it did not take a role in the Lang Xianping debate in 2004, just as it took a backseat in the Sun Zhigang case in 2003. Still, at the end of 2003, CCTV, trying to sustain itself as the most far-reaching hegemonic voice in Chinese society, positioned itself on the side of popular opinion by listing the abolishment of the detention regulation as the top news story of the year. In 2004, however, CCTV's annual list of China's Top 10 Economic Figures—individuals who had made a major impact on China's economic life—excluded Lang Xianping. Lang was not even among the qualifying candidates determined by a group of "experts," mainly economists selected by CCTV. This was particularly odd in the minds of many media and Internet commentators, especially since CCTV had modified its previous selection criteria to foreground the values of "Innovation, Responsibility, and Wholesomeness" and declared that it privileged events over personalities in its 2004 selection. If this was the case, as one print media commentator put it, "what other event had a more profound social impact than this great debate in 2004?"[62]

As one journalist noted, people were waiting for an official take on the debate, and CCTV's 2004 annual economic figures award was seen as such a forum. The process apparently has some popular basis, because television audiences and Internet users can put forward initial nominations. Lang received popular nomination, but he failed to pass the test of the CCTV's nomination committee, which consists of more than 100 "well-known economists, former award winners, scholars from domestic and international economics research institutes, deans of well-known business schools, the chief economic advisers of foreign agencies in China, as well as media elites."[63] Tellingly, Liu Donghua, a nomination committee member and publisher of the *Chinese Entrepreneurs* journal, stated,

> It is perfectly normal for Lang Xianping not to be selected. A great many panelists believed that he was not qualified at all. . . . I believe what Lang Xianping created were basically noises, noises in the economic life of 2004, and moreover, are counterrevolutionary to reform. . . . CCTV's annual selection got rid of some noises, got rid of some individuals who are boisterous. [Let's] quickly flip over noises that do not have any value.[64]

Reflecting the diverging views of the Chinese media, Lang was selected by the *Nanfang People Weekly* (*Nanfang renwu zhoukan*) as the Person of the Year for 2004 and by the *Southern Wind* (*Nanfeng chuang*) magazine as the winner of its annual personality award for "public interest." The *Nanfang Weekend* justified Lang's selection not only because he provoked an intense debate about the SOE property rights reform, but also because the debate went beyond this topic and led to "the rethinking of the orientations of the reform."[65] The *Nanfang People Weekly*, a sister publication of the *Nanfang Weekend*, elaborated further:

> China's economic stage in 2004 belongs to Lang Xianping; Lang Xianping is indisputably China's most influential figure in 2004. . . . [H]e had the most influence. . . . [H]e dared to challenge authority. He had the widest popular support. He caused the broadest controversy, which in itself influenced China's progress. . . . Lang's probe led us to give more thought to our ongoing reform.[66]

CCTV's failure to select Lang as an economic figure of influence became the subject of criticism by print media and Internet commentators. For some, this underscored the fact that CCTV and the mainstream economists it relies upon as its panelists are constituent components of crony capitalism. Because Lang was seen as standing for the interests of small and medium-sized investors and laid-off workers, his exclusion was perceived as an insult to the value of social justice: "Lang Xianping's views have deep roots in popular opinion. Countless ordinary investors and laid-off workers are behind him. . . . What is being denied is not just fairness for Lang Xianping, but also discursive rights of the grassroots strata."[67] For Zhang Tianwei, the director of the *Beijing Youth Daily's* commentary department, CCTV's failure to acknowledge Lang is a return to the "no debate" policy. Rather than condemning CCTV, however, Zhang tried to explicate the rationality of this policy on behalf of neoliberal economists and their vision of China's reform:

> Although it is increasingly difficult to cover up the long-standing contradictions of Chinese social development, "to cover up or not to cover up" remains a difficult choice. Mainstream economists are the hard-core supporters of the "to cover up" school. . . . [T]hey insist on their original views even in the context of today's social reality. . . . They believe that although this has a price . . . as long as this path is surmounted, at the end is a wonderful order: clearly delineated property rights, fair exchange, legal justice, and a harmonious society. The premise of "surmounting," however, is that those who are doomed to be sacrificed as the "price" during the process better be "spent" without knowing it. In the calculation of mainstream economists, this is the lowest cost option for China to march toward its glorious future. . . . Therefore, it is unfair for many people to criticize mainstream economists for speaking on behalf of the propertied class or for their own self-interests. If he had not believed that he had a grand principle, Zhang Weiying could not have braved the tide. . . . [W]e are used to solving problems behind doors and then opening the door to announce miracles. The rejection of Lang Xianping means that not only have we not sorted out the "to cover up or not cover up" dilemma, but also the possibility that even the debate about whether "to cover up or not to cover up" will be covered up.[68]

This is a significant statement. Its contrast with the *Nanfang People Weekly*'s justification for choosing Lang as its Person of the Year is revealing of the conflicting visions of China's reform. Zhang Tianwei's explication of the neoliberal logic and its vision of a perfect market society at the end of a reform process in which the interests of certain groups are to be sacrificed without discussion, let alone protestation, and the attribution of a grand nationalistic objective (China's glorious future) beyond the personal interests of the Zhang Weiyings and the propertied class they speak for are reflective of a right-wing nationalistic and market authoritarian perspective in which the interests of the low social classes are to be sacrificed in the name of a "greater national rationality" (*minzu dayi*). The implications of this perspective for communication politics are clear: in order to realize China's national glory and to achieve the market society utopia, it is better not to have any public debate, including any debate about the necessity of such a debate itself.

CCTV's decision not to acknowledge Lang and comments like Zhang Tianwei's assume particular significance in light of neoliberal economists' concerted media assault against Lang Xianping after he and his supporters put them on the defensive at the initial stage of the debate. In his keynote speech entitled "Creating a Favorable Media Environment for the

Development of Private Businesses" at the China entrepreneur forum in Shenzhen on August 28, 2004, Zhang Weiying made a distinction between the political environment and the public opinion environment for private entrepreneurs. He claimed that while the political environment for private capitalists had progressively improved, "the public opinion environment has reached the worst point since 1992" for private entrepreneurs. In Zhang's view, "the media, in collaboration with professors and scholars, under the banner of upholding academic freedom and protecting state assets and the interests of small investors, are sparing no effort in negating SOE reform and property rights reform of the past 10 years."[69] Zhang called upon private entrepreneurs to pay special attention to public opinion in the Internet age because

> The Internet era is one in which information can be easily biased, and it is an era in which the opinions of a minority can be taken as that of the majority, and it is an era when many people can speak without having to take responsibility. Therefore, we must pay particular attention to this. We should not underestimate the detrimental impact of public opinion for the survival and development of Chinese enterprises. . . . [E]ven more serious, in our country, public opinion in society can easily become political pressure force, and the political environment itself.[70]

Zhang blamed the media for lacking a core value system and for stirring up controversies and misleading the public. He called upon the media to think "about their own responsibility and credibility," to "become mature," and to stay out of what he considers "academic" debates. He warned against the "abuse of media freedom" if Chinese journalists failed the urgent task of improving their qualifications.[71] Zhang even resorted to a nationalistic appeal: "If our society and our media are constantly demonizing Chinese entrepreneurs, I think the possibility of foreign companies dominating the Chinese economy will significantly increase."[72]

Whether coordinated or not, as soon as the debate took off, there was clearly a concerted effort on the part of private entrepreneurs and their academic supporters to take the intellectual offensive to steer public opinion and to make the media "responsible" to them. The editorial position of Sohu and the role of its proprietor are particularly illustrative here. Sohu had appointed Lang Xianping as its chief financial commentator in 2004 because of his outspokenness and his popularity with medium-sized and small stock investors. Lang was also a panelist for Sohu's Top 10 News Stories in 2004. Although the website was at the forefront in promoting the debate from the very beginning, it quickly attempted to narrow the scope of the debate with its selection of the debate's "relevant" articles and with its editorial call for "efficiency" in the debate. By early 2005, the website had become rather blunt in its bias toward the propertied class. Lang was not reappointed as its chief financial commentator in 2005. Moreover, Sohu CEO Zhang Chaoyang's dislike of Lang's perspective was directly responsible for the burst of an "anti-Lang storm" in Sohu's "Annual Summit Forum" on January 5, 2005.[73] Lang was excluded from the forum, where his opponents, as well as many of China's richest private capitalists, launched a counterattack. More significantly, they did so without even wanting to give Lang's name any more publicity.[74] One famous capitalist declared, "I completely disagree with the conclusion of a certain scholar last year. I firmly believe 'state retreats and people advance' is a must in competitive industries!" Afterward, leading capitalists spoke out one after another, with Zhang Weiying, who had declared previously that he did not even want to mention the debate anymore "because it upsets one's stomach,"[75] repeating his plea for society to treat private entrepreneurs well and provide further incentives for their wealth accumulation. One media commentator concluded that Sohu's wholesale one-sided reversal of the debate was truly unprecedented for "an Internet medium of authority and neutrality."[76]

FROM THE "LANG XIANPING STORM" TO THE "THIRD DEBATE ON REFORM"

Although Lang lost his battle at Sohu, he appeared, at least for a moment, to have won his war in contesting neoliberal hegemony in Chinese economics. As the "Lang Xianping Storm" gathered force largely from the bottom up, the central leadership called for vigilance against neoliberalism as a hostile ideology force, while reaffirming the strategy of "doing a good job in gatekeeping and maintaining the appropriate degree of intensity" in propaganda control.[77] This set the political and ideological context for the intensification of what the "new mainstream" Chinese media referred to as the "third debate on reform," a debate that began with the outbreak of the "Lang Xianping Storm" in August 2004, although the timing of its conclusion remains a matter of controversy, as I will discuss shortly in this chapter and in more detail in the conclusion. The year 2005, which was initially set to be a "year of reform" with deepened market reforms and "new breakthroughs in some key areas," was turned into a "year of revisiting the reform," with one headline after another making discursive and realpolitik confrontations.[78]

On March 24, 2005, the venerable 82-year-old economist Liu Guoguang, a former vice president of the Chinese Academy of Social Sciences whose advocacy of market reforms earned him the nickname "Market Liu" as early as 1979, shocked China's economics circles with his concern for the future of socialism in China. In his speech accepting an inaugural "Prize in Chinese Economics," Liu argued that although "socialist market economy" should be a singular concept, he was worried that more emphasis had been put on "market economy" than on "socialism" and that some people wanted to replace Marxist economics with mainstream Western market economics.[79] On July 15, 2005, Liu further provoked China's economics field by publishing a long critique of the dominance of mainstream Western economics in research and teaching in the leftist website Utopia. The article not only gained wide circulation and positive responses on the web, but also led to supportive articles on central party publications such as the *Guangming Daily* and *Research on Economics*, triggering the "Liu Guoguang Storm" in Chinese macroeconomic theory.[80]

Two further developments added fuel to the fire of "revisiting" the market reforms: on July 28, 2005, the State Council Research Development Center issued a report on health care reform, criticizing its market-oriented trajectory and declaring it "basically a failure." On July 29, 2005, Gu Chujun and two business associates were arrested on charges of misappropriating state funds, lending credence to Lang Xianping's charge against Gu and boosting the critique of the negative consequences of market reforms in health care, education, housing, and other areas.[81]

Most dramatically, signifying resistance against the consolidation of capitalistic social relations in the legal system and "the resurgent influence of a small but vocal group of socialist-leaning scholars and policy advisers,"[82] an August 12, 2005, online petition letter by "old leftist" Peking University law professor Gong Xiantian forced the party-state to make further revisions to the Property Rights Law that was expected to be rubber-stamped by the NPC in March 2006. This law, viewed by market reformers and the rising capitalist class as instrumental in consolidating a market transition and securing private property rights, had been in the making since the early 1990s and had gone through seven revisions. On July 1, 2005, the Xinhua News Agency released a draft for society-wide consultation, opening up the space for Gong's unexpected intervention. Gong accused the legal experts who authored the draft of "copying capitalist civil law like slaves," offering equal protection to "a rich man's car and a beggar's stick," and violating the Chinese Constitution because it did not reaffirm that "socialist property is inviolable."[83] Although the law's drafters and proponents were outraged, accusing Gong of attempting to "turn back the wheel of history," of being "ignorant" and "absurd,"[84] even the *New York Times* observed, "Those who dismissed his attack as a throwback to an earlier era underestimated the continued appeal of socialist ideas in a country where glaring disparities between rich and poor, rampant corruption, labor abuses and land seizures offer daily reminders of how far China has strayed from its official ideology."[85] Like the Wang Binyu case, the controversy brought into sharp focus a fundamental question about the nature of law, or "the issue of whose law," which is a profound democratic parameter that goes beyond the liberal discourse on legality and "the rule of law."[86] Perhaps reflective of the central leadership's ambivalence and caution, Gong was invited to speak to NPC leaders and on September 26, 2005, NPC chairman Wu Bangguo set three principles for the law's further revision: maintaining a "correct political orientation," grounding in Chinese reality and not simply imitating the West, and insisting upon public ownership as the economic basis of Chinese socialism.[87]

As can be seen from the "Lang Xianping Storm" at the onset, proponents of further market reforms have been aggressively organizing their communicative counteroffensive in an attempt to rein in a mobilized oppositional public opinion that threatened to put pressure on the central leadership to radically reorient the reform process. The business press played a leading role and the "cast" of opinion leaders shifted quickly from economists and entrepreneurs to prominent members of the political and ideological elite. On October 3, 2005, the *Economic Observer* published an interview with Gao Shangquan, director of the State Council–affiliated Research Society for the Reform of China's Economic System. Like Zhang Weiying, Gao was "deeply disturbed by the direction of public opinion" and was determined to shape it in his own direction. Gao denied a neoliberal influence on China's economic reforms, arguing that the debate over neoliberalism should be merely an academic exercise and warning against the derailing of the reform process by the critique of neoliberalism.[88] On November 25, 2005, *Finance (Caijing)* magazine published interviews with Gao, economists Wu Jinglian and Xu Xiaonian, and legal scholar Jiang Ping under the provocative title "Shooting at the Rich Will Result in Very Grave Social Consequences," advocating further market reforms.[89] On January 25, 2006, *Finance* escalated the stakes by publishing a commentary entitled "Reform Is Unshakable" under the highly symbolic name of Huang Puping—the very same pen name used by former *Liberation Daily* editorialist Zhou Ruijin in late 1991 and early 1992 in a series of famous editorials that served as Deng's mouthpiece in calling for accelerated market reforms and a closure to the capitalist versus socialist debate.[90]

Behind the public media, and revealing that powerful elite intellectuals were taking their arguments against opposition to further market reforms to the highest level of party-state power and in a clear attempt to influence the judgment of the central leadership on the nature of the debate, Liu Ji, a former vice president of the Chinese Academy of Social Sciences and an adviser to former party general secretary Jiang Zemin, had a talk with "a high level central leader" and "upon the encouragement of this leader," "Liu wrote up an article of more than 6,000 words and placed it on the desks of central leaders through a special channel."[91] In the article,

Liu accused Lang Xianping of "fundamentally negating SOE reform," characterized ongoing popular criticisms of the reform as "reactionary ideological trends" that aimed to oppose Deng's and Jiang's theories, and invoked the specter of the Cultural Revolution to discredit these criticisms. Liu further discredited the critique by framing it as the result of foreign ideological penetration and strangely, as "the coalescing between domestic leftists and overseas right-wing forces."[92] Clearly, elite intellectuals such as Liu were escalating the political stakes of the debate by setting up an opposition between any new leadership endorsement of Lang Xianping and the critique of the reforms, and a repudiation of the Deng and Jiang era and a return to the Cultural Revolution. And once again, the Cultural Revolution as the most powerful negative political trope was called upon to delegitimate criticisms of market reforms.

However, underscoring the level of elite intellectual division and the potential role of the Internet in undermining elite communication, Gao Shangquan invited members of the intellectual and policy elites to a resort in Beijing's West Hill on March 4, 2006, for a secret forum to assess obstacles to further market reforms and to advise the leadership on the next steps—suggestions included splitting the Communist Party to privatizing farming lands—and leftists upset the rules of elite politics by posting the leaked transcripts of the whole forum on the Internet.[93]

By then, the central leadership seemed to have made up its mind as to which side of the debate it supported, and the party-state's media control regime had been reined in. Lang Xianping, together with the three leftist websites discussed in chapter 1, became a casualty of this regime, as it tried to suppress further public controversies and prepare the "correct" public opinion environment for the annual NPC and NPPCC meetings. Lang last appeared as the host of a popular business television talk show in the Shanghai-based China Business Network on March 3, 2006, two days before the opening of NPC meeting in Beijing. Although the apparent reason for his removal was that he did not qualify for a certificate for TV and radio hosts, he had hosted the program for some time, and the authorities were clearly concerned that "his words intensified social conflicts."[94] Nevertheless, the March 2006 NPC meeting, in the words of a *New York Times* report, was "consumed with an ideological debate over socialism and capitalism that many assumed had been buried by China's long streak of fast economic growth."[95]

In an attempt to put an end to the debate and with pronouncements that clearly appeased and signaled its alliance with the dominant political, economic, and intellectual elites, Hu Jintao and Wen Jiabao, in their respective remarks made on March 6 and March 14, 2006, at the NPC meeting, reaffirmed the new leadership's determination to "deepen reform and expand openness, and unswervingly adhere to the reform direction."[96] Subsequently, in a March 16, 2006, article, the *Nanfang Week-end* declared the closure of the "third debate on reform," claiming victory for the market reform agenda, while marginalizing reform critics by sin-gling out extreme leftists and characterizing them as the supporters of the "Gang of Four."[97] Other influential media outlets followed the lead and quickly rushed to publish "retrospective" articles and interviews with neo-liberal reformers such as Zhou Ruijin about "the beginning and end" of the "third debate."[98] By then, Gong Xiantian was fighting a losing battle over the politics of his representation by the influential *Nanfang Weekend*.[99] Gong had been warned of potentially hostile media treatment, but in the end, he could not resist being interviewed by the *Nanfang Weekend*, which portrayed Gong as a poor, isolated, and disruptive extremist, as well as an unaccomplished academic.[100] Instead of challenging the paper for its po-tential political bias, Gong ended up feeding into the rising "new" main-stream media outlets' own legitimating regime of professionalism by positing the question "Where Have *Nanfang Weekend* Journalist's Profes-sional Ethics Gone?"[101]

On June 4, 2006, as a further sign of the leadership's determination to discourage the widening of the debate, the Xinhua News Agency released an editorial to be published in the June 5 issue of the *People's Daily*. Signed by Zhong Xuanli—the pen name for the Central Propaganda Department Theoretical Bureau, the editorial, entitled "Unswervingly Adhering to the Reform Direction," elaborated upon the leadership's reaffirmation of the achievements of 28 years of reform and openness and its intention to stay with the path of building a "socialist market economy," while further pro-moting the basic role of the market in resource allocation on the one hand and insisting on the reform's socialist direction on the other. At the same time, to appease the left while reminding the rightists that the current leadership's reaffirmation of the socialist direction was not new, the edi-torial cited Jiang Zemin as saying that the term "socialist" is not an un-necessary add-on, but what "defines the nature of our market econ-omy."[102] That this editorial was released on the politically sensitive date of the June 4 Tiananmen repression, which inaugurated the post-1989 mar-ket reforms and the Deng-Jiang regime of "neoliberalism with Chinese characteristics," was significant.

Nevertheless, China remains a place where "the trees want to be quiet but the winds won't stop," as Ma Guochuan, a journalist who chronicled the milestones of the "third debate," puts it. In particular, Ma noted left-ist calls at the launching of a book about the "Liu Guoguang Storm" on July 1, 2006—the anniversary date of the party's founding—for "a broad debate on insisting on Marxist guidance and the socialist direction of the reform"; arguments about "the existence of class struggle" in the political, economic, and ideological spheres; and reaffirmations about "the working-class nature" of the party, and how, from Ma's perspective, "the lack of signs of closure to the debate on reform have made some people of intelligence deeply worried."[103] To Ma, that such a call was issued after the June 5, 2006, *People's Daily* editorial was especially unsettling. As I will discuss in the conclusion, more intense ideological confrontations were in the making in the run-up to the 17th Party Congress in October 2007.

Notwithstanding the leadership's affirmation of the "reform direction"—an ambivalent term that connotes both "the direction of market-oriented reform" and "the socialist direction of the reform"—the substance of the process continues to face challenge, just as faction struggles within the ruling elite and the display of the central leadership's determination to root out corruption remain crucial. By September 25, 2006, smaller media storms had been upstaged by a major political storm. In a development that was widely seen as the continuation of the succession struggles between the Hu Jintao and Jiang Zemin leaderships, the central party-state shook up Shanghai's political establishment by dismissing Chen Liangyu from Shanghai's top party-state positions and the Politburo on charges pertaining to his collusion with a real estate developer and involvement in the misuse of Shanghai's huge pension fund to make illegal loans and investment in real estate and other infrastructure deals.[104] Chen, a Jiang protégé and the beneficiary of Jiang's political maneuvers to strengthen the loyalty of his Shanghai power base before he transferred central leadership power to Hu in late 2002, was seen as politically at odds with the Hu Jintao leadership and an obstacle to its attempt to pursue macroeconomic controls.

Demonstrating how much the central leadership was concerned not only with the threats posed by Chen Liangyu and the excesses of his crony capitalism on its grip on power, but also with the necessity of "unifying thoughts" before the NPC and NPPCC meetings in March 2007, or conversely, perhaps indicative of the potential lack of ideological unity at the very top, Premier Wen Jiabao took the unusual step of publishing a signed article, "Our Historical Tasks at the Primary Stage of Socialism and Several Issues Concerning China's Foreign Policy," on February 26, 2007. Wen defines the mission of "consolidating and developing socialism" in terms of balancing the task to "liberate and develop the productive forces" with the task to "achieve social fairness and justice." He repeats the party-state's "no democracy, no socialism" slogan and acknowledges that China has yet to accomplish its own democratic project, arguing that "we see a high degree of democracy and well-developed legal system as the inherent requirement of socialism and a key important feature of a mature socialist system." Addressing rising nationalistic ambitions and balancing the implicit expression of China's big power ambition in CCTV's *The Rise of Great Powers* series, Wen reiterates that "we will not seek a leadership role in the international arena" while reaffirming that "China opposes hegemonism and power politics."[105]

Wen's article provided the basis for the orchestration of party-state hegemony through the NPC and NPPCC meetings by the media, old and new mainstream outlets alike. On March 16, 2007, following heightened rhetoric on redistributive politics and pronouncements to uphold equity and social justice and pursue sustainable development throughout the two-week NPC and NPPCC meetings, the NPC passed a revised Property Right Law without any debate.[106] Although provisions were made to protect state, collective, as well as private property, the passage of this law was a clear victory for the market reform agenda, marking a major step toward the legitimation and consolidation of the economic power of China's rising propertied class under the Hu Jintao leadership. The low-key official media treatment of the law's passage underscores a deliberate propaganda strategy of not provoking the law's opponents.

CONCLUSION

The debate on SOE reform between late 2004 and early 2005 and its aftermath, like cases in the previous chapter, provided an unprecedented opportunity to look into the structure, dynamics, and substance of intellectual, media, and Internet discourses, as well as the intricate and explosive politics of elite and popular communication in China. First, the debate revealed the extent of neoliberal hegemony in Chinese economics and the power of elite economists in shaping China's transformation. Although this power did not emerge independently, and its ascendancy was secured by a politically imposed "no debate" policy, the operation of this regime of expert knowledge, bureaucratic power, and economic capital challenges any one-sided emphasis on the state's repression of liberal humanistic intellectuals in discussing Chinese communication politics. The economic, social, and intellectual spheres are equally important sites of power.

Second, the debate reveals a more dynamic and conflictual, rather than a static and monolithic, Chinese party-state. Real struggles are being fought both within and through the party-state over concrete public policies, different class interests, and ultimately, the fundamental directions of China's transformation. Although the reform-era Chinese party-state is structured in favor of the interests of the ruling political class and its incorporated business and intellectual allies, this does not mean that there are no differences in policy orientations within the ruling political class. The protracted succession struggle between the Jiang Zemin and Hu Jintao leaderships accentuated potential differences. More importantly, China's subordinate social groups continue to fight out their interests through the state and make political, moral, and redistributive claims on it. In turn, these struggles feed into existing divisions within the state itself and inflect the parameters of elite power struggles. In order to stay in power, the leadership must either step up repression or force the ruling political class and the ascending economic class to make the necessary compromises, or combine both strategies.[107]

Although the central leadership remained silent on the debate throughout 2004 and 2005, the debate took place within the context of the Hu Jintao leadership's theoretical initiative of critically assessing neoliberalism as the ideology of "internationalizing monopoly capitalism" and its attempt to not only acquire a "sober" understanding of it, but also to "guard against" it—as a November 9, 2004, *Guangming Daily* article put it. At a more concrete policy level, officials at the State Assets Management Bureau were paying close attention to different voices in the debate.[108] As the debate took off, this agency, which, like other government departments, has seen its policy objectives influenced by neoliberalism and its proclaimed mandate to safeguard the interest of "the people" as an agency of the government of the "People's" Republic undermined by corruption and bureaucratic self-interest, undertook a series of regulatory and administrative initiatives to tighten up its supervision of the privatization process. Although a bureau official denied that these actions were prompted by the debate,[109] the debate had clearly created a favorable media environment for these policy moves. Significantly, in April 2005, the State Assets Management Bureau and the Ministry of Finance jointly issued a regulation explicitly prohibiting the privatization of large SOEs and state shares in state-controlled shareholding companies through MBO. Although this policy did not rule out other SOE privatization schemes, it at least halted the most predatory form.

Third, that Lang Xianping was able to pose a challenge against the dominance of mainstream economists and provide an opportunity for long-marginalized voices in the domestic economic and social spheres in Chinese public communication is a testimony to the multifaceted and contradictory nature of media commercialization and globalization. Although the Hu Jintao leadership had instructed elite intellectual circles to critically assess neoliberalism, these criticisms, made by official theoreticians in traditional official organs such as the *Guangming Daily*, did not have any popular reach and resonance. Whether the central leadership likes it or not, commercialized media outlets and the Internet—the very products of the Chinese communication system's neoliberal-oriented developments since the 1990s—helped to "ground" the critique of neoliberalism in China and trigger a broad public debate on reform. Similarly, just as the global reintegration of the Chinese communication system has generated nationalistic sentiments, China's neoliberals cannot expect the inflow of foreign capital and neoliberal ideas without encountering their Western-trained critics. Although marginalized domestic leftist economists not only considered the debate too little and too late, but also viewed Lang's success in stirring up the controversy as a sign of continuing American ideological influence, they clearly had nothing to gain by ignoring Lang.[110] They had no choice but to welcome and seize the discursive space opened up from the above and opportunely grabbed by Lang. Yet just as Gong Xiantian ended up being marginalized by *Nanfang Weekend*, leftists' voices, apart from having to face party-state censorship, are at the mercy of market-oriented media and capitalist-controlled commercial websites. Lang's involvement is also contradictory. For example, while his star status and his relative independence from vested domestic political economic interests allowed him to challenge China's mainstream economists, his celebrity and his transnational linkages also provided opportunities for his intellectual opponents to discredit him, although the overwhelming popular resonance of his arguments made such attempts not only futile but also counterproductive in many ways.

Fourth, the debate reveals the coexistence of a multiplicity of "public spheres" in "socialism with Chinese characteristics." These "public spheres," each with their own media outlets, constitute an unevenly structured complex of sometimes overlapping, sometimes antagonistic, discursive fields. Although the "old mainstream" party organs set the broad ideological boundaries of the debate—with the *Guangming Daily* signaling the central leadership's opening toward a critique of neoliberalism on the one hand and CCTV's refusal to acknowledge Lang Xianping's role in triggering the debate on the other—the most influential part of this cacophony of contending "public spheres" is made up of "new mainstream" commercial urban dailies and popular websites. These outlets, attracted by Lang's sensational messages and his transnational credentials, initiated and led the debate by articulating a nascent notion of "public interest" and arguing for fairness, justice, transparency, and the value of public participation as an essential component of democratic decision making. Such principles are either invoked as ideals that allow the lower social classes (or at least the urban working class) to bargain for a better deal in China's new social order or, more pragmatically, as a form of social compromise on the part of middle-class reformers who are fearful of another radical social revolution.

This "public sphere" has an ambivalent relationship with the party-state. On the one hand, it directly and indirectly draws clues from statist discourses, including the central leadership's reform populist rhetoric and its expressed wariness toward neoliberalism. On the other hand, it continues to operate under the shadow of state censorship and is sometimes in tension with it. Furthermore, because it is materially based on advertising financing of the media and capitalist investment in the Internet, it operates under the disciplining mechanisms of the market and the containment attempts of the propertied class and their organic intellectuals. We have already seen the *NMN*'s appeal to "journalistic professionalism" and Sohu's call for "social responsibility" on the part of the media and Internet gatekeepers themselves. Internet capitalist Zhang Chaoyang's more direct influence on Sohu and Zhang Weiying's blunt calls for the media to guard against the potential abuse of freedom are clear signs of an emerging capitalist instrumentalism in defense of a neoliberal agenda. Between the twin objectives of challenging authoritarian state power from above and containing popular threats from below—from working-class resistance to privatization to citizen claims to access education, health care, and other public goods—social containment has come to the fore and assumed increasing urgency in the constitution of the Chinese "bourgeois public sphere." The contours of this debate, as in the Wang Binyu case, confirm such an assessment. As Lang Xianping won over Gu Chujun, and "the netizens appeared to have defeated the academic elites" in the debate, the Zhang Weiyings were quick to "leave aside the 'Gu-Lang debate'" and turn to attend the more urgent task of containing popular discontent and rein in a "public opinion environment" that threatened to turn against the process of continuing capitalistic development.[111]

In structural terms, this nascent Chinese "bourgeois public sphere" subordinates itself to and partially intersects with a more traditional "party-state media sphere" anchored in the *People's Daily*, the *Guangming Daily*, and CCTV, while dominating and partially intersecting with various old and new special interest media outlets. Within the "party-state media sphere," the *People's Daily* and the *Guangming Daily* speak the official position of the party-state, while CCTV, perhaps because of its entrenched commercialism, represents the realpolitik discursive position of the alliance of bureaucratic power, business power, mainstream economists, and commercialized state media outlets themselves. At the same time, one witnesses a complete asymmetrical balance of media power among different social groups and different intellectual positions. Influential business journals explicitly argued for the interests of China's rising propertied class and further capitalistic development. The role of *Finance* and the *Economic Observer* as the "mouthpieces" of powerful pro-market voices in the "third debate" was particularly obvious. The voices of left-leaning intellectuals and state enterprise workers, who had no representation in the official working-class organ, the *Workers' Daily*, were largely relegated to marginal websites. Women, farmers, and migrant workers, who each make up a numerical majority in Chinese society, had no voice whatsoever in the debate.

Finally, the debate revealed a profound dilemma about the further transformation of the Chinese political economy. The critiques targeted neoliberal economists, SOE managers, and private capitalists. Thanks to the *People's Daily* website, local officials who colluded with capitalists to advance their own interests were also brought into the picture. The central party-state and its policies, however, were excluded from critical scrutiny. In a sense, neoliberals are correct in pointing out that Lang, by defending state ownership, played into the hands of the state, which will not let go of major SOEs as an economic power base. Notwithstanding the recurring affirmation by Lang and his supporters that the SOEs belong to the Chinese people, unaccountable bureaucratic control of state capital remains a fundamental problem of the state socialist legacy and the rationale for the neoliberal solution of privatization and its vision of a privately owned and market-regulated capitalist economy. Instead of privatizing the means of production, there is the alternative of democratizing the state, reimagining and remaking the economy in nonstate socialist and noncapitalist forms, and at the enterprise level, promoting workers' ownership and democratic management—as workers at 3403 Factory had attempted. These more radical solutions, however, were beyond the discursive boundaries of the media and Internet debate.

Still, the debate is significant in reinserting the stakes of China's subordinate social classes into the reform process. Through the debate, China's popular media and the Internet community were not only able to reclaim the economic field and reinject a moral dimension into an emerging market society, but also to raise fundamental questions about the future of Chinese socialism. Moreover, as I have demonstrated, intern reporters at popular urban dailies, left-leaning intellectuals both within and outside state academic institutions, and netizens were at the frontlines of challenging "neoliberalism with Chinese characteristics." Because these social forces are part of China's urban "middle social strata" or "middle class" and are not in the ranks of the vast majority of Chinese workers and farmers they claim to speak for, this revealed a disturbing truth for China's reconstituted dominant social bloc of party-state officials, capitalists, their intellectual supporters, as well as the "silent majority" of the well-off, urban "middle class": the complicity of the entire "middle class" in supporting further capitalistic developments cannot be taken for granted. Interestingly, contrary to Zhang Weiying, who believed that the debate reflected a deep problem in Chinese society—that the public is irrational and "is still easily gullible"[112]—Lang Xianping was impressed with the quality of the Internet discussion, acknowledging how the public's participation moderated his elitism:

From this discussion, I have come to realize that the direction of a society's public opinion is to be determined by the public in the end, rather than the so-called experts and scholars. I have never had such a high opinion toward the society's public. I was profoundly touched by the dynamism of the public, their appeal against social injustice, and their resistance against the repression of coercive power.[113]

NOTES

1. Qin Hui, *"Lang Xianping xuanfeng: You 'anli' er 'wenti' er 'zhuyi'"* (The Lang Xianping Storm: From "Case Studies" to "Problems" to "isms"), *Nanfang zhoumo*, 9 Sept. 2004, www.dushu.net/bbs2/dispbbs.asp?boardID=8&ID=2615&page=1 (accessed 22 Jun. 2006).

2. The SOEs' restructuring processes are complicated and there are enormous constraints on any attempt at straightforward privatization. For detailed discussions, see Jean C. Oi, "Patterns of Corporate Restructuring in China: Political Constraints on Privatization," *China Journal* 53 (Jan. 2005): 115–136; Ross Garnaut Ligang Song and Yang Yao, "Impact and Significance of State-Owned Enterprise Restructuring in China," *China Journal* 55 (Jan. 2006): 35–63.

3. As the *People's Daily* claimed, from 1998 to 2003, the number of state-owned enterprises reduced from 238,000 to 150,000, or a decrease of 40 percent, but profits increased from 21.37 billion yuan to 495.12 billion yuan, or a 23-fold increase. *Guowuyuan Guoyou Zichan Jiandu Guanli Weiyuanhui Yanjiushi* (Research Office of the State Capital Supervision and Management Committee of the State Council), *"Jianchi guoqi gaige fangxiang, guifan tuijin guoqi gaizhi"* (Adhere to the Direction of SOE Reform, Regularize and Push Forward the System Transformation of SOEs), *People's Daily*, 29 Sept. 2004, www.chinanews.com.cn/news/2004/2004-09-29/26489316.shtml (accessed 15 Apr. 2005).

4. Qin, *"Lang Xianping xuanfeng."*

5. Li Ruiying, *"Jingti xinziyouzhuyi dui woguo de yingxiang"* (Beware of the Influence of Neoliberalism in Our Country), bjb-van.cas.cn/html/Dir/2004/06/14/0314.htm.

6. Li, *"Jingti xinziyouzhuyi dui woguo de yingxiang."*

7. One journalist, for example, did not fail to notice that Lang's office was decorated with four "All Star Paper" certificates and that two of his papers were among "the 28 most important papers of the world on corporate governance." Ren Tian, *"Lang Xianping: Wode yijian buneng chengwei zhuliu nashi guojia de bei'ai"* (It Will Be a Sad Thing for the Country If My Opinion Cannot Become the Mainstream), *Nanfang renwu zhoukan*, 23 Sept. 2004, www.blogchina.com/new/display/45631.html (accessed 26 May 2005).

8. *"Lang Xianping qiwen Gu Chujun baoguang Greencoool binggou shenhua"* (Lang Xianping's Seven Questions for Gu Chujun), 16 Aug. 2004, business.sohu.com/20040816/n221548398.shtml (accessed 24 Apr. 2005).

9. Zhang Tian, *"Tiaochu Lang Xianping yu Gu Chujun zhi zheng"* (Move beyond the Debate between Lang Xiaoping and Gu Chujun), *Beijing qingnian bao*, 18 Aug. 2004, www.china.org.cn/chinese/OP-c/638602.htm (accessed 8 Jun. 2005).

10. Pei Ying, *"Lang Xianping: Wo weiyi de yihan shi gujun fenzhan"* (Lang Xianping: My Only Regret is Fighting Alone), *Beijing chenbao*, 18 Aug. 2004, www.beelink.com/20040818/1656717.shtml (accessed 5 May 2005).

11. Wang Han, *"Gu Lang gong'an fansi: Jingji xuejie weihe jitishiyu?"* (Rethinking the Gu-Lang Controversy: Why Is the Economist Circle Collectively Speechless?), *Beijing chenbao*, 20 Aug. 2004, finance.sina.com.cn/financecomment/20040820/0527962197.shtml (accessed 7 Jun. 2005).

12. It is a common strategy for media to use an intern to write a critical piece in China, as this minimizes the political risk for regular staff.

13. Zhong Weizhi, *"2005 zhongguo gaige jiaofeng lu"* (A Memo on the Debates about Reform in 2005), business.sohu.com/20051010/n240506803.shtml (accessed 29 Apr. 2007).

14. Wang Han, *"Beijing jingjixuejie huiying 'Lang-Gu gong'an,' Zhao Xiao huida 'shiyushuo'"* (Beijing Economic Circles Respond to the Lang-Gu Controversy: Zhao Xiao Responds to "Loss of Speech"), *Beijing chenbao*, 23 Aug. 2004, business.sohu.com/20040823/n221673872.shtml (accessed 7 Jun. 2005).

15. *"Zhang Weiying huiying Lang Xianping: Shandai weishehui zhouchu gongxian de ren"* (Zhang Weiying Responds to Lang Xianping: Treat Well Those Who Have Made Contributions to Society), *Jingji guancha bao*, 28 Aug. 2004, tech.sina.com.cn/it/2004-08-28/1036414014.shtml (accessed 5 May 2005).

16. Lang Xianping, *"Shi yue yi ri zai Mo'erben de yanjiang"* (October 1 Speech at Melbourne), www.wyzxsx.com/ShowArticle2.asp?ArticleID=14704&ArticlePage=5 (accessed 14 Nov. 2005).

17. Lang's ideas are widely disseminated by the media and Internet. See, for example, *"Lang Xiaoping: Pipan zhudao Zhongguo chanquan gaige de xinziyouzhuyi"* (Lang Xiaoping: A Critique of the Neoliberalism That Has Dominated Property Rights Reform in China), business.sohu.com/20040829/n221787731.shtml (accessed 9 Jun. 2005).

18. Wang Han and Pei Ying, *"Wu Xuezhe Beijing shengyuan Lang Xiaoping"* (Five Scholars Support Lang Xianping in Beijing), *Beijng chenbao*, 30 Aug. 2004, biz.163.com/40830/9/0V18JBSS00020QC3.html (accessed 7 Jun. 2005).

19. *"'Lang Jufeng' jiaoban xinziyouzhuyi"* ("Lang Tornado" Challenges Neoliberalism), *Waitan huabao* (The Bund), www.cc.org.cn/newcc/browwenzhang.php?articleid=1837 (accessed 5 May 2005).

20. Huang Yongchang and Cui Peisheng, *Wangshi bingbu ruyan* (Past Events Are Not Like Smoke) (Beijing: Zhongguo jingji chubanshe, 2005), excerpts posted at forum.stock.sina.com.cn/cgi-bin/view.cgi?gid=6&fid=1453&thread=7322&date=20050124 (accessed 15 Jun. 2004).

21. *"Zuo Dapei, Yang Fan, Han Deqiang jiu zuzhi guoyou zichan liushi, gaohao guoyouqiye zhi dang he goujia lingdaoren de gongkaixin"* (An Open Letter by Zuo Dapei, Yang Fan, Han Deqiang to the Party and Government Leadership Regarding the Prevention of State Asset Loss), www.chinastudygroup.org/index.php?action=article&type-view&id=91 (accessed 8 Oct. 2004).

22. *"Qing gengduo de 'Lang Xianping' he 'Zhang Weiying' zhanchulai"* (Let More "Lang Xianping" and "Zhang Weiying" Stand Out), *Nanfang dushi bao*, 31 Aug. 2004, www.nanfangdaily.com.cn/southnews/spqy/200408310014.asp (accessed 25 May 2005).

23. Xue Limai, "*Women xuyao Lang Xianping zheyang de 'xueshumingxing'*" (We Need "Academic Stars" Such as Lang Xianping), *Xinjing bao*, 2 Sept. 2004, www.beelink.com/20040902/1668892.shtml (accessed 15 Jun. 2005).

24. "*Jingji shiping: Jingjiquan gewushengping buzhengchang*" (Economic Commentary: It Is Not Normal for the Economic Circles to be Topsy-Turvy), *Zhongguo qingnian bao*, 2 Sept. 2004, www.beelink.com/20040902/1668627.shtml (accessed 16 Jun. 2005).

25. "*Jingjiquan yituanheqi shi yizhong bing*" (The Harmony in the Economic Circles Is a Sickness), www.beelink.com/20040901/1667984.shtml (accessed 16 Jun. 2005). The piece was attributed to *Zhengquan zhixing*, which cited *Yanzhao Dushibao* as its source.

26. Qiu Feng, "*Lang Xianping shijian: Yichang jiqing zhebi lixing de bianlun*" (The Lang Xianping Event: A Debate in Which Passion Overtakes Rationality), www.chinanews.com.cn/news/2004/204-09-27/26/488730.shtml (accessed 26 May 2005).

27. Yang Ruifan and Li Jian, "*Zhang Weikui fanbo Lang Xianping: Guoqi gaige fangxiang burong fouding*" (Zhang Weikui Rebuked Lang Xianping: The Direction of SEO Reform Is Not to be Negated), *Ershiyi shiji jingji baodao*, 21 Aug. 2004, business.sohu.com/20040821/n221655453.shtml (accessed 15 Jun. 2005).

28. Jia Nan, "*Zhang Wenkui: Wo yu Lang Xianping de fenqi shi genbenxing de*" (Zhang Weikui: My Disagreement with Lang Xianping Is Fundamental), finance.beelink.com.cn/20040903/1669968.shtml (accessed 15 Jun. 2005).

29. Wen Zhao and Cheng Mingxiang, "*Zhou Qiren: Wo weishime yao huiying Lang Xianping*" (Zhou Qiren: Why Did I Want to Respond to Lang Xianping), finance.beelink.com.cn/20040913/1677202.shtml (accessed 5 Jun. 2005).

30. "*Gelu 'yingxiong' jiti quexi, yantaohui shang Lang Xianping chang dujiaoxi*" ("Heroes" of All Brands Absent, Lang Xianping Played Alone at Seminar), *Zhongguo gongshang shibao*, 30 Aug. 2004, economy.big5.enorth.com.cn/system/2004/08/30/000853759.shtml (accessed 11 Jun. 2005).

31. Lin Huadi, "*Guozi liushi, zui buzai minqi*" (Private Enterprises Are Not Responsible for State Asset Losses), *Zhonghua gongshang shibao*, 7 Sept. 2004, www.boraid.com/darticle3/list.asp?id=15255# (accessed 25 Apr. 2005).

32. Ma Hailing, "*Puxie Shanghai caijing chuanmei moshi*" (Charting a New Model for Shanghai's Business Media), www.woxie.com/article/list.asp?id=17211 (accessed 11 Jun. 2005).

33. Such a situation is highly consistent with the discursive position of this paper in the Chinese press system. For example, in the coverage of China's WTO deal with the United States in 1999, while *Chinese Commercial and Industrial News* consistently advocated the interests of business, the *Workers' Daily* followed the official and commercial media's overwhelming neoliberal logic. See Yuezhi Zhao, "'Enter the World': Neo-Liberalism, the Dream for a Strong Nation, and Chinese Press Discourse on the WTO," in *Chinese Media, Global Contexts*, ed. Chin-Chuan Lee, 32–56 (London: RoutledgeCurzon, 2003).

34. Matthew Forney, "Women in the Workforce," *Time*, www.time.com/time/asia/covers/1101020617/women.html (accessed 16 Dec. 2003).

35. Liu Qinli, "*Daodi shei yanghuo shei?*" (Who on the Earth Feeds Whom?), *Zhongguo funü bao Meizhou pinglun*, 18 Nov. 1998, 6.

36. Liu, *"Daodi shei yanghuo shei?"*

37. See business.sohu.com/s2004/guoqigaige.shtml (accessed 11 May 2005).

38. *"Wang Xiaoming Shengyuan Lang Xianping: Zheng de bushi jingji"* (Wang Xiaoming Supports Lang Xianping: The Debate Is Not about Economics), www.southcn.com/finance/financenews/guoneicaijing/200409020098.htm (accessed 15 Jun. 2005).

39. Gao Yu, *"Chaoyue jingjixue kandai Lang Xianping shijian"* (Viewing the Lang Xianping Event beyond Economics), *Shangwu zhoukan*, 8 Sept. 2004, www.beelink.com/20040908/1674098.shtml (accessed 15 Jun. 2005).

40. *"Lang Gu zhizheng de zhenzheng shiyuzhe shishei?"* (Who Are the Real Ones to Lose Speech in the Lang-Gu Controversy?), *People's Net*, finance.beelink.com.cn/20040902/1668937.shtml (accessed 22 Jun. 2005).

41. *"'Lang Gu zhizheng' yu shiyu de daduoshu"* (The Lang-Gu Controversy and the Majority Who Lost Speech), www.people.com.cn/GB/guandian/1036/2761379.html (accessed 22 June 2005).

42. Zuo Dapei, *"Zhuyao de wenti shi guan tai 'da'"* (The Main Problem Is That the Officials Are Too "Big"), www.guancha.gmw.cn/shw.aspx?id=1283 (accessed 5 May 2005).

43. See business.sohu.com/s2004/guoqigaige.shtml (accessed 5 May 2005).

44. *"Yulun huanjing shinianlai zuihuai?"* (The Worst Public Opinion Environment in 10 Years?), www.qzwb.com/gb/content/2004-08/31/content_1343625.htm (accessed 5 May 2005).

45. *"Weihu quanli yu quanli de pingheng dian—2004 nian de gonggong shenghuo"* (Maintaining a Balance between Rights and Power—Public Life in 2004), *Nanfang zhoumo*, 30 Dec. 2004, www.nanfangdaily.com.cn/southnews/zt/2004zmnztk/2004zggc/200412300119.asp (accessed 25 May 2005).

46. Richard Madsen, "One Country, Three Systems: State-Society Relations in Post-Jiang China," in *China After Jiang*, ed. Gang Lin and Xiaobo Hu, 91–114 (Stanford, Calif.: Stanford University Press, 2003).

47. Stanley Rosen, "Chinese Media and Youth: Attitudes toward Nationalism and Internationalism," in *Chinese Media, Global Contexts*, ed. Chin-Chuan Lee, 97–118 (London: RoutledgeCurzon, 2003).

48. *"Chaoyue Lang Gu zhizheng"* (Beyond the Lang and Gu Controversy), finance.sina.com.cn/financecomment/20040929/17311057159.shtml (accessed 13 Jun. 2005).

49. Wang Zihui, *"Chanquan gaige de 'feizijue' gongshi yu meiti zeren"* (The Unconscious Consensus on Property Rights Reform and the Responsibility of the Media), business.sohu.com/20040923/n222190761.shtml (accessed 5 May 2005).

50. See www.qglt.com/bbs/Readfile?whichfile=697746&typeid=17 (accessed 5 May 2005). I have deleted some entries and conflated the different layers of responses to streamline the presentation.

51. China Labour Bulletin, "Thousands of Textile Factory Workers Enter 4th Week of Strike in Xianyang City against Unfair Contracts Imposed after Buyout by Hong Kong Conglomerate," www.china-labour.org.hk/iso/article_pv.adp?article_id=5832 (accessed 19 Oct. 2004).

52. Huchangjinkuang, *"Liangyi guozi, zhixu 2200 wan maichu, yinfa liuxue chongtu"* (200 Million Yuan State Assets Sold for 22 Million Only, Resulting in

Bloody Conflict), www.gongnong.org/bbs/read.php?f=3&i=81327&t=81327 (accessed 14 Dec. 2005).

53. See www.gongnong.org/bbs/read.php?f=3&i=81658&t=81327 (accessed 14 Dec. 2005).

54. With the Chinese state's new regulation that compels bloggers to use real names, one wonders whether this type of blogging activity is still possible.

55. See www.gongnong.org/bbs/read.php?f=3&i=81658&t=81327 (accessed 14 Dec. 2005).

56. Chongqing3403gongchang, *"Guoqi si[you]hua zhongjiangjifa geming—Zhi Zhonggong shiliujiesizhongquanhui de gongkaixin"* (The Privatization of the SOEs Will Eventually Lead to Revolution—An Open Letter to the 4th Plenary of the 16th National Congress of the CCP), www.gongnong.org/bbs/read.php?f=7&i=1866&t=1866 (accessed 14 Dec. 2005).

57. *"3403gongchangzhigong: Zhiwen zichanjieji de fazougou—Zhang Wenkui zhi liu"* (Questioning the Running Dogs of the Bourgeois Class—Zhang Wenkui and His Type), *China and the World* 91, 1 Nov. 2004, www.zgysj.com/2004/200410f1.htm (accessed 5 Jun. 2005).

58. Personal interview with a participant of this seminar, 30 Oct. 2006, Beijing.

59. See www.gongnong.org/bbs/read.php?f=3&i=81658&t=81327 (accessed 5 Jun. 2005). I have deleted entries and conflated different levels of responses to streamline the presentation.

60. *"Liu Jipeng cheng Langxianping xiashou taihen, Jiangping zhiyi xingzheng jiaoting MBO"* (Liu Jipeng Charging Lang Xianping for Being Too Harsh, Jiang Ping Questioning the Halt of MBO through Administrative Means), *Zhongguo gongshang shibao*, 20 Dec. 2004, www.china.org.cn/chinese/jingji/732795.htm (accessed 12 Jun. 2005).

61. *Guowuyuan Guoyou Zichan Jiandu Guanli Weiyuanhui Yanjiushi, "Jianchi guoqi gaige fangxiang, guifan tuijin guoqi gaizhi."*

62. *"Lang Xianping weihe quexuan jingji niandu renwu"* (Why Didn't Lang Xianping Win the Title of the Annual Economic Figure?), *Shanghai zhengquan bao*, www.cnradio.com/wcm/caijing/cjxw/t20041207_161983.html (accessed 5 May 2005).

63. Zhu Zheng, *"Shei yilou le Wang Shi? Ba Lang Xianping zaoyin tichu chuqu"* (Who Neglected Wang Shi? Get Rid of the Lang Xianping Noise), biz.163.com/41223/6/18A5M16000020QEO.html (accessed 22 Jun. 2005).

64. Zhu Zheng, *"Guoqi piping zhe? Zaoyin zhizao zhe?"* (A Critic of State Enterprises or a Noise Maker?), biz.163.com/41223/6/18A5M16000020QEO.html (accessed 22 Jun. 2005).

65. Zhu, *"Guoqi piping zhe? Zaoyin zhizao zhe?"*

66. Nanfang renwu zhoukan bianjibu, *"2004 nian Nanfang renwu zhoukan niandu renwu—Lang Xianping"* (*Nanfang People Weekly* Person of the Year: Lang Xianping), oldblog.blogchina.com/article_110742.511595.html (accessed 12 Jun. 2005).

67. Tang Yajie, *"Niandu jingji renwu pingxuan wei 'dan' dangdao, Yangshi daiyan guanshang?"* (Annual Economic Figure Award Dominated by "Beauties," CCTV Stands for Officials and Entrepreneurs?), www.media.163.com/04/1221/09/184880000014180L.html (accessed 25 May 2005).

68. Zhang Tianwei, *"Cong lingyige jiaodu kan jingji renwu pingxuan zhong Lang Xianping luoxuan"* (Another Perspective on the Failure to Select Lang Xianping as an Economics Figure), *Jiangnan shibao*, news.sina.com.cn/o/2004-12-10/03534481437s.shtml (accessed 25 May 2005).

69. *"Zhang Weiying paohong Lang Xianping"* (Zhang Weiying Bombards Lang Xianping), www.blogchina.com/new/display/42430.html (accessed 25 May 2005).

70. *"Zhang Weiying paohong Lang Xianping."*

71. Gu Xue, *"Zhang Weiying: Xuezhe yaoyou gongxinli: Wo buyu wuchi de ren lunzhan"* (Zhang Weiying: Scholars Must Have Credibility: I Am Not Debating with a Shameless Individual), *Beijing qingnian zhoukan*, finance.beelink.com.cn/20040928/1689418.shtml (accessed 22 Jun. 2005).

72. *"Zhang Weiying paohong Lang Xianping."*

73. *"'Ting Langpai' zai Zhongguo zhuyao wangluo meiti shiqu huayuquan"* (Lang's Supporters Lost Discursive Power in China's Main Internet Sites), economy.enorth.com.cn/system/2005/01/07/000940119.shtml (accessed 25 May 2005).

74. *"Lang Xianping youzao dangtou banghe"* (Lang Xianping Once Again Received a Blow), *Beijing chenbao*, 7 Jan. 2005, www.cqcb.com/gb/map/2005-01/07content_454472.htm (accessed 26 May 2005).

75. Gu, *"Zhang Weiying."*

76. *"Lang Xianping youzao dangtou banghe."*

77. *"Zhongxuanbu 29 hao wenjian chuixiang piping xinziyou zhuyi de zhandou haojiao"* (PD Document 29 Trumpeted the Critique of Neoliberalism), www.wyzxwyzx.com/2005/printpage.asp?ArticleID=7983 (accessed 25 Apr. 2007).

78. Ma Guochuan, *"Disanci gaige zhenglun"* (The Third Debate on Reform), www.chinaelections.com/NewsInfo.asp?NewsID=99482 (accessed 15 Apr. 2007); see also Li Liang and Xu Tonghui, *"2004–2006 'Disanci gaige zhenglun' shimo"* (The Beginning and End of the "Third Debate on Reform," 2004–2006), *Nanfang zhoumo*, 16 Mar. 2006, www.nanfangdaily.com.cn/zm/20060316/xw/tb/200603160002.asp (accessed 17 Mar. 2006).

79. Ma, *"Disanci gaige zhenglun."*

80. Ma, *"Disanci gaige zhenglun."*

81. Zhang Yan and Shi Wenfu, *"Shexian nuoyong zijin Gu Chujun beibu chuanwen huo duofang zhengshi"* (Involved in Misappropriation of Funds, News about Gu Chujun's Arrest Verified by Multiple Sources), it.people.com.cn/GB/42891/42893/3582027.html (accessed 25 Oct 2005).

82. Joseph Khan, "A Sharp Debate Erupts in China over Ideologies," *New York Times*, 12 Mar. 2006, www.nytimes.com/2006/03/12/international/asia/12china.html?pagewanted=2&_r=1&th&emc=th (accessed 12 Mar. 2006).

83. Khan, "A Sharp Debate."

84. Lü Juan and Lu Nan, *"Beida jiaoshou shangshu fandui dao wuquan fa cao'an tuichi biaojue"* (Peking University Professor Petition to Oppose Draft Property Rights Law, Leading to Delayed Voting), news.21cn.com/luntan/shidian/2006/02/10/2460982_1.shtml (accessed 12 Mar. 2006).

85. Khan, "A Sharp Debate."

86. Lin Chun, *The Transformation of Chinese Socialism* (Durham, N.C.: Duke University Press, 2006), 185–186.

87. Ma, *"Disanci gaige zhenglun."*

88. Zhong Weizhi, *"Gao Shangquan: You lishi weiwu zhuyi pingjia Zhongguo gaige"* (Gao Shangquan: Using Historical Materialism to Assess China's Reform), www.xinhuawz.com/zw.asp?title_id=50841 (accessed 20 Apr. 2007).

89. *"Wu Jinglian: Xiangfuren kaiqiang jianghui daozhi heng yanzhong de shehui houguo"* (Wu Jinglian: Shooting at the Rich Will Lead to Very Grave Social Consequences), biz.163.com/05/1126/13/23G3JLQU00020UPH.html# (accessed 25 Apr. 2007).

90. Huang Puping, *"Gaige buke dongyao"* (Reform is Unshakable), finance.sina.com.cn/g/20060125/13042306080.shtml (accessed 25 Apr. 2007). For discussions of previous Huang Puping editorials, see Joseph Fewsmith, *China since Tiananmen: The Politics of Transition* (Cambridge: Cambridge University Press, 2001), 45–55; Yuezhi Zhao, *Media, Market and Democracy in China: Between the Party Line and the Bottom Line* (Urbana: University of Illinois Press, 1998), 6–7.

91. Ma, *"Disanci gaige zhenglun."*

92. Ma, *"Disanci gaige zhenglun."*

93. For the full transcripts, see www.wyzxsx.com/ShowArticle.asp?Article ID=18307 and www.wyzxsx.com/ShowArticle.asp?ArticleID=18308 (accessed 24 Mar. 2006). The meeting is dubbed by online leftists the "Xishan Conference" in reference to the historical Xishan Conference of 1925, when the rightists within the Nationalist Party held the conference before Sun Yat-sen's tomb at Xishan to reject Sun's policies and efforts and to establish a separate Party Central Department from the one existing.

94. Don Lee, "China Pulls Plug on Controversial Hong Kong Talk Show King," *Vancouver Sun*, 16 Mar. 2006, A14.

95. Khan, "A Sharp Debate."

96. Ye Tieqiao, *"Hu Jintao: Jianchi gaige buke dongyao"* (Hu Jintao: Insistence on Reform is Unshakable), news.phoenixtv.com/special/dengxp/200702/0212_669_75653.shtml (accessed 17 Oct. 2007).

97. Li and Xu, *"2004–2006 'Disanci gaige zhenglun' shimo."*

98. See Ma, *"Disanci gaige zhenglun"*; Chen Baocheng, *"Zhuanfang Zhou Ruijin: Zaitan 'gaige buke dongyao'"* (Special Interviews with Zhou Ruijin: Once Again on "Reform Is Unshakable"), news3.xinhuanet.com/politics/2006-03/15/content_4304640.htm (accessed 21 Oct. 2007).

99. Andy Hu, "Swimming against the Tide: Tracing and Locating Chinese Leftism Online" (master's thesis, School of Communication, Simon Fraser University, 2006), 72, 105.

100. Zhao Lei, *"Gong Xiantian: Yingxiong haishi zuiren?"* (Gong Xiantian: Hero or Sinner?) www.nanfangdaily.com.cn/zm/20060223/xw/fz/200602230017.asp (accessed 26 Feb. 2006).

101. Gong Xiantian, *"Nanfang zhoumo jizhe de zhiye daode nali qu le?"* (Where Have *Nanfang Weekend* Journalist's Professional Ethics Gone?), host378.ipowerweb .com/~gongnong/bbs/read.php?f=3&i=149569&t=149569 (accessed 26 Feb. 2006).

102. Zhong Xuanli, *"Haobu dongyao jianchi gaige faxiang"* (Unswervingly Adhere to the Reform Direction), news.xinhuanet.com/newscenter/200606/04/content_4644203.htm (accessed 30 Apr. 2007).

103. Ma, "*Disanci gaige zhenglun.*"

104. "Top China Leader Fired for Graft," BBC News, 25 Sept. 2006, news.bbc.co.uk/1/hi/world/asia-pacific/5376858.stm.

105. Wen Jiabao, "Our Historical Tasks at the Primary Stage of Socialism and Several Issues Concerning China's Foreign Policy," www.bjreview.com.cn/document/txt/2007-03/12/content_58927.htm (accessed 30 Apr. 2007).

106. "China Passes New Law on Property," BBC News, 16 Mar. 2007, news.bbc.co.uk/2/hi/asia-pacific/6456959.stm (accessed 30 Apr. 2007).

107. Jonathan Manthorpe, for example, observed two "radically different and perhaps contradictory responses" to the growing social upheaval in the Hu Jintao–Wen Jiabao leadership, with Wen blaming the reckless exploitation of farmers as a source of instability and Hu calling for security forces to "strike hard" against rising public unrest. Jonathan Manthorpe, "Communist Party Divided on Dealing with Dissidents," *Vancouver Sun*, 30 Jan. 2006, E3.

108. Deng Yuwen, *Feichang jiaofeng: Guoqi chanquan gaige dataolun shilu* (Special Contention: The Great Debate on Property Rights Reform of State-Owned Enterprises) (Beijing: Haiyang chubanshe, 2005), 78–87.

109. "*Guoyou zichan zhenglun rijian susha, guanfang cheng qingcha xingdong yu Lang wuguan*" (Debate on State Assets Becomes Increasingly Serious, Government Claims that Inspection Actions Unrelated to Lang), biz.163.com/41022/9/139OKPBT00020QC3.html (accessed 10 Jun. 2005).

110. "*Dafan fubai: Jiang guoyou qiye gaige dataolun tuijin xin jieduan*" (Anticorruption at Large, Carry the Grand Debate on SEO Reform to a New Stage), www.snzg.net/shownews.asp?newsid=2209 (accessed 13 Jun. 2005).

111. Ma Ling, "*Disanci gaige da zhenglu yiqi zouxiang*" (The "Third Debate on Reform" and Its Directions), www.chinaelections.org/NewsInfo.asp?NewsID=93700 (accessed 21 Oct. 2007).

112. Gu, "*Zhang Weiying.*"

113. "*Zhuanfang Lang Xianping: Wo weishenme fandui muqiande chanquan gaige siwei*" (Interview with Lang Xianping: Why I Oppose the Current Thinking about Property Rights Reform), *Nanfang renwu zhoukan*, 20 Dec. 2004, business.sohu.com/20041220/n223561701.shtml (accessed 13 Jun. 2005).

Conclusion

The Trees Want to Be Quiet
but the Winds Won't Stop

As China's post-Mao "reform and opening up" process enters its 30th year in 2008, Chinese state and societal forces, left and right, elite and popular, organized and unorganized, seem to have never vested such high stakes in public communication. Communication, in turn, seems to have never been so central to the processes of political legitimation, capital accumulation, social relations restructuring, and cultural transformation. The party-state has accelerated and strengthened its efforts to secure the "commanding heights" in the political economy of a marketized and globally integrated communication system, while negotiating the terms of its engagement with transnational and domestic private capital. In turn, these efforts have simultaneously deflected and deepened the political economic, ideological, and cultural contradictions of the system.

On the one hand, an expanded realm of commoditized media and popular culture—from watchdog journalism to popular television dramas and Internet chat rooms—has provided a much-needed buffer zone for the party-state to redefine and reestablish hegemony over a deeply fractured and rapidly globalizing Chinese society. The party has embraced the marketized provision of media and culture more consciously. Market-oriented media outlets, in turn, have emerged as the "new mainstream" and become adept at marginalizing "old" and "new" leftists, moderating popular nationalistic sentiments, and selectively deploying "journalistic professionalism" as a means of both social legitimation and class containment. The party leadership, so long as it manages to stay unified and continues to commit to market reforms and stabilize the conditions for domestic and transnationalized capitalist accumulation, can perhaps sustain its monopoly of power inside China and continue to contribute to bolstering the global capitalist order.

On the other hand, the party's revolutionary legacy, its socialist pretensions, as well as popular demands for social justice and equality continue to feed into multifaceted elite and popular resistance against the further installation of capitalistic social relations within and through the communication system. If the problem for China's "old" and "new" left alike is that they could not pursue economic and social justice without confronting the daunting tasks of democratizing the Chinese state and challenging the global capitalist order, one of the main problems for capitalist integrationists both inside and outside China is that the Chinese party-state is not willing to officially repudiate its communist legacy and give up socialism as a legitimating ideology. Above all, China's popular classes are not willing to be sacrificed for a neoliberal-envisioned market society utopia without protesting and calling upon the state to live up to its socialist and anti-imperialist pretensions. Furthermore, although Gong Xiantian and his "old leftist" supporters were not able to block the eventual passage of the Property Rights Law, Gong's limited success in challenging its provisions and delaying its passage demonstrates that appealing to constitutional authority is no longer exclusively a liberal strategy. In fighting for discursive space and their vision of China's future and its place in the world, "old leftists," for example, have not only championed democratic principles—from accusing Jiang Zemin of pushing through his "three represents" undemocratically to questioning Zheng Bijian's personal authority in declaring the party's foreign policy directions vis-à-vis the U.S.-led global capitalist order in the 21st century—but also have taken the constitutional commitment to socialism and anti-imperialism seriously.

In his speech at the March 4, 2006, forum organized by Gao Shangquan, He Weifang, Gong's colleague at the Peking University Law School and his opponent, provided an interesting description of the political and ideological and, above all, communicative constraints for a liberal democratic capitalist prospect in China. According to He, the leftists are "rampant" (*changjue*) online because they hit the party-state's "soft ribs" (or more precisely, Achilles' heel?) and are empowered to utilize the socialist discourse in critiquing the reform with moral authority. Rightists, on the other hand, have always felt that they have something to hide. As a result, although they all have clear aims, that is, liberal political objectives such as a multiparty system, press freedom, democracy, and individual rights, they have been hesitant to respond to the leftists "because some words can't be articulated." That is, as He put it, these political objectives "are in fact currently unspeakable."[1] As I will discuss shortly, He Weifang underestimated the determination of the rightists to speak the "unspeakable" as leftist and popular critiques of the reform continued to gain strength and as the debates over the party's political orientations intensified in the run-up to the 17th Party Congress in October 2007. He also failed to acknowledge that the party has always claimed to strive for democracy, and at issue is not whether one speaks the language of democracy, but the actual meaning of the term. Nevertheless, He's remarks underscored the communicative challenges for the ideological proponents of a liberal democratic capitalist future in a postrevolutionary China that has taken 30 years (1978–2008) to "reform" 29 years of state socialism (1949–1978) and is still under the control of a political party that calls itself "communist."

Yiching Wu has argued that "*a coherent dual criticism*" of China's ongoing transition—"a critique of both capital and state, of economic accumulation and bureaucratic power, and a fuller understanding of their structural and historical connections"—"is not only imperative but also possible."[2] My objective in this book has been to continue to advance such a dual critique in relation to the institutional and symbolic transformation of the Chinese communication system, one of the most crucial sites of political economic and cultural power, and a key battleground for China's future. Moreover, I have moved beyond a negative, ahistorical, and static critique to show how this system transformation has been haunted and mediated by the revolutionary legacies of party-state formation on the one hand and robustly contested by various social forces on the other. I have also demonstrated how one of the much-desired alternatives, that is, the development of a liberal capitalist constitutional democracy, and in media and communication a relatively autonomous "bourgeois public sphere," has, from the onset, been suppressed by the party-state's reconfigured regime of political, bureaucratic, and ideological control from above and instrumentalized by rapidly constituting capitalist class interests from within, while being contested and challenged by various counterpublics from below. These counterpublics have included popular nationalist, socialist, workers', farmers', women's, and religious and quasi-religious discourses. In particular, in addition to whatever remains in the party-state's attempt at frustrating capitalist class formation within and through the media and cultural realm, as the resurgence of popular online leftism and as He Weifang's previously cited comments testify, various socialist discourses have reemerged to serve as a powerful ideological and moral constraint on the further capitalistic development of the Chinese political economy. Finally, from the respective roles of private television series producers in sustaining the party's revolutionary legacies through the "red classics" to the Internet and market-oriented urban dailies in both spearheading and policing the boundaries of public debates on the directions of the reform, and from the influence of Western media and neoliberal economics to the cosmopolitan credentials of provocateur Lang Xianping and the overseas bases of websites that have contributed to the revival of leftist and popular nationalistic discourses inside China, I have demonstrated the contradictory implications of media commercialization, globalization, and information technology explosion in the transformation of China's social order.

Along with "old left" calls for the party to return to a state-directed economy based on public ownership and a reversal of the policy of opening its membership to capitalists, liberal intellectuals have called for the party to openly embrace capitalism and reinvent itself as a Western-style social democratic party. I will return to both positions shortly. Meanwhile, domestic and overseas intellectuals within a revitalized Chinese "new left," encouraged by the Hu Jintao leadership's emphasis on social justice and a more balanced developmental path after it came to power in late 2002, have articulated radical socialist alternatives to capitalist reintegration. Instead of applying the boilerplate of capitalist liberal democracy to China or clinging to a Maoist past, "new left" intellectuals are arguing for the democratic renewal of Chinese socialism as part of a contemporary, worldwide, and open movement, drawing lessons not only from indigenous Chinese socialist experiments with economic democracy and "people's democracy," but also from socialist thoughts and movements abroad. In this way, they are attempting to make "socialism" not just a "noun in official documents" or a "name without substance," but "a pursuable objective in reality."[3] Echoing Lin Chun's examination of China's socialist legacies from abroad in her 2006 book *The Transformation of Chinese Socialism*, Huang Ping, Yao Yang, and Han Yuhai, for example, have articulated a "new socialism" at the ethical-political, institutional, and cultural levels within China in their book-length three-way dialogue *Our Times* (*Women de shidai*), which explicitly aims to popularize "new left" thinking in a nonacademic form. Their vision of an alternative socialist modernity is at once more democratic than the party leadership's "propeople" paternalist redistributive politics and more forward-looking than the largely frozen vision of the "old left."[4] In late October 2006, "new left" playwright Huang Jisu's play *We Walk on a Broad Path* (*Women zouzai dalushang*) took the "third debate"—which had been declared over by the "new mainstream" media outlets in March 2006—to a new high with both his devastating critique of the neoliberal jungle logic of survival of the fittest (*hulang zhitao*, "the way [*tao*] of tigers and wolves") and its corrosive impact on the Chinese nation since the early 1990s, and his faith in a noncapitalist alternative Chinese modernity. Furthermore, Huang, reversing long-standing Chinese liberal intellectual aspirations to import Western values to transform China and reflecting a regained Chinese national "self-confidence," perhaps even some aspects of Chinese cultural essentialism, asserted the "lofty inspiration" of the Chinese nation—which in his view "has long engraved 'the heavenly way' [*dao*] and 'the great commons' in its soul"—"to use the power of the tigers and wolves to subvert the way [*tao*] of the tigers and wolves, to chart a new course for humanity, and to open a new page in history."[5] Underscoring the fact that "new left" intellectuals outside the ruling political elite are not alone in envisioning new forms of socialism and that there is no lack of progressive alternatives inside the party-state, Pan Yue, a deputy director of the State Environmental Protection Agency and perhaps China's leading "green" politician, for example, has passionately advocated a "Green GDP" and "ecological socialism" or "socialist ecological civilization." Pan called for the formation of a new coalition between the "reds" (communists) and "greens" (environmentalists), arguing that socialism in essence should be ecologically more sustainable than capitalism and that China should "externally unite developing countries in opposing a world economic order that has led to environmental injustices, and internally establish a whole set of institutions to prevent the ecological crises resulting from uneven development."[6]

In short, although the progressive implementation of market reforms in the 1990s and early 2000s has made China's self-proclaimed socialist state in many ways "an ideal capitalist state" of world historical proportions— "freedom for the capital, with the state doing the 'dirty job' of controlling the workers" and "everything subordinated to the ruthless drive to develop and become the new superpower"[7]—China's communist legacies and the ongoing rearticulations of socialist ideals at both the state and societal levels have made this not only a highly contested, but an unfinished project. Along with the substantive reconstitution of bureaucratic and capitalist class power within and beyond the borders of the Chinese nation, and indeed, partly because of it, Chinese society, especially many among the subordinate social classes who have regained a new appreciation of the values of equality and justice in the wake of neoliberal developmental excesses, is being activated, making economic and social justice claims on the state on the one hand and calling for political protection against the destructive impact of the market on the other. If "socialism is the subordination of market and state to the self-regulating society"[8] or the "establishment of a society with the working people as the primary subjects" (*yi laodongzhe wei zhuti de shehui*),[9] then perhaps not only the party's official socialist slogans per se, but also their reappropriation by various Chinese social forces and the unfolding societal processes of subordinating both state and market to the social needs of the working people, are what the struggle for socialism in China is about.

Lin Chun has divided up China's post-Mao reform process into three phases in making her case for socialist renewal in China. In this view, the first phase, from 1978 to 1989, was a period of socialist self-adjustment with the objective of realizing rather than reversing the socialist cause. This reformist socialist path, however, was derailed in the second phase, or what she called the "long decade" of elite compliance with capitalist impositions from 1989 to 2003, with developments that "amounted to a near-'revolutionary' transformation aimed at repealing the Chinese revolution and socialist alternative."[10] Lin posited a third turn of the reform since 2003 and suggested that the "emergence of a 'Beijing consensus,' the introduction of a 'green GDP,' and the pledging of attending 'social harmony' by bettering the plight of peasants and migrant workers are among the signs of a resumption of reform socialism."[11]

Lin has perhaps vested too much hope in the Hu Jintao leadership. Moreover, to reach a definitive evaluation of both the significance and effectiveness of the Hu Jintao leadership's rearticulation of the party's socialist hegemony and its expressed vigilance against transnational capitalist integration is probably premature. Nevertheless, I do agree with her that there is no preordained path for China's social transformation. As she put it, "Insofar as this collective effort [of searching for a socialist alternative to capitalist modernity] has persisted, the chance of the Chinese model to succeed cannot be ruled out."[12]

Although the "third debate on reform" has not quite amounted to what Lin had called for, that is, determining the concrete meaning of the "third phase" of the reform process "through open, informed, and widely acted out deliberation and experimentation,"[13] there is clearly an ongoing, fundamental conflict over different visions of China's future and its place in the global capitalist order. Unlike the covert debates in the early 1980s and early 1990s between the "conservatives" and the "reformers" within the ruling elite that ended up with accelerated market reforms, the current debate, which to a large extent has been facilitated by the Internet from the bottom up, has a much broader resonance within Chinese society. The critics of capitalistic developments are no longer confined to the so-called conservatives or old leftists within the party-state—after all, once powerful "conservatives" were either dead or no longer in power. Rather, marginalized "old leftists" within the party have been joined by a wide range of intellectual and popular voices. That is, although the current debate continues to be framed around the highly normalizing binaries between "capitalism" versus "socialism," "pro-reform" versus "anti-reform," and "left" versus "right," it did not originate from a political confrontation at the high echelons of party-state power (after all, the succession between the Jiang Zemin and Hu Jintao leaderships did not involve an open power struggle), but primarily from social discontents from below. Consequently, the terms of the debate are no longer constrained by elite power struggles. Profound questions regarding the stakes of different social classes in the evolving Chinese social formation, including the vested interest of an emerging "power, money, and knowledge regime"—known as the "iron triangle alliance" (*tiesanjiao tongmeng*) of political, economic, and media/intellectual elites, or perhaps more accurately, a reconstituted and transnationally linked capitalist class—in hijacking the reform process, have been posited. And yet, precisely because the current debate no longer pits one faction of the ruling political elite against another in an open power struggle, but pits an emerging and rapidly reconsolidating "iron triangle" of dominant social forces against the popular classes in a seemingly smooth, but protracted, party leadership succession process in a rapidly globalizing context, the conflict is less dramatic, the playing field more uneven, the process more opaque, the intersection between class and nation more complex, and its immediate impact more difficult to assess.

Richard Robison, in assessing the dramatic confrontations against neo-liberal globalization worldwide, has noted that there was ambivalence among scholars as to "whether such dramatic confrontations represent shifts in power within the neo-liberal camp or whether they reflect a more structural challenge to the neo-liberal order."[14] Although I would like to conclude that the Chinese case seems to represent more a shift in power within the reform camp, I also must underscore the unsettled nature of the ongoing confrontations. As I have discussed previously, the market-oriented media have been quick to put closure on the "third debate," claiming victory on behalf of an agenda of further market reform and capitalist reintegration. The passage of the Property Rights Law in March 2007 was a definitive step toward the consolidation of the market reform agenda. However, as I mentioned in chapter 3, also passed at the 2007 NPC meeting was a Corporate Income Taxation Law that promises to facilitate a shift away from a foreign investment–dependent and export-driven economy.[15] In the ideological and cultural realm, as I discussed in the first half of this book, the Hu Jintao leadership has rearticulated the party's ideological hegemony around a developmental path that initiates a shift from growth to social equity, promising to increase public investment in the cultural sector and in the rural cultural infrastructure, and there have been various government efforts to reassert more domestic control in different sectors of the communication and cultural industries since 2005.

Again, whether these developments constitute a fundamental challenge to further neoliberal developments in China remains to be seen. Such a challenge, as Lin Chun hopes, would amount to "a redefinition of the reform and development" and the forging of "yet even a newer social contract (after the Maoist and Dengist allocation of freedom and security respectively) while rebuilding the country's national and social strength."[16] In communication and culture, such a redefinition would amount to nothing short of reinventing the party's cultural system reform program around the twin objectives of democratization and decommodification, including a redefinition of an "advanced socialist culture" that centers neither on reified cultural objects and commodities nor the party's predetermined "core value systems," but on the cultivation of nonexploitative human relationships and, as Huang Ping, Yao Yang, and Han Yuhai hope, "the development of the culture of the working people."[17]

The party-state's reform program and the implementation of "neoliberalism with Chinese characteristics" in the post-1989 era have clearly boosted China's *national* strength as measured by the size of the domestic Chinese economy—now the fourth largest in the world—within the global capitalist system. The growing "China's rising" rhetoric at least partly reflects this reality. However, the goals of building China's *social* strength and cultivating social harmony remain elusive. Despite heightened rhetoric and visible achievements, the Hu Jintao leadership has had difficulty implementing policies aiming at bridging the gaping fissures between rich and poor, protecting the environment, controlling endemic corruption, and reducing the Chinese economy's dependence on foreign investments and labor-intensive exports. Although Pan Yue's idea of establishing a "Green GDP" that accounts for natural resources depletion and environmental degradation received official endorsement, it has met vehement resistance from local officials. Consequently, a plan for the idea's trial implementation has been indefinitely postponed.[18] Not surprisingly, Hu Jintao has been compelled to acknowledge in his October 15, 2007, report to the 17th Party Congress that the party's achievements "still fall short of the expectations of the people" and that "the governance capability of the party falls somewhat short of the need to deal with the new situation and tasks."[19]

In the media and communication sector, along with attempts at reasserting political control and protecting domestic markets, conflicting bureaucratic capitalist self-interests, growing academic and social critiques against the excesses of commodification, as well as the scandals involving the *Guangzhou Daily* and the *Beijing Youth Daily* groups as the trailblazers on the road to media conglomeration and stock market listing had temporarily slowed down the further marketization and privatization of the party-state media sector. In the area of media restructuring, as of the end of October 2007, there had not been a wave of stock market listing of major party-state print media groups, just as no more state broadcasting channels have been partially privatized since the trial phase of the cultural system reform program. In broadcasting and popular culture, the supremacy of market populism as measured by "audience ratings" has begun to be challenged by at least some media professionals and media managers, and arguments have been made for a "correct understanding of audience ratings," that is, not to make them absolute criteria in programming. Cui Yongyuan, a popular CCTV talk show host, even declared that "audience ratings are the source of all evil."[20] In an attempt to contain the challenge posed by *Super Girl* and other *American Idol*–type synergized reality shows on CCTV's market share, as well as what broadcast regulators considered to be the negative social impacts of these reality programs, new regulations were issued in 2007 to ban voting by cell phone or on the Internet for contestants in these shows. Nor are these shows allowed to be aired on prime time after October 2007.[21] For their part, some party-state media conglomerates, facing the challenges of trying to meet both the party line and the bottom line at the same time amid the tough realities of market competition, have even pressured the central state, which had progressively cut subsidies to media and cultural institutions in the 1980s and early 1990s, to increase the level of subsidies, thus partially reversing the process of commodification. Most notably, the official Xinhua News Agency has been able to press the party-state to significantly increase the level of subsidies since the second half of the 1990s, enabling it to refocus on its core journalistic mission in some ways.[22] One leading domestic advertising expert has even observed that the party-state, after an extended period of rapid commercialization, may "buy back" the media with increased subsidies.[23]

Meanwhile, the party-state is determined to boost the strength of China's cultural industry and increase its global competitiveness. Echoing the tenor of the party's January 2006 decision on cultural system reform, Hu Jintao's 17th Party Congress report calls for "mobilizing a new tidal wave of socialist cultural construction, stimulating the cultural creativity of the entire nation, promoting the state's cultural soft power, and enabling the better fulfillment of the people's basic cultural rights."[24] Nevertheless, "new socialist" ideas such as "the development of the culture of the working people" remain antithetical to the current leadership. Moreover, from Rupert Murdoch's loud outcry against a "paranoid" Chinese state bent on controlling its media to domestic liberal media outlets such as the *Nanfang Metropolitan News'* mobilization of the market populist discourse to challenge the state's legitimacy to "regulate audience's preference,"[25] not to mention the powerful market imperative that has already been set in motion by the party-state itself and the domestic and transnational capitalist class interests such a process has already engendered, any attempt on the part of the party-state to seriously decommodify media and cultural production—which would amount to a substantive reorientation of the party-state's cultural system reform program—will set it up on a collision course with powerful capitalist class interests.

In short, the structure of the media and communication industries and the unfolding politics of elite and popular communication regarding China's current problems and its future developments remain crucial, and this is why the "third debate" has not only assumed great importance, but also defied any politically calculated, premature pronouncements about its closure. Control of media outlets and media discourses continues to be at the center of the "third debate." To be sure, the party continues to resist escalating pressures from within for a wholesale political and ideological embrace of liberal democratic capitalism, that is, to adopt Western-style constitutional democracy to "match" an economic foundation that is already capitalistic, and to give up its communist ideological pretensions. For example, contrary to He Weifang's March 2006 observation that the rightists had been reluctant to speak out about their political vision, 86-year-old party theorist Xie Tao, a former vice president of Chinese People's University, issued a blunt call for the party to embrace such a vision in an essay in the February 2007 issue of the well-established liberal journal *Chinese across the Ages* (*Yanhuang chunqiu*), which is run by a group of influential liberal party intellectuals and former state officials headed by Du Daozheng, a former head of the GAPP.[26] Clearly written in response to the upsurge of leftist and grassroots criticisms of the reform, the essay embraced the ideas of Eduard Bernstein (1850–1932)—who had long been criticized by the party as being a "revisionist"—as "true" Marxism, arguing that Marx and Engels gave up on communistic ideals and violent revolution toward the end of their lives and that Leninism, Stalinism, and Maoism are all forms of "leftist revisionism." Further, Xie repudiated the Bolshevik Revolution, and, by implication, the Chinese communist revolution, as wrongheaded from the very beginning. Most significantly and in an apparent attempt to neutralize leftist critiques of social inequality while positioning himself within the party's legitimating discourse of Marxism, Xie credits Western and North European–style welfare capitalism, particularly Swedish social democracy ("democratic socialism" in Xie's terminology), as the "highest achievement of Marxism" and sets it as the only model for China's future.[27] Revealing the rightists' understanding of the party's continuing proclaimed allegiance to the communist ideology as a real threat to the further capitalistic transformation of the Chinese political economy, Xie blamed the continued strength of leftism as "the natural outcome of our ideological compromise." Thus, Xie, like He Weifang, not only realized the danger posed by elite leftist and grassroots critiques of capitalistic developments, but also made it clear that the party's communist legacy and its continuing communistic pretensions had legitimated these critiques.

Xie's article stirred up a major controversy among China's political and intellectual elites. Liberal intellectuals applauded it because it resonated with their thoughts.[28] Leftists denounced it for being "antiparty, antisocialism, and anti-Marxist" and an attempt by bourgeois liberals to "put their mark on the flag of the 17th Party Congress, so as to achieve the objective of capitalist restoration."[29] Significantly, the central leadership did not openly criticize the article, nor did it punish *Yanhuang chunqiu* for publishing it, thus allowing liberal intellectuals considerable space to further elaborate their perspectives.[30] Although Hu Jintao's June 25, 2007, speech at the Central Party School, which foreshadows the tenor of his 17th Party Congress report, offered an implicit response to Xie by reemphasizing the "Sinification" of Marxism and the slogan of "socialism with Chinese characteristics," the party clearly did not want to break out into open ideological warfare by publicly discussing the content of the essay.[31] Moreover, in the aftermath of the censorship fiasco over *Freezing Point*, discussed in chapter 1, the party probably does not have the political will to face a frontal confrontation with the powerful alliance of domestic and international liberal anticensorship forces, provoking a domestic liberal backlash at its 17th National Congress and courting further foreign accusations of repression before the 2008 Beijing Olympics.

At the same time, reflecting the coalescing pro-capitalist political economic and intellectual power that I have described in this book, leftists—both "old" and "new"—found their public communication further undermined in the months leading to the 17th Party Congress. In July 2007, capitalizing on popular outrage in response to the parent- and Internet-led exposure of the massive kidnapping and enslavement of laborers, including hundreds of children, at brick kilns in Shanxi Province,[32] and aiming to influence the party's political directions as it convened its 17th National Congress in October 2007, "old leftists" once again issued an Internet appeal to the party's Politburo Standing Committee, urging it to face the grave consequences of a derailed reform that, among other things, has engendered the extreme forms of labor exploitation and the deprivation of basic human freedoms in the Shanxi kilns. The authorities, who had issued a specific order to prohibit communication using the event to question fundamental party-state policies, once again temporarily shut down the Maoflag.net website, which had posted the appeal letter, and forced it to remove the letter.[33]

Perhaps more significantly, during the same month of July 2007, "new left" voices—which have been accused by liberal intellectuals of being complicit with the party-state's authoritarianism—suffered a major blow when the central state-controlled Sanlian Publishing House, a subsidiary of the China Publishing Group, dismissed Tsinghua University professor Wang Hui and Chinese Academy of Social Sciences researcher Huang Ping—two leading "new left" intellectuals—as the executive editors of *Reading* (*Dushu*), the flagship Chinese intellectual journal, and put it under the control of more liberal-oriented staff editors. Established in 1979 with a liberal orientation at the onset of the "reform and opening up" process, *Reading* began to explore critical issues such as China's rural problems and the Asian financial crisis in 1997 and turned to the left in its intellectual orientation after Wang Hui became its editor-in-chief in 1996. This development had long brewed discontent among liberal intellectuals who have engaged in a protracted struggle with Wang Hui and other "new left" scholars for ideological hegemony in China since the mid-1990s. Coincidentally, in February 2007, as Xie Tao's embrace of Swedish welfare capitalism struck a responsive chord among liberal intellectuals and perhaps even the central party leadership itself, *Reading* published one of its most critical essays on the relevance of class politics, thus further antagonizing liberal intellectuals. Commenting on Huang Jisu's abrupt and unconvincing appeal to a common Chinese identity ("we are brothers and sisters, we belong to the same clan") as the means to heal the deep wounds of a fractured Chinese nation resulting from neoliberal capitalistic developments in *We Walk on a Broad Path*, "new left" intellectual Kuang Xinnian offered a powerful critique of left popular nationalism. He called attention to the internally repressive nature of the nation-state and the problematic formation of national identity in the age of transnationalized capitalism, warning against any illusion of social harmony in an increasingly class-divided and globalized Chinese society.[34]

No evidence suggests that Kuang's article was the final straw that led the state owner to finally push out Wang Hui and Huang Ping under the publicly stated rationale of strengthening the journal's corporate management and "rectifying" the situation of letting outsiders serve as the journal's chief editors—a phenomenon that contradicts the GAPP's periodical industry management guidelines.[35] However, this still begs the question about the timing of the decision. Moreover, many believed that the highly controversial decision—which was internally resisted by the journal's staff, because of the lack of transparency in the decision-making process, especially the controversial and unprofessional role played by the *Beijing News* in creating the media and elite intellectual pressure that eventually led to this decision[36]—amounted to a coup staged by liberal journalists and intellectuals outside the journal as well as bureaucratic capitalists at the Sanlian Publishing House. In the view of a number of observers, "the *Reading* event" underscored the dominant liberal intellectual elites' determination to undermine any remaining left-oriented print media outlet within the party-state media sector. This would prevent it from playing a potential role in forging a counterhegemonic alliance between the central party leadership, the politically active segment of the "middle social strata" or "middle-class" reading public—who have demonstrated their critical stance against the dominant power bloc both in the Wang Binyu case and in the "Lang Xianping Storm"—and the low social classes.[37] One analyst has even argued that the event marked the end of the so-called Hu-Wen New Deal, symbolizing the Hu Jintao leadership's final alliance with the entrenched "iron triangle" ruling class bloc.[38] To frame this analyst's account in the Gramscian language of hegemony and counterhegemony and correlate it at least partially with the discussions in this book, I would like to construct the following interpretation of recent Chinese communication politics: When Hu Jintao and Wen Jiabao came to power in 2002, they faced the explosive social tensions created by the excesses of the neoliberal reforms of the Jiang Zemin era. At the same time, they needed to rein in powerful cadres who were both loyal to the previous leadership at the central and provincial levels and deeply entrenched in the bureaucratic capitalist order. To consolidate their own personal power and keep the party as a whole in power, Hu and Wen were compelled to address popular concerns and tackle the issues that have been on the agenda of the leftist critics of the reform process. However, this put the central leadership in a conflictual relationship with the dominant bureaucratic, economic, and media/intellectual elites. These elites were quick to sense the potential threat of an anti-neoliberal, counterhegemonic alliance among the central leadership, leftist intellectuals, and mobilized masses demanding social justice and equality. Consequently, they quickly rallied themselves around the objective of social containment, while putting pressures on the Hu-Wen leadership to hold back on any radical reorientation of the reform process, including a critical assessment of neoliberalism.[39] Eventually, the Hu-Wen leadership yielded to elite pressures, because a radical reorientation of the reform would ultimately undermine their own place within the dominant "iron triangle" ruling class power bloc. In this view, the fight against SARS signaled the beginning of a potential realignment of Hu-Wen central leadership power with the critical "middle-class" media and Internet public and the party's grassroots social bases; the "Lang Xianping Storm" marked the climax of this potential rearticulation of central leadership and popular power in a potential anti-neoliberal counterhegemony; while the passage of the Property Rights Law marked the beginning of the end of the potential formation of an anti-neoliberal counterhegemony.[40]

The above interpretation risks placing Hu and Wen "outside" the bureaucratic capitalist power structure to begin with. It also probably vests too much potential in Hu and Wen as individual leaders able to break with such a structure and with the political will to forge an anti-neoliberal, counterhegemonic alliance. As I demonstrated in chapter 1, although the Hu Jintao leadership projects a reform populist image, its suppression of grassroots leftist voices was consistent from the beginning. Moreover, although no evidence is available regarding whether the central authorities were directly involved in the decision at *Reading*, an argument can be made that the party-state's project of rationalizing the bureaucratic capitalist control of media—a consistent policy under both the Jiang and Hu leaderships—was precisely what provided the legitimating rationale for the publisher's decision. In fact, the decision at *Reading* is highly consistent with the ways in which other leftist and anti-neoliberal voices—from the closure of leftist websites for lack of capitalization to Lang Xianping's removal from his television show—were suppressed.

Nevertheless, we must move beyond any static and one-dimensional discussion centering on a monolithic party-state driven by a single-minded will to power. More importantly, the previously discussed interpretation helps to ground the dynamics of Chinese communication politics around the party-state's conflictual relationship with a rapidly constituting capitalist class formation on the one hand and the interests of China's subaltern classes on the other. It not only reveals the deep fear and sense of vulnerability among China's rising capitalist class and its organic intellectuals, but also underscores the almost insurmountable structural challenges the party-state must face in pursuing its "scientific concept of development" and building a "harmonious society" within the framework of a transnationally reintegrated capitalist economy. At a time when the widening gap between rich and poor has become a primary societal concern and when nearly 59.1 percent of the respondents answered negatively a Huang Jisu–inspired question on a *China Youth News* survey about whether "we" (i.e., members of the Chinese nation) can still "walk together" (i.e., share a common national destination), class conflict has become a social reality, not simply a leftist intellectual fantasy.[41] Within this context, the complicated intersections between class and nationalistic politics, and the debate between the "old leftists" and Zheng Bijian over whether China should accommodate the U.S.-led global capitalist order (which I discussed in chapter 3), continue to assume paramount importance.

David Harvey, in assessing the future of "neoliberalism with Chinese characteristics," wrote in 2005 that whether the ongoing transformation of internal party structure "will consolidate the ascendance of the same sort of technocratic elite that led the Mexican PRI towards total neoliberalization remains to be seen" and that "it cannot be ruled out either that the masses will seek a restoration of their own unique form of class power" by demanding the party live up to its revolutionary promises.[42] In light of the latter prospect and the interpretation about a moment of potential openness for an anti-neoliberal hegemony from 2003 to 2005, perhaps there is indeed a grain of truth in the evocations of the Cultural Revolution by neoliberal reformers such as Liu Ji and Zhou Ruijin (aka Huang Puping) in their framing of mounting leftist and popular opposition against further neoliberal reforms. Behind such evocations is their fear of an anti-authoritarian, and even potentially democratic, inspiration on the part of China's low social classes to reassert their class power and take control of the direction of the reform, enacting what the term "people's democracy," in its most radical form of the pre–Cultural Revolution era, is supposed to mean. Post-Mao official party history and Chinese liberal intellectuals understood the Cultural Revolution as nothing but the torture of officials and intellectuals—a plot hatched by Mao to purge his political rivals. The party (and, I would add, the capitalists and intellectual elites), in turn, "benefits enormously from the continuing fear of social upheaval that the Cultural Revolution has left" in the reform era.[43] However, as even an open-minded Western journalist would readily admit, "another bequest of the Cultural Revolution is that it spawned a period of questioning party authority and even the search for a measured program of political reforms," which "found expression in the Democracy Wall movement of 1978 and later in the nationwide demonstrations generated by Tiananmen Square protests in 1989."[44] The relationship between the Cultural Revolution and two conflicting understandings of democracy came into full play in October 2007, during the party's 17th National Congress. A liberal and procedural one was invoked by Jiangsu provincial party chief and new political star Li Yuanchao, when he said that the Cultural Revolution could have been avoided if there had been democracy. A day earlier in Hong Kong, a substantive and populist concept was implied, in a negative way, by Hong Kong chief executive Donald Tsang Yam-kuen, who said in a radio interview that democracy "taken to its full swing" had led to episodes such as the Cultural Revolution. Underscoring just how much damage the Cultural Revolution had done to any notion of radical democracy and the hegemony of liberal democracy, Tsang had to apologize for his remarks.[45]

The much anticipated 17th Party Congress between October 15 and 21, 2007, did not produce any surprises in terms of the party's political directions. Although Du Daozheng was quick to offer a spin in the overseas Chinese press by claiming that Hu Jintao's report to the congress did not "yield a single inch or a single word of concession to the leftists,"[46] the party also frustrated any hope for "bourgeois liberalization" and Western-style liberal democracy in China. Hu's report claimed to hold high the banner of "socialism with Chinese characteristics," while placing "the scientific concept of development," with its focus on redistributing growth more equally, on par with Mao Zedong Thoughts, Deng Xiaoping Theory, and Jiang Zemin's "Three Represents." At the same time, the report addresses the growing demands for political participation by elevating the discourse on "people's democracy" to a new high, claiming that "people's democracy is the life of socialism" and that "the development of socialist democracy is our unwavering goal," while promising to achieve an "organic unity" among party leadership, the people's mastering of the state, and the rule of law and to improve the functioning of existing political institutions.[47] However, the report offered no concrete policy initiatives. Nor did the new leadership lineup promise any prospect for departing from market authoritarian politics. The foreign media focused on the balance of power between the "princelings faction" and the "Youth League faction" in their analysis of the new party leadership lineup, while ignoring the fact that the preservation of the interests of the "iron triangle," and through it, the interests of transnational capital, has been the most important criterion in personnel selection by the party. For example, although Hu Jintao has written Pan Yue's idea of a "socialist ecological civilization" into his report, and Pan may continue his position as a deputy ministerial–level official, it is unimaginable that Pan—who is both a princeling and a former Communist Youth League official—or somebody else who truly embraces a radical socialist policy orientation will be elevated to the party's inner circle of power.

There are formidable structural forces against any substantive reorientation of China's developmental path around the goals of human-centered and balanced development, environmental sustainability, social harmony, and "people's democracy"—if these are to be more than hollow rhetoric. Moreover, the extent of China's reintegration with the global capitalist system means that such structural forces are transnational in nature and scope. And yet, as Raymond Williams pointed out in a different context, "real determining factors—the distribution of power or of capital, social and physical inheritance, relations of scale and size between groups—set limits and exert pressures" on social practices, but these factors "neither wholly control nor wholly predict the outcome."[48] Human agency and historical contingencies remain important.

Since I start the book with the agency of newspaper vendor Feng Xiujü, let me continue to engage with her agency and subjectivity. As the world waits for China to stage the 2008 Olympics in Beijing, Feng is vigilant against being finally pushed off her street corner in the name of "One World, One Dream."[49] She did not read Xie Tao, nor did she follow the "third debate." However, her understanding of socialism precludes an embrace of a capitalist welfare state, with individuals like her being cast in the ranks of "vulnerable social groups" and welfare recipients—leaving aside whether the state will ever be able to provide a meaningful welfare handout on par with Swedish standards. She stated explicitly to me during my July 1, 2007, conversation with her that she wanted to be engaged in socially useful labor and be self-reliant (*zishi qili*) and that she did not want to become a burden on society. In fact, she has tried her best to preserve her own dignity and is extremely proud of her work in selling newspapers to the public. Of course, she had no idea that a group of old communists would be outraged by the exploitations at the Shanxi kilns and appeal to the central leadership to address the structural conditions that had led to the scandal a few days after I talked to her. And yet, her understanding of the Shanxi kilns scandal resonated with that of the old communists: something was fundamentally wrong in a reform process that has engendered such extreme forms of oppression and exploitation. Will this outrage and this framework of interpretation die away with the passing of the old communists and Feng's generation?

NOTES

1. *"He Weifang Xishan huiyi fayan jilu"* (Transcript of He Weifang's Speech at the Xishan Conference), *Kaifang*, Jun. 2006, 67.

2. Yiching Wu, "Rethinking 'Capitalist Restoration' in China," *Monthly Review*, Nov. 2005, 62, emphasis original.

3. Huang Ping, Yao Yang, and Han Yuhai, *Women de shidai* (Our Times) (Beijing: Central Compilation & Translation Press, 2006), 408.

4. Huang, Yao, and Han, *Women de shidai*, chapter 12, 405–427.

5. Huang Jisu, "Dedication" to *We Walk on a Broad Path* (*Women zouzai dalushang*). I attended the premiere of the play on October 27, 2006, Beijing. For an excellent discussion of Huang Jisu's play and the broader debate surrounding the play, see Tao Qingmei, *"'Dalu' tongxiang hefang"* (Where Does the Broad Road Lead), taoqingmei.blshe.com/post/2392/47588 (accessed 19 Oct. 2007).

6. Heng Baofeng, *"Pan Yue zhuzhang honglu jiemeng, shiqida shang renran meixi"* (Pan Yue Advocated Alliance between Reds and Greens, Still No Hope at the 17th Party Congress), club.backchina.com/main/viewthread.php?tid=560623 (accessed 23 Oct. 2007).

7. Slavoj Žižek, *Welcome to the Desert of the Real* (London and New York: Verso, 2002), 146–147.

8. Michael Burawoy, "For a Sociological Marxism: The Complementary Convergence of Antonio Gramsci and Karl Polanyi," *Politics and Society* 31, no. 2 (2003): 198.

9. Huang, Yao, and Han, *Women de shidai*, 411.

10. Lin Chun, *The Transformation of Chinese Socialism* (Durham, N.C.: Duke University Press, 2006), 271.

11. Lin, *Transformation of Chinese Socialism*, 5.

12. Lin, *Transformation of Chinese Socialism*, 1.

13. Lin, *Transformation of Chinese Socialism*, 271.

14. Richard Robison, "Introduction," in *The Neo-Liberal Revolution: Forging the Market State*, ed. Richard Robison (New York: Palgrave Macmillan, 2006), xiv.

15. "China Passes New Law on Property," BBC News, 16 Mar. 2007, news.bbc .co.uk/2/hi/asia-pacific/6456959.stm (accessed 30 Apr. 2007).

16. Lin, *Transformation of Chinese Socialism*, 271.

17. Huang, Yao, and Han, *Women de shidai*, 411.

18. Heng, "*Pan Yue zhuzhang honglu jiemeng, shiqida shang renran meixi.*"
19. Jonathan Watts, "Hu Admits Communist Shortcomings," www .guardian.co.uk/china/story/0,,2191475,00.html?gusrc=rss&feed=network front#article_continue (accessed 17 Oct. 2007).
20. Li Ge, "*Dianshi shoushilu tanxi*" (An Exploration on Television Audience Ratings), 202.102.170.235/tv/sdst/info.jsp?id=600 (accessed 23 Oct. 2007).
21. Aileen McCabe, "China Targets Reality TV," *Vanouver Sun*, 26 Sept. 2007, A13.
22. Conversation with a Xinhua correspondent, 1 Jun. 2007, Vancouver; see also, Xin Xin, "Xinhua News Agency and Globalization: Negotiating between the Global, the Local, and the National," in *Communications Media Globalization and Empire*, ed. Oliver Boyd-Barrett (Eastleigh, U.K.: John Libbey Publishing, 2006), 122.
23. Personal conversation, 28 Oct. 2006, Beijing.
24. "*Zhongguo Gongchandang dishiqi ci quanguo daibiao dahui*" (The 17th National Congress of the Chinese Communist Party), www.xinhuanet.com/zhibo/ 20071015/wz.htm (accessed 16 Oct. 2007).
25. McCabe, "China Targets Reality TV."
26. "*Xietao zai Xiang Gang daxue tan 'minzhu zhehuizhuyi moshi yu Zhongguo qiantu' fabiao qianhuo*" (Xie Tao Discussed What Happened before and after the Publication of "Democratic Socialism and China's Future"), wlc.blogbus .com/logs/10000161.html (accessed 19 Oct. 2007).
27. Xie Tao, "*Minzhu shehui zhuyi yu Zhongguo de qiantu*" (Democratic Socialism and China's Future), economy.guoxue.com/article.php/11416 (accessed 19 Oct. 2007).
28. Joseph Fewsmith, "Democracy Is a Good Thing," *China Leadership Monitor* 22, media.hoover.org/documents/CLM22JF.pdf; see also, "In China a Call for Democracy Stirs Secretive Storm," Reuters, 7 May 2007, en.eochtimes.com/news/ 7-5-7/5004.html (accessed 19 Oct. 2007).
29. Nong Nuji, "*Shanghai, Zhejiang zhaokai 'minzhu shehui zhuyi yu Zhongguo de qiantu' wenti zuotanhui*" (Shanghai and Zhejiang Held Seminars on "Democratic Socialism and China's Future"), www.wyzxwyzx.com/Article/Class17/ 200704/17977.html (accessed 19 Oct. 2007).
30. *Yanhuang chunqiu* published more articles in support of Xie Tao from April to July 2007. Fewsmith, "Democracy Is a Good Thing," 6–7.
31. For a further discussion of Hu's speech, see Fewsmith, "Democracy Is a Good Thing," 7–8.
32. See Howard W. French, "Reports of Forced Labor Unsettle China," www.nytimes.com/2007/06/16/world/asia/16china.html?_r=2&partner=rssnyt &emc=rss&oref=slogin&oref=slogin (accessed 16 Oct. 2007).
33. Agence France-Presse, "Old Guard Communists Complain of Being Muzzled," *Vancouver Sun*, 5 Oct. 2007, A5.
34. For a discussion of Kuang Xinnian's comments, see Tao Qingmei, "'*Dalu' tongxiang hefang.*"
35. The fact that Wang Hui and Huang Ping are not only outsiders, but also well-known intellectuals, made it hard for the journal's management to exercise editorial control.

36. A *Beijing News* report first broke the story with little factual base and long before the decision was actually made. Moreover, the report interviewed those with strong opinions against Wang and Huang. The report claimed to get the idea that *Reading* was considering the replacement of Wang and Huang from the blog of *Reading* editor Meng Hui, who subsequently accused the newspaper of fabrication. Zhang Hong, "*Dushu zazhi yunniang huanshuai*" (*Reading* Journal Planning a Change of Guard), culture.thebeijingnews.com/0820/2007/06-21/015@085457 .htm (accessed 19 Oct. 2007). Meng Hui, "*Kangyi xinjingbao zhizhao jiaxinwen*" (Protesting *Beijing News* for Fabricating False News), www.eduww.com/Article/Class4/200706/13932.html (accessed 19 Oct. 2007). According to one very credible interpretation, *Beijing News*, by prematurely publishing the story without an official announcement and by interviewing those who disliked Wang and Huang, created the public opinion pressure for the result it desired.

37. See Lao Tian, "*Dushu zhubian 'renxian' youguan 'tiesanjiao' jingying tongmen de qianqiu daye?*" (Does the Choice of *Reading*'s Chief Editor Concern the "Iron Triangle" Elite Alliance's Long Term Cause?), www.wehoo.net/jgcn/dispbbs .asp?boardID=3&ID=3971; Fang Dehao, "*Dushu zazhi yishuai, Zhongguo 'xin zuopai' shishi xianzhao?*" (Is *Reading*'s Change of Guard a Sign of China's New Left's Loss of Political Favor?).

38. Davietone [*sic*], "*Cong 'Dushu' shijian toushi dangdai Zhongguo*" (What the *Reading* Event Reveals about Contemporary China), truworld.yculblog.com/post.1728520.html (accessed 21 Oct. 2007).

39. The following remark, made to me by a transnationally located real estate tycoon from Harbin over a dinner conversation in summer 2007, revealed how the political and business sides of the "iron triangle" interacted over the consequences of the "Hu-Wen New Deal": "I told the deputy provincial governor of [Heilongjiang], Premier Wen's pro-people policy is good. However, it has created a swamp of wicked citizens [*yiqun diaomin*] [who demanded a proper compensation for the land he had acquired for real estate development]."

40. Davietone, "*Cong 'Dushu' shijian toushi dangdai Zhongguo*." The inflection of the Gramscian language of "hegemony" and "counterhegemony" in this analysis is mine.

41. A total of 89.3 percent of the 10,250 respondents to the survey identified the gap between rich and poor as a very serious problem, while 80.7 percent believed that the situation of the widening wealth gap must be changed. Furthermore, contrary to the claim that a scholarly consensus has identified rural/urban division as the primary source of inequality, popular opinion identifies the existence of "special interest groups" as the primary cause for income inequality. The fact that most of the respondents are between 20 and 30 years old, and either Internet users or *China Youth News* readers with a monthly income between 1,000 to 3,000 yuan, is also significant. See Zhang Ling, "*80.7% deren renwei pingfu caoju yuelai yueda de wenti bixu gaibian*" (80.7% of the People Believe That the Problem of the Widening Gap between Rich and Poor Must Be Solved), news.xinhuanet.com/fortune/2006-12/25/content_5528105.htm (accessed 22 Oct. 2007).

42. David Harvey, *A Brief History of Neoliberalism* (Oxford: Oxford University Press, 2005), 150–151.

43. Jonathan Manthorpe, "A New Era of Leadership in China Doesn't Mean Change," *Vancouver Sun*, 24 Oct. 2007, A15.

44. Manthorpe, "A New Era of Leadership."

45. "Democracy 'Was Answer,'" *South China Morning Post*, 18 Oct. 2007, www .scmp.com/portal/site/SCMP/menuitem.2af62ecb329d3d7733492d9253a0a0a0/ ?vgnextoid=2f0cb0bc3eea5110VgnVCM100000360a0a0aRCRD&s=News (accessed 19 Oct. 2007). I am grateful to Ariane Pele for sending this piece of news.

46. "*Du Daozheng: Shiqida baogao du zuopai 'cunbu burang, cunzhi burang'*" (17th Party Congress Report Made Not a Single Inch and Single Word of Concession to the Left), www5.chinesenewsnet.com/gb/MainNews/Forums/BackStage/2007_ 10_18_17_13_36_920.html (accessed 20 Oct. 2007).

47. "*Zhongguo Gongchandang dishiqi ci quanguo daibiao dahui*" (The 17th National Congress of the Chinese Communist Party), www.xinhuanet.com/zhibo/ 20071015/wz.htm (accessed 16 Oct. 2007).

48. Raymond Williams, *Television, Technology, and Cultural Forum* (London: Fontana, 1974), 130.

49. This is the official slogan of the 2008 Beijing Olympics.

Index

About the Author

Yuezhi Zhao is associate professor and Canada Research Chair in the Political Economy of Global Communication at the School of Communication, Simon Fraser University, Canada. She received her Ph.D. in 1996 from Simon Fraser University and taught at the University of California, San Diego, between 1997 and 2000. She is the author of *Media, Market, and Democracy in China: Between the Party Line and the Bottom Line* (1998), coauthor of *Sustaining Democracy? Journalism and the Politics of Objectivity* (1998), and coeditor of *Democratizing Global Media: One World, Many Struggles* (2005) and *Global Communications: Toward a Transcultural Political Economy* (2008).